SYSTEM/370
JOB CONTROL LANGUAGE

SYSTEM/370
JOB CONTROL LANGUAGE

Second Edition

GARY DeWARD BROWN

A Wiley-Interscience Publication

JOHN WILEY & SONS

New York • Chichester • Brisbane • Toronto • Singapore

Library of Congress Cataloging in Publication Data:

Brown, Gary DeWard.
  System/370 job control language.

  "A Wiley-Interscience publication."
  Includes index.
    1. IBM 370 (Computer)—Programming.   2. Job Control
Language (Computer program language)
I. Title.

QA76.8.I123B76   1987   005.4'3   87-14228
ISBN 0-471-62435-7 (pbk.)

PREFACE

· This is the new edition of the JCL book, and it comes ten years after the first edition. This edition incorporates all the minor changes and additions to JCL. It's amazing how few there have been in the past decade, especially considering that there has been a revolution in the way that a computer is used, mainly because of the personal computer.

More important than the minor changes and additions that have been made to the book are the new chapters that have been added. To use System/370, you may also need to be familiar with JES2 and JES3, TSO, and ISPF/PDF. Chapters have been added describing these. I've also included more illustrations and tried to explain the System/370 concepts more clearly.

My goal in this book is to explain the MVS and VS1 operating systems and provide the reader with most of the information they need to use them. This is why there are also chapters on Sort/Merge, the Utilities, and VSAM.

My special thanks to Sandra Audero for her help in preparing the book and her insistence that things be made clear. I'd also like to thank John Jensen for his thorough review. Of course, any errors in the book are my sole responsiblility.

GARY DeWARD BROWN

Los Angeles, California
June 1987

CONTENTS

Chapter 1

INTRODUCTION

I. *THE SHOCK OF JCL*

Your first use of JCL (Job Control Language) will likely be a shock. You probably have used personal computers that cost one or two thousand dollars with wonderfully human-engineered software, and this gives you expectations of how easy a computer should be to use. Now that you are to use a computer costing several million dollars, it may come as a shock to you that its software is not wonderfully human engineered.

The design of the hardware and software for large IBM mainframe computers dates back to the days when Kennedy was President. JCL is a language that may be older than you are, and it was designed at a time when the "user friendly" concept was not even a gleam in the eye of its designers. To demonstrate that point, let's contrast a JCL function with a comparable one on the IBM personal computer. To copy a file on an IBM personal computer, you type:

```
COPY old-name new-name
```

To do the same thing with JCL, you might write:

```
//COPY#1 JOB 2215,'COPY',CLASS=A
//STEP1   EXEC PGM=IEBGENER
//SYSPRINT DD SYSOUT=A
//SYSUT1   DD DSN=old-name,DISP=SHR
//SYSUT2   DD DSN=new-name,DISP=(NEW,CATLG),
//            UNIT=SYSDA,VOL=SER=PACK12,
//            DCB=(RECFM=FB,LRECL=80,BLKSIZE=6400),
//            SPACE=(6400,(100,20),RLSE)
//SYSIN    DD DUMMY
```

JCL is inherently difficult. It can be made less difficult, but it can't be made easy. Much of the difficulty is due to the inherent weaknesses of an aging operating system.

The large mainframe computer is an extremely conservative environment. The basic hardware architecture and operating system appear to the user almost exactly as they did a quarter of a century ago. Programs written back then could still run unchanged today, which is the great strength of large IBM mainframe com-

1

puters—their compatibility. The strongest force in the computing universe is compatibility. Billions of dollars are tied up in application software, and many companies would not accept an incompatible computer with modern design and software features even if it were free because software is the dominant cost in computing, not hardware.

II. THE ROLE OF JCL

JCL is not used to write computer programs. Instead, it consists of control statements that introduce a computer job to the operating system, provide accounting information, direct the operating system on what is to be done, request hardware devices, and execute the job. JCL is most concerned with input/output—telling the operating system everything it needs to know about the input/output requirements.

III. THE DIFFICULTY OF JCL

The role of JCL sounds complex and it is—JCL is downright difficult. It provides the means of communicating between an application program and the operating system and computer hardware. Measured according to the number of moving parts, the System/370 operating system is one of mankind's most complex creations. The computer hardware is less complex, but complex nonetheless.

JCL is difficult because of the way it is used. A normal programming language, however difficult, soon becomes familiar through constant use. In contrast, JCL has language features used so infrequently that many never become familiar.

JCL is also difficult because of its design. It is not a procedural language like COBOL or FORTRAN in which complex applications are built up step-by-step from simple statements. JCL consists of individual parameters, each of which has an effect that may take pages to describe. JCL has few defaults. It makes no assumption for the user, but must be told exactly what to do. For example, virtually every computer program ever written prints some output, but the system doesn't assume this. You must supply a JCL statement to print output.

JCL requires you to supply an extraordinary amount of information to the operating system. For example, to save a file on disk storage, you may have to tell the system the amount of space to allocate, the record type, the record length, the block size, the type of I/O unit, the volume serial number of the disk pack, and more. Some of the information, such as the amount of space to allocate, may have to be estimated. Other information, such as the block size, depends on the type of disk device, and while the operating system is in a much better position to supply this, it won't. JCL was designed at a time when people were relatively cheap and computers expensive. In 1965, the cost of one million computer instructions was roughly equivalent to 15 minutes of a person's time. Today the opposite is true. People are expensive and computers are cheap. A million instructions today buys about two milliseconds of a person's time. Consequently, JCL, designed to be efficient in computer time, is an extremely inefficient language today because it costs so much in terms of a person's time. Much of the discussion of efficiency in this book will dwell on saving you time, not just saving computer time.

IV. THE APPROACH TO JCL

The first few chapters describe the individual language statements, tell how to write them, explain what they do, and suggest how to use them. With this as background, the book shifts to functional descriptions of the hardware devices, access methods, and other topics.

The overall goal is to provide you with all the information needed to program on System/370, aside from the programming language used. To accomplish this, the book goes far beyond JCL. The concepts and facilities of the operating system are introduced from the application programmer's point of view. Several non-JCL operating system facilities are also described, including the IBM utility programs, the Sort/Merge program, the linkage editor, VSAM (Virtual Sequential Access Method), and TSO (Time-Sharing Option.)

This book will explain JCL, but it won't try to make you like it because JCL is not a likable language. The book will also show you how to use JCL. Almost no one, even programmers with years of experience, can sit down and write JCL statements the way they could COBOL or FORTRAN statements. Consequently, people who write JCL generally know what they want to do and then consult some existing JCL to use as a prototype to write the new JCL statements. This book provides many examples to serve as prototypes.

The book gives special attention to the use of JCL with COBOL, FORTRAN, PL/I, and assembler language. The interface of JCL to these languages is described wherever appropriate.

The book is based on the VS1 (Virtual System 1) and MVS (Multiple Virtual System) versions of the operating system. Although IBM occasionally releases new versions of System/370, the new releases seldom change existing JCL. However, IBM may add minor new features, and you should consult each new system release.

If you are just learning System/370, you can use this book as an introduction to the operating system and JCL. The book presumes you have some familiarity with a higher level language. If you are an experienced System/370 programmer, you can use this book to learn unfamiliar JCL features or to refresh your memory on seldom-used features. Finally, the book serves as a reference for all who program in System/370.

For classroom usage, Chapters 1 to 13 should be read in sequence, working in the installation's particular requirements. Topics can then be selected from the remaining chapters as needed. Exercises are included at the end of the chapters to help in the instruction. The exercises consist of short, simple problems to be run on a computer. They are designed as much to teach you about your installation and the problems of actually running jobs as they are to teach you about JCL as a language.

Chapter 2

INTRODUCTION TO JCL AND SYSTEM/370

I. JCL STATEMENTS

The JCL statements are:

1. The JOB statement. This is the first control statement; it marks the beginning of a job.
2. The EXEC (Execute) statement. This statement follows the JOB statement and names the program or procedure to execute.
3. The DD (Data Definition) statement. This statement describes each data set (a file on a direct-access storage device, tape, or printed output) and requests the allocation of I/O devices.
4. The Delimiter (/*) statement. This is the "end-of-file" statement for marking the end of data that is included with the JCL statements.
5. The Comment (//*) statement. Comments are coded in columns 4 to 80 as an aid to documenting JCL.
6. The Null (//) statement. The null may be used to mark the end of a job.
7. The PROC statement. This statement begins a cataloged or in-stream procedure and assigns default values to symbolic parameters.
8. The PEND statement. This statement marks the end of an in-stream procedure.
9. The Command statement. This statement is used by computer operators to enter operator commands from the input stream.
10. The CNTL statement. This statement is used to mark the beginning of program control statements in the input stream.
11. The ENDCNTL statement. This statement marks the end of program control statements in the input stream.
12. The OUTPUT statement. This statement is used with JES2 or JES3 to specify processing of output data sets.

In practice, you usually use only JOB, EXEC, DD, and Comment statements. The remainder of this chapter describes the System/370 concepts and facilities to give

4

you a better understanding of the operating system and its relationship to these JCL statements.

II. COMPUTER ARCHITECTURE

A. Major Components

While large mainframe computers have essentially the same hardware components as all other computers, including personal computers (PCs), the terminology is totally different. The formidable-sounding "Direct Access Storage Device" (or DASD as it is usually called) on a mainframe becomes the more unassuming "diskette" on a PC. Likewise, the impressive term "data set" on a mainframe turns out to be just a "file" on the PC.

The computer is essentially a device that reads some data sets, does some computing or processing, and writes some data sets. The main computer hardware that concerns you consists of:

- The CPU, or Central Processing Unit.
- Real storage, or computer memory.
- Input and output devices, such as disks, tapes, and printers.

Figure 1 illustrates a typical computer:

- The Central Processing Unit (CPU) executes instructions to perform computations, initiates input/output, and directs the operation of the computer. It is the part of the computer that does the computing.
- The computer memory holds both the instructions and data during computations and is termed *real storage* or simply *storage*. It corresponds to Random Access Memory (RAM) on a PC.
- The Input/Output (I/O) devices contain external data. A collection of data stored on an external device is called a *data set* or *file*. I/O devices consist of a recording device and access mechanism, a control unit (actually a small computer itself), and a channel to transmit the data between the I/O device and the computer's storage.

B. Forms of Computer Data

Computer data consists of bits, bytes, and words. A *bit* is a single binary digit, 0 or 1. Think of it as a light switch that can have two values: on and off. A *byte* is the minimal addressable element in System/370 and consists of eight bits. All storage sizes and capacities in System/370 are expressed in bytes. A byte is also the amount of storage required to contain a single alphabetic character, such as an A, B, C, etc. A *word* is 32 bits, or four bytes, or the amount of storage required to store a single-precision integer or real number.

Since it is very cumbersome to write binary numbers (a byte containing a binary 1 is written as 00000001), *hexadecimal* (base 16) notation is used. A hexadecimal digit occupies four bits and two hexadecimal digits equal one byte. The binary equivalences of the hexadecimal digits are:

Binary	Hex	Decimal	Binary	Hex	Decimal
0000	0	0	1000	8	8
0001	1	1	1001	9	9
0010	2	2	1010	A	10
0011	3	3	1011	B	11
0100	4	4	1100	C	12
0101	5	5	1101	D	13
0110	6	6	1110	E	14
0111	7	7	1111	F	15

For example, we would represent the binary digits 1111000011011011 as F0DB in hexadecimal, which saves space and reduces the chance for error in copying the number. Hexadecimal notation is generally used to represent System/370 binary data.

The System/370 representation of a character is eight bits so that one character can be contained in a byte. The Extended-Interchange Code (EBCDIC) is used to represent the characters internally in the computer. System/370 can also process the

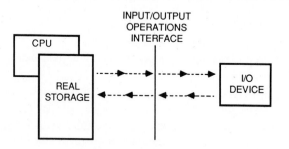

CPU — The Central Processing Unit executes all the computer instructions. It does the actual computing.

REAL STORAGE — This is the computer's memory. Programs are placed here when they are executed.

I/O (or INPUT/OUTPUT) DEVICE — This stores the data and consists primarily of disk, tape, and printers.

Figure 1. A typical computer.

ASCII (American Standard Character Code for Information Interchange) character set that is standard on PCs. The characters are subdivided into several character sets which vary, depending on the context. JCL defines *alphanumeric* characters as A to Z and 0 to 9; *national* characters as @, $, and #; and *special* characters as blank , . / ') (* & + − = .

III. SYSTEM/370 CONCEPTS AND VOCABULARY

System/370 consists of a computer (the model 370, 4300, and 30xx series), an Operating System (OS), and a vocabulary. In fact, people who work on System/370 form a separate culture. You need to understand the concepts and speak the language to fit within the culture.

A. The People

One difference between a large IBM mainframe and other computers is the number of people required to support it. Computer operators run the computer, schedule jobs, mount tapes, and distribute output. One of the advantages of a large computer is that you don't have to worry about hardware problems or paper jams—the operators do this. Needless to say, it pays to stay on the good side of computer operators.

There are also system programmers on large IBM mainframe computers. They install, maintain, and tune the operating system software. The software on large IBM mainframe computers is extremely difficult to install, and once installed, is even more difficult to maintain and tune for good performance. System programmers are generally highly skilled and valuable—and aware of this. It pays to stay on their good side, too.

B. Operating System (OS)

The IBM System/370 *Operating System* introduces programs to the computer, initiates their execution, and schedules all the resources and services they require, such as printers, memory, and disk storage space. The operating system is made up of a general library of programs that can be tailored to accommodate a variety of applications on a wide range of hardware configurations. Each installation selects the portions that it needs through a system generating process (*SYSGEN*), adds its own procedures, and updates its procedures as the needs change.

The programs and routines that compose the operating system are classified either as control programs or processing programs. The *control programs* perform six main functions:

- Job Management controls the reading, scheduling, initiation, allocation, execution, and termination of all jobs in a continuous flow. Job management is accomplished through the Job Entry Subsystems (JES).

- Task Management supervises the dispatching and service requests of all work in the system.
- Data Management stores and retrieves all the data.
- Storage Management controls the use of virtual, real, and auxiliary storage.
- Resource Management allocates the computer's resources.
- Recovery Termination Management ensures proper recovery from system and hardware failures.

Although the operating system is composed of these, you don't see them as entities when you use the computer. You see the system as a whole, and needn't worry about what each component does.

The *processing programs* consist of *language translators* (such as the COBOL and FORTRAN compilers), *service programs* (such as the linkage editor and sort programs), and *application programs* (such as the programs that you write).

C. OS/370 Concepts

System/370 was designed as a batch system that can run on-line jobs. This is in contrast with the PC and the other popular system on large IBM mainframe computers, VM/CMS, which were designed as on-line systems that can run batch jobs. With a *batch* system, you prepare a complete job and submit it to the computer. The computer's operating system schedules the job and executes it at its convenience, which may be hours later. You have no control over the job once you submit it. It is not unusual to submit a job and then hours later, when you get your output, to find that a minor JCL error caused the entire job not to run. With JCL, there is no such thing as a "minor" error.

On-line jobs are submitted from your computer terminal and you stay at the terminal while the job runs, usually interacting with the job to supply necessary information as the program runs. You can quickly correct any errors.

Batch execution is great for long-running jobs, especially those run on a routine basis—*production* jobs. There are several advantages to batch jobs:

- You needn't wait at your terminal for your job to complete to obtain your output.
- The job can be run off-shift, when computer rates are usually lower.
- You can set up a complex job once and then keep resubmitting it rather than having to retype all the run commands each time.
- The job may run more efficiently because you don't require the computer resources that on-line jobs require.

- The computer can schedule the jobs at its convenience to make the most effective use of the computer hardware.

Of course, there are also disadvantages to running jobs in batch with JCL.

- You don't get immediate turnaround, as a rule.
- You must learn to use JCL.
- If something goes wrong while a job is running, you don't get a chance to correct it and continue.
- You must set the entire job up in advance. You can't play it by ear.

On-line is great for jobs requiring interaction while the job runs, jobs that change frequently, and jobs requiring quick turnaround. In practice, on-line is usually used for program development, and batch for production of the programs once they are developed.

Since many jobs are run concurrently on a large computer, the resources of the computer must be shared so that each job eventually gets the resources it needs. This is done by multiprogramming and time sharing—terms often confused.

Time sharing allows many people to use a computer simultaneously in such a way that each is unaware that the computer is being used by others. The usual case is an on-line system with several consoles using the main computer at the same time. Time sharing attempts to maximize an individual's use of the computer, not the efficiency of the computer itself. Time sharing is supported on System/370 by such systems as the Time-Sharing Option (TSO), CICS (Customer Information Control System), IMS/VS (Information Management System/Virtual Storage), and VTAM (Virtual Telecommunications Access Method).

Multiprogramming is just the opposite of time sharing in concept. It attempts to maximize the efficiency of the computer by keeping all the major components busy—such as the CPU, I/O devices, and real storage. Most jobs running on a large general-purpose computer do not use all the I/O devices or storage. Moreover, not all of the CPU is used since time is spent waiting for some I/O action to complete. Rewinding a tape is an extreme case in point.

Since most jobs do not use all of the storage, all of the I/O devices, or all of the CPU, a multiprogramming system can keep several jobs inside the computer at the same time and switch back and forth between them. Several jobs are loaded into storage and the operating system gives control to one job. It then switches control to another whenever one becomes idle. By balancing I/O-bound jobs with the compute-bound jobs, several jobs can be completed in little more time than it would take to complete a single job.

At any given time, several programs may be running in real storage. The programs are placed in areas called "regions" (Figure 2).

Multiprogramming adds to the complexity of the operating system. The system has to protect each job in storage from other jobs. It also has to dole out the computer's resources so that the mixture of jobs in storage do not contend for nonsharable resources such as tape drives. The system has to hold back a job if it needs an unavailable resource and schedule another job instead whose resource requirements could be met. This is in contrast to the typical PC that has only a single user. The fact that the large mainframe computer is shared is a major reason it is so complex and difficult to use.

The system, since it schedules jobs based on their resource requirements, has to be told what resources each job needs. This is done with JCL statements. For example, if a job needs a tape, a JCL statement must describe the tape unit needed. The system will not schedule the job to be run until such a tape unit becomes available. This prevents the job from sitting idle in storage waiting for an available tape unit.

IBM provides two versions of the multiprogramming system, VS1 and MVS. *VS1* (Virtual System 1) is generally for smaller computers and *MVS* (Multiple Virtual System) for larger computers.

Figure 3 illustrates a multiprogramming system on System/370. Each job occupies a contiguous section of storage called a *region* (in MVS) or *partition* (in VS1), and the jobs remain in storage until they complete. Some regions (a region is equivalent to a partition in the following discussion) such as the readers or writers may never complete and always reside in storage. Each region is protected against being destroyed by another region. The system decides which region to run and for how long, and has been made as crash proof as possible so that, although a particular job may fail, the system is not disturbed. Unfortunately, the system is not perfect, and system crashes do occur.

The first region contains the *nucleus* or resident portion of the operating system (those portions of the system not kept on a direct-access storage device). The

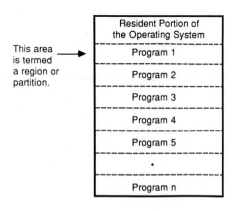

Figure 2. Real storage.

reader/interpreter (or *reader*) reads in jobs and queues them on a direct-access volume. (The term *volume* refers to a specific storage unit such as direct-access storage volume or a tape reel. A direct-access storage device [called DASD and pronounced daz-dee] is usually a disk pack—a large version of the diskette on a PC.) The *writers* write output from the direct-access volume where it has been queued, onto the proper output device. Queuing the input and output on direct-access volumes is called spooling. You might equate it to the take-up reel of a movie projector. Spooling is an acronym for Simultaneous Peripheral Operation On-Line; one of those rare cases where an acronym conveys more meaning than that for which it stands. The sequence of lines read by the reader is called the *input stream*, and the sequence of output written by the writers is called the *output stream*.

The *unit record* devices (printers, and, rarely today, card readers and card punches) are normally assigned to the readers and writers. All other I/O units except tapes can be used concurrently by any of the regions. A tape unit can be assigned to only one region at a time. This is one reason for using direct-access storage devices—jobs will not be kept waiting for a tape unit to become free.

To capsulate the operating system: The reader/interpreter reads jobs from the input stream and queues them on a direct-access volume. When a job comes to the top of its queue, a system program called the *initiator/terminator* loads it into a region and executes it. If the job reads data from the input stream, the system gets the lines from a direct-access volume where they have been stored. If the job prints output, this output is again queued on a direct-access volume. A job never prints directly—it is all

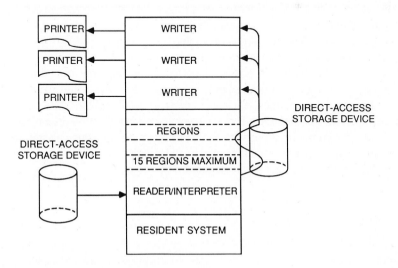

Figure 3. A multiprogramming system.

done by queuing on a direct-access volume. The job will not be aware of this since it is done automatically by the system. After the output is queued on a direct-access volume, the writers write it out to the appropriate output device. Figure 4 illustrates how spooling works.

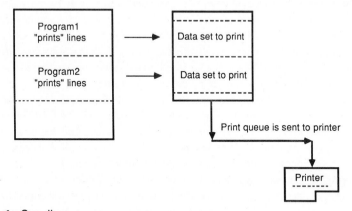

Figure 4. Spooling.

Although the running of a single region was described here, several regions can be kept running at the same time in a similar manner.

Multiprogramming, which divides the computer's internal storage into regions or partitions, creates several problems. A job is limited to the size of the largest region. Storage is often wasted. In VS1, storage within a partition is wasted if the job does not fill the partition. In MVS, storage becomes fragmented, wasting storage because jobs can only be run in contiguous storage. And inevitably, some applications need more storage to run than the computer has available.

Two applications aggravate these problems: time sharing and teleprocessing. Time sharing must give many people access to a computer at the same time with fast response to all. Teleprocessing connects remote devices to the main computer through communication lines. The applications are often real time, as typified by an airline reservations system in which an agent at a remote location reserves a seat on an airliner by communicating with the central computer. Time-sharing and tele-processing applications are both characterized by long periods of inactivity and then brief periods when fast response is required.

D. Virtual Storage

A major architectural component in System/370 is virtual storage. With virtual storage, the storage addresses of an application program are independent of the addresses of the computer's real storage. A hardware feature translates the user's virtual storage addresses to the computer's real storage addresses during execution.

When a program begins execution, the system first "loads" it onto a direct-access volume, the *virtual storage*, rather than directly into the computer's memory or *real storage*. The system divides the application program into small parts called *pages*. Real storage is likewise divided into parts termed *page frames* to contain the pages on the direct-access volume. A *paging supervisor* in the operating system loads each page from the direct-access volume into real storage on demand, as illustrated in Figure 5. Thus large portions of an application program may reside on a direct-access volume rather than in real storage at any given time during execution. (The direct-access storage is called the *external paging storage*.) The implications of this are twofold—the program's size can exceed that of real storage, and little real storage is wasted by inactive portions of programs.

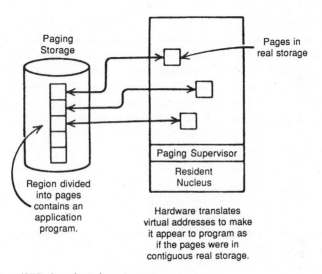

Figure 5. System/370 virtual paging storage.

When a page is needed, the paging supervisor is notified by the hardware detecting the reference to a virtual storage address of a page that is not in real storage. This event is termed a *page break*. The paging supervisor looks around in real storage for a free page frame in which to load the page. If no free page frame is found, the system looks for an inactive page in real storage to swap out.

With virtual storage, a program needs to occupy only a relatively small amount of real storage. This lets you run programs whose size exceeds the real storage available on the computer. It has one other important benefit. Virtual storage allows a larger number of programs to be run on the computer at the same time. The virtual storage contains your entire program while it is executing. You request the maximum region size your program needs through your JCL.

In VS1, the entire operating system can be mapped onto virtual storage with a maximum address space of 16 million bytes. The fixed-size partitions are allocated within this area. In MVS, each individual region is mapped onto virtual storage with a maximum address space of 16 million bytes (2 billion bytes for computers with Extended Architecture). Thus, in VS1 the total system including all of the user partitions or regions cannot exceed 16 million bytes. In MVS, each individual region can have an address space of up to 16 million bytes. With MVS/XA—Extended Architecture—the address space can be up to 2 billion bytes.

E. System/370-XA

One of the problems in any computer is the amount of storage it can address. The amount of storage a computer can address, termed its *addressable space*, depends on the number of bits used to contain addresses. One of the main limitations of the original 8-bit personal computers, such as the Apple II, was the size of its address space. The original IBM PC was a 16-bit computer, and had a larger addressable space. The IBM 370 computer is a 32-bit computer, as are some personal computers. On the 370 computer, only 24 bits are used to contain addresses, and the maximum size of the address space is 2 to the 24th power, or roughly 16 million bytes.

Sixteen million bytes of address space seemed like a lot of memory back when the typical computer had only half a million bytes of memory. (A million bytes is termed a megabyte or just a meg. One billion bytes is termed a gigabyte.) But large computers today have several million bytes of real storage, and with virtual storage, programs can be as large as the address space of the computer. The System/370-XA (Extended Architecture) lets 32 bits be used for addressing in the computer. This gives an address space of roughly 2 to the 32nd power, or 2 billion bytes.

The Extended Architecture also consists of more sophisticated Input/Output channels for faster I/O. The channels are more or less complete computers in themselves for controlling input/output. This not only speeds up the I/O, but relieves the CPU from having to get involved in input/output.

Computers with Extended Architecture require a separate version of the operating system: MVS/XA. Although the internals of a computer with the Extended Architecture feature are considerably different, most of the differences are buried deep inside the operating system. About the only difference that you need to be concerned with as a user is the maximum size of the program that you can write: 16 million bytes for System/370 and 2 billion bytes for System/370-XA.

F. Real Storage

The real storage in the computer is divided into three areas. The system's nucleus or *resident supervisor* is loaded first. A second area of real storage may be reserved for programs that cannot be paged. Such programs include those that use Magnetic Ink Character Recognition (MICR) devices and those that dynamically modify channel programs during I/O operations. The remainder of the real storage is available for loading pages. Figure 6 illustrates VS1 and Figure 7 MVS.

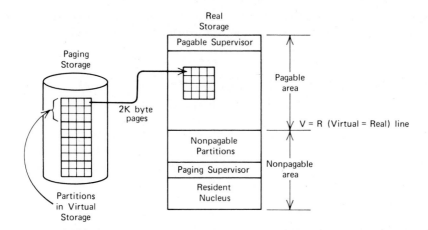

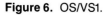

Figure 6. OS/VS1.

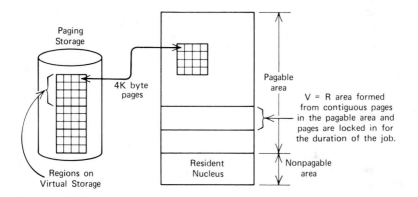

Figure 7. OS/MVS.

G. Job Entry Systems

The Job Entry Subsystem in both VS1 and MVS interfaces with JCL. The Job Entry Subsystem in VS1 is termed *JES* (for Job ENTRY System); in MVS it is either JES2 or JES3. JES2 and JES3 are systems that provide similar functions for installations with several computers that are linked together. They schedule jobs through a central input queue and route the output to the appropriate devices. For example, you may submit a job through a terminal to a remote computer and have the output printed at a local printer. This *remote job entry* permits remote users to submit jobs as easily as those located near the computer.

Although JES2 and JES3 provide similar functions, the statements that you write for them have little in common. They are different products that happen to provide similar functions. JES2 lets each processor or computer operate independently, selecting jobs as needed from the central queue. By contrast, JES3 exercises central control over the processors and assigns jobs to them from the central job queue.

H. Computer Jobs

A computer *job* is the basic independent unit of work. It begins as a group of computer language statements (often called *source language* statements) which are stored on a direct-access volume and submitted to the computer. A set of source language statements that are executed together within a job is often referred to as a *program*. Programs are usually divided into functional parts called modules, sub-routines, or procedures, so that the various parts can be tested and changed without affecting other parts.

JCL statements direct the operating system on the processing to be done on a job and describe all the I/O units required. Since these JCL statements are numerous and complex, the statements for frequently used procedures are kept on a direct-access volume. The user invokes these *cataloged procedures* by giving the system the name of the cataloged procedure rather than submitting all the JCL statements.

Each job must begin with a single JOB statement. (The JOB statement, along with all other JCL statements, is described in subsequent chapters.)

```
//TEST#9 JOB 5542,'JONES',CLASS=A
```

This statement tells the operating system that a job named TEST#9 is charged to account 5542, belongs to a programmer named Jones and belongs to Job Class A.

1. Job steps

By the classic definition, a computer is a device that reads some input, processes it, and writes some output, as shown in Figure 8.

INPUT ⟶ Process ⟶ OUTPUT

Figure 8. Input, process, output.

You specify the process part with EXEC statements. The EXEC statement tells the computer what computer program to execute. Each program execution within a job is called a *job step* or simply a *step*; a job may consist of several steps. A typical job might consist of a compile step to convert the source language statements into machine language, a linkage editor step to combine the compiled program with other programs in subroutine libraries, and an execution step to actually run the program. This entails the execution of three separate programs: the compiler and linkage editor, which are system programs, and the user's job. All are executed with JCL statements.

Each job step begins with a single EXEC statement that names a program or cataloged procedure.

```
//STEP1 EXEC PGM=PL1COMP
//STEP2 EXEC PLIXCLG
```

STEP1 executes a program named PL1COMP; STEP2 requests a cataloged procedure named PLIXCLG. Steps within a job are executed sequentially, so that the output from one step can be input to a following step. For example, Figure 9 illustrates a job with three steps. STEP1 performs some calculations, STEP2 sorts some data, and STEP3 produces some statistics.

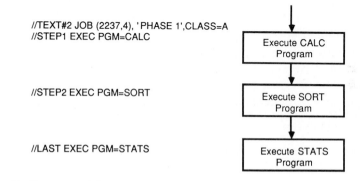

```
//TEXT#2 JOB (2237,4), 'PHASE 1',CLASS=A
//STEP1 EXEC PGM=CALC
```
Execute CALC Program

```
//STEP2 EXEC PGM=SORT
```
Execute SORT Program

```
//LAST EXEC PGM=STATS
```
Execute STATS Program

Figure 9. Three-step job.

The following example illustrates the difference between jobs and job steps.

```
//RUNA JOB 7233,LINCOLN           <== First job
//COMP EXEC PGM=FORTCOMP
//LKED EXEC PGM=LINKEDIT
//TRY#1 JOB 6221,DOUGLAS          <== Second job
//PL1  EXEC PGM=PL1COMP
//LKED EXEC PGM=LINKEDIT
```

Two distinct jobs, RUNA and TRY#1, are executed. The steps within each job are executed sequentially. However, the jobs may not run sequentially. TRY#1 might execute before RUNA, after RUNA, or both jobs might run concurrently.

2. Compilation

A group of source language statements is called a *source module*. A System/370 program called the *compiler* reads the source module and translates the language statements into machine instructions. The output from the compiler, which consists of these machine instructions, is called an *object module*. The compiler writes the object module on a direct-access volume for subsequent execution.

3. Linkage editor

Before the object module can be executed, it must be processed by the *linkage editor*. The linkage editor is a service program that determines which subprograms call other subprograms and resolves these *external references* (symbols contained in one subprogram that are referred to in another). The linkage editor also searches various *subroutine libraries* to gather additional subroutines required to complete the job. A subroutine library is a partitioned data set, a form of System/370 data set organization (described later in this chapter) that can contain several subroutines as members.

Public libraries, such as the FORTRAN or PL/I libraries, are usually searched automatically. You may also create a *private library* containing your own sub-routines and instruct the linkage editor to search it by the inclusion of JCL statements.

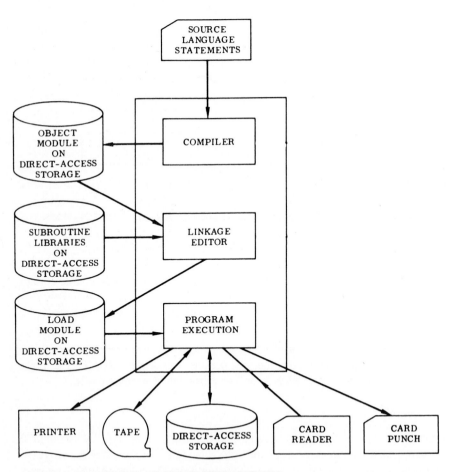

I/O MAY BE PERFORMED ON ANY OF THESE DEVICES.

Figure 10. System/370 job execution.

The linkage editor combines these subroutines into a complete program called a *load module* and writes the load module onto a partitioned data set on a direct-access volume. The load module is a complete program ready to be entered (*loaded*) into storage for execution.

4.   Execution

After the program is link edited, it is loaded into real storage and executed. This step is usually called the *execute* or *go step*. When the program is completed, you may keep it on a direct-access volume in load module form, saving compile and link edit costs. Only a fraction of a second is needed to begin executing a load module, whereas several seconds may be required to compile and link edit the same program. Figure 10 illustrates the entire compile, link edit, and execute steps.

A job need not consist of a compile, link edit, and execute step. Perhaps only a single step is needed to compile source statements for error checking. Or perhaps several related execution steps are required, with each step performing an operation on some data and passing the results on to a subsequent step. For example, the first step of an automated address labeling system might update the names and addresses in a master file. The second step could select all names and addresses with a given zip code. The final step could then print these names and addresses for mailing labels.

5.   The loader

A special service program called the *loader* combines linkage editing and execution into one step. Like the linkage editor, the loader accepts object modules passed to it from the compiler, resolves external references, and searches subroutine libraries.

The loader differs from the linkage editor by not producing a load module. Instead it processes all object modules in storage. Enough storage must be provided for both the loader and the program. When processing is complete, the loader passes control to the program for execution. This process is called *load and go*.

The advantage of the loader is its speed; it is about twice as fast as the linkage editor. Time is also saved by the reduced overhead of a single job step. The disadvantage is that a load module cannot be saved for later execution.

I.   Input/Output

A program, while executing, may read data from tapes or direct-access storage devices and write output to the printer, tapes, or direct-access storage devices.

1.   Data organization

A *record* is a logical unit of data and may consist of any number of bytes; for example, a payroll record might be all the payroll data relating to an individual, such as name, salary, and exemptions. The words *record* and *logical record* are used interchangeably.

System/370 records have three forms: fixed, variable, and undefined. *Fixed* records are all of the same length; for example, a data set containing card images is fixed length because the old punched cards contained 80 characters.

Variable records have varying lengths, with the first four bytes of the record specifying the record length. For example, a personnel file containing employee information might have variable-length records because different information might be retained for each person.

Undefined records have varying lengths, but the record length is not contained in the record. Records are separated by a physical gap on the storage device called an *interblock gap* (IBG). The computer is able to sense this gap when transmitting a record and thus can distinguish between records. Undefined-length records might be used where there is no predetermined unit of data, such as in a load module.

Data is transferred between storage and I/O devices in blocks; each block is separated by an interblock gap. Several fixed- or variable-length records may be contained in a single block; an undefined-length record is equivalent to a block. A block then consists of one or more records to be transmitted at a time. Fixed-length records can be processed slightly faster than variable-length records because they are easier to block and unblock. In a block containing variable-length records, the first four bytes specify the number of bytes in the block.

Data can be transmitted very quickly (up to 3 million bytes per second) between storage and direct-access volume or tape once the transmission of data actually begins. However, it may take quite long (more than 60 milliseconds) to start the transmission because of mechanical inertia, time to position the access mechanism, and the rotation time of the direct-access volume. Blocking allows large, efficient groups of data to be transmitted at one time. It is rather like filling an airliner with people and flying them all coast to coast rather than flying them one person at a time. Blocking further conserves storage space on the volume by limiting the number of interblock gaps.

The number of records per block is called the *blocking factor*. A block is sometimes called a *physical record*, but this term is easily confused with logical record. Blocking is done only for hardware efficiency and is unrelated to the way you want to process your data. The system usually does all blocking and unblocking, but you have to tell it the block size by writing JCL statements.

A block of data is read into an area of storage called a *buffer*. When the last record of a block is processed, the system reads in another block. The reverse occurs when data is written. Several internal buffers can be requested so that while data is being processed in one buffer, the system is reading the next block of data into another buffer. This results in considerable efficiency since I/O is *overlapped*; that is, data is read or written simultaneously with computations being done in the computer. This is one main difference between a large mainframe computer and a PC. The mainframe computer can perform calculations while it is doing I/O, whereas a PC can usually perform only one operation at a time.

Data sets must be opened before they can be used and closed after processing is completed. When a data set is *opened*, the system creates all the internal tables needed to keep track of the I/O, positions the data set to the starting point, and generally readies the data set for processing. *Closing* a data set releases all buffers and tables associated with the data set, frees any tape drive used, releases temporary direct-access storage, and generally cleans up after processing the data set.

2. Data set organization

Any named collection of data (source modules, object modules, or data) is called a *data set*. The words data set and *file* are synonymous. Organization of data sets can be sequential, partitioned, directed, or indexed sequentially. To understand the difference, visualize several decks of cards. *Sequential* organization consists of stacking the decks one on top of the other and processing the cards one at a time in the order in which they appear in the stack. The tape, the printer, the card reader, and direct-access storage devices can contain sequential data sets. Sequential organization is most appropriate when the data set is processed in the order in which it is stored. A payroll file in which all employee records are processed is an example. Figure 11 illustrates sequential organization.

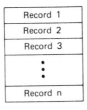

Figure 11. Sequential organization. Records can only be read in the order they are stored.

If the card decks are left in separate stacks, you could pick up a particular deck and process it by reading it sequentially. This *partitioned* organization, where the individual card decks are called *members,* is used most often for subroutine and program libraries since one subroutine or program (member) can be selected or replaced without disturbing the others. A partitioned data set can be processed sequentially by *concatenating* the members, that is, effectively stacking the members end to end. Partitioned data sets can be used only from direct-access volumes. Figure 12 illustrates partitioned data sets.

If all the cards are spread out on the table so that each individual card can be seen, you could select or replace any card directly, without disturbing the others. *Direct* data set organization can exist only on direct-access volumes and is appropriate when records are processed *randomly;* that is, the next record to be processed bears no physical relationship to the record just processed. An example would be an on-line telephone directory in which a person's telephone number is retrieved by that person's name. COBOL, FORTRAN, PL/I, and assembler language all support direct data set organization. Figure 13 illustrates direct organization.

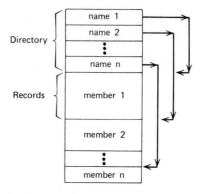

Figure 12. Partitioned organization. Member, after being located through the directory, is read sequentially.

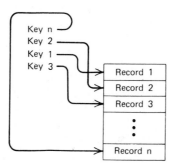

Figure 13. Direct organization. Key is supplied to locate a specific record. Data set can also be read sequentially.

The Indexed-Sequential Access Method (ISAM) provides both sequential and random access. A better analogy for *indexed-sequential* data sets is the public library where each book is assigned a *key* (a Dewey decimal number) and the books are arranged in *collating sequence* (the sequence in which the character set of the computer is ordered) based on the key, such as A-Z, 0-9, etc. Books are placed on shelves and can be removed or added without disturbing other books on other shelves. You can process the "data set" sequentially by strolling through the stacks, or access a book directly by looking it up in the *index*. Indexed-sequential data sets can be created by COBOL, PL/I, and assembler language. They can reside only on direct-access storage volumes. Figure 14 illustrates ISAM organization.

System/370 also provides the Virtual Storage Access Method (*VSAM*) for storing data on direct-access volume. VSAM data sets can be organized as an *entry-sequence* data set, which is functionally equivalent to a sequential data set; as a *relative record* data set, which is functionally equivalent to a direct data set; and as a *key-sequenced* data set, which is functionally equivalent to an indexed-sequential data set. COBOL,

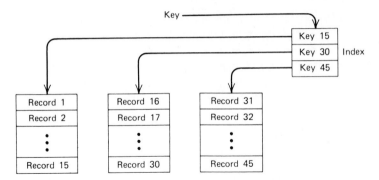

Figure 14. Indexed-sequential organization. Key is supplied to locate a specific record through the index. Data set can also be read sequentially.

PL/I, and assembler language support VSAM key-sequenced data sets. Its advantage over ISAM is that it is generally more efficient.

3. Access techniques

An *access technique* is a method of moving data between real storage and an I/O device. Two ways of reading or writing are provided in System/370, basic and queued. In the *basic access* technique, a read or write command starts the transfer between real storage and the I/O device. Since I/O operations are overlapped, the program can continue execution while the I/O action completes. It is the user's responsibility to provide buffers and to *synchronize* the I/O (that is, detect that a buffer is completely written before moving more data into it). The basic technique gives relatively complete control over I/O, but it requires more effort to use, and is rarely used.

In the *queued access* technique, the system does all buffering and synchronization. The program receives or sends a record and the system does all the I/O, buffering, blocking, and deblocking. The queued access technique is the easiest to use and is provided in all languages.

J. Data Storage

The two most common means of storing data are on tapes and direct-access storage devices.

1. Magnetic tapes

Tapes used for storing computer data are similar to those used in home tape recorders, although the recording method and content are quite different. A single reel of tape can contain up to 170 million bytes; an infinite amount of information can be stored using multiple reels. Tapes contain sequential data sets. Several data sets can be stored on a single tape reel by separating them with file marks. Because tapes are updated by copying the old tape and the changes onto a new tape, an automatic backup is obtained by keeping the old tape and a copy of the changes.

Tape makes excellent long-term storage because a reel of tape is inexpensive and can contain a great deal of information in a small storage space. Tapes may be faster or slower than direct-access storage devices, depending on the particular device. Tape reels are more portable than direct-access storage devices, and are often used for mailing data.

2. Direct-access storage devices

Direct-access storage devices, the most versatile I/O device, can contain sequential, partitioned, direct, ISAM, and VSAM data sets. Direct-access storage derives its name from the way data is accessed. Unlike tape, you don't need to read the first nine records to get to the tenth. Direct-access storage devices are usually disks, similar to the diskettes on PCs, but much larger.

In addition to containing general data, direct-access storage devices are used for subroutine libraries and for storing complete programs in load-module form. Non-resident portions of the operating system are also stored on direct-access volumes.

3. The DD statement

Each program may use various input/output devices. The JCL DD statements tell the system which I/O devices each program needs. The system then coordinates the use of the I/O devices with the programs. Figure 15 illustrates this.

Figure 16 shows the way a DD statement works.

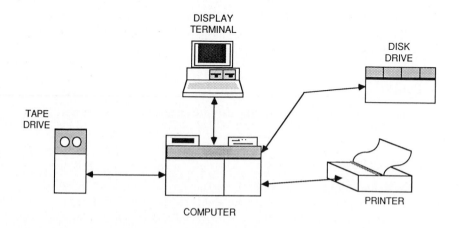

Figure 15. Coordination of I/O devices.

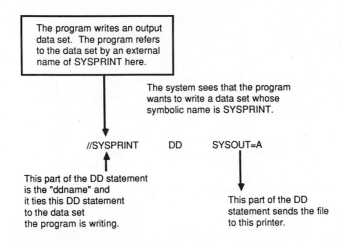

Figure 16. The way a DD statement works.

You usually write JCL using a text editor, such as ISPF/PDF. There is a JCL statement that lets you enter lines of data along with your JCL. (Your JCL and lines of data are termed the "input stream.") The statement for this is:

```
//ddname DD *
     [ The * means that the data immediately follows this JCL
     statement. ]
```

Figure 17 shows the flow of a typical job with the input and output specified by DD statements.

The JCL to process the transactions looks like this:

```
//TEST#2 JOB (2237,4),'PHASE1',CLASS=A    <== JOB statement
//STEP1   EXEC PGM=CALC                    <== Executes the CALC program.
//INPUT   DD *                             <== Defines the input data.
     [ Data placed here ]
//OUTPUT DD many parameters                <== Specifies where the output
                                               data is to be written.

//STEP2   EXEC PGM=SORT                    <== Executes the SORT program.
//INPUT   DD many parameters               <== Can point to the OUTPUT data
                                               written in the previous job
                                               step.
//OUTPUT DD many parameters                <== Specifies where the new OUTPUT
                                               data is to be written.

//LAST    EXEC PGM=STATS                   <== Executes the STATS program.
//INPUT   DD many parameters               <== Can point to the OUTPUT data
                                               written in the previous job
                                               step.
//OUTPUT DD SYSOUT=A                        <== Specifies that the output
                                               data is to be printed.
```

Each data set used within a job step must be described by a DD (Data Definition) statement. The DD statement tells the system which I/O device to use, the volume

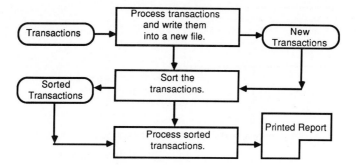

Figure 17. Flow chart of a typical job.

serial number of any specific volumes needed, the data set name, whether old data is being read or new data generated, and the disposition of the data when the job step completes. The following DD statement is typical:

```
//DATAIN DD DSN=MYDATA,DISP=(OLD,KEEP),UNIT=3380,VOL=SER=PACK12
```

The DD statement is named DATAIN and requests a data set named MYDATA. MYDATA is an OLD data set to KEEP after it is read. It is contained on a 3380 disk pack with a volume serial number of PACK12.

Data sets may also be *cataloged* by asking the system to record the data set name, type of I/O unit, and volume serial number containing the data set. This permits the data set to be referred to by name without specifying where the data set is stored. If the MYDATA data set is cataloged, the DD statement could be written as:

```
//DATAIN DD DSN=MYDATA,DISP=(OLD,KEEP)
```

The data set name, type of I/O unit, and volume serial number are recorded in the system's catalog. The *catalog* is itself a data set that contains an entry for each cataloged data set. A cataloged data set should not be confused with a cataloged procedure. A cataloged procedure is a named collection of JCL kept in a data set; a cataloged data set has its name, type of I/O unit, and volume serial number recorded by the system. Thus the special data set containing cataloged procedures may be cataloged.

With this background, we are now ready to go on to the next chapter to see how the JCL is used within a complete job.

Chapter 3

JCL WITHIN A JOB

This chapter gives an overview of how JCL is used within a job. It goes rather fast and is intended only to give the flavor of using JCL. Don't worry about understanding all the details because they will be covered later.

I. SORT EXAMPLE

We'll start with a simple example to illustrate the concepts and then move to a more complicated example that illustrates a language compiler and linkage editor. For our first example, we'll write a step to execute a program named SORT to sort some data in the input stream. Then a second step will execute a program named REPORT to read the sorted file and print a report. The job begins with a JOB statement.

```
//SORT#1 JOB (2217,6),'SORT',CLASS=A
```

An EXEC statement is needed to specify the following:

```
       Stepname:     STEP1
       Program:      SORT
       Region Size:  256K
```
```
//STEP1 EXEC PGM=SORT,REGION=256K
```

We need a DD statement for this step to print some output. It must have a *ddname* (data definition name) of SYSPRINT and be assigned to output class A.

```
//SYSPRINT DD SYSOUT=A
```

Next, we need a DD statement with a ddname of SYSIN to read lines from the input stream.

```
//SYSIN DD *
```

We've added some lines of data and a DD statement with a ddname of SORTOUT to write the sorted output into a disk data set. Our job so far consists of:

```
//SORT#1 JOB (2217,6),'SORT',CLASS=A
//STEP1 EXEC PGM=SORT,REGION=256K
//SYSPRINT DD SYSOUT=A
//SYSIN    DD *
     [ Lines of data ]
/*
//SORTOUT DD DSN=&&OUT,DISP=(NEW,PASS),
//            UNIT=SYSDA,SPACE=(6400,(20,10)),
//            DCB=(RECFM=FB,LRECL=80,BLKSIZE=6400)
```

Let's briefly explain the DD statement as a preview to later chapters where it is described in detail.

```
//SORTOUT DD DSN=&&OUT,DISP=(NEW,PASS),
     [ DSN=&&OUT specifies the data set name.  The && makes it a
     temporary data set.  The data set name is OUT.
     DISP=(NEW,PASS) specifies the data set disposition.  NEW
     means the data set is to be created and PASS means the data
     set is passed to a following step. ]
//            UNIT=SYSDA,SPACE=(6400,(20,10)),
     [ UNIT=SYSDA specifies the type of device to write the data
     set on, and each installation assigns its own names.
     SPACE=(6400,(20,10)) specifies the amount of disk space to
     allocate to the data set. ]
//            DCB=(RECFM=FB,LRECL=80,BLKSIZE=6400)
     [ This specifies the record format (Fixed Blocked), the
     logical record length (80), and the block size (6400).  More
     on this later. ]
```

Symbolically, our step looks like Figure 18.

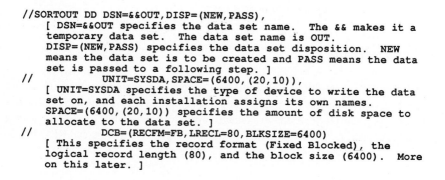

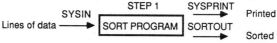

Figure 18. Sort step.

The next EXEC statement is needed to execute a program named REPORT. We give the step a *stepname* of STEP2 and assign it a region of 512K.

```
//STEP2 EXEC PGM=REPORT,REGION=512K
```

A DD statement is added with a ddname of PRINT to print the output. We'll assign the output to class A—the printer.

```
//PRINT DD SYSOUT=A
```

We'll assume that the REPORT program expects the input DD statement to have a ddname of INPUT.

```
//INPUT DD DSN=&&OUT,DISP=(OLD,DELETE)
   [ DSN=&&OUT names the data set--the same data set created in
   STEP1.  DISP=(OLD,DELETE) gives the disposition of the data
   set.  OLD means it already exists.  DELETE means to delete it
   at the end of the step. ]
```

Symbolically, Figure 19 shows the way our job looks.

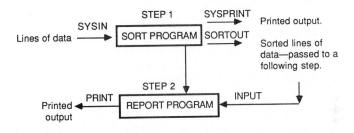

Figure 19. Sort and report steps.

II. COMPILE, LINKAGE EDIT, EXECUTE EXAMPLE

Now let's take a more complicated example that is equally typical—compiling some computer language statements, link editing them to create a program, and loading and executing the program. We'll go into the JCL parameters in more detail in this example.

A. Compile Step

For our example, suppose that some PL/I source language statements are to be compiled. Assume the PL/I compiler is a system program named PLICOMP that requires three data sets: an input data set consisting of source language statements to compile, an output data set to print the compilation listing, and an output data set to contain the *object module*—that is, machine language instructions produced by the compiler. Figure 20 illustrates this.

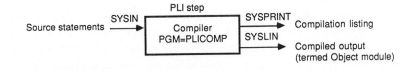

Figure 20. Compile step.

This program might be executed by the following JCL.

```
//TEST JOB 5542,'SMITH',CLASS=A
//PL1 EXEC PGM=PL1COMP,REGION=256K
//SYSPRINT DD SYSOUT=A
//SYSLIN   DD DISP=(NEW,PASS),UNIT=SYSSQ,SPACE=(80,250)
//SYSIN    DD *
     [ source language statements to compile ]
/*
```

Let's examine each statement individually to see what it does.

```
//TEST JOB 5542,'SMITH',CLASS=A
```

The job is named TEST, the JOB marks this as the start of a job, the account number is 5542, and the programmer's name is SMITH. The job class is A.

```
//PL1 EXEC PGM=PL1COMP,REGION=256K
```

The *stepname* or name of the job step is PL1. The EXEC is the statement name. The PGM = PL1COMP means that a program named PL1COMP is to be executed. It is given 256K bytes of storage in which to execute.

```
//SYSPRINT DD SYSOUT=A
```

SYSPRINT is the ddname of the DD statement. The PL1COMP program must internally define a data set with the ddname of SYSPRINT. When you write your own programs, you are free to choose any ddname; you must know the ddnames required by existing programs.

SYSOUT = A defines a print data set. Print data sets are used so often that a special abbreviation, SYSOUT, is provided. The SYSOUT keyword instructs the system to queue the output on a direct-access volume. The general form is SYSOUT = *class*, where the *class* is defined by the installation. Traditionally, SYSOUT = A is a printer, but other classes may be established as needed for special forms, high-volume output, and so on.

```
//SYSLIN DD DISP=(NEW,PASS),UNIT=SYSSQ,SPACE=(80,250)
```

The SYSLIN DD statement describes the data set to contain the object module produced by the compiler. The DISP (disposition) keyword describes the status of the data set at the start of the job step and its disposition after the step is completed. NEW indicates the data set is new—it will be created in the job step. PASS causes the data set to be passed on to the next job step.

The UNIT keyword specifies the I/O unit to be used. There are three ways of specifying I/O units: by hardware address, by device type, and by device group. Each I/O unit attached to the computer has a unique three-character *hardware address*. For example, if three tapes are attached to the computer, they might have hardware addresses of 0C1, 0C2, and 0C3. UNIT = 0C2 would request a particular tape unit. (This is equivalent to the way you specify the *a* or *b* diskette drive on a PC.) In multiprogramming systems, it is better to use device type rather than specify hardware addresses; a specified unit might already be busy. The *device type* is the generic type of unit. For example, UNIT = 3380 permits the use of any available 3380 disk drive. The *device group* permits the installation to classify groups of I/O units under one name. SYSSQ is traditionally used to include I/O devices that can contain sequential data sets (tapes and direct-access storage devices). SYSDA is likewise used to refer to direct-access storage devices.

The SPACE keyword allocates storage on the direct-access volume for the data set. SPACE = (80,250) requests space for 250 80-byte blocks. All NEW data sets on direct-access volumes must be allocated space. Space allocation is unnecessary for data sets stored on tape.

```
//SYSIN DD *
```

The asterisk (*) is a special code telling the system that lines of data immediately follow the DD statement in the input stream. The end of the data is indicated by the /* statement. The lines of JCL and data are termed the *input stream*.

B. Linkage Editor Step

Next, the program must be link edited to create a load module that can be executed. Assume that the linkage editor is a system program named IEWL that requires three data sets: an input data set containing the object modules produced by the compiler, an output data set for printing error messages, and an output data set to contain the load module produced. Figure 21 illustrates this.

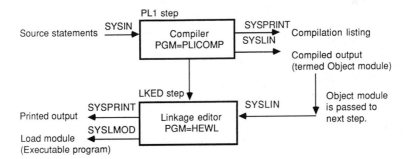

Figure 21. Compile and linkage edit steps.

Here are our statements so far with the linkage editor step.

```
//TEST JOB 5542,'SMITH',CLASS=A
//PL1 EXEC PGM=PL1COMP,REGION=256K
//SYSPRINT DD SYSOUT=A
```

```
//SYSLIN    DD DISP=(NEW,PASS),UNIT=SYSSQ,SPACE=(80,250)
//SYSIN     DD *
      [ source language statements to compile ]
/*
//LKED EXEC PGM=IEWL,REGION=104K
//SYSPRINT DD SYSOUT=A
//SYSLIN    DD DSN=*.PL1.SYSLIN,DISP=(OLD,DELETE)
//SYSLMOD   DD DSN=&&TEMP(GO),DISP=(NEW,PASS),
//             UNIT=SYSDA,SPACE=(1024,(200,20,1))
```

Now examine the added statements in detail.

```
//LKED EXEC PGM=IEWL,REGION=104K
      [ This executes the IEWL program. The region size is 104K
      bytes. ]
//SYSPRINT DD SYSOUT=A
      [ The SYSPRINT DD statement defines a print data set. ]
//SYSLIN SS DSN=*.PL1.SYSLIN,DISP=(OLD,DELETE)
      [ The SYSLIN DD statement describes the input data set
      containing object modules for the linkage editor--the data
      set created in the preceding job step. DSN=*.PL1.SYSLIN
      tells the system that this is the same data set described in
      the step named PL1 with a DD statement named SYSLIN.  (The
      *.step.ddname parameter is called a referback parameter.)
      Since the data set already exists, the current status is
      OLD.  The data set is not needed after this step, so we
      can DELETE it, releasing the space on the direct-access
      volume. ]
//SYSLMOD DD DSN=&&TEMP(GO),DISP=(NEW,PASS),
//          UNIT=SYSDA,SPACE=(1024,(200,20,1))
      [ This DD statement is similar to the SYSLIN DD statement in
      the first step except for the DSN (Data Set Name) keyword
      parameter.  Load module output must be placed on a
      direct-access volume as a member of a partitioned data set.
      A partitioned data set is a special data set that contains
      several sequential data sets termed members.  It is
      analogous to a file cabinet that contains several file
      drawers.  GO is chosen as the member name, and the data set
      is given a name of TEMP.  The ampersands (&&) in front of
      the data set name mark it as temporary--to be deleted at the
      end of the job.  Space is requested for 200 1024-byte
      blocks, and additional 20 1024-byte blocks can be allocated
      if more space is needed, and 1 block is reserved for storing
      the member names of the partitioned data set. ]
```

C. Execution Step

The load module is now ready to be executed. Figure 22 illustrates the complete job.

```
//TEST JOB 5542,'SMITH',CLASS=A
//PL1 EXEC PGM=PL1COMP,REGION=256K
//SYSPRINT DD SYSOUT=A
//SYSLIN    DD DISP=(NEW,PASS),UNIT=SYSSQ,SPACE=(80,250)
//SYSIN     DD *
      [ source language statements to compile ]
/*
//LKED EXEC PGM=IEWL,REGION=104K
//SYSPRINT DD SYSOUT=A
//SYSLIN    DD DSN=*.PL1.SYSLIN,DISP=(OLD,DELETE)
//SYSLMOD   DD DSN=&&TEMP(GO),DISP=(NEW,PASS),
//             UNIT=SYSDA,SPACE=(1024,(200,20,1))
//GO EXEC PGM=*.LKED.SYSLMOD,REGION=52K
//SYSPRINT DD SYSOUT=A
```

Again we can examine the added statements in detail.

```
//GO EXEC PGM=*.LKED.SYSLMOD,REGION=52K
     [ The referback parameter tells the system that the load
     module to execute is described in the LKED step on the SYLMOD
     DD statement.  The program will execute in 52K bytes of
     storage. ]
//SYSPRINT DD SYSOUT=A
     [ The SYSPRINT DD statement defines a print data set.  Output
     printed by the job would be written into this data set. ]
```

Of course, you won't actually write all these statements when you compile, link edit, and execute a program. Instead, you invoke existing JCL statements contained in a cataloged procedure.

III. CATALOGED PROCEDURE

All JCL statements are now provided to compile, link edit, and execute the program—but there are a great number of them. We should now make them a cataloged procedure so that several people can use the JCL. The JCL statements are made a *cataloged procedure* by storing them on a direct-access volume as a member of a special partitioned data set. A name, one to eight characters long, is chosen for the

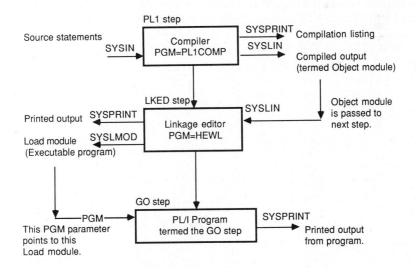

Figure 22. Compile, linkage edit, and go steps.

cataloged procedure. PLIXCLG might be an appropriate name for the PL/I compile, link edit, and execute procedure. The following statements constitute the procedure.

```
//PLIXCLG PROC
     [ The PROC statement is the first statement in a cataloged
     procedure. ]
//PL1 EXEC PGM=PL1COMP,REGION=256K
//SYSPRINT DD SYSOUT=A
//SYSLIN   DD DISP=(NEW,PASS),UNIT=SYSSQ,SPACE=(80,250)
//LKED EXEC PGM=IEWL,REGION=104K
//SYSPRINT DD SYSOUT=A
//SYSLIN   DD DSN=*.PL1.SYSLIN,DISP=(OLD,DELETE)
//SYSLMOD  DD DSN=&&TEMP(GO),DISP=(NEW,PASS),
//           UNIT=SYSDA,SPACE=(1024,(200,20,1))
//GO EXEC PGM=*.LKED.SYSLMOD,REGION=52K
//SYSPRINT DD SYSOUT=A
```

The JOB statement, //SYSIN DD * statement, the source language statements, and the /* statements are omitted; they must be included when the job is submitted. The JCL statements can now be called forth by giving the name of the cataloged procedure on an EXEC statement.

```
//TEST JOB 5542,'SMITH',CLASS=A
// EXEC PLIXCLG
//PL1.SYSIN DD *
       [ source language statements ]
/*
```

The absence of a PGM= keyword on the EXEC statement indicates that a cataloged procedure is requested. The PL1. prefixed to the SYSIN ddname tells the system that the DD statement is for the step named PL1. Now the JCL has become manageable.

We've covered the JCL statements very fast here to just give the feel for their use. The next chapters go into them in detail.

Chapter 4

JCL STATEMENT FORMATS AND RULES

I. JCL STATEMENT FORMAT

All JCL statements (except for the /* statement) begin with a // in columns 1 and 2, followed by a name, operation, operand, and comments field.

```
//name operation operand comments
```

The name field is optional for some statements and begins immediately after the second slash, while the other fields are separated from each other by one or more blanks. The fields, except for the comments, must be coded in columns 3 to 71. The comments field can be extended through column 80.

The *name field* identifies the statement so that other statements or a computer program can refer to it. The name can range from one to eight characters in length and can contain any alphanumeric (A to Z, 0 to 9) or national (* $ #) characters. For JCL, the *, $, and # characters are considered to be alphabetic characters, and you can write them wherever you can write an alphabetic character. However, the first character of the name must be in column 3 and be alphabetic (A to Z) or national (*, $, #). Choose names that convey meaning in the JCL just as you would if you were writing an application program.

```
        Correct                      Incorrect

    //A                  //1TEST    [ first character not A-Z, @ $ # ]
    //TEST#10            //SPACECRAFT  [ more than 8 characters ]
    //PAYROLLS           //TEST-6    [ dash not legal ]
```

The *operation field* specifies the type of statement: JOB, EXEC, DD, PROC, PEND, or an operator command.

```
//TEST20 JOB
//STEP EXEC
//PRINT DD
```

The *operand field* supplies the information in the form of parameters separated by commas. Parameters are composites of prescribed words (keywords) and variables for which information must be substituted. The operand field has no fixed length or column requirements as long as it does not extend beyond column 71, but it must be preceded and followed by at least one blank.

```
//TEST20 JOB 9205,CLASS=A
//STEP1 EXEC PLIXCLG
//PRINT DD SYSOUT=A
```

The *comments field* is optional, and is used for notes and comments. It must be separated from the operand field by at least one blank, and can only be coded if there is an operand field.

```
//TEST20 JOB 9205,CLASS=A     THIS IS A COMMENT
```

II. PARAMETERS IN THE OPERAND FIELD

The operand field is made up of two types of parameters: *positional parameters* characterized by their position in the operand field in relation to other parameters, and *keyword parameters*, positionally independent with respect to others of their type and consisting of a keyword followed by an equal sign and variable information. The following example contains both a positional parameter (3645) and a keyword parameter (CLASS = A).

```
//TEST JOB 3654,CLASS=A
```

A positional parameter or the variable information in a keyword parameter is sometimes a *list of subparameters*. Such a list may comprise both positional and keyword subparameters that follow the same rules and restrictions as positional and keyword parameters. Enclose a subparameter list in parentheses unless the list reduces to a single subparameter. The following JOB statement illustrates positional subparameters.

```
//TEST JOB (3645,100,40),COND=(9,LT)
```

The (3645,100,40) is a positional parameter containing three positional sub-parameters. COND = (9,LT) is a keyword parameter containing two positional subparameters. Subparameters can also be keywords. DCB = (LRECL = 80,BLKSIZE = 1600) represents a keyword parameter consisting of two keyword subparameters.

III. PARAMETER RULES

1. Both positional and keyword parameters must be separated by commas; blanks are not permitted.

Correct	Incorrect
`6,CLASS=A,REGION=104K`	`6,  CLASS=A,REGION=104K` `[ blanks not permitted ]`
`(6,106),CLASS=A` `CLASS=A,REGION=104K`	`(6,106)CLASS=A   [ no comma ]` `CLASS=A,REGION=104K,   [ extra comma ]`

   Misplaced blanks in JCL statements lead to errors. In the following statement, a blank is inadvertently left between two parameters. The ,CLASS = A parameter is treated as a comment and is ignored.

```
//TEST20 JOB 9205 ,CLASS=A
```

2. Positional parameters must be coded in the specified order before any keyword parameters in the operand field.

Correct	Incorrect
`(6,106),CLASS=A`	`CLASS=A,(6,106)`

3. The absence of a positional parameter is indicated by coding a comma in its place. The second positional subparameter in the following JOB statement is to be omitted.

```
//TEST JOB (3645,100,40),CLASS=A
//TEST JOB (3645,,40),CLASS=A
```

4. If the absent positional parameter is the last parameter, or if all later positional parameters are also absent, subsequent replacing commas need not be coded.

```
//TEST JOB (3645,,),CLASS=A
     or
//TEST JOB (3645),CLASS=A
```

5. The enclosing parentheses can be omitted if a subparameter consists of a single value.

```
//TEST JOB (3645),CLASS=A
  or
//TEST JOB 3645,CLASS=A
```

6. Nothing need be coded if all positional parameters are absent.

```
//TEST JOB CLASS=A
```

7. Keyword parameters may be coded in any order in the operand field, after any positional parameters.

```
//TEST JOB 3645,MSGLEVEL=1,REGION=104K,CLASS=A
     or
//TEST JOB 3645,CLASS=A,MSGLEVEL=1,REGION=104K
```

These rules appear complex, but a little practice makes their application automatic. The following examples should help to establish the rules in your mind.

```
//A DD DCB=(LRECL=80,RECFM=F),
//      SPACE=(TRK,(100,80,30),RLSE,CONTIG,ROUND)
```

This statement does not fit onto one line so it is continued onto another. The rules for continuation are given in the next section. The example that follows shows how the statement is coded as the underlined parameters are omitted.

```
//A DD DCB=(LRECL=80,RECFM=F),
//      SPACE=(TRK,(100,,30,RLSE,,ROUND)

//A DD DCB=LRECL=80,SPACE=(TRK,100,RLSE)

//A DD SPACE=(TRK,100)
```

IV. GENERAL JCL RULES

1. Start all statements in column 1 with the appropriate // or /*.
2. An entry (sometimes optional) in the name field must begin in column 3 and be followed by at least one blank.

```
//TEST12 JOB    but not    // TEST12 JOB    or    //TEST12JOB
```

3. Fields must be separated by at least one blank.

```
//STEP1 EXEC PLIXCLG    but not    //STEP1EXEC PLIXCLG
                                          or
                                   //STEP1 EXECPLIXCLG
```

4. There must be no imbedded blanks within fields, and parameters must be separated by commas.

5. Comments may be written on JCL statements that have an operand field by leaving a blank between the operand and the comments.

```
//STEP1 EXEC PLIXCLG THIS IS A COMMENT.
```

6. Columns 1 to 71 contain the JCL information. If more than one line is needed or if you wish to place parameters on separate lines, interrupt the fields after a complete parameter (including the comma that follows it) at or before column 71, code // in columns 1 and 2 of the following line, and continue the interrupted statement beginning anywhere in columns 4 to 16. (The accounting information on JOB statements, ACCT and PARM parameters on EXEC statements, COND parameters on JOB and EXEC statements, and DCB, VOL = SER, and VOL = REF parameters on DD statements can also be interrupted after a complete subparameter and any comma following it.)

```
//TEST JOB 6245,CLASS=A,MSGLEVEL=1,
//   REGION=104K
        or
//TEST JOB 6245,
//   CLASS=A,MSGLEVEL=1,
//   REGION=104K
```

7. Some parameters apply only to specific systems or hardware devices. Parameters are ignored if they are inappropriate for a system or hardware device.

8. In this book, fields containing upper case or special characters [PARM (, / . , etc.] are coded exactly as shown. Lower case fields must be filled in with values you select. For example, TIME = *minutes* could be coded as TIME = 10 to request a time of 10 minutes.

9. As a convention in this book, items stacked vertically above a dashed line indicate that one of the items must be chosen. If one of the stacked items is underlined, it is the default. For example:

```
        NEW   KEEP
        OLD   DELETE
DISP=(---,  ------)
```

could be coded as DISP = (NEW,KEEP), DISP = (OLD,KEEP), etc. DISP = (,DELETE) is equivalent to DISP = (NEW,DELETE) because NEW is the default. If both positional subparameters were optional, you could code DISP = (,KEEP), DISP = OLD, etc.

V. COMMENTING JCL

JCL should be commented as you would any programming language. The comments statement contains //* in columns 1 to 3, with the remaining columns containing any desired comments. They can be placed before or after any JCL statements following the JOB statement to help document the JCL. Comments can also be coded on any JCL statement by leaving a blank field after the operand field.

```
//A DD UNIT=SYSDA,  A DISK IS USED.
//* THE FOLLOWING STATEMENTS REQUESTS THE
//* SPECIFIC VOLUME TO USE.
//     VOL=SER=PACK12  PACK 12 IS USED.
```

The system lists the comments but ignores them when interpreting the JCL. This statement is interpreted as:

```
//A DD UNIT=SYSDA,VOL=SER=PACK12
```

As an example of the use of comment statements, suppose the JCL must be changed each time it is run. You could place comment statements after the JOB statement to remind yourself of the changes.

```
//TEST#9 JOB (5542,30),CLASS=A
//******** TAPE MOUNTS: 003845, 003900-WRITE ENABLE.
//******** JCL CHANGES: LAST LINE IS RUN DATE.
```

Use comment statements as necessary throughout the job to describe what the reader may need to know. A solid line of asterisks as comment statements preceding each job step makes the start of the step easier to locate.

```
//***********************************************************
//******** SORT THE PAYROLL MASTER
//***********************************************************
//STEP6 EXEC SORTD
```

VI. PLACEMENT OF JCL STATEMENTS

Many of the JCL statements have not been described yet, but their placement is described here for completeness. JCL statements must be placed in the following order:

1. JOB statement.
2. Any JOBLIB statement.
3. Any JOBCAT or SYSCHK statements.
4. Any in-stream procedures.
5. The first EXEC statement.
6. Any STEPCAT, STEPLIB, or ordinary DD statements belonging to the step.

7. Any more EXEC statements and their associated DD statements.
8. Any null statement.

In addition to these rules, the following items must be considered in placing JCL statements:

- If DD statements in a step have the same ddname, the first statement is used and subsequent DD statements in that step with the same ddname are ignored. (In JES3, the job is terminated with a JCL error.)
- Data sets are concatenated in the order of the DD statements.
- Multiple SYSOUT DD statements to the same output class are printed in the order of the DD statements.
- DD statements overriding cataloged procedures must be in the same order as the statements within the procedure. Added DD statements must follow any overriding DD statements.
- EXEC or DD statements with referback parameters must follow the statement to which they refer.
- DD statements describing an ISAM data set must define the index area, prime area, and overflow area, in that order.
- The PROC statement must be the first statement in a cataloged or in-stream procedure.
- The PEND statement must follow the last JCL statement in an in-stream procedure.
- Any comments statement must be placed after the JOB statement, but can be placed before or after any other JCL statements.
- Command statements can be placed before a JOB, EXEC, null, or another command statement. However, it cannot be placed before the first JOB statement in a jobstream.

Chapter 5

THE JOB STATEMENT

The JOB statement informs the operating system of the start of a job, gives the necessary accounting information, and supplies run parameters. Each job must begin with a single JOB statement. Installations usually establish a fixed JOB statement format that must be used, and some JOB statement parameters described in this chapter may be forbidden.

The JOB statement has the following form:

```
//jobname JOB (acct-number,acct-information),name,keyword-parameters
```

- *jobname* is a name you assign to the job.
- *acct-number,acct-information* is the account number to which the job is charged and any additional accounting information established by the installation.
- *name* is a name you select to identify the run.
- *keyword-parameters* are the following:

CLASS   Specifies the job class.

GROUP   (MVS only.) Allows users to share Resource Access Control Facility (RACF) protected data sets. (Seldom needed. Description deferred until Chapter 17.)

MPROFILE   (VS1 only.) Assigns job scheduler messages to Installation Specified Selection Parameters (ISSP). (Seldom needed. Description in Chapter 17.)

MSGCLASS   Specifies the job scheduler output class.

MSGLEVEL   Specifies whether or not to list all the JCL statements.

NOTIFY   (MVS only.) Notifies you at a time-sharing terminal when the batch job completes. (Description in Chapter 17.)

PASSWORD   (MVS only.) Identifies a current RACF password or assigns a new password. (Seldom needed. Description in Chapter 17.)

PROFILE   (VS1 only.) Assigns a job to a job class and priority by use of ISSP. (Seldom needed. Description in Chapter 17.)

PRTY | Specifies the job's priority in the input queue.

RESTART | Submits a job for restart. (Seldom needed. Description in Chapter 17.)

TYPRUN | Holds the job in the input queue or allows JCL to be checked without executing job. Seldom needed.

USER | (MVS only.) Specifies a RACF userid. (Seldom needed. Description in Chapter 17.)

The following optional keyword parameters may be coded on both the JOB and EXEC statements. They are discussed in Chapter 7.

ADDRSPC | Specifies that the job cannot be paged. Seldom needed.

COND | Specifies conditions for executing subsequent job steps if a previous step fails.

PERFORM | (MVS only.) Assigns the job to a performance group for execution priority. (Seldom needed. Description in Chapter 17.)

RD | Request restart of a job step. (Seldom needed. Description in Chapter 17.)

REGION | Specifies region size to allocate to job.

TIME | Imposes a time limit on the job.

The start of a job is defined by the JOB statement. The following is typical:

```
//TEST#6 JOB (2215,16),'TEST6',CLASS=A
```

The system reads the entire job in and checks your JCL statements for syntax errors. Then it stores the job on disk in a job queue to await execution. Actually, the system keeps several queues, termed job classes. Jobs are directed into the queues by the CLASS parameter. This is illustrated in Figure 23.

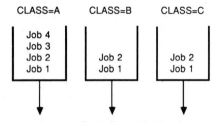

Jobs are selected on a first-in-first-out basis to be executed.

Figure 23. Job classes.

There are several reasons for an installation to set up separate job classes.

- To balance the running of jobs that do many calculations with jobs that do lots of input/output.
- To set aside jobs that require a special setup, such as requiring a tape to be mounted.
- To control when some jobs are run, such as overnight or on weekends.

Actually, the JOB statement is easy because most of the items on it are specified by your installation, which will tell you what to write. Figure 24 illustrates the usual JOB statement.

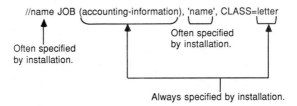

Figure 24. Typical JOB statement.

Now let's examine the parameters in detail.

I.   JOBNAME: NAME OF JOB

The *jobname* is selected by you to identify the job to the operating system. It can range from one to eight alphanumeric (A to Z, 0 to 9) or national (@ $ #) characters. The first character must begin in column 3 and be alphabetic (A to Z) or national. Jobs should be given unique names because the system will not run jobs concurrently having the same name. It will hold up a job until any job having the same jobname completes execution. Unique names can be achieved by assigning job names or by coding some unique characters as a part of the jobname, for example, initials, job number, or employee id.

```
    Correct              Incorrect

//GDB406      //6J    [ first character not A to Z, @ $ #. ]
//A8463       //SUPERCOMP  [ more than 8 characters. ]
//B8750#12    // RUN#6   [ does not begin in column 3. ]
```

Many installations prescribe the jobname you must use.

II. ACCOUNTING INFORMATION

Accounting information is coded as:

```
(acct-number,additional-acct-information)
```

The *account number* and *additional accounting information* must be defined by an installation. Subparameters must all be separated by commas.

The account number is optional but can be made mandatory when the system is generated. The total number of characters in the account number and additional accounting information (including commas that separate the subparameters) cannot exceed 142. If the account number or additional accounting information contains any special characters except a hyphen [that is, blank . , / ') (* & + =], enclose the subparameter in apostrophes ('). The apostrophes are not passed as part of the information. A legitimate apostrophe is coded as two consecutive apostrophes; for example, I'M is coded as 'I' 'M'. Ampersands (&) should also be coded as two ampersands (&&).

The usual rules of omitting commas and parentheses in lists of subparameters apply. If the account number is omitted, its absence is indicated by a comma: (, *additional-acct-information*). If there is no additional accounting information, the parentheses around the account number may be omitted. Accounting information can be continued onto another line after a complete subparameter, including the comma that follows it.

```
//jobname JOB 2011

//jobname JOB (20746,30,
// 6,94)

//jobname JOB 3042,6   [ Wrong!  Parentheses needed if more than one
                         positional parameter. ]
```

Alternatively, you may enclose the accounting information in apostrophes rather than parentheses. This obviates having to enclose subparameters containing special characters in apostrophes, but the accounting information must then be coded completely on one line.

```
//jobname JOB '2256/2240'
```

In JES2, the accounting information is usually specified as follows:

```
(acct,room,time,lines,cards,forms,copies,log,linect)
```

- *acct* is the account number, one to four alphanumeric characters.
- *room* is your room number, one to four alphanumeric characters.
- *time* is the CPU time estimate in minutes, one to four numeric digits.
- *lines* is the estimated lines of printed output, one to four numeric digits.
- *cards* is the estimated number of cards punched, one to four numeric digits.
- *forms* requests special forms for printing the entire job, one to four alpha-numeric characters.
- *copies* is the number of copies to print, 1 to 255; 1 is default.
- *log*; code an N if no joblog is wanted.
- *linect* is the lines per page, one to three digits.

III. NAME: PROGRAMMER NAME

The name is a one- to twenty-character name selected by you to identify yourself or the job. It must be enclosed in apostrophes if it contains special characters other than a period [that is, blank . , / ') (* $ + − =]. Rather than trying to remember all these rules, just enclose the name in apostrophes and forget about them. A legitimate apostrophe is coded as two consecutive apostrophes; for example, O'BRIAN is coded as 'O' 'BRIAN'.

The name parameter can be made mandatory by an installation when the system is generated.

```
//FIRST JOB (4562,200,10),SMITH
//SECOND JOB ,A,SMITH
    [ If the account number is not coded, indicate its absence
    with a comma. ]
//THIRD JOB 6542,'O''REILLY'
//FOURTH JOB 5642,AL GOLL
    [ Wrong!  Need enclosing apostrophes if name contains special
    characters other than the period. ]
```

IV. CLASS: JOB CLASS

CLASS = *class* specifies the job class. Your installation will specify which of the 36 possible job classes to use. Job classes can range from A to Z, 0 to 9. The installation establishes a default job class that is in effect if CLASS is omitted.

Installations usually attempt to establish job classes that achieve a balance between I/O-bound jobs and CPU-bound jobs, between big jobs and little jobs, etc. The job class may depend on such things as the amount of CPU time required by the job, tape mounts, when the job is to be run, and the region size.

Job classes also determine the overall priority of a job, along with the PRTY parameter. (The PRTY parameter is a JCL parameter that you can write to establish the priority for a job. It is described later.) The operator can start and stop various job classes, thus controlling the time they are run.

Jobs within the same job class are queued together in the input queue to await execution. The installation may assign priorities to jobs within the same class, based on such resource requirements as CPU time. You may code the PRTY parameter on the JOB statement to give special priority to a job (it may also be set by the operator), but your installation will likely control this. Jobs of equal priority are executed in the order they are submitted.

V.   MSGCLASS: SYSTEM MESSAGES

A.   The MSGCLASS Parameter

MSGCLASS = *class* specifies job scheduler message output class. The system first writes print output onto direct-access volumes, and output writer procedures later write the output onto printers. The output class is a single character, A to Z, or 0 to 9. The installation sets the default if MSGCLASS is omitted, usually MSGCLASS = A, the printer.

Job scheduler messages include all messages not printed by the actual job steps being executed; that is, JCL statements and error messages, device allocations, data set dispositions, and accounting information. Since the operator must start output writers to specific output classes, an active output class must be used; otherwise the output will not be printed.

Special output classes may be established for high-volume output, for special forms, or to separate output (all output of a specific class is printed together). You should seldom need to use a special output writer for job scheduler messages.

```
//BIG JOB 2564,JONES,PRTY=2,MSGCLASS=V
```

B.   MSGCLASS Output

JCL statements submitted in the input stream are listed with // in columns 1 and 2, comment statements are listed with *** in columns 1 to 3, cataloged procedure statements are listed with XX in columns 1 and 2, and in-stream procedure statements are listed with + + in columns 1 and 2. DD statements overriding cataloged procedures are listed with X/ in columns 1 and 2, and DD statements overriding in-stream procedures are listed with +/ in columns 1 and 2. Within a cataloged procedure, JCL statements considered by the system to contain only comments are listed with XX* in columns 1 to 3; within in-stream procedures they are listed with + + * in columns 1 to 3.

The output from your job is actually divided into two categories:

- Job scheduler messages, which include your JCL statements and error messages, device allocations, data set disposition, and accounting information.
- The output generated by the programs you execute with your JCL.

The job scheduler message output you receive varies with the version of the operating system you're using and is often customized by the individual installation, so it may be a little different from that shown here. You first receive a general summary of the job execution, called a job log, such as this:

```
15.49.39 JOB nnnn jobname STARTED - CLASS A
       [ This tells you the time your job started, the job number
       assigned to the job internally, your jobname, and the job
       class. ]
15.50.04 JOB nnnn IEF233A M 562,942731,,jobname,stepname
15.50.13 JOB nnnn IEF234E K 562,942731,,jobname,stepname
       [ For tapes:  The M above tells you that tape 942731 was
       mounted.  The K means it was kept--dismounted--at 15.50.13. ]
```

If your job ABENDs, you get a system code message.

```
15.49.39 JOB 1724 TEST#1 STARTED - CLASS A
15.50.04 JOB 1724 IEF233A M 562,942731,,TEST#1,STEP1
15.50.13 JOB 1724 IEF234E K 562,942731,,TEST#1,STEP1
15.50.20 JOB 1724 IEF450I TEST#1 STEP2 - ABEND 322 U0000
15.50.23 JOB 1724 TEST#1 ENDED
```

There are thousands of possible messages, but most of them rarely occur. Following the job log will be a listing of your JCL. It will include a listing of any cataloged procedures you use. This listing can go on for pages, so we'll show only a few statements.

```
//TEST#1 JOB (2215,15),'TEST',CLASS=A
// EXEC FORTCLG
       [ The JCL statements you actually write--the JCL statements in
       the input stream--display with // in the first two columns. ]
XXFORT EXEC PGM=FORTVS,REGION=128K
XXSYSPRINT DD SYSOUT=A
       [ If you invoke a cataloged procedure, it is listed after the
       EXEC invoking it.  You can tell the cataloged procedure
       statements because they display with XX in the first two
       columns.  ]
```

Following the JCL will be a list of all the symbolic parameter substitution done within the step of the cataloged procedure. The output might look like this:

```
STMT NO.        MESSAGE
   4            IEF653I SUBSTITUTION JCL - TIME=3
   5            IEF653I SUBSTITUTION JCL - DISP=SHR
   .            .   .   .   .   .   .   .   .   .
```

When you override a DD statement in a cataloged procedure, both the overriding statement and the original statement are shown. The cataloged procedure statement displays with an X/ in the first two columns:

```
//LKED.SYSLMOD DSN=Y0000.PGM.LIB(COMPUTE),DISP=(OLD,PASS)
X/SYSLMOD DD DISP=(MOD,PASS),DSN=&&GOSET(MAIN),
X/             SPACE=(1024,(200,0,1)),UNIT=SYSDA
```

Notice that you don't get a display of how the overridden step actually appears to the system. The SYSLMOD DD statement will be treated as if it were written as:

```
//SYSLMOD DD DSN=Y0000.PGM.LIB(COMPUTE),DISP=(OLD,PASS),
//             SPACE=(1024,(200,0,1)),UNIT=SYSDA
```

You must visualize how the statement will appear. The system doesn't display it this way. The system also lists comment statements differently if they come from the input stream than if they come from a cataloged procedure. A comment statement such as this:

```
//* THIS IS A COMMENT.
```

appears with asterisks in the first three columns if it comes from the input stream.

```
*** THIS IS A COMMENT.
```

It appears with XX* in the first three columns if it comes from a cataloged procedure:

```
XX* THIS IS A COMMENT.
```

Then you get the allocation messages for each data set in the step:

```
IEF236I ALLOC. FOR TEST#1
IEF237I 452 ALLOCATED TO STEPLIB
IEF237I 450 ALLOCATED TO SYSLIN
IEF237I JES2 ALLOCATED TO SYSPRINT
   .      .         .
```

The 450 and 452 are hardware device addresses. From this, you know that the data set specified with a ddname of SYSLIN was placed on hardware address 450, which is a specific disk pack. The JES2 in place of the hardware address for

SYSPRINT means that the printed output was spooled rather than being written to a particular hardware device. Then you get a line telling you the condition code for the step, such as this:

```
IEF142I TEST#1 FORT - STEP WAS EXECUTED - COND CODE 0012
```

Following the COND CODE message, you get a disposition message for each data set used in the step.

```
IEF285I SYS1.PROCLIB                                    KEPT
IEF285I VOL SER NOS= SYSPGM.
IEF285I JES2.JOB00258.S00102                           SYSOUT
IEF285I SYS85178.T085249.RA000.TEST#1.LOADSET          PASSED
IEF285I VOL SER NOS= PACK12.
```

From this you know that a data set named SYS1.PROCLIB on a volume named SYSPGM was kept. The JES2.JOB00258.S00102 for SYSOUT represents your spooled output. The SYS85178.T085249.RA000.TEST#1.LOADSET is the data set name made up for a temporary data set when you wrote DSN = &&LOADSET. The system makes up names like this, incorporating the date, time, and jobname to ensure that the temporary data set name is unique. The LOADSET data set was stored on PACK12 and was passed.

And, finally, you get a message telling you when the step started, when it ended, how much virtual storage you used, and how much storage the system needed to execute the step.

```
IEF373I TEST#1  /FORT    / START 85178.1549
IEF374I TEST#1  /FORT    / STOP  85178.1553
        CPU   0MIN 01.79SEC SRB  0MIN 00.13SEC
        VIRT 256K SYS 240
```

From this, you can tell that your FORT step used 1.79 seconds of CPU time. You used a virtual region size of 256K. It is this number that determines what you must specify in the REGION parameter. Unfortunately, you don't get this number until you execute the job step.

The final item printed for the step is usually the accounting information for the job step. This will differ for each installation. All of the information is then repeated for each step:

- A list of your JCL statements interspersed with any cataloged procedure statements you invoked.
- The allocation message for each data set.
- The condition code for the job step.
- The disposition messages for the data sets.

- The elapsed time, CPU time, and region used.
- Any accounting information.

After you wade through all the job scheduler messages for the entire job, you finally get to the output generated by your job.

VI. MSGLEVEL: PRINT JCL STATEMENTS

MSGLEVEL = (*jcl,allocations*) specifies the printing of JCL statements and allocation messages. *Allocation messages*, if requested, appear at the beginning of each job step to show the allocation of data sets to devices, and at the end of each step to show the data set disposition. Default values set by the installation are in effect if MSGLEVEL is omitted.

The values for jcl and allocations are as follows:

```
   jcl                              Meaning
    0          Print only the JOB statement.
    1          Print all JCL in the input stream and all the JCL
               in any cataloged procedures invoked, including
               the internal representation of statements after
               symbolic parameter substitutions.
    2          Print only the JCL in the input stream.

allocations                        Meaning
    0          Do not print allocation messages unless the job
               abnormally terminates.
    1          Print all allocation messages.
```

```
//TEST JOB 6542,'LEWIS N. CLARK',MSGLEVEL=(1,0)
    [ All JCL is printed.  No allocation messages are printed. ]

//RUNFAST JOB 5540,STOCK,MSGLEVEL=2
    [ Only the JCL in the input stream is printed.  Printing of
    allocation messages depends on the default. ]

//AFTERIT JOB 5522,STACK,MSGLEVEL=(,1)
    [ Printing of JCL statements depends on the default.
    Allocation messages are printed. ]
```

The reason for the MSGLEVEL parameter is to save paper. After a job is debugged, there may be no need to print all the JCL and allocation messages each time it runs. To reduce printing to a minimum, code MSGLEVEL = (0,0).

VII. PRTY: JOB PRIORITY

PRTY = *priority* specifies the *job execution priority*, the priority with which jobs are selected from the queue to be executed. The *priority* may range from 0 (lowest) to 13 (in VS1 and MVS JES3) or 15 (in JES2). A priority established by the installation defaults if PRTY is omitted. The default priority may also be changed by the operator or by the system as the job ages in the input queue. Your installation will likely control the use of this parameter.

Priority is within job class. When several jobs of a given class are queued up waiting to be executed, the job with the highest priority within a class is selected first. Jobs with equal priority are selected on a first-in/first-out order. The job scheduler determines which job classes have the highest priority for job selection.

Dispatching priority, the priority with which each job in storage gets the CPU, is set by the installation. (The dispatching priority can also be set with the DPRTY parameter on the EXEC statement.)

VIII. TYPRUN: SPECIAL JOB PROCESSING

TYPRUN = HOLD holds a job in the input queue for later execution. The job is held until the operator releases it. Be sure the operator is told when to release the job or it will just sit in the input queue.

TYPRUN = HOLD can be used when one job must not be run until another job completes, or to ensure that all mountable volumes are located before the job is released for execution. However, the operators are usually kept busy by the system, and operator intervention should be minimized.

```
//XR15 JOB (2001,10),'J.K.L.',CLASS=M,TYPRUN=HOLD
```

TYPRUN = JCLHOLD (JES2 only) also holds the job until the operator releases it, but differs from TYPRUN = HOLD in that the JCL is not checked until the operator releases the job. Perhaps the only use for JCLHOLD is when a preceding job updates a cataloged procedure.

```
//XR15 JOB (2001,10),'J.K.L.',CLASS=M,TYPRUN=JCLHOLD
```

TYPRUN = SCAN checks the JCL for syntax errors and suppresses execution of the job. This checking does not include checking for duplicate data sets on volumes, insufficient direct-access storage space, or an insufficient region size for the job steps. You can use this to check for JCL syntax errors without executing the job.

```
//XR15 JOB (2001,10),'J.K.L.',CLASS=M,TYPRUN=SCAN
```

TYPRUN = COPY (JES2 only) lists or duplicates the lines placed after the JOB statement. The system routes the output to the message class specified by the MSGCLASS parameter. Class A is traditionally the printer. You can use this to list your JCL statements.

```
//XR15 JOB (2001,10),'J.K.L.',MSGCLASS=A,TYPRUN=COPY,CLASS=A
       [ Lines to be printed are placed here. ]
```

EXERCISES

1. Find out your installation's requirements for the JOB statement, including the following parameters:

   - jobname
   - acct-number,acct-information
   - name
   - CLASS. Find out all the permissible job classes and the requirements for assigning a job to a class. Note the default job class.
   - MSGCLASS. List all the output classes and their use. Note the default.
   - MSGLEVEL. Note the default.
   - PRTY. Note the default.
   - TYPRUN

2. Make up a JOB statement and run the following job. Code the MSGCLASS parameter to produce both JCL and allocation messages.

```
// JOB statement
// EXEC PLIXCG
//PL1.SYSIN DD *
  TEST: PROC OPTIONS(MAIN);
    DCL CARD CHAR(80);
    ON ENDFILE(IN) STOP;
  START:
    READ FILE(IN) INTO (CARD);
    WRITE FILE(OUT) FROM (CARD);
    GO TO START;
    END TEST;
//GO.OUT DD SYSOUT=A,DCB=BLKSIZE=80
//GO.IN DD *
  LINE 1
  LINE 2
/*
```

3. Have someone explain all the system messages and the accounting information produced by your installation. Be sure you can tell how much it costs to run the job.

Chapter 6

THE EXEC STATEMENT

Each job step begins with an EXEC statement that either names the program to execute (compiler, linkage editor, applications program, utility, etc.) or invokes a cataloged procedure. A cataloged procedure can contain several job steps, each beginning with an EXEC statement naming a program to execute. There may be as many as 255 EXEC statements in a job, each followed by DD statements defining the data sets required by the job step. The general form of the EXEC statement is:

```
                    procedure
                    PGM=program
                    PGM=*.referback
//stepname EXEC ---------------,keyword-parameters
```

- *stepname* is the name you choose for the job step.
- *referback* names a previous DD statement describing the program to execute.
- *program* names the program to execute.
- *procedure* is the cataloged procedure to use.
- *keyword-parameters* are the following:

ACCT	Provides accounting information for the job step. Seldom needed.
DPRTY	(MVS only.) Sets the dispatching priority of the job step. Seldom needed.
DYNAMNBR	(MVS only.) Specifies the number of dynamically allocated resources. (Seldom needed. Discussion deferred until Chapter 17.)
PARM	Passes parameters to the job step.

The following optional keyword parameters may be coded on both the EXEC and JOB statements; a discussion of them is deferred until Chapter 7.

ADDRSPC	Specifies that the step cannot be paged. Seldom needed.

COND Specifies conditions for executing subsequent job steps if previous steps fail.

PERFORM (MVS only.) Assign the step to a performance group for execution priority. (Seldom needed. Described in Chapter 17.)

RD Specifies the step restart conditions. (Seldom needed. Described in Chapter 17.)

REGION Specifies the region size to allocate to job step.

TIME Imposes a time limit on the job step.

Although there are several parameters, the only ones you are likely to need are PARM, COND, REGION, and TIME.

I. STEPNAME: NAME OF JOB STEP

//stepname EXEC names the job step. The stepname is an optional one- to eight-alphanumeric (A to Z, 0 to 9) or national (@ $ #) character name you select. It must begin in column 3 with an alphabetic or national (A to Z @ $ #) character. Stepnames within a job or cataloged procedure should be unique so that you can reference them in other JCL statements. A stepname is required if subsequent JCL statements refer to the job step or if you wish to restart the job from the step. All EXEC statements in cataloged procedures should have stepnames so that the statements can be modified.

```
//STEP10 EXEC
//COMPUT EXEC
//(GO EXEC
        [ Wrong!  First character not alphabetic. ]
```

II. PGM: NAME OF PROGRAM

//stepname EXEC PGM=program names the program to execute. Programs can reside in a system library named SYS1.LINKLIB, in temporary libraries, and in private libraries. A program is a load module and must be a member of a partitioned data set on a direct-access volume. If the program name cannot be found in the libraries, the system abnormally terminates the job with an 806 completion code. This completion code will be listed with the system messages in your printed output.

In JES3, you can write PGM=JCLTEST to test the JCL without executing any program. This does the same thing as TYPRUN=SCAN on the JOB statement.

A. Programs in System Library

A system library named SYS1.LINKLIB contains all the IBM-supplied system programs, such as compilers, linkage editor, and service programs. An installation may add its own programs to SYS1.LINKLIB as long as it chooses names that do not conflict with the names of the IBM programs. (If a program is added to a partitioned data set with the same name as an existing program, the old program is replaced.)

A system program in SYS1.LINKLIB is executed by naming the program on the EXEC statement.

```
//STEP1 EXEC PGM=IEFBR14
```

In the absence of other instructions, the system searches SYS1.LINKLIB for the program. IBM programs have names similar to that shown to decrease the likelihood of someone duplicating the name.

B. Programs in Private Libraries

Private program libraries are created as output from the linkage editor. Chapter 14 describes how to retain this output as a private library. Programs within a library must have unique names; programs in separate libraries may have the same name. A private program is executed by including a special JOBLIB DD statement immediately after the JOB statement. (DD statement parameters are fully described in later chapters.)

```
//TEST JOB 62545,'SMITH',CLASS=A
//JOBLIB DD DSN=COMPLIB,DISP=SHR
//GO EXEC PGM=COMP1
```

C. JOBLIB DD Statement

The previous JOBLIB DD statement defines COMPLIB as a private library that presumably contains the program COMP1. The JOBLIB statement is placed immediately after the JOB statement and is effective for all the job steps. It cannot be placed in a cataloged procedure. If the program is not found in the named library, the system searches SYS1.LINKLIB. Libraries must be concatenated if several programs from different libraries are executed. The libraries are searched in the order in which they are named in the DD statements.

```
//TEST JOB 6245,'SMITH',CLASS=A
//JOBLIB DD DSN=COMPLIB,DISP=SHR
//       DD DSN=PRINTLIB,DISP=SHR
    [ PRINTLIB is concatenated to COMPLIB by omitting the ddname
      on the DD statement.  The system treats COMPLIB and PRINTLIB
      as if they were one data set. ]
//STEP1 EXEC PGM=COMP1
    [ COMP1 might be a program contained in COMPLIB. ]
//STEP2 EXEC PGM=PRINTX
    [ PRINTX could be contained in PRINTLIB. ]
//STEP3 EXEC PGM=IEA001
    [ IEA001 could be a system program contained in SYS1.LINKLIB. ]
```

You must specify the unit and volume serial number of the direct-access volume containing the data set if the library is not cataloged; that is, if its name and location are not recorded by the system.

```
//JOBLIB DD DSN=COMPLIB,DISP=SHR,UNIT=3380,VOL=SER=PACK12
      [ COMPLIB is not cataloged and is contained on volume PACK12
      of a 3380 disk unit. ]
```

D. STEPLIB DD Statement

The STEPLIB DD statement, similar in form and function to the JOBLIB statement, is placed after an EXEC statement and is effective only for that job step. STEPLIB provides an alternative means of specifying a private library.

```
//TEST JOB 6245,'SMITH',CLASS=A
//STEP1 EXEC PGM=COMP1
//STEPLIB DD DSN=COMPLIB,DISP=SHR
//STEP2 EXEC PGM=PRINTX
//STEPLIB DD DSN=PRINTLIB,DISP=SHR
```

If JOBLIB and STEPLIB DD statements are both included in a job, the STEPLIB statement overrides the JOBLIB statement for the step. To negate the effect of the JOBLIB statement for a particular step, name SYS1.LINKLIB on the STEPLIB statement.

Like the JOBLIB statement, the STEPLIB statement may be concatenated, and unit and volume parameters must be given if the library is not cataloged. Unlike the JOBLIB statement, the STEPLIB statement can be placed in a cataloged procedure. The following example shows the use of both JOBLIB and STEPLIB DD statements.

```
//TEST JOB 6245,'SMITH',CLASS=A
//JOBLIB   DD DSN=COMPLIB,DISP=SHR
//         DD DSN=PRINTLIB,DISP=SHR
//STEP1 EXEC PGM=ONE
//STEPLIB DD DSN=LIB1,DISP=SHR
      [ LIB1 and SYS1.LINKLIB are searched in that order for a
      program named ONE. ]
//STEP2 EXEC PGM=TWO
      [ COMPLIB, PRINTLIB, and SYS1.LINKLIB are searched in that
      order for a program named TWO. ]
//STEP3 EXEC PGM=THREE
//STEPLIB DD DSN=SYS1.LINKLIB,DISP=SHR
      [ SYS1.LINKLIB is searched for a program named THREE. ]
//STEP4 EXEC PLIXCLG
//PL1.STEPLIB DD DSN=LIB2,DISP=SHR
//             DD DSN=LIB3,DISP=SHR
      [ PLIXCLG is a cataloged procedure.  LIB2, LIB3, and
      SYS1.LINKLIB are searched in that order for the program
      requested in the PL1 step of the procedure.  COMPLIB,
      PRINTLIB, and SYS1.LINKLIB are searched in that order for
      programs requested in any remaining job steps in the
      procedure. ]
```

If several steps execute programs from the same library, it is generally better to use a JOBLIB statement. But if the steps execute programs from different libraries, you should probably use STEPLIB statements. There is another advantage to STEP-LIB statements. Quite often you will use a text editor to piece together steps from different jobs to create a new job. When you use STEPLIB statements, each step is complete. But if you use JOBLIB statements, you must remember to also copy the JOBLIB statement, which may be located far away from the EXEC statement and is thus easy to overlook.

E. Programs in Temporary Libraries

Often the output from one job step becomes the program to execute in a subsequent step. Linkage editor output is usually executed in a following step. If the load module output from the linkage editor is needed only for the duration of the job, it is placed in a temporary library. Then, rather than naming the program to execute, it is easier to refer back to the DD statement describing the data set containing the program. The step executing the program need not immediately follow the step creating the program.

```
//LK EXEC PGM=LINKEDIT
//LKEDOUT DD DSN=&&TEMP(GO),DISP=(NEW,PASS),
//              UNIT=SYSDA,SPACE=(1024,(200,20,1))
//STEP2 EXEC PGM=IEA001
//STEP3 EXEC PGM=*.LK.LKEDOUT
```

The backward reference (or *referback*) names the step and then the ddname of a DD statement within the step. If a cataloged procedure is invoked, the referback must include the cataloged procedure stepname. Suppose the previous LK step was part of a cataloged procedure named LKED.

```
//LKED PROC
//LK EXEC PGM=LINKEDIT
//LKEDOUT DD DSN=&&TEMP(GO),DISP=(NEW,PASS),
//              UNIT=SYSDA,SPACE=(1024,(200,20,1))
```

If the LKED procedure were invoked, you would refer back to the step with *.STEP1.LK.LKEDOUT:

```
//STEP1 EXEC LKED
//STEP2 EXEC PGM=IEA001
//STEP3 EXEC PGM=*.STEP1.LK.LKEDOUT
```

The referback parameter is not limited to temporary data sets. A program may be executed from any library using the referback.

```
//STEP1 EXEC PGM=IEFBR14
//PROGRAM DD DSN=COMPLIB(RUN6),DISP=SHR
//STEP2 EXEC PGM=*.STEP1.PROGRAM
```

STEP2 executes a program named RUN6 contained in the COMPLIB cataloged data set. The PGM = IEFBR14 is not arbitrary; it is a null program contained in SYS1.LINKLIB. The program executes a single end-of-program statement and is useful in writing a null job step to provide a place for DD statements. As is shown in subsequent chapters, you may want to allocate space to a data set on a direct-access volume or delete data sets without executing a program. Or, as the previous example shows, you may define data sets for subsequent referbacks. (The previous program could also be executed using a JOBLIB or STEPLIB statement.)

III. PROCEDURE: NAME OF CATALOGED PROCEDURE

//stepname EXEC procedure names a cataloged or in-stream procedure to use. Chapter 13 explains how to create procedures.

```
//STEP1 EXEC PLIXCLG
//STEPA EXEC FORTGCL
//EXEC COBUC
```

The stepname is often omitted on the EXEC statement invoking a procedure. You may code just the procedure name or the keyword PROC = *procedure*:

```
// EXEC PLIXCLG     same as     // EXEC PROC=PLIXCLG
```

In practice, the PROC = form is almost never used. It only increases the chance for a typing error.

IV. KEYWORD PARAMETERS

The keyword-parameters (PARM, TIME, etc.) are coded on the EXEC statement following the program or procedure name and apply only to the step being executed. The PGM parameter must appear first. (It looks like a keyword parameter, but is actually a positional parameter.)

```
//STEP1 EXEC PGM=STUDY,TIME=4,PARM=LIST
     [ The TIME and PARM parameters apply to STEP1 only.  The
     keyword parameters may be coded in any order after the PGM
     parameter or procedure name. ]
```

Parameters can be added to any step of a cataloged or in-stream procedure by appending the stepname to the keyword. (The PGM parameter cannot be overridden in a procedure.)

```
// EXEC PLIXCLG,TIME.GO=4
    [ The TIME parameter is added to the GO step of the PLIXCLG
    procedure.  Any TIME parameter already coded on the GO step
    in the procedure is overridden.  Other parameters on that or
    other steps in the procedure are not affected. ]
```

Each parameter may be coded as many times as there are steps in the procedure. However, the parameters for each step must appear on the EXEC statement in the order the steps appear in the procedure. If the PLIXCLG procedure had a PL1 step, a LKED step, and a GO step, the following might be coded.

```
// EXEC PLIXCLG,PARM.PL1=DECK,TIME.PL1=6,
//       TIME.LKED=7,TIME.GO=4
```

The following is invalid because the LKED step precedes the GO step.

```
// EXEC PLIXCLG,TIME.GO=24,TIME.LKED=7
```

If the stepname is omitted, a parameter applies to all steps of a procedure with the following exceptions.

- The PARM parameter applies only to the first step in the procedure, and any PARM parameters in subsequent steps within the procedure are nullified.
- The TIME parameter sets the total time for all the job steps, nullifying those on individual job steps.

Omitting the stepname for all other parameters causes them to be applied to all the job steps individually. Parameters with a stepname appended must appear before any parameters coded without appended stepnames. To nullify an existing parameter within a step in a procedure, code just the keyword and appended stepname, and an equal sign.

```
// EXEC PLIXCLG,TIME.PL1=,PARM.PL1=MAP,PARM.LKED=DECK,ACCT=6
    [ The TIME parameter in the PL1 step is nullified, the PARM
    parameters apply to the PL1 and LKED steps, and the ACCT
    parameter applies to all steps. ]
```

V. PARM: PASS PARAMETERS TO JOB STEPS

PARM = *value* passes control information to the job step when the step is initiated.

```
//STEP1EXEC PGM=ONE,PARM=XREF
```

There may be from one to a hundred characters of data in the PARM. If the value consists of several subvalues separated by commas, or if it contains special characters [blank , . / ') (* & + − =], enclose the value in apostrophes. Code a legitimate apostrophe as two consecutive apostrophes:

PARM = 'O' 'CLOCK,XREF,SIZE = 100'.

Parentheses may also be used to enclose several subvalues; any subvalues containing special characters must then be enclosed in apostrophes:

PARM = ('O' 'CLOCK',XREF,'SIZE = 100').

An ampersand must also be coded as two consecutive ampersands unless it designates a symbolic parameter in a procedure. The value may be interrupted for continuation only by enclosing it in parentheses and interrupting it after a complete subvalue, including the comma following it:

```
//STEP1 EXEC PGM=ONE,PARM=('K=6'
//          FIVE,'I=3','J=4',SEVEN)
     [ K=6,FIVE,I=3,J=4, and SEVEN are passed to the step. ]
//STEP2 EXEC PLIXCLG,PARM=STOP
     [ STOP is passed to the first step of the procedure; any PARM
     values in subsequent steps within the procedure are
     nullified. ]
//STEP3 EXEC PLIXCLG,PARM.LKED=MAP,PARM.GO=LIST
     [ MAP is passed to the LKED step, and LIST is passed to the GO
     step of the procedure. ]
```

You must know what values the processing program expects to be passed to it. If PARM is omitted, no values are passed. Programs supplied by IBM, such as the compliers and linkage editors, expect the value to represent various run options. Programs written in COBOL, PL/I, and assembler language can accept PARM values as follows:

COBOL:

```
//STEP1 EXEC COBUCLG,PARM.GO='string'
    .      .       .    .     .    .
  LINKAGE SECTION.
  01 PARM
     05 LNGTH PIC S9(4) COMP.
     05 VAL   PIC X(100).
     PROCEDURE DIVISION USING PARM.
     [ The length of the string is stored in LNGTH, and the string is
     stored in VAL.  Any valid data names may be used in place of
     PARM, LNGTH, and VAL. ]
```

PL/I:

```
//STEP1 EXEC PLIXCLG,PARM.GO='/string'
   .     .     .       .       .    .     .
  name: PROC(PARM) OPTIONS(MAIN);
```

```
DCL PARM CHAR(100) VAR;
    [ The string is stored in PARM and the PARM length is set to
    the length of the string.  Any valid data name may be used in
    place of PARM. ]
```

Assembler Language:

```
//STEP1 EXEC ASMFCLG,PARM.GO='string'
    [ When the system gives control to the program, general
    register 1 points to a full word containing the address of an
    area in storage.  The first half word of this area contains
    the number of characters in the string, the remainder of the
    area contains the string itself. ]
```

IBM processing programs may have three levels of values: default values generated into the system, PARM values in cataloged procedures that override the defaults, and PARM values coded on EXEC statements invoking the procedures. If a single PARM value is overridden in a procedure step, all PARM subparameters in the procedure step are nullified and the default values are reestablished. For example, a FORTRAN compile procedure might contain:

```
//FORTGC PROC
//FORT EXEC PGM=IEYFORT,PARM='LIST,MAP'
```

If the PARM is overridden when the procedure is invoked, all PARM subparameters are overridden.

```
//EXEC FORTGC,PARM.FORT=DECK
```

The LIST and MAP subparameters are replaced by DECK, and the FORT step appears in the run as:

```
//FOR EXEC PGM=IEYFORT,PARM=DECK
```

The loader program combines link edit and program execution into one job step. Parameters must be coded for both the loader and the program being loaded in a single PARM field. Values for the loader must be coded first, and any program values must be separated by a slash (/).

```
//LKEDGO EXEC PGM=LOADER,PARM='MAP,PRINT/RUN'
        [ MAP and PRINT are passed to the loader.  RUN is passed to
        the program being loaded. ]
//LKEDGO EXEC PGM=LOADER,PARM=MAP
        [ MAP is passed to the loader. ]
//LKEDGO EXEC PGM=LOADER,PARM='/RUN'
        [ RUN is passed to the program being loaded. ]
```

VI. ACCT: JOB STEP ACCOUNTING INFORMATION

Any accounting information for job steps must be defined by the installation. To supply step accounting information, you write ACCT = (*acct-information*), where the accounting information may be one or more subparameters separated by commas but cannot exceed 142 characters including the commas: ACCT = (2645,30,17). The outer parentheses may be omitted if there is only one subparameter: ACCT = 6225.

If subparameters contain any special characters except hyphens [blank , . / ') (* & + =], enclose the subparameters in apostrophes. Code a legitimate apostrophe as two consecutive apostrophes: ACCT = (2645,'O' 'CLOCK','T=7').

```
//STEP1 EXEC PGM=ONE,ACCT=(24,53,
//          45,'A=17')
     [ Accounting information may be continued onto another line
     by interrupting it after a complete subparameter, including
     the comma that follows it. ]

// EXEC COBUCLG,ACCT=2647
     [ The accounting information applies to each step of the
     COBUCLG procedure. ]

// EXEC PLIXCLG,ACCT.PL1=('T=7','K=9'),ACCT.GO=('T=9')
     [ T=7 and K=9 are supplied to the PL1 step; T=9 is supplied to
     the GO step of the PLIXCLG procedure. ]
```

VII. DPRTY: DISPATCHING PRIORITY (MVS ONLY)

Code DPRTY = (*v1,v2*) to set the dispatching priority. *Dispatching priority* is the priority with which the several steps in storage from different jobs are given control of the CPU. (The PRTY parameter sets the priority for selection of jobs in the input queue for execution.) The step with the highest priority is given the CPU until it must wait for an I/O action to complete or until a task with a higher priority needs the CPU. Your installation will generally control the use of DPRTY.

The dispatching priority assigned to the step is computed as $16(v1) + v2$ where $v1$ and $v2$ may have values from 0 to 15. If $v1$ is not coded, an installation default is assumed, but if $v2$ is not coded, a value of 6 is assumed. Thus DPRTY = (10,2) yields a dispatching priority of 162 and DPRTY = 10 a priority of 166. If DPRTY is not coded the system assumes an installation-defined default.

```
//STEP 1 EXEC PGM=ONE,DPRTY=(5,2)
     [ The dispatching priority is set to 82. ]

//EXEC PLIXCLG,DPRTY.LKED=(4,6),DPRTY.GO=(3,6)
     [ The dispatching priority of the LKED step is set to 70 and
     the GO step to 54 in the PLIXCLG cataloged procedure. ]

// EXEC PLIXCLG,DPRTY=(13,6)
     [ The dispatching priority of each step in the PLIXCLG
     cataloged procedure is set to 214. ]
```

VIII. SYSUDUMP, SYSABEND: ABNORMAL TERMINATION DUMPS

Sometimes it is difficult to find the source of an error when a program abnormally terminates (This is called an *ABEND*, and means ABnormal End). The SYSUDUMP DD statement provides a formatted dump of the program area in hexadecimal, including the contents of registers, a traceback of subroutines called, and information about all the data sets used. The SYSABEND DD statement additionally dumps the system nucleus—the resident portion of the operating system. If you want a storage dump, use SYSUDUMP unless you have a particular reason for examining the nucleus. A storage dump can be extremely valuable when you need it, but wastes paper and printer time if you do not need it. You should never need to use SYSUDUMP.

Place either the SYSUDUMP or SYSABEND DD statement after each EXEC statement in a step in which a dump is wanted. If both SYSUDUMP and SYSABEND appear in one step, the last statement is effective. A dump results only if the step abnormally terminates.

```
//STEP1 EXEC PGM=ONE
//SYSUDUMP DD SYSOUT=A
//STEP2 EXEC PGM=TWO
//SYSABEND DD SYSOUT=A
```

For cataloged procedures, append the name of the step for which a dump is wanted. See Chapter 9 for a complete description of adding DD statements to procedures.

```
// EXEC PL1XCLG
     .   .   .   .
//GO.SYSUDUMP DD SYSOUT=A
    [ The SYSUDUMP statement is effective for the GO step of the
    PLIXCLG procedure. ]
```

SYSUDUMP and SYSABEND are both DD statements; their parameters are described in later chapters. Although many special parameters may be coded on the DD statement if the dump is to be saved on disk or placed on tape, SYSOUT = A usually suffices if the dump is to be printed.

To request the dump to be printed in high-density format (204 characters per line, 15 lines per inch) on a 3800 printer (JES3 only), add CHARS = DUMP on the DD statement:

```
//SYSUDUMP DD SYSOUT=A,CHARS=DUMP
```

In MVS, there is also a SYSMDUMP DD statement that dumps the system nucleus and program area but doesn't format it. The dump can then be read by a computer program, but it can't be printed.

```
//SYSMDUMP DD DSN=SAVE,DISP=(NEW,CATLG),UNIT=SYSDA,SPACE=(TRK,(20,5))
```

Chapter 7

PARAMETERS COMMON TO JOB AND EXEC STATEMENTS

Several parameters may be coded on either the JOB or EXEC statements.

ADDRSPC	Specifies that the step cannot be paged. Seldom needed.
COND	Specifies conditions for executing subsequent job steps.
PERFORM	Assigns the job or step to a performance group for execution priority. (Seldom needed. Description deferred until Chapter 17.)
RD	Request restart of a job step. (Seldom needed. A discussion of RD and checkpoint/restart is deferred until Chapter 17.)
REGION	Specifies the region size to assign to the job or individual steps.
TIME	Imposes a limit on the job or individual job steps.

You will likely write the REGION and TIME parameters for most of your jobs, and you may write the COND parameter often, but you'll likely never need to write ADDRSPC, PERFORM, and RD.

If a particular parameter is coded on the JOB statement, it applies to each step within the job and takes precedence over any corresponding parameters on EXEC statements. This is convenient if there are many steps in the job; the parameter need be coded only once on the JOB statement.

I. COND: CONDITIONS FOR BYPASSING JOB STEPS

Each job step may pass a return code to the system when it reaches completion. The COND parameter permits the execution of steps to depend on the return code from previous steps. For example, if a compilation fails, there is no need to attempt subsequent linkage editor or execution steps in the job. If the COND parameter is omitted, no tests are made and steps are executed normally. If a step is bypassed, it returns a code of zero.

65

Programs can issue return codes as follows:

COBOL:

```
MOVE return-code TO RETURN-CODE.
```

FORTRAN:

```
STOP return-code
```

PL/I:

```
CALL PLIRET(return-code);
```

Assembler Language: Place the return code in general register 15.

Return codes can range from 0 to 4095. The return codes issued by the compilers and linkage editor are:

0   No errors or warnings detected.
4   Possible errors (warnings) detected but execution should be successful.
8   Serious errors detected; execution likely to fail.
12   Severe error; execution impossible.
16   Fatal error; execution cannot continue.

The COND parameter on an EXEC statement can test any or all return codes from previous steps. If any test is satisfied, the step making the test is bypassed. The COND parameter on the EXEC statement can also make step execution depend on the abnormal termination of previous steps. When the COND parameter is coded on the JOB statement, any successful test causes all subsequent steps to be bypassed. A COND parameter on the JOB statement nullifies any COND parameters on EXEC statements.

A. COND on EXEC Statements

The parameter is coded on the EXEC statement as:

```
COND=((number,comparison),...,(number,comparison))
```

Each number is compared against the return code from each prior step. If any comparison is true, the step is bypassed. For example, if you code COND = (4,LT), the step is bypassed if 4 is less than the return code of any previous step. Up to eight tests may be coded.

Any one of the tests may also be coded as (*number,comparison,stepname*) to compare the number against the return code of a specific step. Coding COND = (4,GT,STEP2) bypasses the step if 4 is greater than the return code issued by STEP2, a previous step. Code *stepname.procstep* to apply the test to the return code from a specific step within a procedure. Coding COND = (4,LT,STEP2.LKED) bypasses the step if 4 is less than the return code issued by the LKED step of the procedure executed by STEP1.

When a specific step is not named and only (*number,comparison*) is coded, the comparison is made against the return codes from all previous steps. The comparisons are:

GT	Greater Than	LT	Less Than
GE	Greater than or Equal	LE	Less than or Equal
EQ	EQual	NE	Not Equal

For example, COND = (8,LT) is read "if 8 is less than the return code from any previous step, bypass this step." COND parameters are difficult to read and write because their written expression is the reverse of the way you think. The COND may be easier to understand when stated in the reverse: "execute the step if all the return codes from previous steps have values 0 to 8." Be careful writing COND, for what you write may turn out to be the opposite of what you want.

```
//STEPA EXEC PGM=ONE
//STEPB EXEC PGM=TWO,COND=(4,EQ,STEPA)
     [ STEPB is bypassed if 4 is equal to the return code issued by
     STEPA.  The outer parentheses may be omitted if one test is
     made. ]
//STEPC EXEC COBUCLG,COND.GO=((12,GE),
//             (8,EQ,STEPB),(4,EQ,STEPA))
     [ The GO step of the COBUCLG procedure is bypassed if 12 is
     greater than or equal to the return code of any previous
     step, if 8 is equal to the return code of STEPB, or if 4 is
     equal to the return code of STEPA.  The COND parameter can be
     continued onto a new line after a complete test, including
     the comma that follows it. ]
//STEPD EXEC PLIXCLG,COND=(4,NE,STEPC.GO)
     [ Any step in the PLIXCLG procedure is bypassed if 4 is not
     equal to the return code of the GO step in the previous COBUCLG
     cataloged procedure invoked by STEPC. ]
//STEPE EXEC PGM=FOUR,COND=(4095,LT)
     [ STEP E is executed regardless of the return codes.  A return
     code cannot exceed 4095 so the condition can never be met. ]
//STEPF EXEC PGM=FIVE,COND=(0,LE)
     [ STEPF is not executed regardless of the return codes.  A
     return code cannot be less than zero and so the condition is
     always met. ]
```

If the job has a JCL error, the system will not attempt to execute it. If a step abnormally terminates, no return code can be issued and all subsequent steps are bypassed—unless the EVEN or ONLY subparameters are used.

COND = EVEN permits the job step to execute even if previous steps abnormally terminate. COND = ONLY causes the step to execute only if previous steps abnormally terminate. EVEN and ONLY can be coded with up to seven return code tests.

The step making the test COND = ((EVEN,(8,EQ),(7,LT,STEPA)) is bypassed if 8 equals the return code from any previous step or if 7 is less than the return code from STEPA; if not, it is executed even if previous steps abnormally terminate. The relative position in which the individual tests are coded does not matter. COND = ((2,EQ),EVEN) and COND = (EVEN,(2,EQ)) are equivalent.

EVEN and ONLY cannot be coded in the same step because they are mutually exclusive. The tests for EVEN and ONLY are made only if the job goes into execution; JCL errors or the inability to allocate space on I/O devices cause the remainder of the job steps to be bypassed regardless of the COND parameters.

```
//STEPA EXEC PGM=ONE
//STEPB EXEC FORTGCLG,COND.LKED=EVEN,
//           COND.GO=((ONLY,(4,EQ,STEPB.LKED))
     [ The LKED step of the FORTGCLG procedure is executed EVEN if
     a previous step abnormally terminates.  The GO step is
     bypassed if 4 is equal to the return code of the LKED step;
     it is then executed ONLY if a previous step has abnormally
     terminated. ]
```

For most steps that depend on the successful execution of a program, a return code of 4 or less means that a previous step has executed successfully, perhaps with only some warning messages. For this usual case, you code the COND parameter as:

```
//stepname EXEC PGM=program,COND=(4,LT)
     [ This executes the step if no previous step has issued a
     return code of greater than 4. ]
```

B. COND on JOB Statements

Although the COND parameter can be written on the JOB statement, it rarely is because you usually want to write it for individual job steps. A COND parameter on the JOB statement is applied to each step in the job. COND parameters on EXEC statements within the job are nullified. The parameter is coded on the JOB statement as:

```
COND=((number,comparison),..., (number,comparison)).
```

A stepname cannot be used, and EVEN and ONLY are also prohibited. The tests are made at the end of each step against the return code of the step. If any test is satisfied, all remaining steps are bypassed. The comparisons are the same as for the EXEC statement, and up to eight tests may be coded.

```
//TEST JOB 6245,SMITH,COND=((4,GT),(6,LT)),CLASS=A
     [ Terminate the job if 4 is greater than a return code or if 6
     is less than a return code (that is, terminate the job unless
     the return code equals 4, 5, or 6). ]

//RUN#10 JOB (6452,200),JONES,COND=((4,EQ),(5,EQ),(6,EQ))
     [ Terminate the job if a return code equals 4, 5, or 6.  This
     is just the opposite of the previous JOB statement. ]
```

II. TIME: TIME LIMIT

The TIME parameter sets a CPU time limit for an entire job when it is coded on the JOB statement. CPU time is the time the CPU is actually executing your job. It is not the same as clock time. TIME may also be coded on the EXEC statement to set a CPU time limit for a specific step. In practice, though, it is usually written on the JOB statement. The forms are:

```
TIME=minutes
TIME=(minutes,seconds)
```

The *minutes* may range from 1 to 1440 (24 hours); *seconds* must be less than 60. If the total CPU time for the job exceeds the limit set on the JOB statement, or if the elapsed CPU time within a step exceeds the time limit for that step, the entire job is abnormally terminated (called an ABEND— ABnormal END) with a 322 completion code. (Coding TIME = 0 will abnormally terminate a job.)

You may wish to estimate the CPU time for two reasons:

- Your installation may require it. They may also limit you to certain job classes based on the CPU time you estimate.
- If you are debugging a program and you think a bug in your program may prevent your program from reaching completion, you can cut the job off after a certain length of time.

When you estimate CPU time, be generous. Allow more time than you think you need. For example, suppose you have a job you estimate will run for five minutes of CPU time.

- If you estimate five minutes of CPU time and your job runs a fraction over this (which always seems to happen), your job ABENDS at the worst possible time—after you have incurred all your run costs but before the job terminates and you get your results. You have wasted five CPU minutes.
- If you estimate eight minutes of CPU time and, in the unlikely event your job goes into an endless loop, you have wasted only three CPU minutes.

The TIME parameter sets a limit for CPU time, not clock time. *CPU time*, the time a job is executing instructions, does not include wait time (when the job is waiting for I/O actions to complete), system time, and time that other jobs in the multiprogramming environment are using the CPU. The time is not exact. The system only checks the time for jobs every 10.5 seconds clock time. If your job were the only job running, it could execute up to 10.5 seconds longer than what you specified in the TIME parameter.

A job is abnormally terminated if it is in the wait state for 30 consecutive minutes. (The installation may change this limit.) Code TIME = 1440 to eliminate this limit, and any CPU time limit. A default time limit set by the reader procedure is effective if the TIME parameter is omitted.

A. TIME on EXEC Statements

The TIME parameter on an EXEC statement applies to specific steps.

```
//STEP1 EXEC PGM=ONE,TIME=(10,30)
     [ The time limit for the step is set to 10 minutes, 30
     seconds.  The step may be terminated sooner if a time limit
     set on the JOB statement is exceeded. ]

//STEP2 EXEC PGM=ONE,TIME=7
     [ The limit is set to 7 minutes.  The outer parentheses may be
     omitted if seconds is not coded. ]

// EXEC PLIXCLG,TIME.LKED=(,15),TIME.GO=1
     [ The limit is set to 15 seconds in the LKED step and 1 minute
     in the GO step of the PLIXCLG cataloged procedure. ]

// EXEC COBUCLG,TIME=3
     [ The limit of each step of the COBUCLG cataloged procedure is
     nullified, and the total limit for all the steps is set to 3
     minutes.  That is, if the cumulative time for all the steps
     exceeds 3 minutes, the job is abnormally terminated. ]
```

B. TIME on JOB Statements

TIME coded on the JOB statement sets the limit for the entire job. It does not override the limits set on EXEC statements—it is in addition to them.

```
//TEST JOB (5421,5),'LIMIT JOB',TIME=9,CLASS=A
     [ The job is abnormally terminated after 9 minutes of CPU
     time.  It will be terminated sooner if a time limit set on an
     EXEC statement within the job is exceeded. ]
```

III. REGION SIZE

The system allocates storage to programs as requested by the REGION parameter. REGION on the EXEC statement requests storage for a specific step; REGION coded on the JOB statement allocates a region size to all steps, overriding any region size on EXEC statements. A default region size specified in the reader procedure is used if the REGION parameter is omitted.

In MVS, REGION is the total amount of storage needed, virtual or real. When ADDRSPC = REAL is coded in MVS, REGION allocates an area of real storage. When ADDRSPC = VIRT is coded or assumed in MVS, REGION sets an upper bound of the virtual storage size. In VS1, REGION is the amount of real storage and is ignored if ADDRSPC = VIRT is coded.

REGION is coded as REGION = nK, where n is the number of 1024-byte (K—on the computer, K represents 1024, a power of 2, rather than 1,000) areas of storage to allocate. The maximum value of n depends on the address space of the computer—15625 for MVS and 2096128 for MVS/XA. Storage is allocated in 2K block units. If n is odd, the system rounds it up to make it even. (REGION = 65K is treated as REGION = 66K.)

In MVS/XA, you can also write REGION = nM, where n is in units of 1,024,000 bytes (megabytes). The REGION can range from 1M to 2047M. The n can be even or odd.

If a job step requires more storage than specified by REGION, the job is abnormally terminated with an 804 or 80A completion code. Remember that storage is allocated dynamically, and that a job's requirement may increase during execution. Thus the job may be terminated for exceeding its region size after the step has begun execution. For example, a COBOL job might fit nicely into its region, do some calculations, and then open a data set. Since COBOL obtains storage dynamically for buffers, the program could then abnormally terminate. There are numerous ways of alleviating this problem (checkpoint/restart, opening all data sets first), but the simplest solution is to allow a safety margin in estimating region size.

A. REGION on EXEC Statements

The REGION parameter on the EXEC statement requests storage for individual steps.

```
//STEPA EXEC PGM=ONE,REGION=64K
     [ STEPA is allocated 64K bytes of storage. ]

// EXEC PLIXCLG,REGION.LKED=128K,REGION.GO=64K
     [ The LKED step of the PLIXCLG procedure is allocated 128K of
     storage.  The GO step is allocated 64K of storage. ]

//EXEC COBUCLG,REGION=192K
     [ Each step in the COBUCLG procedure is allocated 192K bytes
     of storage. ]
```

B. REGION on the JOB Statement

The REGION parameter on the JOB statement must allow enough storage for the maximum region required by any step. For example, a COBOL job may require 228K to compile, 104K to link edit, and 52K to execute. A REGION parameter on the JOB statement must allow enough storage for the largest step (228K).

```
//JOB27 JOB 4625,MEDICI,REGION=192K,CLASS=A
     [ All steps within the job are allocated 192K bytes. Any
     REGION parameters on EXEC statements within the job are
     ignored. ]
```

IV. ADDRSPC: PROHIBIT PAGING

The ADDRSPC parameter prevents a job or job step from being paged. ADDRSPC = REAL locks the job or step into real storage during execution. ADDRSPC = VIRT allows the job or step to be paged.

ADDRSPC = VIRT is usually a default if it is not coded, although an installation can generate the system with ADDRSPC = REAL as default. The installation will generally control the use of ADDRSPC = REAL because of its adverse effect on the system's performance. Generally it is required only for programs that are time dependent and those that dynamically modify channel programs during I/O operations.

A. ADDRSPC on EXEC Statements

ADDRSPC coded on the EXEC statement applies to specific job steps.

```
//STEP6 EXEC PGM=ONE,ADDRSPC=REAL
     [ STEP6 would not be paged. ]

//STEP7 EXEC COBUCLG,ADDRSPC.GO=REAL
        [ Only the GO step of the cataloged procedure is not paged. ]

//STEP8 EXEC COBUCLG,ADDRSPC=REAL
        [ None of the steps of the cataloged procedure is paged. ]
```

B. ADDRSPC on JOB Statements

ADDRSPC coded on the JOB statement applies to all steps within the job, overriding any ADDRSPC parameters coded on EXEC statements.

```
//FIRST JOB (1776,18),'A JOB',CLASS=A,ADDRSPC=REAL
       [ No steps in the job would be paged. ]
```

EXERCISES

Execute the PL/I compile, link edit, and GO procedure from Chapter 5 twice within the same job. This will require the following JCl statements:

```
//JOB statement
//STEP1 EXEC PLIXCLG
//PL1.SYSIN   DD *
    [ source statements ]
/*
//GO.SYSUDUMP DD ...
//GO.OUT      DD ...
//GO.IN       DD ...
    [ lines of data ]
```

```
//STEP2 EXEC PLIXCLG
//PL1.SYSIN   DD *
    [ some source statements ]
/*
//GO.OUT      DD ...
//GO.IN       DD ...
    [ lines of data ]
/*
```

Before you run the job, modify the JCL to do the following:

- In STEP1 set the PARM values of the PL1 step to be XREF, GOSTMT, COUNT, MAP, and LIST.
- In STEP1 set the TIME parameter of the GO step to zero.
- Include a SYSUDUMP DD statement in STEP1 for the GO step. The preceding JCL shows where to place the SYSUDUMP DD statement.
- Override all the steps in STEP2 to execute even if a STEP1 step abnormally terminates.
- Set the region size of STEP1.GO to 80K and of STEP2.GO to 82K.

Chapter 8

THE DD STATEMENT

A DD (Data Definition) statement must be placed after the EXEC statement for each data set used in the step. The DD statement names the data set, requests an I/O unit and perhaps a specific volume to use, and gives the data set disposition. The system ensures that requested I/O devices can be allocated to the job before execution is allowed to begin. A maximum of 255 (1635 in MVS) DD statements are permitted per step.

The DD statement may also give the system various information about the data set: its organization, record length, blocking, and so on. If a new data set is created on a direct-access volume, the DD statement must specify the amount of storage to allocate. A specific file on a multiple-file tape is also indicated on the DD statement.

A great deal of information must be supplied to read or write a data set: the data set organization, record type, record length, and block length. Supplying this information is one of the things that makes JCL so difficult. System/370 permits this information to come from three sources: a data control block (DCB), DD statements, and data set labels.

I. DATA CONTROL BLOCK

A *Data Control Block* (DCB) is a table of data in storage that describes each data set used by the program. It is usually supplied default values by the language compiler, but values may be changed in COBOL, PL/I, and assembler language.

When a data set is opened, information is taken from the DD statement and merged into blank fields of the data control block. The data set label is then read (if it is an existing data set with a label), and any data from it is merged into any remaining blank fields of the data control block. The hierarchy is:

- Data control block first
- DD statement second
- Data set label third

For example, the record format need not be coded in the data control block; it can be supplied on a DD statement to make the program more flexible. Record length and blocking are often omitted in the data control block, and the information is supplied later by either the DD statement or the data set label. You must know which data control block fields are left blank by the compiler so that you can supply them on the DD statement. Refer to the appropriate programmer's guide for this information.

Since there may be several data control blocks, one for each data set used, a data definition name (*ddname*) is assigned to each. A DD statement with a corresponding ddname must be included for each data set used. The ddname forms the connection between the program and the data set. The system may then read the data set label for further information.

II. DD STATEMENT FORMAT

The format of the DD statement is:

```
//ddname DD optional-parameters
```

The *ddname* is the name given to the DD statement. The optional parameters consist of four positional parameters (DUMMY, DATA, DYNAM, and *) and several keyword parameters.

*	Indicates that lines of data immediately follow the DD statement. Described in Chapter 10.
DATA	Indicates that lines of data with // in columns 1 and 2 immediately follow the DD statement. Seldom needed. Described in Chapter 10.
DUMMY	Gives the data set a dummy status. Described in Chapter 9.
DYNAM	Indicates that the data set is to be dynamically allocated. Seldom needed. Described in Chapter 17.

The following keyword parameters may be coded in any order, after any positional parameter.

ACCODE	(MVS/XA only.) Requests an access code for ANSI tapes. Seldom needed. Described in Chapter 12.
AFF	(VS1 only.) Requests channel separation. Seldom needed.
AMP	Provides information for VSAM data sets. Seldom needed. Described in Chapter 18.
BURST	Bursts the output on the 3800 printer. That is, it tears the paper apart at the perforations. Seldom needed. Described in Chapter 10.

CHARS	Specifies a character set for the 3800 printer. Seldom needed. Described in Chapter 10.
CHKPT	Requests checkpoints and end-of-volume. Seldom needed. Described in Chapter 17.
COMPACT	(VS1 only.) Compacts the data sets sent to a work station. Seldom needed. Described in Chapter 17.
COPIES	Requests copies of an output data set. Seldom needed. Described in Chapter 10.
DCB	Specifies data control block parameters. Described in this chapter.
DDNAME	Postpones definition of a data set. Seldom needed. Described in Chapter 10.
DEST	Routes output to a specified destination. Seldom needed. Described in Chapter 10.
DISP	Specifies the data set disposition. Described in this chapter.
DLM	Specifies an alternative delimiter. Seldom needed. Described in Chapter 10.
DSID	Supplies the 3540 diskette reader id. Seldom needed. Described in Chapter 10.
DSN	Names the data set. Described in this chapter.
FCB	Specifies forms control image for a printer or card punch. Seldom needed. Described in Chapter 10.
FLASH	Specifies a forms overlay for the 3800 printer. Seldom needed. Described in Chapter 10.
FREE	Deallocates I/O device when data set is closed. Seldom needed. Described in Chapter 17.
HOLD	Holds the output data set in a queue. Seldom needed. Described in Chapter 10.
LABEL	Provides label information and data set protection. Described in Chapter 12.
MODIFY	Modifies print lines on the 3800 printer. Seldom needed. Described in Chapter 10.
MSVGP	Requests a 3540 Mass Storage System device. Seldom needed. Described in Chapter 11.
OUTLIM	Limits the lines of printed or punched output. Seldom needed. Described in Chapter 10.
OUTPUT	(MVS/XA only.) Used to associate a DD statement with an OUTPUT statement to specify special output processing in JES2 or JES3. Seldom needed. Described in Chapter 20.
PROTECT	(MVS only.) Requests password protection for data sets. Seldom needed. Described in Chapter 18.

QNAME	Gives access to messages received through TCAM. Seldom needed. Described in Chapter 17.
SEP	(VS1 only). Requests channel separation. Seldom needed. Described in Chapter 17.
SPACE	Requests the amount of direct-access space to allocate. Described in Chapter 11.
SPLIT	(VS1 only.) Allocates space on a direct-access volume to be suballocated. Seldom needed. Described in Chapter 11.
SUBALLOC	(VS1 only.) Suballocates space on a direct-access volume. Seldom needed. Described in Chapter 11.
SUBSYS	Specifies the subsystem to process the data set. Seldom needed. Described in Chapter 17.
SYSOUT	Routes a data set through the system output stream. Described in Chapter 10.
TERM	Sends or receives a data set from a time-sharing terminal. Seldom needed. Described in Chapter 17.
UCS	Specifies a character set for printing. Seldom needed. Described in Chapter 10.
UNIT	Specifies the I/O device. Described in this chapter.
VOL	Specifies the volume and provides volume information. Described in this chapter.

Although there are many DD statement parameters, only eight are used on a regular basis: DCB, DISP, DSN, LABEL, SPACE, SYSOUT, UNIT, and VOL.

III. DDNAME: DATA DEFINITION NAME

The ddname must be from one to eight alphanumeric or national (A to Z, 0 to 9, @, $, #) characters. The first character must be alphabetic or national (A to Z, @, $, #). Each ddname within a step should be unique; if duplicate ddnames exist within a step, device and space allocations are made for each statement, but all references are directed to the first statement. The required ddnames vary with each language processor.

Language	Data Set Requested by	JCL ddnames
Assembler	DCB = ddname	//ddname DD . . .
COBOL	SELECT file ASSIGN to ddname	//ddname DD . . .
FORTRAN	FORTRAN unit nn	//FTnnF001 DD . . .
PL/I	DECLARE ddname	//ddname DD . . .

IV. REFERBACK: REFERBACK PARAMETER

The referback parameter, similar to the *//EXEC PGM = *.referback* in Chapter 6, is also used on DD statements to copy information from a previous DD statement. The following example in which data control block information is copied from a previous DD statement illustrates the referback.

```
//COMP PROC
//STEP1 EXEC PGM=ONE
//DD1 DD DCB=BLKSIZE=800,...
//DD2 DD DCB=*.DD1,...
     [ To refer back to a DD statement in the same step, code
     *.ddname. ]
//STEP2 EXEC PGM=TWO
//DD3 DD DCB=*.STEP1.DD1,...
     [ To refer back to a DD statement in a previous step, code
     *.stepname.ddname. ]
```

To refer back to a DD statement within a procedure, refer first to the stepname invoking the procedure, next to the stepname within the procedure, and then to the ddname. If the COMP cataloged procedure above is invoked, the following could be coded:

```
//STEP3 EXEC COMP
//STEP4 EXEC PGM=FOUR
//DD4 DD DCB=*.STEP3.STEP1.DD1,...
```

V. DCB: DATA CONTROL BLOCK PARAMETER

Using JCL, you often specify three attributes for the records in the data set:

- RECFM, the record format. Tells what type of record it is.
- LRECL, the logical record length. That is, the length of a record of data.
- BLKSIZE, the block size. For efficiency, several records are usually placed together in a block.

You specify the RECFM, LRECL, and BLKSIZE with a DCB parameter on a DD statement. The following is typical:

```
//OUT DD DCB=(RECFM=FB,LRECL=80,BLKSIZE=3200), ...
```

DCB stands for Data Control Block. It represents an area where the system keeps information about a data set. The DCB parameter is coded as DCB = *subparameter* or DCB = (*subparameter,...,subparameter*). Several of the most frequently used subparameters are described here.

A. DSORG: Data Set Organization

Code DSORG=*organization* to specify the type of organization. The default is DSORG=PS, and since most data sets are Physical Sequential, DSORG is often omitted. The following organization types are the most common.

PS	Physical Sequential
PO	Partitioned Organization
IS	Indexed Sequential
DA	Direct Access
DAU	Direct Access Unmovable

```
//OUTPUT DD DCB=DSORG=DA
```

B. RECFM: Record Format

Code RECFM=*format* to specify the record format. Figure 25 shows the different record formats.

RECFM=F   Fixed-Length Records

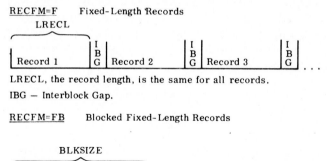

LRECL, the record length, is the same for all records.

IBG — Interblock Gap.

RECFM=FB   Blocked Fixed-Length Records

BLKSIZE, the block size, is a multiple of LRECL.

RECFM=V   Variable-Length Records

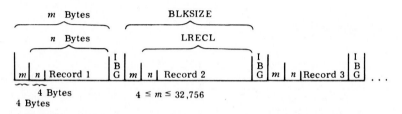

$4 \leq m \leq 32{,}756$

LRECL is the maximum record length in the data set.

(continued)

RECFM=VB   Blocked Variable-Length Records

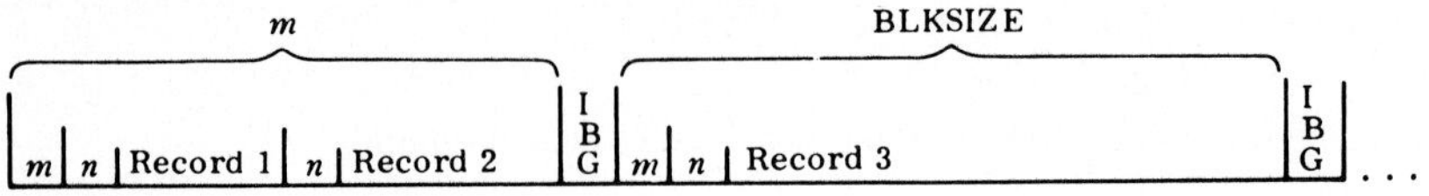

$$8 \leq m \leq 32{,}760$$

BLKSIZE must be equal to or greater than the maximum record length
in the data set.

RECFM U   Undefined-Length Records

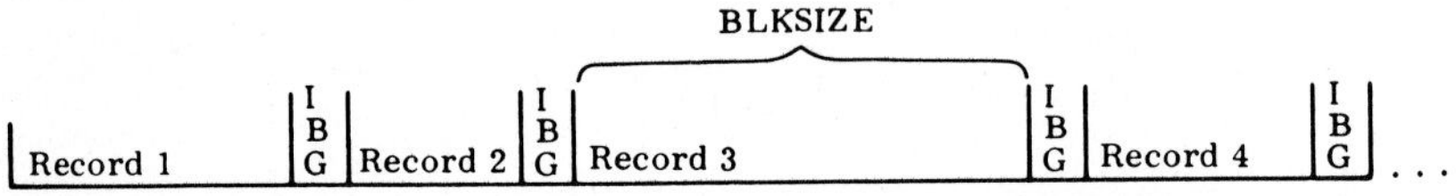

BLKSIZE must be equal to or greater than the maximum record length
in the data set.

Figure 25. Record formats

Records are mainly used to store data and text. Computer data, as illustrated in
Figure 26, is often of fixed length. That is, each record has the same length. Text, as
illustrated in Figure 27, usually varies in length. That is, each record may have a
different line length. You specify fixed- or variable-length records with the DCB
RECFM subparameter. The form is:

DCB=(RECFM=FB, . . .   or   DCB=(RECFM=VB, . . .

Data: (From 1980 Census)

CITY	COUNTRY	POPULATION
SAO PAULO	BRAZIL	12,578,045
SHANGHAI	CHINA	11,000,000
MEXICO CITY	MEXICO	9,200,000
CALCUTTA	INDIA	9,165,650
RIO DE JANEIRO	BRAZIL	9,011,981

Figure 26. Typical data

Text:

Mr. John Q. Smith
The Ajax Company
14 Oak Street
Norogrudo, Byelorussian Soviet Socialist Republic

Figure 27. Typical text

There is a third type of record format occasionally used—the undefined format. You specify it with RECFM = U. The system must read the record to determine its length. For undefined records, you omit the LRECL and specify the BLKSIZE as that of the largest block. The undefined record format is often used to read input from a terminal device.

```
DCB=(RECFM=U,BLKSIZE=120)
```

The format can be one or more of the following characters. First character (only one permitted):

U	Undefined-length records. LRECL should not be coded, and BLKSIZE must be greater than or equal to the largest record.
V	Variable-length records. LRECL must be the length of the longest record plus 4 bytes. BLKSIZE must be at least as large as LRECL + 4.
F	Fixed-length records. BLKSIZE must be a multiple of LRECL of blocked records.
D	Variable-length ASCII tape records.

Next characters:

B	Blocked records. (FB and VB are permitted; UB is not.)
T	Track overflow used. A disk track is completely filled even if it means that a block must be split across two tracks. Used when the BLKSIZE exceeds the track size. T cannot be coded with S or D.
S	Spanned records. For V format records—logical records are spanned over more than one block. For VS or VBS the BLKSIZE is independent of the LRECL. For F format records—no truncated blocks or unfilled tracks within the data set. S cannot be coded with U, T, or D.
A	ASA control character is the first byte of data. Used to control the printer. Cannot be coded with M.
M	Machine code control character is the first byte of data. Used to control the printer. Cannot be coded with D or A.

```
//OUTPUT1 DD DCB=(DSORG=PS,LRECL=80,BLKSIZE=1600,RECFM=FB)
//OUTPUT2 DD DCB=RECFM=FBSA
```

C. LRECL: Logical Record Length

Code LRECL = *length* to specify the length of the logical record in bytes for fixed- or variable-length records. Omit the LRECL for undefined-length records. The LRECL is determined differently for fixed-length and variable-length records.

- Fixed-length records: LRECL is the length of the record. (Each record has the same length.)
- Variable-length records: LRECL is the length of the longest record plus 4. That is, if the longest record were 96, you would specify LRECL = 100.

```
//OUTPUT DD DCB=(DSORG=PS,RECFM=F,LRECL=80)
```

You may wonder why variable-length records are used at all. That is, why not just use fixed-length records with a length large enough to contain the longest line? The reason is that it would waste a lot of file storage space on the computer. With fixed-length data in a fixed-length record, there is no wasted space. Figure 28 illustrates variable-length data stored in a fixed-length record. Space is wasted. Figure 29 shows how variable-length records prevent space from being wasted.

How about the other way around? Why not make all records variable-length? Why have fixed-length records at all? Variable-length records are more complicated to process because the length of each record must be determined to process it. With fixed-length records, the computer always knows how long each record is.

| Mr. John Q. Smith |
| The Ajax Company |
| 14 Oak Street |
| Norogrudo, Byelorussian Soviet Socialist Republic |

Figure 28. Variable-length data stored in a fixed-length record

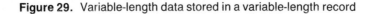

Figure 29. Variable-length data stored in a variable-length record

D. BLKSIZE: Block Size

Blocking concerns how the records are transmitted and stored on an I/O device, such as disk. When records are physically stored on disk and tape, the system leaves a gap between the records so that it can tell where one record ends and the next one begins, as shown in Figure 30. This inter-record gap can take up as much and even more space than the record itself. On a typical disk, the inter-record gap occupies 185 character positions; on tape it occupies 230 character positions.

Figure 30. Record gaps

To regain some of the space used for inter-record gaps, you can "block" the records. That is, you can put several records together in a block. Instead of the records stored as they are in Figure 30, you can block them as shown in Figure 31.

Figure 31. Blocked records

Blocking can save a tremendous amount of data set storage space. But there is another, equally important reason for blocking. Blocked records can be read and written much faster than unblocked records, significantly reducing run costs. It is far more efficient for the computer to transmit (read or write) a group of records in a block than to transmit them one at a time, just as it is far more efficient to carry a number of passengers in an airplane than it is to fly one passenger per plane. The basic cost of the pilot and fuel doesn't change much with each passenger added. Similarly, with the computer the big cost of locating the start of a block in a data set and getting things going doesn't change much with each additional record you place in that block.

For fixed blocked records, the block size must be an even multiple of the record length. It is more complicated for variable-length records:

- Record length must be at least as long as the longest record plus 4.
- Block size must be at least as long as the longest record plus 8.

The actual record length and block length are stored within those extra 4 and 8 bytes. By storing the record length in each record, the operating system always knows how long each record is.

Of course, the block size can also be inefficient if it is too big. The basic unit of storage on disk is a track. A track is analogous to the groove of a phonograph record, except that a track is circular and a record groove is continuous. On a typical disk unit, the IBM 3380, a track can contain 47,476 bytes. If you have 80-byte records and choose a block size of 24,000 bytes, only one block will fit on a track, as shown in Figure 32. Approximately 23,000 bytes on each track are wasted because the block size is too large.

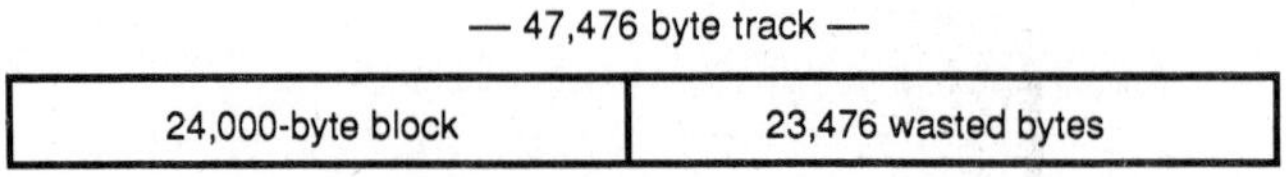

— 47,476 byte track —

24,000-byte block	23,476 wasted bytes

Figure 32. One block stored on a track

Choosing an appropriate block size is very important—and very complicated. The following simple rules should solve most of your blocking problems, assuming your installation doesn't have a standard. Choose a block size of 6233 bytes, or as close as you can get under this. It is big enough to be efficient but it's not too big. It also fits nicely onto the tracks of most models of disk units. The suggested record lengths for data and text are:

- Data records: DCB = (RECFM = FB,LRECL = 80,BLKSIZE = 6160). If the LRECL isn't 80, choose some multiple of it that results in a block size close to 6200.
- Text records: DCB = (RECFM = VB,LRECL = 255,BLKSIZE = 6233)

Code BLKSIZE = *blocksize* to specify the block size in bytes. The block size must be a multiple of the LRECL for fixed-length records; for variable-length records it must be equal to or greater than LRECL plus 4. That is, it must be equal to or greater than the longest record plus 8. For undefined-length records, the block size must be as large as the longest block. The block size can range from 18 to 32,760 bytes. Generally the block size should not exceed the track size of a direct-access volume.

```
//OUTPUT DD DCB=(DSORG=PS,RECFM=FB,LRECL=80,
          BLKSIZE=1600)
     [ DCB parameters can be continued after a complete
     subparameter, including the comma following it. ]
```

E. BUFNO: Number of Buffers

Code BUFNO = *number* to specify the number of buffers. The number of buffers can also be coded in COBOL and PL/I. The installation establishes a default if BUFNO is omitted, and this default is usually sufficient.

```
//OUTPUT DD DCB=(DSORG=PS,LRECL=80,BLKSIZE=1600,BUFNO=2)
```

F.   DCB Information from Data Set Labels

A data set label is created for nontemporary data sets. The DCB subparameters DSORG, RECFM, BLKSIZE, and LRECL are recorded on the label and become part of the data set. The OPTCD, KEYLEN, RKP, and TRTCH DCB subparameters, the EXPDT or RETPD LABEL subparameters, and the volume sequence number are also stored in the label. (These subparameters are described later.) The parameters stored in the label need not be specified when referring to an old data set; the system retrieves them from the data set label. If all required DCB information is contained in the data control block or in the data set label, the DCB parameter may be omitted.

Several DD parameters, some not yet explained, are either stored in the catalog when the data set is cataloged, stored in the data set label, or are retained by the system when the data set is passed. These parameters, except for DSN, need not be coded to retrieve the data set. Table 1 shows the DD parameters that are retained.

Table 1.   Retained DD Parameters

	Retained in Catalog	Retained in Label	Retained if Passed
DSN	Yes†	Yes†	Yes†
UNIT	Yes	No	Yes
VOL = SER	Yes	Yes†	Yes
Volume seq #	Yes	Yes	Yes
DCB = BLKSIZE	No	Yes	Yes‡
DCB = DEN	No	Yes	No‡
DCB = DSORG	No	Yes*	Yes‡
DCB = KEYLEN	No	Yes	Yes‡
DCB = LRECL	No	Yes	Yes‡
DCB = OPTCD	No	Yes	Yes‡
DCB = RECFM	No	Yes	Yes‡
DCB = RKP	No	Yes	Yes‡
DCB = TRTCH	No	Yes	Yes‡
Creation date	No	Yes	No
Generation #	Yes	No	Yes
LABEL = EXPDT	No	Yes	No
LABEL = RETPD	No	Yes	No
LABEL = PASSWORD	No	Yes	No
LABEL = NOPWREAD	No	Yes	No
LABEL = file#	Yes	Yes†	Yes
LABEL = type	No	No	Yes
SPACE = (u,(p,s))	No	Yes	No

* DSORG = IS must be coded.
† Although retained, must still be specified.
‡ For tape, only for standard labels.

G. Copying DCB Values

Often you would like to create a data set with the same DCB subparameters as an existing data set. This is done by either naming the other data set or by referring back to a DD statement containing the desired DCB information.

```
DCB=(dsname,subparameter,...,subparameter)
DCB=(*.referback,subparameter,...,subparameter)
```

If a dsname is coded, the DCB information (DSORG, RECFM, BLKSIZE, LRECL, OPTCD, KEYLEN, and RKP) is copied from the named data set. It must be a cataloged data set on a direct-access volume that is mounted before the step begins execution. The volume sequence number and retention date are copied along with the DCB subparameter unless they are coded on the DD statement.

   If a referback is coded, the DCB subparameters are copied from those coded on the previous DD statement. Note that the DCB parameters are copied from the DD statement, not from the data set label of the data set described by the DD statement. Any subparameters can be coded after the dsname or referback to override or augment the copied DCB subparameters.

```
//INPUT DD DCB=SYS1.LINKLIB,...
      [ DCB subparameters are copied from SYS1.LINKLIB. ]

//INPUT DD DCB=*.DDONE,...
      [ DCB subparameters are copied from the DDONE DD statement.
      DDONE must be a previous statement in this same step. ]

//INPUT DD DCB=(*.STEP1.DDTWO,BLKSIZE=800,BUFNO=3),...
      [ DCB subparameters are copied from the DDTWO DD statement in
      STEP1.  STEP1 must be a previous step.  Any BLKSIZE or BUFNO
      subparameter in the copied DCB is overridden. ]
```

VI. DSN: DATA SET NAME

The DSN parameter names the data set. DSN can also be coded as DSNAME; for example, DSN = MYLIB and DSNAME = MYLIB are equivalent.

   Data sets can be temporary or nontemporary. A temporary data set is created and deleted within the job, whereas nontemporary data sets can be retained after the job completes. All nontemporary data sets must be given names; the name is optional for temporary data sets. If the data set is new, DSN assigns a name to it; if old, DSN gives its existing name.

A. Temporary Data Sets

Temporary data sets are used for storage needed only for the duration of the job. If the DISP parameter does not delete the data set by the end of the job, the system deletes it. Deleting a tape data set dismounts the tape, whereas deleting a data set on a direct-access volume releases the storage.

A data set is marked temporary by omitting the DSN parameter or by coding DSN = &&*dsname*. The system assigns a unique name to the data set when the DSN parameter is omitted, and any subsequent steps using the data set must refer back to the DD statement. (The DSN = *.*referback* parameter can be used to refer back to any data set, temporary or nontemporary.)

```
//STEP1 EXEC PGM=ONE
//DATA1 DD UNIT=SYSSQ,DISP=(NEW,PASS),...
//STEP2 EXEC PGM=TWO
//DATA2 DD DSN=*.STEP.DATA1,DISP=(OLD,PASS)
```

A temporary data set is assigned a name by coding DSN = &&*dsname*; the ampersands mark it as temporary. The *dsname* is a one- to eight-character name beginning with an alphabetic or national (A to Z, @, $, #) character. The remaining characters may be alphanumeric or national (A to Z, @, $, #, 0 to 9), the hyphen (-), or +0 (12-0 multipunch). The temporary data set can be referred to later by coding either DSN = &&*dsname* or DSN = *.*referback*.

```
//STEP1 EXEC PGM=ONE
//DATA1 DD DSN=&&STUFF,...
//STEP2 EXEC PGM=TWO
//DATA2 DD DSN=&&STUFF,...
     or
//DATA2 DD DSN=*.STEP1.DATA1,...
```

B. Nontemporary Data Sets

Nontemporary data sets can be retained after the completion of the job. A data set label created along with the data set is filled with the dsname and DCB sub-parameters. The data set may also be cataloged so that the system records the unit and volume on which the data set resides, along with the file number if the data set is on tape. Although a nontemporary data set may be created and deleted in the same step, it is wasteful; a temporary data set should be created instead. (But use a nontemporary data set if you need to save the data set in the event of a restart.)

A nontemporary data set is denoted by coding DSN = *dsname* where *dsname* is a one- to eight-character name. NULLFILE should not be used because it gives the data set a dummy status. The first character must be alphabetic or national (A to Z, @, $, or #), and the remaining characters can be either alphanumeric or national (A to Z, 0 to 9, @, $, #), the hyphen (-), or +0 (12-0 multipunch).

The referback is often used to refer back to DD statements so that if the data set name is changed, only one DD statement is affected.

```
//STEP1 EXEC PGM=CREATE
//A DD DSN=OMNIBUS,...
//STEP2 EXEC PGM=READ
//B DD DSN=OMNIBUS
   or
//B DD DSN=*.STEP1.A,...
```

The dsname can contain special characters [blank , . / ') (* & + =] under the following circumstances:

- The name is enclosed in apostrophes. A legitimate apostrophe is coded as two consecutive apostrophes: 'O' 'CLOCK'. A data set name enclosed in apostrophes may contain 44 characters.
- The data set name does not refer to a partitioned, ISAM, or generation data group.
- The data set is not cataloged.
- The name is not used in a referback.
- DSN = &&*dsname* is not coded.
- The data set name is not qualified.

Names can be extended or *qualified* by concatenating names. Each level of name, called an *index*, must conform to the above naming conventions and must be separated from other names by a period, for example, A.B.Z. Qualified names can contain up to 44 characters including periods (35 characters if it is a generation data group name), and so 22 levels of qualification are possible. Qualified names are used to group data sets or to ensure unique names. For example, DATA.A27.B74276 is likely to be a unique name, and the data sets named SMITH.SOURCE, SMITH.DATA, and SMITH.REPORT could all belong to Smith. (Qualified names are used in much the same way a directory is used on a PC.)

```
//INPUT   DD DSN=JONES.N2267.TEST6,...
//OUTPUT DD DSN=LAX.UNITED.FT767.SEAT32,...
```

Installations usually impose naming conventions for nontemporary data sets. Check with your installation for its conventions. In TSO and ISPF/PDF (the text editor used in many MVS installations), data set names often have three levels as follows:

```
project.name.type
```

- *project* identifies the project or person owning the data set. It is often a userid.
- *name* names the data set itself.
- *type* is the generic type of the data set. (It is equivalent to the filetype in CMS.)
- Typical generic types are:

ASM	Assembler language source.
CLIST	TSO command procedures.
CNTL	JCL.
COBOL	COBOL language source.
DATA	Data. (Upper case.)

FORT   FORTRAN language source.

PLI   PL/I language source.

TEXT   Text. (Upper and lower case.)

For example, a typical data set name might be:

`X0225.TEST.CNTL`

which might be some JCL given a name of TEST and belonging to X0225.

C. Other Data Sets

The DSN parameter has a slight variation for partitioned, generation, and ISAM data sets. (These data sets are covered in detail in later chapters.) The general form is DSN = *dsname*(*value*) or DSN = &&*dsname*(*value*), depending on whether the data set is nontemporary or temporary. The dsname is the data set name, and the value depends on the type of data set.

To refer to a member of a partitioned data set, code DSN = *dsname*(*member*), giving the member name within the data set; for example, DSN = HOLD(IT) requests member IT in the partitioned data set HOLD. To refer to a particular generation data group (GDG), code DSN = *dsname*(*number*), giving the relative generation number—zero, or a signed integer (such as +1, −1, etc.); for example, DSN = TAX(−1) refers to relative generation −1 of data group TAX. An ISAM data set can consist of an index, prime, and overflow area, and you must code DSN = *dsname*(INDEX), DSN = *dsname*(PRIME), and DSN = *dsname*(OVFLOW), respectively.

VII. UNIT: I/O UNIT

An I/O unit is a particular type of I/O device: a 3380 disk, 3400 tape, 3211 printer, etc. The I/O unit requested by the UNIT parameter should not be confused with the volume. A volume is a specific storage container: a tape reel or a disk pack. Thus a volume is mounted on an I/O unit. Specific volumes are requested by the VOL parameter described later in this chapter.

UNIT requests an I/O unit by hardware address, device type, or group name—or by requesting the unit used by another data set in the same step. Other UNIT subparameters request that multiple volumes be mounted in parallel and that volume mounting be deferred until the data set is opened. UNIT is generally required unless the data set is passed or cataloged. The following list gives other circumstances in which the UNIT is not needed:

- SYSOUT is coded on the DD statement. UNIT is ignored if SYSOUT is coded.

- DUMMY or DSN=NULLFILE is coded on the DD statement. UNIT is ignored if they are coded.
- The data set already exists, either as a cataloged data set or as a data set passed from a previous job step, and the VOL=SER parameter is not coded.
- The data set is assigned volumes used by an earlier data set in the same job with the VOL=REF parameter. The UNIT information is obtained from the previous DD statement.

To request an I/O unit, code UNIT=*address*, UNIT=*type*, or UNIT=*group*. The *address* is the hardware address, the *type* is the numeric model type, and the *group* is a name assigned by the installation to a group of units. To request a unit or units used by another data set, code UNIT=AFF=*ddname*, where the ddname is the name of an earlier DD statement in the same step. The system will select a unit with affinity for the unit specified in the named DD statement.

A. Hardware Address

Code UNIT=*address* to request a specific I/O unit by giving the three-digit hardware address of the device, set when the computer is installed. For example, if a specific tape unit is on 0C4 code UNIT=0C4. Do not use hardware addresses unless you want a specific hardware unit; the system may already have allocated the device to another job. It is better to ask for one of a group of devices and let the system select one that is available. In practice, the hardware address is almost never used.

B. Type

Code UNIT=*type* to request an I/O device by the IBM model number. For example, UNIT=3380 requests an available 3380 disk.

C. Group

Your installation will have several disk packs and will have assigned its own volume serial numbers. The volumes shown in Figure 33 are typical. Either you or the system has to decide which volume (disk pack) to write your data set on.

SYSSQE	TEMP01	TEMP02	TEMP03	TEMP04
SYSRES	PERM01	PERM02	PERM03	PERM04

Figure 33. Typical disk volumes

The UNIT names are used by your installation to specify one or more disks. For example, an installation may use these unit names:

```
SYSTEM -- for system data sets--volumes SYSSQE and SYSRES.
SYSDA  -- for storage of permanent data sets--volumes PERM01-PERM04.
TEMP   -- for storage of temporary data sets--volumes TEMP01-TEMP04.
```

Figure 34 shows how the volumes are grouped by unit name. Your installation will tell you what UNIT values you can use. If you don't request a specific volume, the system selects a volume on which to store your data set. It's usually best to let the system select a volume for you.

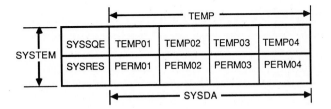

Figure 34. Typical unit names

```
UNIT=TEMP   The system would select TEMP01, TEMP02, TEMP03, or TEMP04.
UNIT=SYSDA  The system would select PERM01, PERM02, PERM03, or PERM04.
```

Code UNIT = *group* to request one of several I/O devices grouped by the installation. UNIT = SYSDA is traditionally defined to be direct-access storage devices, and UNIT = SYSSQ is traditionally units, such as tape and disk, that can contain sequential data sets. An installation can define one group for temporary and another for nontemporary storage on direct-access volumes. Both groups might include different devices. The following examples show the distinction between hardware addresses, type, and group.

Available Devices

	3380#1	3380#2	3350#1	3350#2
Address	130	131	230	231
Type	3380	3380	3350	3350
Group	SYSDA	SYSDA	SYSDA	SYSDA
	SCRATCH	SCRATCH	SCRATCH	

UNIT = 130 selects 3380#1 only, UNIT = 3380 requests either 3380#1 or 3380#2, or UNIT = SYSDA allows any of the four devices to be selected. Either 3380#1, 3380#2, or 3350#1 is selected if UNIT = SCRATCH is coded.

D. AFF: Unit Affinity

Code UNIT = AFF = *ddname* to assign data sets on mountable volumes to the same unit used by another data set. The ddname must be the name of a previous DD statement in the same step. Unit affinity conserves I/O units by forcing data sets onto the same physical device. The unit is used sequentially; that is, each data set must be closed before the next data set is opened. Unit affinity implies deferred mounting (the volume is not requested to be mounted until the data set is opened), and so it can be requested only for units with mountable volumes: disk and tape.

```
//STEP1 EXEC PGM=ONE
//A DD UNIT=3380,...
//B DD UNIT=AFF=A,...
//C DD UNIT=AFF=D,...
        [ Wrong!  Must refer to a previous DD statement. ]
//D DD UNIT=DISK,...
```

If the ddname refers to a dummy DD statement (DUMMY or DSN = NULLFILE), the requesting DD statement is also assigned a dummy status.

E. Special Options

Multiple volumes and deferred mounting can also be specified with the UNIT parameter.

```
        type  P
        group volumes
UNIT=(_____,_____,DEFER,SEP=(ddname,ddname,...))
```

1. Volumes, P: parallel volume mounting

If a data set resides on more than one volume, all volumes can be mounted concurrently by coding UNIT = (*device,volumes,...*). The device can be either a type or group, and "volumes" is the number of volumes (1 to 59) to mount in parallel. The volumes must not exceed the number of drives available.

Mounting volumes in parallel can save time by eliminating the need for the operator to dismount and mount volumes on a single unit as they are needed. However, parallel mounting denies the use of these units to other jobs. Parallel mounting allows data sets contained on more than one direct-access volume to be processed. One unit is assumed if volumes are omitted.

If the data set is cataloged or passed, or if the VOL parameter indicates the number of volumes, code P rather than volumes. The number of volumes is then obtained from the catalog, from the passed data set, or from the VOL parameter. The device type or group should be omitted from cataloged or passed data sets since this information is contained in the catalog or passed with the data set.

```
//A DD UNIT=(3380,2),...
     [ Two 3380 disks are mounted in parallel. ]

//B DD UNIT=(,P),...
     [ All volumes containing the cataloged or passed data sets are
     mounted in parallel. ]

//C DD UNIT=(TAPE9,P),VOL=SER=(000200,000300),...
     [ Two volumes (000200 and 000300) are mounted in parallel. ]
```

2.   DEFER: deferred volume mounting

To defer volume mounting until the data set is opened, code UNIT = (*device*,,
DEFER). The system will not request the volume to be mounted until the data set is
opened. DEFER can be used to prevent needlessly mounting a volume because a
particular run does not require it. DEFER is ignored if the volume is already
mounted; in addition, it is ignored for new data sets on direct-access volumes because
space must be allocated before the step is initiated. DEFER cannot be coded for
ISAM data sets.

```
//A DD UNIT=(TAPE,,DEFER),...
//B DD UNIT=(DISK,2,DEFER),...
//C DD UNIT=(,P,DEFER),...
```

A volume might be deferred when a tape volume is not immediately required,
when successive volumes must be mounted on the same unit, or when several files are
to be read in succession from the same tape reel.

3.   SEP: unit separation (VS1 only)

To separate a data set on a direct-access volume from other data sets, code
UNIT = (...,SEP = (*ddname,ddname,...,ddname*)). Since SEP is a keyword subparameter, it is coded after the last positional subparameter. One to eight ddnames of
previous DD statements in the same step may be listed from which to separate this
data set.

SEP limits arm contention by forcing concurrently used data sets onto I/O devices
with separate access arms; thus it may significantly reduce processing time. For
example, if the same direct-access volume contains an input and output data set, the
access arm must be moved whenever reading and writing alternate. When the data
sets are separated, the arm contention is eliminated. (There may still be arm
contention with data sets used by other jobs in the system, but this is beyond your
control unless you request a private volume.)

```
//STEP1 EXEC PGM=ONE
//A DD UNIT=SYSDA,...
//B DD UNIT=(SYSDA,SEP=A),...
//C DD UNIT=(SYSDA,SEP=D),...
     [ Wrong!  Must refer to a previous DD statement. ]
//D DD UNIT=(SYSDA,3,DEFER,SEP=(A,
//      B,C))
     [ The SEP subparameters can be continued after a complete
     ddname, including the comma following it. ]
```

If the SEP request cannot be satisfied, the system ignores it. If one of the ddnames defines a dummy data set (DUMMY or DSN = NULLFILE), the unit separation for the ddname is ignored.

VIII. DISP: DATA SET DISPOSITION

The DISP parameter describes the current status of the data set (old, new, or to be modified) and directs the system on the disposition of the data set (pass, keep, catalog, uncatalog, or delete) either at the end of the step or if the step abnormally terminates. DISP is always required unless the data set is created and deleted in the same step. The general form of the DISP parameter is:

```
DISP=(status,normal-disp,abnormal-disp)
```

```
The various options are:

          KEEP
          NEW DELETE   KEEP
          MOD PASS     DELETE
          OLD CATLG    CATLG
          SHR UNCATLG UNCATLG
    DISP=(___,_____,_____)
```

A. Status

The *status*, NEW, MOD, OLD, or SHR, is the status of the data set at the beginning of the step. If the data set is new, the system creates a data set label; if it is old, the system locates it and reads its label.

1. NEW: new data sets

DISP = (NEW,...) creates a data set. The UNIT parameter is required, the VOL parameter can be used to place the data set on a specific volume, and the SPACE parameter is required for data sets on direct-access volumes. The step abnormally terminates if a data set with the same name already exists on the same direct-access volume.

NEW is default if nothing is coded; for example, DISP = (,KEEP) is the same as DISP = (NEW,KEEP). If DISP is omitted entirely, NEW is also assumed.

2. MOD: modifying data sets

DISP = (MOD,...) modifies a sequential data set. When the data set is opened, MOD positions the read/write mechanism after the last record in the data set, as shown in Figure 35. This provides a convenient means of adding data to sequential data sets.

If the data set does not exist, the system changes MOD to NEW—unless the VOL parameter requests a specific volume. When VOL is coded, the system expects to find the data set on the specified volume and terminates the step if it cannot find it. If VOL is not coded, the system looks to see whether the data set was passed or is in the catalog; if neither is the case, it assumes the data set does not exist and creates it as if NEW had been coded.

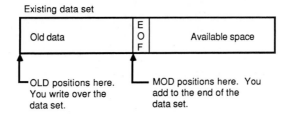

Figure 35. Disposition of MOD

A new data set does not contain an end-of-data-set marker until it is opened and closed for output. Space is often allocated on a direct-access volume with the expectation that subsequent jobs will add data to it with a disposition of MOD. An attempt to read the data set yields unpredictable results unless the data set has been opened and closed for output to write an end-of-data set marker.

MOD can be used to add to a data set that extends onto several volumes; it is the usual way of extending data sets onto several direct-access volumes. Always specify a disposition of CATLG with MOD for cataloged data sets, even if they are already cataloged, to record additional volume serial numbers in the catalog. If the volumes onto which the data set extends are not already mounted, specify either a volume count with the VOL parameter or deferred mounting with the UNIT parameter so that the system will request dismounting and mounting of volumes.

DCB parameters contained in the data set label of a data set being extended with MOD should not be coded on the DD statement extending the data set because a data set must not be written with conflicting sets of DCB parameters. If DCB parameters are coded on the DD statement, be sure that they do not conflict with the data set.

3. OLD: old data sets

DISP = (OLD,...) designates an existing data set; it can be an input data set or an output data set to rewrite. The step is given sole access to the data set. (In multi-programming environments, several jobs have the potential of concurrently reading the same data set on a direct-access volume.)

If the old data set is cataloged or passed from a previous step, the DSN parameter is usually the only other DD parameter needed. (The LABEL parameter may also be needed for tapes.) If the old data set is not cataloged or passed from a previous step, UNIT and VOL parameters are required.

4. SHR: sharing input data sets

DISP = (SHR,...) permits old data sets to be shared. SHR is identical to OLD except that several jobs may read the data set concurrently in multiprogramming environments. SHR must be used only for input data sets; use OLD or MOD if the data set is modified. Sharing data sets is necessary because public libraries like SYS1.LINKLIB or the subroutine libraries should be available to every job in the system. Generally, SHR should be used for all input data sets. (If the data set is being modified by another job, that job will have a disposition of OLD to prevent the data set being shared.)

```
//STEP1 EXEC PGM=FIRST
//A DD DSN=RECORDS,DISP=(NEW,PASS),UNIT=SYSDA,SPACE=(1600,100)
        [ The data set named RECORDS is created. Since it now exists,
        any later usage of it must be with the disposition, MOD, SHR,
        or OLD. ]
//STEP2 EXEC PGM=SECOND
//B DD DSN=BOOKS,DISP=(MOD,CATLG),UNIT=SYSDA,SPACE=(1600,100)
        [ If data set BOOKS is not found in the catalog, the system
        assumes it does not exist and creates it. If it does exist,
        any new data written into it is placed after the last record
        in the data set. ]
//C DD DSN=LIBRARY,DISP=(MOD,CATLG),UNIT=SYSDA,VOL=SER=PACK12
        [ Because of the VOL, LIBRARY must be an existing data set.
        Any new data written into it is placed after the last record
        in the data set. ]
//STEP3 EXEC PGM=THIRD
//D DD DSN=PRIVAT.FORTLIB,DISP=OLD
        [ PRIVAT.FORTLIB must be an existing data set, and the step is
        given sole use of it. If the system cannot locate it in the
        catalog, the step is terminated. ]
//E DD DSN=SYS1.FORTLIB,DISP=SHR
        [ The only difference between D and E is that E permits other
        jobs to read SYS1.FORTLIB concurrently. ]
```

B. Normal Disposition

Normal disposition, the second term in the DISP parameter, indicates the disposition of the data set when the data set is closed or when the job terminates normally. The normal disposition can be omitted if the status of the data set is not to change— existing data sets (MOD, OLD, or SHR) continue to exist; NEW data sets are deleted.

Disposition for data sets on direct-access and tape volumes differs. Space on direct-access volumes remains intact if the data set is kept, and space is released for other use if the data set is deleted. Keeping and deleting a tape data set is similar; the tape is rewound and unloaded. The computer operator is then told whether the tape is to be kept or deleted. Presumably the operator will reserve a kept tape and put a deleted tape back into circulation, but nothing actually happens to the data on the tape.

A data set passed between job steps on a direct-access volume is retained. Passing tape data sets rewinds the tape to the load point between steps but does not dismount it.

Under the following special circumstances, disposition is not performed, leaving data sets as they were prior to the job step.

- The step is not initiated because of JCL errors or JCL checking.
- The step is bypassed because of the COND parameter on JOB or EXEC statements. Disposition is performed only for passed data sets.
- The data set is not opened and either a nonspecific request was made for a tape (VOL = SER not coded), or deferred mounting is specified for direct-access volumes [UNIT = (...,DEFER) is coded].
- The step abnormally terminates after devices have been allocated but before the step begins execution because space on a direct-access volume cannot be obtained. Existing data sets (OLD, MOD, and SHR) continue to exist; NEW data sets are deleted.
- DUMMY or DSN = NULLFILE is coded on the DD statement.

1.   PASS: pass data sets

DISP = (..,PASS,..) passes the data set on to subsequent job steps, and each step can use the data set once. PASS saves time because the system retains the data set location and volume information, and a mountable volume containing the data set remains mounted. Both temporary and nontemporary data sets can be passed. Table 1 lists all the DD parameters passed with the data set.

Final disposition is left to a subsequent step. If the data set is not referred to by an intervening step, the data set continues to be passed. If PASS is coded in the last step or no disposition is given, temporary data sets are deleted, and nontemporary data sets assume their original status: existing data sets (MOD, OLD, or SHR) continue to exist; NEW data sets are deleted.

PASS passes the file number and label type of a tape data set. The tape density is not passed.

Subsequent steps can refer to a passed data set by name or by referback. UNIT and VOL parameters need not be coded since this information is passed with the data set.

```
//STEP1 EXEC PGM=ONE
//A DD DSN=&&IT,DISP=(NEW,PASS),
//      UNIT=SYSDA,VOL=SER=PACK10,SPACE=(1600,100)
//STEP2 EXEC PGM=TWO
//B DD DSN=&&IT,DISP=(OLD,PASS)
     or
//B DD DSN=*.STEP1.A,DISP=(OLD,PASS)
```

Several data sets having identical names can be passed in successive steps. DD statements referring to these identically named passed data sets retrieve them in the order they were passed.

2. KEEP: keep data sets

DISP = (..,KEEP,..) keeps nontemporary data sets. A data set residing on a direct-access volume is retained, and a data set residing on tape is rewound and dismounted. A keep message is issued to the operator if the data set resides on a mountable volume. If KEEP is attempted for a temporary data set, the disposition is changed to PASS. (The data set is deleted if no DSN parameter is coded and DEFER is specified in the UNIT parameter.) If KEEP is used for a NEW data set, a data set label is created for the data set.

```
//READ DD DSN=LEDGER,DISP(NEW,KEEP),
//        UNIT=SYSDA,VOL=SER=PACK10,SPACE=(1600,100)
    [ LEDGER is created and is kept after the step terminates.
    Since LEDGER is not passed or cataloged, any later use of the
    data set, either in a subsequent step or in a later job, must
    be given the volume and unit. ]

//LATER DD DSN=LEDGER,DISP=(OLD,KEEP),UNIT=SYSDA,VOL=SER=PACK10
    [ The system locates LEDGER on the volume and unit specified.
    OLD, MOD, or SHR must be used to refer to an existing data
    set.  If NEW has been used instead of OLD, the system would
    terminate the step because a data set with the same name
    already exists on the volume. ]
```

3. DELETE: delete data sets

DISP = (..,DELETE,..) deletes data sets. Storage on a direct-access volume is released; a tape is rewound and unloaded, and the operator is told that the tape data set is deleted (nothing actually happens to the data on tape). If the data set is located through the catalog (UNIT and VOL not coded), the data set is also uncataloged. If the retention period of a data set on a direct-access volume has not expired, the data set is not deleted.

4. CATLG: catalog data sets

DISP = (..,CATLG,..) catalogs a nontemporary data set. CATLG is similar to KEEP except that the unit and volume of the data set are recorded in the catalog along with the data set name. The file number of a tape data set is also recorded in the catalog, but the type of tape label and the tape density is not. (The system assumes standard labels, so you need code the LABEL parameter only for nonstandard labels.)

If the data set is already cataloged, the disposition is the same as PASS. If CATLG is attempted for temporary data sets, the disposition is changed to PASS. (The data set is deleted if no DSN parameter is coded and DEFER is specified in the UNIT parameter.) All volumes of a multivolume data set are recorded in the catalog. If a multivolume data set is being expanded onto more volumes, DISP = (MOD,CATLG) records the additional volumes in the catalog.

```
//CARDS DD DSN=BALANCE,DISP=(NEW,CATLG),UNIT=TAPE,VOL=SER=000500
     [ BALANCE is created and cataloged.  A later DD statement can
     refer to the data set by its name, omitting the unit and
     volume. ]
```

```
//LATER DD DSN=BALANCE,DISP=(OLD,CATLG)
     or
//LATER DD DSN=BALANCE,DISP=(OLD,KEEP)
     [ CATLG and KEEP are equivalent if the data set is already
     cataloged.  However, if a multivolume data set is expanded
     onto more volumes, use CATLG to record the additional volumes
     in the catalog. ]
```

```
//SAVE DD DSN=BUDGET,DISP=(OLD,CATLG),UNIT=TAPE,VOL=SER=000300
     [ An existing data set can also be cataloged. ]
```

5.   UNCATLG: uncatalog data sets

DISP = (..,UNCATLG,..) uncatalogs a data set. UNCATLG is the same as KEEP except that the data set name is removed from the catalog. If the data set is not cataloged, UNCATLG is equivalent to KEEP. In practice, there is rarely a need to uncatalog a data set.

```
//RID DD DSN=BALANCE,DISP=(OLD,UNCATLG)
     [ BALANCE is removed from the catalog.  If BALANCE were not
     cataloged, the system could not locate the data set and would
     terminate the step. ]
```

```
//A DD DSN=DT,DISP=(OLD,UNCATLG),UNIT=SYSDA,VOL=SER=PACK06
     [ DT is removed from the catalog.  If DT is not cataloged,
     UNCATLG is treated as KEEP. ]
```

C. Abnormal Disposition

The *abnormal disposition*, effective only if the step abnormally terminates, is the same as a normal disposition except that PASS is not allowed. KEEP, CATLG, UNCATLG, and DELETE are all permitted:

DISP = (NEW,PASS,DELETE), DISP = (OLD,DELETE,CATLG), etc.

If an abnormal disposition is not specified and the step terminates abnormally, the normal disposition is assumed; for example, DISP = (OLD,KEEP) is equivalent to DISP = (OLD,KEEP,KEEP); DISP = (OLD,PASS) is equivalent to DISP = (OLD,PASS,KEEP). The abnormal termination disposition for temporary data sets is always DELETE, regardless of what is coded.

A passed data set assumes the conditional disposition specified the last time it was passed if a step abnormally terminates. If no conditional disposition was specified, the data set is deleted if it was new when first passed; otherwise it is kept. The following example illustrates the use of the abnormal disposition.

```
//STEP1 EXEC PGM=CREATE
//A DD DSN=JUNK,DISP=(NEW,KEEP),
//     UNIT=SYSDA,VOL=SER=PACK02,SPACE=(1600,100)
```

If STEP1 abnormally terminates, the data set named JUNK is kept. If the program is corrected and the job resubmitted with the same JCL, it will abnormally terminate again—this time because the data set JUNK already exists on the volume. You must change the disposition of the A DD statement to DISP = (OLD,KEEP). This inconvenience is avoided by deleting the data set if the step abnormally terminates.

```
//STEP1 EXEC PGM=CREATE
//A DD DSN=JUNK,DISP=(NEW,KEEP,DELETE),
//     UNIT=SYSDA,VOL=SER=PACK02,SPACE=(1600,100)
```

Now if STEP1 abnormally terminates, JUNK is deleted and the disposition need not be changed to OLD when the job is resubmitted. The abnormal disposition is very useful for data sets on direct-access volumes because, as the above example illustrates, subsequent runs may depend on the disposition of the data sets in previous runs. The abnormal disposition, in addition to deleting unwanted data sets, can also retain information about the data set. Here's how:

```
//STEP1 EXEC PGM=ONE
//X DD DSN=SAVEIT,DISP=(NEW,PASS),UNIT=SYSDA,SPACE=(1600,100)
```

If STEP1 abnormally terminates, SAVEIT is deleted because PASS is assumed, and passed nontemporary data sets assume their original disposition if the step abnormally terminates.

```
//STEP2 EXEC PGM=TWICE
//B DD DSN=SAVEIT,DISP=(OLD,DELETE,CATLG)
     [ If STEP2 abnormally terminates, SAVEIT is cataloged and the
     unit and volume information are retained in the catalog.  If
     the restart feature is used to restart the job from STEP2,
     the B DD statement need not be changed. ]
```

The current status, normal disposition, and abnormal disposition are all optional. The following examples show the actual dispositions in effect if parameters are omitted. You should reread the description of the dispositions if the assumed dispositions are not clear.

```
//A DD UNIT=3380,SPACE=(1600,100)
     [ DISP=(NEW,DELETE,DELETE) is assumed. ]

//B DD DISP=NEW,UNIT=SYSDA,SPACE=(1600,100)
     [ DISP=(NEW,DELETE,DELETE) is assumed. ]

//C DD DSN=LIB,DISP=SHR
     [ DISP=(SHR,KEEP,KEEP) is assumed. ]

//D DD DSN=TURNON,DISP=MOD,UNIT=SYSDA,SPACE=(1600,100)
     [ DISP=(OLD,KEEP,KEEP) is assumed if TURNON is cataloged or
     passed from a previous step.  DISP=(NEW,DELETE,DELETE) is
     assumed if TURNON does not exist. ]
```

```
//E  DD DSN=IT,DISP=(,KEEP,DELETE),UNIT=SYSDA,SPACE=(1600,100)
    [ DISP=(NEW,KEEP,DELETE) is assumed. ]

//F DD DSN=&&IT,DISP=(OLD,PASS,KEEP)
    [ DISP=(OLD,PASS,DELETE) is assumed. ]

//G DD DSN=IT,DISP=(OLD,,CATLG),UNIT=SYSDA,VOL=SER=PACK02
    [ DISP=(OLD,KEEP,CATLG) is assumed. ]

//H DD DSN=&&IT,DISP=(,KEEP),UNIT=SYSDA,SPACE=(1600,100)
    [ DISP=(NEW,PASS,DELETE) is assumed. ]
```

IX. VOL: VOLUME PARAMETER

The VOL parameter requests a specific volume, multiple volumes, specific volumes of a multivolume cataloged data set, and private volumes. A volume is the portion of a storage device served by one read/write mechanism, such as a tape reel or disk pack. The VOL parameter can also be coded as VOLUME; for example, VOL = SER = 000200 and VOLUME = SER = 000200 are equivalent.

Each volume can have a label. There are two types of labels (actually three if one includes the external label pasted on a tape reel or disk pack): a volume label and a data set label. Both the volume and data set labels are contained in the volume itself as data. The volume label contains the volume serial number and is read by the system to ensure that an expected volume is actually mounted.

Volumes can be permanently mounted, mounted by the operator, or mounted because they are required by your job. Volumes become permanently mounted if critical portions of the system reside on them, if the volume cannot be physically dismounted, or if they are so designated by the installation. Direct-access volumes are almost always permanently mounted. Tapes are usually mounted when they are required by user jobs.

Volumes are *private* or *public*. The space on public volumes is suballocated to many users. Private volumes are assigned to a single user. Tapes can only be used by one user at a time and are always private. Other devices such as disk can be made private by coding PRIVATE in the VOL parameter described in this chapter.

For the two types of volumes there are two types of requests, *specific* and *nonspecific*. A nonspecific request, which can be made only for new data sets, is made by not requesting a specific volume with the VOL parameter and by requesting an appropriate UNIT name. The installation must define which UNIT names may be nonspecific. For example, UNIT = SYSDA might be nonspecific, in which case the VOL parameter could be omitted. UNIT = PRIV might be specific, requiring the VOL parameter to be coded. Check with your installation to find out which UNIT names are specific and nonspecific.

A nonspecific request is satisfied either by the system selecting an on-line volume or by the system requesting the operator to select and mount a mountable volume. The DISP parameter tells the operator what to do with the volume. A disposition of KEEP or CATLG requests the operator to assign the volume to the user; a disposition of DELETE tells the operator that the volume is available for reuse.

A.   SER, REF: Request a Specific Volume

To request specific volumes, code VOL = SER = *volume* for one volume or VOL = SER = (*volume,...,volume*) if several volumes (up to 255) are needed. The volume serial numbers are one to six alphanumeric (A to Z, 0 to 9) or national (@ $ #) characters, or the hyphen (-). Special characters [blank , . / ') (* & + =] can also be used by enclosing the volume in apostrophes; code a legitimate apostrophe as two consecutive apostrophes. If the volume serial number has fewer than six characters, it is extended on the right with blanks to six characters.

```
//A DD DSN=SAVE,DISP=(NEW,CATLG),
//    UNIT=3340,VOL=SER=PACK12,SPACE=(1600,100)
     [ A 3340 disk pack labeled PACK12 is requested.  If the pack
     is not mounted, the system will request the operator to mount
     it. ]

//B DD DSN=MANY,DISP=(OLD,KEEP),VOL=SER=(TP1,
//    TP2,TP3),UNIT=(TAPE,3)
     [ Three tape volumes are requested to be mounted in parallel:
     volumes TP1, TP2, and TP3.  A DD statement specifying several
     volumes can be continued after a complete serial number,
     including the comma following it. ]
```

Rather than specifying volume serial numbers, you can request the same volumes used by another data set. If the other data set is cataloged or passed from a previous step, code VOL = REF = *dsname* to name the data set. The dsname cannot contain special characters. If the data set is not cataloged, passed, or assigned a temporary name, code VOL = REF = *.referback* to refer back to a previous DD statement describing the data set. If the earlier data set resides on multiple volumes, only the last volume is assigned for tapes; all volumes are assigned for direct-access volumes. If a referback is made to a DD statement defining a dummy data set, the DD statement making the referback is also assigned a dummy status.

```
//STEP1 EXEC PGM=START
//A DD DSN=HOLDUP,DISP=(NEW,PASS),
//    UNIT=SYSDA,VOL=SER=PACK02,SPACE=(1600,100)
//B DD DSN=REPORT,DISP=(NEW,PASS),VOL=REF=*.A,SPACE=(1600,100)
     [ Disk volume PACK02 is also assigned to REPORT.  No unit
     parameter is needed since the system already knows to which
     unit the pack is assigned. ]
//STEP2 EXEC PGM=FINISH
//C DD DSN=MORE,DISP=(NEW,CATLG),VOL=REF=*.STEP1.A,SPACE=(1600,100)
     or
//C DD DSN=MORE,DISP=(NEW,CATLG),VOL=REF=HOLDUP,SPACE=(1600,100)
     [ The data set named MORE is also assigned to PACK02. ]
```

B.   Special Options

Options are provided to request private volumes, to ensure that the private volumes remain mounted between steps, to request multiple volumes, and to request a specific volume of a multivolume data set. All subparameters are optional and can be coded in any combination. Code commas to omit any positional subparameters.

```
                                        SER=..
                                        REF=..
    VOL=(PRIVATE,RETAIN,sequence,volumes,_____)
```

1. PRIVATE: private volumes

To give exclusive use of a mountable volume to a particular data set during a step, code VOL = (PRIVATE,...). No other data sets are assigned to the volume, and it is dismounted after its last use in the step. Another job may now specifically request this volume. Either a specific or a nonspecific request can be made; the system asks the operator to select a private volume if the volume serial number is not specified. If a permanently mounted volume is requested, the volume is assigned, but PRIVATE is ignored. Tape data sets are always assumed to be PRIVATE.

```
//STEP1 EXEC PGM=PRIMARY
//A DD DSN=ALL,DISP=(NEW,CATLG),UNIT=3380,
//     VOL=(PRIVATE,SER=PACK12),SPACE=(1600,100)
    [ The system will request the operator to mount pack PACK02.
    No other data sets are assigned to the pack, and it is
    dismounted after its last use in the step. ]
```

2. RETAIN: retain private volumes

To keep a volume mounted between steps, code VOL = (PRIVATE,RETAIN,...). The volume remains mounted until it is used in a subsequent step or until the end of the job. Only the last volume of a multivolume data set is retained. RETAIN is often used when a tape is needed in several job steps, thereby minimizing mounting.

```
//A DD DSN=DISKFILE,DISP=(NEW,CATLG),UNIT=SYSDA,
//     VOL=(PRIVATE,RETAIN,SER=PACK03),SPACE=(1600,100)
    [ Pack PACK03 is not dismounted at the end of the step. ]
```

The PASS disposition also keeps the volume mounted between steps. RETAIN is generally required only when PASS cannot be used—when CATLG is specified or when a subsequent step retrieves a different file from a tape volume.

If RETAIN is not coded and the data set is not passed, a mountable volume is dismounted at the end of the step. Then if a subsequent step requests the volume, the operator may have to mount it on another I/O unit. (The CLOSE statement in several languages has precedence over DD statement parameters and may specify a different disposition.)

3. Sequence

When a multivolume data set is cataloged, all volume serial numbers are recorded in the catalog. To begin processing at other than the first volume, code VOL = (..,..., sequence,...), giving the sequence number (1 to 255). If the sequence number is omitted, processing begins with the first volume.

```
//A DD DSN=MULT,DISP=OLD,VOL=(PRIVATE,RETAIN,2)
     [ Processing begins with volume 2 of the MULT data set.  The
     volume serial numbers and I/O unit are omitted since they are
     contained in the catalog. ]

//B DD DSN=IRS,DISP=OLD,VOL=(,,3)
     [ Processing begins with volume 3 of the cataloged IRS data
     set. ]
```

4.   Volumes

If a data set extends onto more than one volume, you can either list the volume serial numbers with SER for specific volumes or give the number of volumes for a nonspecific request. To request nonspecific volumes, code VOL = (..,..,..,*volumes* ,...), giving the number (1 to 255) of volumes needed. The number of volumes can also be given for a cataloged or passed data set to indicate that additional volumes may be required. If *volumes* is omitted, one volume is assumed.

```
//A DD DSN=IRS,DISP=(NEW,CATLG),UNIT=TAPE9,VOL=(PRIVATE,,,2)
     [ The operator will be requested to assign and mount a maximum
     of 2 tapes. ]
```

If a multivolume data set is created or extended and the number of volumes the data set requires is unknown, a maximum number can be specified.

```
//A DD DSN=FILE,DISP=(NEW,CATLG),
//    UNIT=TAPE,VOL=(,,,6,SER=(000100,000200))
     [ Tape volumes 000100 and 000200 are assigned to the data set.
     Since a maximum of 6 volumes was requested,  the operator may
     be  requested to assign and mount up to 4 additional  volumes
     if they are needed.  The volume serial numbers of all volumes
     used are recorded in the catalog. ]
```

Alternatively, deferred mounting can be used.

```
//A DD DSN=FILE,DISP=(NEW,CATLG),
//     UNIT=(TAPE9,,DEFER),VOL=SER=(000100,000200)
     [ The effect of this statement is the same as that above
     except that the data set is not limited in the number of
     volumes onto which it can extend.  If more than the 2
     volumes are required, the DEFER requests the operator to
     assign additional volumes as needed.  The assigned volumes
     are then cataloged. ]
```

If the number of volumes exceeds the number of direct-access units requested with the UNIT parameter, PRIVATE must also be coded, that is, UNIT = (3380,2), VOL = (PRIVATE,,,3). If PRIVATE is not coded and the job requires more than the specified number of units, the job is abnormally terminated. Coding PRIVATE is not required for tape units.

Now consider two special problems. Suppose you wish to write a data set on a volume, but you do not know the volume serial number. The following must be coded on the DD statement.

```
VOL=PRIVATE,DISP=(NEW, ...),UNIT=(address,,DEFER)
```

For example, suppose the external label pasted on a tape reel is lost and we do not know the volume serial number. The following job opens the data set for output and catalogs the tape. The volume serial number is then listed in the system data disposition messages and is recorded in the catalog.

```
//STEP1 EXEC PGM=OPEN
     [ Assume that OPEN is a program that opens the data set. ]
//A DD DSN=WHAT,DISP=(NEW,CATLG),UNIT=(0D0,,DEFER),VOL=PRIVATE
```

Next, suppose that a data set is used twice in the same step; perhaps it is first opened for output, closed, and then opened for input. Normally one DD statement would suffice, but the program might be coded to require two DD statements. The second DD statement must contain:

```
DSN=*.ddname,DISP=(OLD, ...),VOL=REF=*.ddname
```

The following example illustrates a program that uses a data set twice in the same step.

```
//STEP1 EXEC PGM=INOUT
//A DD UNIT=3380,SPACE=(1600,100)
     [ DD statement A creates a temporary data set. (No DISP
     parameter means it must be temporary.) ]
//B DD DSN=*.A,DISP=OLD,VOL=REF=*.A
     [ DD statement B refers to the temporary data set. ]
```

EXERCISES

1. Find out your installation's conventions for disk and tape data set names.
2. Make a list of the type and group names for all the I/O devices at your installation. Note which ones require specific volume requests, and which permit nonspecific requests.
3. Make a list of all the public disk volumes at your installation.
4. Find out how private tape volumes are obtained and how you request them to be mounted. Also find out if your installation has any public tape volumes for temporary data sets.

Chapter 9

MORE ON THE DD STATEMENT

With the basics of the DD statement in hand from the preceding chapter, we are ready to discuss dummy data sets, concatenated data sets, overriding the DD statement in procedures, and the placement of DD statements.

I. *DUMMY, NULLFILE: DUMMY DATA SETS*

A sequential data set may be assigned a dummy status in which all I/O operations are bypassed, and device allocation, space allocation, and data set disposition are ignored. An attempt to read a dummy data set results in an immediate end-of-file exit: a write request is ignored. Only sequential and VSAM data sets can be assigned a dummy status.

Dummy data sets are used to test program flow without actually processing data. Unwanted output (listings, data sets, etc.) may also be suppressed by giving the output data sets a dummy status.

A data set is assigned a dummy status by coding either DUMMY as the first parameter in the DD statement or DSN = NULLFILE. Other parameters may also be coded on the DD statement as they would be for a real data set, but except for the DCB parameter they are ignored. BLKSIZE is required in the DCB parameter if it must be coded for the normal data set—the BLKSIZE is required by the OPEN to obtain buffers. The following examples illustrate the use of dummy data sets.

```
//SYSPRINT DD DUMMY
     [ Any output produced by SYSPRINT is suppressed. ]

//SYSIN DD DUMMY
     [ Any  attempt to read data from SYSIN results in an immediate
     end-of-file exit. ]

//OUTPUT DD DSN=NULLFILE,DISP=(NEW,CATLG),UNIT=SYSDA,
//          VOL=SER=PACK12,SPACE=(200,100),DCB=BLKSIZE=800
     [ The   requested  volume  need not be  mounted,   no  space  is
     allocated,  and the data set is not cataloged.   OUTPUT  must
     describe  a sequential data set because only sequential  data
     sets can be given a dummy status. ]

//OUTPUT DD DUMMY,DSN=REAL,DISP=(NEW,CATLG),UNIT=SYSDA,
//          VOL=SER=PACK12,SPACE=(200,100),DCB=BLKSIZE=800
     [ This statement is equivalent to the preceding statement. ]
```

A sequence of concatenated data sets is broken by an intervening dummy data set. (Concatenated data sets are described next.) In the following example, only the first data set is read.

```
//DD1 DD DSN=ONE,DISP=SHR
//     DD DUMMY,DCB=BLKSIZE=800
//     DD DSN=TWO,DISP=SHR
```

II.   CONCATENATING DATA SETS

A.   Sequential and Partitioned Data Sets

Sequential data sets are made up of records that are ordered sequentially—that is, one record follows another in the order they are entered. A partitioned data set is made up of several sequential data sets grouped together. Each sequential data set is called a *member* of the partitioned data set. Each member has a unique name. The entire partitioned data set also has a name. An example of a partitioned data set name is:

`Y2222.STUDENTS.DATA`

Here is an analogy that further illustrates sequential and partitioned data sets. Suppose we have a four-drawer file cabinet, with a drawer for each class—freshmen, sophomores, juniors, and seniors. Each piece of paper in the file represents a record. A single file drawer represents a sequential data set as shown in Figure 36.

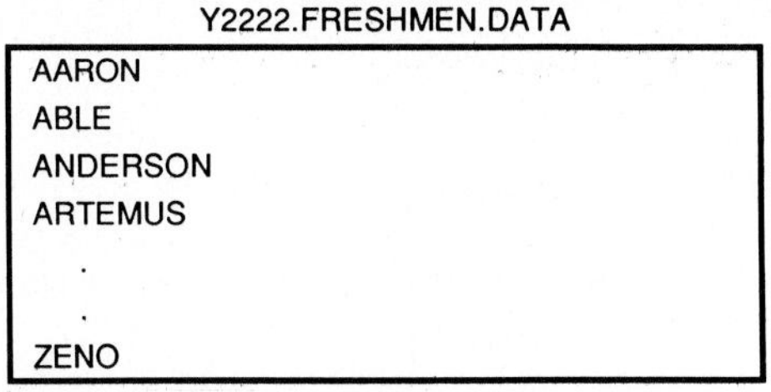

Y2222.FRESHMEN.DATA

```
AARON
ABLE
ANDERSON
ARTEMUS

    .
    .
ZENO
```

Figure 36. A sequential data set as a file drawer

The file drawer (sequential data set) is named Y2222.FRESHMEN.DATA. There is a record for each student. Figure 37 represents a partitioned data set as a file cabinet:

Y2222.STUDENTS.DATA

```
FRESHMEN      |   SOPHS
              |
──────────    |  ──────────
              |
JUNIORS       |   SENIORS
```

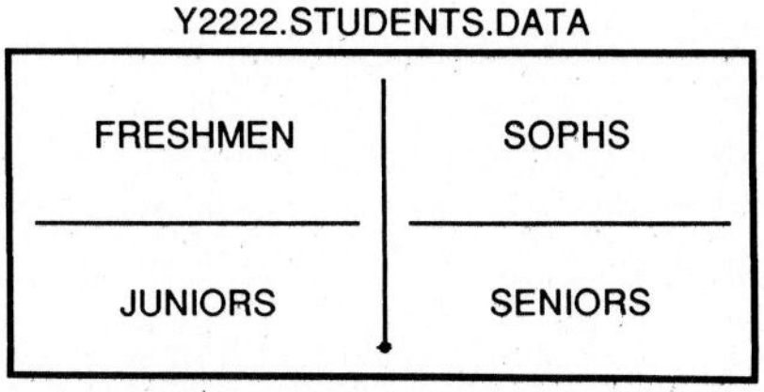

Figure 37. A partitioned data set as a file cabinet

The file cabinet (partitioned data set) is named Y2222.STUDENTS.DATA. The file drawers (members) are named FRESHMEN, SOPHS, JUNIORS, and SENIORS. Each member contains a record for each student in that class. Partitioned data sets are perhaps most often used for program libraries. The load module created by the linkage editor must be stored in a partitioned data set.

B. Concatenating Data Sets

Several input data sets can be read in sequence as if they were a single data set by concatenating them. Concatenating data sets consists of treating two or more data sets as if they were placed end to end to form one long sequential data set. Suppose we had three separate sequential data sets as shown in Figure 38.

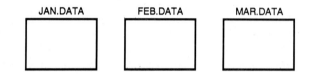

Figure 38. Three sequential data sets

To generate a quarterly report, we would need all three data sets. We want the system to see them as shown in Figure 39.

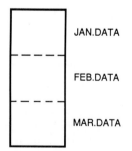

Figure 39. Three concatenated data sets

To concatenate data sets, you write a normal DD statement for the first data set, and then add a DD statement without a ddname for each data set to be concatenated. We want to concatenate three data sets:

```
JAN.DATA
FEB.DATA
MAR.DATA
```

The concatenated data sets must have the same characteristics (RECFM and LRECL). They must also reside on the same type of device, disk or tape.

```
//IN DD DSN=JAN.DATA,DISP=SHR
//   DD DSN=FEB.DATA,DISP=SHR
//   DD DSN=MAR.DATA,DISP=SHR
```

Here, JAN.DATA will be read first, then FEB.DATA, and last MAR.DATA. If the BLKSIZE is not the same for all data sets, the data set with the largest BLKSIZE must come first.

Data sets are concatenated by coding a DD statement for each data set in the order they are to be read. A ddname is coded on the first DD statement only. NAMES, ADDRESS, PHONES, and the lines of data in the input stream are read sequentially in the following example:

```
//DATAIN DD DSN=NAMES,DISP=SHR
//       DD DSN=ADDRESS,DISP=SHR
//       DD DSN=PHONES,DISP=SHR
//       DD *
   [ lines of data ]
/*
```

The DD statements need not be aligned as shown, but aligning them makes the statements easier to read.

Data in the input stream can be concatenated with other data sets. The other data sets must have a LRECL of 80. The input stream must also be spooled onto a direct-access volume; you cannot concatenate input read directly from the card reader.

You can also concatenate partitioned data sets. This is often done for program libraries to have the system search in several libraries for a member:

```
// EXEC PGM=CREATE
//STEPLIB DD DSN=LIB1.LOAD,DISP=SHR
//        DD DSN=LIB2.LOAD,DISP=SHR
```

The STEPLIB DD statement tells the system which library contains the program you want to execute. Here, the system will first search the LIB1.LOAD partitioned data set to find the CREATE program. If it doesn't find it, it then searches the LIB2.LOAD data set.

You can also concatenate the individual members of a partitioned data set. It will appear to the system as if they were one long sequential data set when you write:

```
// EXEC PGM=REGISTER
//IN DD DSN=STUDENTS.DATA(FRESHMEN),DISP=SHR
//   DD DSN=STUDENTS.DATA(SOPHS),DISP=SHR
//   DD DSN=STUDENTS.DATA(JUNIORS),DISP=SHR
//   DD DSN=STUDENTS.DATA(SENIORS),DISP=SHR
```

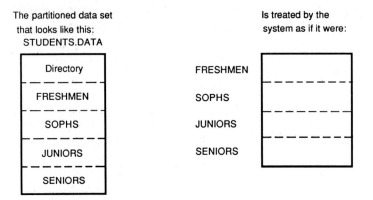

Figure 40. Concatenating data sets

Figure 40 shows how the data set is treated.

The next example concatenates sequential data sets with a member of a partitioned data set.

```
//DATAIN DD DSN=LIB(ONE),DISP=SHR
//       DD *
    [ lines of data ]
/*
//       DD DSN=NAMES,DISP=SHR
    [ Member ONE in LIB is read first, then the lines of data, and
    finally the sequential data set NAMES. ]
```

A member name must be given for any partitioned data set concatenated with a sequential data set. In the following example, an I/O error occurs when DATAIN is read because LIB is a partitioned data set.

```
//DATAIN DD DSN=NAMES,DISP=SHR
//       DD DSN=LIB,DISP=SHR
```

To read LIB in its entirety, concatenate each member.

The following rules apply to concatenating data sets:

- You can concatenate as many as 255 sequential data sets. They must have the same RECFM and LRECL and must also reside on the same type of device. If the BLKSIZE is not the same for all the data sets, the data set with the largest BLKSIZE must be placed first.
- You can concatenate as many as 16 partitioned data sets.
- You can concatenate as many as 255 members of partitioned data sets to form what appears to a program to be one sequential data set.
- You can't concatenate sequential data sets with members of partitioned data sets.

III. MODIFYING DD STATEMENTS IN CATALOGED PROCEDURES

Parameters on DD statements in procedures can be overridden, nullified, or added, or an entire DD statement can be added. The stepname is placed in front of the ddname to override or add DD statements to procedures. If the ddname of the submitted statement matches a ddname within the procedure, parameters on the DD statement are overridden; if the names do not match, the submitted statement is added. DD statements must be overridden in the order they appear in the procedure, and added DD statements must follow any overriding statements.

DD statements are added in their entirety, whereas an overridden DD statement is modified parameter by parameter. Parameters are overridden if parameters on the overriding statement match parameters on the procedure statement; parameters are added if they do not match. The order of parameters on overriding DD statements does not matter. The changes made to a cataloged procedure by overriding DD statements are effective only for the run and do not change the cataloged procedure permanently. The following example illustrates DD statements overridden in a procedure named RUN. The RUN procedure consists of:

```
//RUN PROC
//FIRST EXEC PGM=ONE
//INPUT    DD DSN=PIANO,DISP=OLD
//SCRATCH DD DSN=&&TEMP,SPACE=(1600,200),UNIT=SYSDA,
//              VOL=SER=PACK12,DCB=(RECFM=FB,LRECL=80,BLKSIZE=1600)
//SECOND EXEC PGM=TWO
//OUTPUT DD DUMMY,SYSOUT=A
```

The RUN procedure is invoked, and statements are overridden and added.

```
// EXEC RUN
//FIRST.INPUT DD DSN=GUITAR,UNIT=TEMP,VOL=SER=PACK16
         [ INPUT  matches a ddname in step FIRST so that parameters are
         overridden or added:   DSN is overridden,   DISP is unchanged,
         and UNIT and VOL are added. ]
//FIRST.SCRATCH DD UNIT=TEMP
         [ The UNIT parameter is overridden.   The statement overriding
         SCRATCH  must follow the statement overriding  INPUT  because
         SCRATCH follows INPUT in the procedure. ]
//SECOND.OUTPUT DD SYSOUT=B
         [ The SYSOUT parameter is overridden. ]
//SECOND.MORE DD DSN=DRUM,DISP=SHR
         [ Since the  DD  statement  is  added,  it  must  follow  the
         statement overriding OUTPUT. ]
```

The cataloged procedure is interpreted as follows for the run:

```
//FIRST EXEC PGM=ONE
//INPUT    DD DSN=GUITAR,DISP=OLD,UNIT=TEMP,VOL=SER=PACK16
//SCRATCH DD DSN=&&TEMP,SPACE=(1600,200),UNIT=TEMP,VOL=SER=PACK12,
//              DCB=(RECFM=FB,LRECL=80,BLKSIZE=1600)
//SECOND EXEC PGM=TWO
//OUTPUT DD DUMMY,SYSOUT=B
//MORE    DD DSN=DRUM,DISP=SHR
```

The following example shows a common error caused by misplaced DD statements.

```
// EXEC RUN
//SECOND.MORE    DD DSN=DRUM,DISP=SHR
//SECOND.OUTPUT DD DSN=VIOLIN,DISP=OLD
```

MORE should follow OUTPUT since it is an added DD statement. However, the system does not detect this error and assumes that OUTPUT is also to be added. Since two DD statements in the step now have the same ddname, the second OUTPUT DD statement is ignored. Thus a statement that was meant to override a DD statement is ignored with no error message printed.

A stepname prefixed to a ddname has no effect if a cataloged procedure is not invoked. The following two steps are treated the same.

```
// EXEC PGM=ONE
//IN DD DSN=LIB,DISP=SHR
```

```
    Same as:
```

```
// EXEC PGM=ONE
//GO.IN DD DSN=LIB,DISP=SHR
```

Parameters can be coded on overriding DD statements in any order: those appearing in the procedure are overridden; those not appearing are added. All except the DCB parameter are overridden in their entirety. DCB subparameters rather than the entire DCB parameter must be overridden or added.

```
// EXEC RUN
//FIRST.SCRATCH DD DCB=BLKSIZE=800,VOL=SER=PACK07
```

The SCRATCH DD statement is interpreted as:

```
//SCRATCH DD DSN=&&TEMP,SPACE=(1600,200),UNIT=SYSDA,VOL=SER=PACK07,
//              DCB=(RECFM=FB,LRECL=80,BLKSIZE=800)
```

Nullify parameters by coding the keyword followed by an equal sign but omitting the value. To nullify the entire DCB parameter, nullify each subparameter. (DCB= cannot be coded to nullify the entire DCB parameter.) To nullify a dummy data set (DUMMY or DSN=NULLFILE), code a DSN parameter on the overriding DD statement. If the DD statement does not require a data set name, code just DSN=.

```
// EXEC RUN
//FIRST.SCRATCH DD DSN=,DCB=(RECFM=F,BLKSIZE=)
//SECOND.OUTPUT DD DSN=
```

SCRATCH and OUTPUT are interpreted as:

```
//SCRATCH DD SPACE=(1600,200),UNIT=SYSDA,
//            VOL=SER=PACK12,DCB=(RECFM=F,LRECL=80)
//OUTPUT   DD SYSOUT=A
```

If a DD statement is overridden with parameters mutually exclusive from ones on the overridden DD statement, such as SYSOUT and DISP, the mutually exclusive parameters on the overridden DD statement are nullified. Do not attempt to nullify them on the overriding DD statement.

Concatenated DD statements within a cataloged procedure must be overridden individually in the same order they appear in the procedure. The following procedure contains a concatenated data set.

```
//WALK PROC
//STEP1 EXEC PGM=PRIMARY
//WORK DD DSN=LIBA,DISP=SHR
//     DD DSN=LIBB,DISP=SHR
```

To leave a particular DD statement unchanged, leave the operand field blank in the overriding DD statement.

```
// EXEC WALK
//STEP1.WORK DD DSN=LIBRARY,DISP=SHR
//           DD
//           DD DSN=LIBC,DISP=SHR
```

The first DD statement is overridden, the second is left unchanged, and a third data set is concatenated. The WORK DD statement is interpreted as:

```
//WORK DD DSN=LIBRARY,DISP=SHR
//     DD DSN=LIBB,DISP=SHR
//     DD DSN=LIBC,DISP=SHR
```

If you override a single DD statement, the other concatenated DD statements are undisturbed.

```
// EXEC WALK
//STEP1.WORK DD DSN=LIBRARY,DISP=SHR
```

The cataloged procedure is interpreted as:

```
//STEP1 EXEC PGM=PRIMARY
//WORK DD DSN=LIBRARY,DISP=SHR
//     DD DSN=LIBB,DISP=SHR
```

EXERCISES

Execute the PL/I program from Chapter 5 twice in succession within the same job. Name the first EXEC statement STEP1 and the second EXEC statement STEP2. Override STEP1 as follows:

```
//GO.OUT DD DISP=(NEW,PASS),UNIT=public-disk,
//            DCB=(RECFM=FB,LRECL=80,BLKSIZE=800),SPACE=(800,(1,1))
```

Override STEP2 to concatenate its stream input to the end of the temporary data set from STEP1. Verify that the job is correct by the output printed from STEP2.

Chapter 10

DD STATEMENTS FOR PERIPHERAL I/O DEVICES

This chapter discusses the DD statements required to read and write data for input stream data sets, output stream data sets, and unit record devices. The DDNAME parameter used to postpone the definition of a data set is also described.

I.   *, DATA: INPUT STREAM DATA SETS

Data in the form of 80-byte lines is perhaps the most common type of input. The 80-byte length is historic. Punched cards had 80 columns. Today, terminal screens are usually 80 columns wide as well. To include lines of data in the input stream, code:

```
//ddname DD *
     [ lines of data ]
/*
```

SYSIN is traditionally used as a ddname for lines of data in the input stream. The /* marks the end of the lines. The lines of data cannot contain // or /* in columns 1 and 2 if DD * is used. If the lines contain // in columns 1 and 2, as it would if the data included JCL, code DATA in place of *.

```
//ddname DD DATA
     [ lines of data which may contain // in columns 1 and 2. ]
/*
```

DATA is the same as * except that lines with // in columns 1 and 2 may be included. Both * and DATA are positional parameters and must be coded before any other parameters on the DD statement. DD * and DATA cannot be placed in cataloged procedures because they must immediately precede the lines of data in the input stream.

There may be several DD * or DATA statements with different ddnames because input is queued on a direct-access volume before the job is executed. If the system encounters lines of data (any lines not having // or /* in columns 1 and 2) not preceded by a DD * or DATA statement, it automatically provides a DD * statement with a ddname of SYSIN. If a cataloged procedure is invoked, the generated SYSIN statement applies to the first step of the procedure. If DD * is specified or assumed and the /* statement is omitted, the system assumes a /* when the next statement with a // in columns 1 and 2 is encountered. This means that you can usually omit the /*.

```
//STEP1 EXEC PGM=PRIMERO
     [ lines of data ]
//STEP2 EXEC PGM=SEGUNDO

   These steps are equivalent to:
//STEP1 EXEC PGM=PRIMERO
//SYSIN DD *
     [ lines of data ]
/*
//STEP2 EXEC PGM=SEGUNDO
```

Note that the /* delimiter is required for a DD DATA statement because DD DATA treats lines containing // in columns 1 and 2 as data.

A. DLM: Delimiter Parameter

If the data itself contains /* in columns 1 and 2, which could occur if the data consisted of JCL statements, code the DLM = 'cc' parameter on the DD statement to specify any two characters as the delimiter. If the delimiter contains an ampersand or apostrophe, code it as two consecutive characters: DLM = '&&"' specifies the delimiter characters as &'. DLM can be coded on either a DD * or DATA statement.

```
//SYSIN DD *,DLM='ZZ'
     [ lines of data which may contain /* in columns 1 and 2. ]
ZZ
```

B. DCB Subparameters

The system normally blocks input stream data automatically. The DCB = BLKSIZE subparameter may be coded to specify a different block size, as long as it is a multiple of 80. The DCB = BUFNO subparameter may also specify the number of buffers, and the DCB = LRECL subparameter can specify the logical record length. (Except in JES2, DCB = MODE = C may be coded to specify column binary data—an old format used for punched cards.)

```
//SYSIN DD *,DCB=BLKSIZE=80
     [ The block size is set to 80. ]

//SYSIN DD DATA,DCB=(BLKSIZE=800,BUFNO=2)
     [ The block size is set to 800 and two buffers are provided
     for reading the input. ]
```

II. DDNAME: POSTPONING DEFINITION OF DATA SETS

The DDNAME = *ddname* parameter, often used in cataloged procedures for input stream data sets, postpones the definition of the data set until a subsequent DD statement is encountered with the specific ddname. DCB subparameters BLKSIZE, BUFNO, and DIAGNS may be coded with the DDNAME parameter; no other parameters or subparameters are permitted. The following step requires both BLKSIZE and BUFNO on the DD * statement.

```
//GO EXEC PGM=INITIAL
//TWO DD *,DCB=(BLKSIZE=80,BUFNO=3)
     [ lines of data ]
/*
```

You can make this step a cataloged or in-stream procedure, but DD * and DATA statements cannot be placed in procedures, so the TWO DD statement cannot be in the procedure. If the procedure is named JOG, the step would consist of:

```
// EXEC JOG
//GO.TWO DD *,DCB=(BLKSIZE=80,BUFNO=3)
     [ lines of data ]
/*
```

The lengthy DCB parameter makes this procedure inconvenient. The TWO DD statement, with BLKSIZE and BUFNO subparameters, can be included in the procedure by using the DDNAME parameter. The procedure is coded as:

```
// JOG PROC
//GO EXEC PGM=INITIAL
//TWO DD DDNAME=TWO,DCB=(BLKSIZE=80,BUFNO=3)
```

The step is simplified to:

```
// EXEC JOG
//GO.TWO DD *
     [ lines of data ]
/*
```

BLKSIZE and BUFNO subparameters coded on the DD statement pointed to by DDNAME override any subparameters on the DDNAME statement. Since DDNAME can refer to any name, SYSIN can be used as well as TWO.

```
//TWO DD DDNAME=SYSIN,DCB=(BLKSIZE=80,BUFNO=3)
```

The step is now executed with BLKSIZE set to 800.

```
//EXEC JOG
//GO.SYSIN DD *,DCB=BLKSIZE=800
     [ lines of data ]
/*
```

DD statements with a ddname matching a DDNAME parameter in a cataloged procedure can precede or follow any overriding or added DD statements. A maximum of five DDNAME parameters, each referring to unique ddnames, may be included in a single job step. DDNAME cannot be used on JOBLIB, JOBCAT, or STEPCAT DD statements.

A referback parameter on subsequent DD statements must refer to the statement containing the DDNAME parameter, not to the statement with the matching ddname, and must follow the statement with the matching ddname; otherwise it refers to a dummy data set. The following example illustrates such an error for the JOG procedure.

```
//STEP1 EXEC JOG
//GO.ALPHA DD DSN=WHAT,DISP=OLD,UNIT=TAPE9,VOL=SER=000200
//GO.BETA   DD DSN=*.STEP1.GO.ALPHA,DISP=OLD
     [ BETA results in a dummy data set ]
//GO.GAMMA DD DSN=*.STEP1.GO.TWO,DISP=OLD
     [ GAMMA is coded correctly. ]
```

A DDNAME parameter coded in a concatenated data set must be coded first, before the other concatenated data sets.

```
//INPUT DD DDNAME=SYSIN
//       DD DSN=SYS1.PROCLIB(LIST),DISP=SHR
```

The following is in error because DDNAME is not coded first.

```
//INPUT DD DSN=SYS1.PROCLIB(LIST),DISP=SHR
//       DD DDNAME=LATER
```

The DD statement that matches a DDNAME statement cannot be concatenated. The next example illustrates this. Assume that a cataloged procedure contains the following DD statement.

```
//INPUT DD DDNAME=SYSIN
```

Next, SYSIN is defined as a concatenated data set, resulting in an error.

```
//GO.SYSIN DD DSN=ONE,DISP=SHR
//         DD DSN=TWO,DISP=SHR
```

To correct the error, override the INPUT DD statement with the concatenated data set.

```
//GO.INPUT DD DSN=ONE,DISP=SHR
//         DD DSN=TWO,DISP=SHR
```

III. SYSOUT: OUTPUT STREAM DATA SETS

The SYSOUT parameter provides a convenient means of routing output to printers. To route an output data set to an output device, code:

```
//ddname DD SYSOUT=class
```

The *class* can be any alphanumeric (A to Z, 0 to 9) character (or the asterisk * in MVS). An installation may define separate output classes for special forms, high-volume output, high-priority output, etc. SYSOUT = A is traditionally the printer and SYSOUT = B the card punch.

```
//SYSPRINT DD SYSOUT=A
//SYSPUNCH DD SYSOUT=B
```

The asterisk in MVS specifies the same class as specified on the MSGCLASS parameter on the JOB statement.

```
//RUN#12 JOB (5542,30),'PRINT JOB',CLASS=A,MSGCLASS=E
  .      .       .
//SYSPRINT DD SYSOUT=*
     [ Same as SYSOUT=E. ]
```

Output is queued onto a direct-access volume, and system output writers later write the output onto the appropriate I/O device. The computer operator must start an output writer to a specific device, and each writer may write several classes of output. Be sure to use an output class that will have a writer started to it or the output will remain queued on the direct-access volume. If several data sets are written on the same output class, each data set is printed separately in the order of the DD statements.

A. Special Processing

You may also specify a special program to write the output and request special output forms. For this, the SYSOUT parameter is coded as:

```
SYSOUT=(class,program,form)
```

The *program* is the name of a program contained in SYS1.LINKLIB that is to write the output. The *form* requests special output forms and ranges from one to four alphanumeric or national characters. Each installation must establish its own form numbers. The system requests the operator to mount the special form just before the data set is printed, and requests the original form to be remounted when printing is complete.

```
//PRINT DD SYSOUT=(A,MYPRINT)
     [ The system loads the MYPRINT program and passes control to
     it so that it can print the output. ]

//PRINT DD SYSOUT=(A,,1001)
     [ The operator is requested to mount form 1001 before the
     output is printed. ]

//PUNCH DD SYSOUT=(B,MYPUNCH,2)
     [ The output is written on punched cards. The operator is
     requested to mount form 2 prior to program MYPUNCH punching the
     output. ]
```

Instead of coding the form in the SYSOUT parameter, JES2 lets you specify the one- to four-alphanumeric or national character code of an OUTPUT statement from which to copy the output characteristics.

```
//SYSPRINT DD SYSOUT=(A,,code)
     [ The output characteristics are obtained from a JES2 OUTPUT
     statement that matches the code. ]
```

In JES2 and JES3, you can specify a *program* as INTRDR to cause the output to be sent to the internal reader as a job in the input stream.

```
//OUTPUT DD SYSOUT=(A,INTRDR)
```

B. COPIES: Multiple Copies

COPIES = *copies* specifies the number of copies (1 to 254) of the output to produce. One copy is assumed if COPIES is omitted. The number of copies may also be requested in the JES2 JOBPARM statement, but then the number of copies is the product of the JOBPARM and COPIES values.

```
//SYSPRINT DD SYSOUT=A,COPIES=3
     [ Three copies are produced. ]
```

C. OUTLIM: Limit the Lines of Output

OUTLIM = *lines* limits the number of logical records (print lines or cards punched). The limit can range from 1 to 16777215. The job is terminated if this limit is exceeded. In JES2 there is no limit if OUTLIM is omitted; JES3 has an installation-defined limit.

```
//SYSPRINT DD SYSOUT=A,OUTLIM=20000
     [ The job is terminated if more than 20,000 lines are
     produced. ]
```

D. HOLD: Hold the Output

For time-sharing users, HOLD = YES holds the output in the output queue rather than printing it. This allows you to retrieve the output from the queue and display it on a terminal rather than waiting for it to be printed.

```
//SYSPRINT DD SYSOUT=A,HOLD=YES
```

The output is held until you free it or until the operator releases it. You can tell the operator whether to print or purge the output with the OPERATOR statement in JES3 or with the JES2 MESSAGE statement. Omitting HOLD or coding HOLD = NO requests the system to process the output normally.

E.   DEST: Route the Output

DEST = *destination* routes the output to a special destination. The destination depends on the job entry system.

1.   MVS.JES2

- DEST = RMT*nnnn*, RM*nnnn*, or R*nnnn* specifies one to four alphanumeric or national characters indicating the destination. R000 is equivalent to LOCAL.
- DEST = U*nnn* specifies a number (1 to 255) indicating the local device with special routing that is the destination.
- DEST = LOCAL routes the output to a local device.
- DEST = *name* specifies a one- to eight-alphanumeric or national character name defined by the installation of a device that is the destination.
- DEST = N*nnnn*, N*nn*R*mmmm*, N*nnn*R*mmm*, or N*nnnn*R*mm* specifies a node (the *n*s) and a remote work station (the *m*s). The maximum number of *n*s and *m*s cannot exceed 6. Coding DEST = N0 results in a specification of LOCAL at node N.

2.   MVS/JES3

- DEST = ANYLOCAL routes the output to a local device.
- DEST = *device-name* specifies a one- to eight-alphanumeric or national character name of a local printer or punch to receive the output.
- DEST = *device-address* specifies a three-character physical device address of a local printer or punch that is the destination.
- DEST = *group-name* specifies a one- to eight-alphanumeric or national character name of a local printer or punch to receive the output.

3.   MVS/TSO

- DEST = (*node,userid*) specifies a one- to eight-character *node* to which to direct the output. The *userid* is the userid assigned by the installation.

4.   VS1

- DEST = *userid* specifies a valid userid established by the installation. The userid must be from one to seven alphanumeric characters.

F. DCB Subparameters

The DCB parameter is generally not required but can be coded if needed. Any DCB parameter must be for the direct-access volume on which the output is queued, not the ultimate unit record device.

```
//SYSPUNCH DD SYSOUT=B,DCB=MODE=C
     [ The MODE subparameter is ignored.  Column binary is a
     feature of the card punch, not a feature of a direct-access
     storage device. ]
```

IV. UNIT RECORD DEVICES

Unit record devices include printers, card readers and punches, typewriter consoles, and paper tape readers. As the name implies, a single record is processed at a time: one card read or punched, one line typed or printed.

Most unit record devices are preempted for system use, and you must be careful in requesting them. Card readers are normally allocated to the readers, and card punches and printers are allocated to the writers. Since the system can allocate only idle unit record devices to a job, the operator may have to stop the readers or writers to free the device. Programs should normally use the input or output stream DD statements (DD *, DATA, or SYSOUT) rather than request the card reader, punch, and printers directly.

The card reader, punch, and printers might be used as unit record devices for security so that sensitive data is not queued on a direct-access volume or for processing quantities of data too large to queue on a direct-access volume. But most likely you will never need to use them. The DD statement for unit record devices is coded as:

```
//ddname DD UNIT=address,DCB=(..),UCS=(..),FCB=(..)
```

The unit may also be requested by type or group, but *address* is often used because you usually want a specific device.

A. DCB Subparameters

The DCB subparameter LRECL can be included for any unit record device. The following DCB subparameters may also be included.

- Printer: PRTSP controls the printer spacing (0 to 3, PRTSP=1 is assumed). RECFM describes the record format (F, V, U), and printer control characters (A for ASA control characters and M for machine code control characters).
- Card reader and punch: MODE=C specifies column binary and MODE=E specifies EBCDIC; MODE=E is assumed. If MODE=C is coded, BLKSIZE, LRECL, and BUFL must be specified as 160. In *column binary* a

card column is treated as 12 binary bits, and each column is read into 2 bytes in storage. The top 6 rows are read into bits 2 to 7 of the first byte and the bottom 6 rows into bits 2 to 7 of the second byte. Bits 0 to 1 of each byte are set to zero. RECFM specifies the record format (F, V, U), and control characters (M or A). STACK selects a particular stacker (1 or 2); STACK = 1 is default. FUNC may be coded for 3505/3525 card reader/punches with the following values.

D   Punch cards with data protection.

I   Punch and print (interpret) cards.

P   Punch cards.

R   Read cards.

T   Print with two-line option.

W   Print data set.

X   Print and punch data set.

- Paper tape: RECFM sets the record format (F or U), and CODE describes special character codes as follows. (CODE = I is assumed if CODE is omitted.)

A   ASCII (8 tracks).

B   Burroughs (7 tracks).

C   National Cash Register (8 tracks).

F   Friden (8 tracks).

I   IBM BCD perforated tape and transmission code (8 tracks).

N   No conversion.

T   Teletype—trademark of Teletype Corporation, Skokie, Ill. (5 tracks).

```
//DD1 DD UNIT=00E,DCB=PRTSP=3
     [ Unit 00E, a printer, is assigned and the spacing is set to
     3. ]

//DD2 DD UNIT=2540-2,DCB=(MODE=C,STACK=1,
//          BLKSIZE=160,LRECL=160,BUFL=160)
     [ A card punch is requested for punching column binary. ]
```

B. UCS: Universal Character Set

The UCS parameter specifies a character set for the 1403, 3203, or 3211 printer. UCS requests a print chain or train for a particular character set to be mounted on the printer. A default character set established by the installation when the system is generated is used unless UCS specifies another character set. UCS may be coded on a SYSOUT DD statement or where the UNIT parameter specifies a printer. To request a special character set, code:

```
UCS=(code,FOLD,VERIFY)
```

- *code* is a one- to four-digit code identifying the character set. Installations may add their own character sets to the system and assign codes to them. Character sets for the following codes can be generated into the system.

3211	3203	1401	
A11	AN	AN	48-character EBCDIC
H11	HN	HN	EBCDIC
G11	—	—	ASCII
—	PCAN	PCAN	Alphanumeric
—	PCHN	PCHN	Alphanumeric
P11	PN	PN	Alphanumeric (PL/I character set)
—	QN	QN	Alphanumeric (PL/I-scientific)
—	RN	RN	FORTRAN/COBOL commercial
—	SN	SN	Text printing
T11	TN	TN	Text printing
—	XN	XN	High-speed alphanumeric
—	YN	YN	High-speed alphanumeric

- FOLD folds the first, second, and third quadrants of the EBCDIC into the fourth quadrant; that is, hexadecimal characters 01, 21, 81, and C1 all print as upper case A's. FOLD is used to print upper- and lower-case characters as upper case.
- VERIFY displays the character set and requests the operator to verify it.

```
//DD1 DD UNIT=1403,UCS=QN
     [ The QN character set is requested. ]

//DD2 DD UNIT=1403,UCS=(PN,FOLD)
     [ The PN character set is requested.  All characters print as
     upper case. ]

//DD3 DD UNIT=1403,UCS=(AN,,VERIFY)
     [ The AN character set is requested and displayed for the
     operator to verify. ]
```

C. FCB: Forms Control Buffer

The FCB parameter specifies the forms control image for the 3211 and 3800 printers that have the Forms Control Buffer feature. The FCB controls the movement of forms on the printer. It may also specify a carriage control tape for printers that have this feature. For the IBM 3525 card punch, FCB specifies the data protection image. FCB is coded as follows:

```
                ALIGN
                VERIFY
    FCB=(image-id,_____)
```

- *image-id* is from one to four alphanumeric or national characters, the first character alphabetic or national. The image id identifies the image to be loaded into the forms buffer, specifies the carriage control tape, or requests the data protection image for the 3525 card punch. IBM supplies four standard images: STD1 and STD6 for six lines per inch on an 11-inch form, and STD2 and STD8 for eight lines per inch on an 8.5-inch form. FCB = STD3 may be used with the 3800 printer to print eight lines per inch.
- ALIGN requests the operator to check the printer for forms alignment before printing the data set. ALIGN is not used by the 3800 printer.
- VERIFY is the same as ALIGN, but it also requests the operator to verify that the image displayed on the printer is the desired one.

V. 3800 PRINTER PARAMETERS

The BURST, CHARS, MODIFY, COPIES, and FLASH parameters may be coded for the IBM 3800 printer. They may appear on either a SYSOUT DD statement or a DD statement in which the UNIT parameter specifies the 3800 printer.

A. BURST: Burst the Output

Coding BURST = Y requests the output to be burst into separate sheets, and BURST = N requests the output to be printed in normal continuous fanfold mode. The default is BURST = N, but the installation can make BURST = Y the default for a particular SYSOUT class.

```
//OUTPUT DD SYSOUT=A,BURST=Y
```

B. CHARS: Specify a Character Set

Coding CHARS = (*table,...,table*) lists from one to four table names that specify the 3800 printer's character sets. Each table is from one to four alphanumeric or national characters. When multiple tables are specified, the DCB = OPTCB = J parameter may be coded to indicate that the second byte of each line, the byte following the printer control character, is a single numeric character (0 to 3) that selects the table to use to print the line. The selection is based on the order in which the tables are listed in the CHARS parameter.

For MVS, CHARS = DUMP may be coded on a SYSUDUMP or SYSABEND DD statement to print storage dumps in 204-character print lines.

C. MODIFY: MODIFY Print Lines

Coding MODIFY = (*module-name,table-no*) specifies the name (from one to four alphanumeric or national characters) of a module contained in SYS1.IMAGELIB supplied by the installation, which replaces blanks or data in the print lines. This feature is often used to print legends and column headings. The *table-no* is a number (0 to 3) that corresponds to the character arrangement table specified by the chars parameter. The table-no is optional and defaults to 0.

```
//OUTPUT DD SYSOUT=A,CHARS=(ALPH,CYRL),MODIFY=(HDR1,1)
     [ Module HDR1 is invoked to replace data in the print lines
     and the lines are printed with the CYRL character set. ]
```

D. COPIES: Specify Copy Groups

Coding COPIES=(,(n,n,...,n)) specifies groups of multiple copies. One to eight groups may be coded. Each *n* specifies the number of copies to print for the group. The total of all the groups cannot exceed 255. Each group is placed in a separate output bin on the 3800 printer. For example, COPIES=(,(2,1,4)) prints three groups. The first group contains 2 copies, the second 1 copy, and the third group 4 copies.

```
//OUTPUT DD SYSOUT=A,COPIES=(, (2,1,4))
```

On a DD statement in which the UNIT parameter specifies the 3800 printer, only the first group is printed. In the preceding example, two copies would be printed.

E. FLASH: Specify a Forms Overlay

Coding FLASH=*overlay-name* specifies the one- to four-alphanumeric or national character name of an overlay form designated by the installation. The operator is requested to mount this form on the printer, and the form is projected on each page of the output.

If you are printing multiple copies and wish to print the forms overlay on a limited number of copies, code FLASH=(*overlay-name,count*). The forms overlay is printed on the first number of copies as specified by the count.

```
//OUTPUT DD SYSOUT=A,COPIES=6,FLASH=(FRM1,3)
     [ The forms overlay specified by FM1 is printed on the first
     3 copies. ]
```

In JES3, you can code FLASH=NONE to set the overlay-name to zero before sending the job to the node.

Chapter 11

DIRECT-ACCESS STORAGE DEVICES

I. DIRECT-ACCESS HARDWARE DEVICES

Direct access, the most versatile storage device, can contain sequential, partitioned, direct, indexed sequential, and VSAM data sets. Direct-access storage derives its name from the way data is accessed. Unlike tape or cards, each record can be read independently of the previous record. Direct-access storage generally consists of disks and drums, with disk devices the most prevalent.

A disk device consists of a stack of rotating recording surfaces similar to a stack of personal computer diskettes. Each disk surface contains many concentric *tracks* radiating inward toward the center, each containing the same amount of data. A set of electronic read/write heads positioned between each disk surface is connected to an access arm as shown in Figure 41. When a specific track is read or written, the access arm is moved to position the read/write head over the track. This arm movement is called a *seek*. The read/write head looks for a special marker on the rotating track to tell it where the track begins. Thus there are two physical delays in accessing a specific track: a *seek delay* which depends on how far the access arm must be moved, and a *rotational delay* which averages one-half revolution.

Since there is a read/write head for each disk surface, several tracks can be read without arm movement. The tracks that lie one on top of the other form an imaginary *cylinder* in which all the tracks are accessible without arm movement. Access arm movement is required if data resides on different cylinders; thus data can be read or written much faster if it resides all on the same cylinder.

Disks are the most versatile direct-access storage devices because of their large storage capacity and speed. The IBM 3330 and 3340 disk devices have removable packs, allowing a disk unit to contain an infinite amount of data, but an installation generally controls the use of private or mountable packs. It requires a few minutes for the operator to change disk packs, and not only are the disk packs relatively heavy, but if dropped they can be destroyed. Tape reels are more convenient to mount than disk packs.

Mass Storage Systems (MSS) have the largest capacity and slowest access of the IBM direct-access storage devices. The IBM MSS contains 4,720 storage volumes or cartridges, each having the capacity of a 3300 Model 1 disk volume. The MSS is a

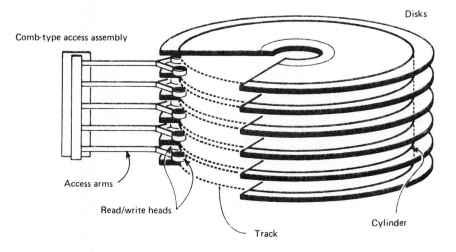

Figure 41.   Direct Access Storage Device. Reprinted by permission from Introduction to IBM Direct-Access Storage Devices and Organization Methods 1974 International Business Machines Corporation

virtual device in that each data cartridge appears to the user as if it were a 3330 disk. When you request a MSS volume, the system copies the data on the cartridge to a dedicated 3330 disk volume. When the job terminates, your data on the 3330 volume is copied back onto the data cartridge.

Table 2 summarizes the capacity of the various IBM direct-access volumes.

A Volume Table of Contents (VTOC) is maintained on each direct-access volume as a directory to existing data sets and free space. The VTOC is usually allocated one or two cylinders and is placed in either the first or middle cylinders. A table of contents in the first cylinders maximizes the largest contiguous amount of space that can be allocated. Placing the table of contents in the middle minimizes seek time since the access arm generally has half as far to travel between the VTOC and any data set. The first track on the volume contains the volume label and points to the VTOC.

The installation must initialize each volume before allowing it to be used. This process is called Direct Access Storage Device Initialization (DASDI, pronounced daz-dee) and is done by the IBM-supplied utility program named IEHDASDR. (It is equivalent to formatting a diskette for a PC.) IEHDASDR writes the volume label, allocates space for the VTOC, and initializes each track on the volume. Generally, a volume need never be reinitialized.

II. SPACE ALLOCATION

Space allocation is somewhat unique to System/370. While you never have to reserve disk space on a PC, on System/370, you must specify the amount of space for each

Table 2.   Direct-Access Storage Device Characteristics

Device	Capacity in Million Bytes	Tracks per Cyl	Number of Cyls	Avg. Seek Time (ms)	Average Rotational (ms)	Data Rate (Kb/sec)
MSS *	100.02	19	404	30	8.4	806
3330	100.02	19	404	30	8.4	806
3330-11	200.04	19	808	30	8.4	806
3340/3344	69.89	12	696	25	10.1	885
3350	317.50	30	555	25	8.4	1198
3375	409.87	12	959	19	10.1	1859
3380	630.24	15	885	16	8.3	3000

* The MSS virtual volume has the characteristics of a 3330 Model 1.

data set created. This is always inconvenient, usually difficult, and often frustrating. Space allocation is an inherent weakness in the operating system, and is the area where the system most shows its age.

All new data sets on direct-access volumes must be allocated space. Storage on direct-access volumes is always allocated in units of tracks, so the minimum space that can be allocated is one track.

When space is requested, the system looks in the VTOC to see if it is available, and allocates the space by updating the VTOC. The system attempts to allocate space in contiguous tracks (tracks on the same cylinder) and adjacent cylinders. If contiguous space is unavailable, the system tries to satisfy the request with up to five noncontiguous blocks of storage. These blocks of storage are termed *extents*.

If enough space still cannot be found and you have not requested a specific volume, the system looks for space on other appropriate volumes. If space cannot be found, the system issues a message to the operator asking whether the job should be canceled or held. Unless the operator is able to mount another volume or wait for some other job to terminate and release its space, the job must be canceled.

The space may be requested as a primary and a secondary amount. The primary amount is allocated when the data set is opened with a disposition of NEW. The secondary amount is allocated if the primary amount is exceeded, even if this is in a later job step or job. The secondary amounts offer the following advantages:

- The primary amount can be conservative, with the secondary amount providing a reserve.
- The secondary amount provides for data set growth over time.
- The secondary amount may be allocated on different volumes. The data set size is not limited to the space available on a single volume.

Space is allocated in extents, that is, contiguous blocks of tracks. There may be 16 extents per volume. The primary amount and 15 secondary amounts may be allocated on the first volume, and 16 secondary amounts on any subsequent volumes. However, if the extent is not large enough to satisfy the amount of space requested, up to five extents will be used to fill the request. Thus for a worst case, five extents could be required to fill the primary amount and each secondary amount. This would limit the space allocation on the volume to a primary and two secondary amounts.

Storage on direct-access volumes allocated in noncontiguous blocks and across different volumes is read and written as if it were one large block; the system compensates for the noncontiguous space. However, data sets can be read or written faster if they reside on the same cylinder because a relatively slow mechanical movement is required to position the access arm between noncontiguous blocks. High-activity data sets should be allocated contiguous space on the same cylinders.

For disk data sets, you can specify all the DD parameters discussed so far:

```
//ddname DD DSN=name,DISP=(beginning-status,ending-status),
//         UNIT=unit,VOL=SER=volume,
//         DCB=(RECFM=type,LRECL=length,BLKSIZE=length)
```

One more parameter is also needed, the SPACE parameter, to specify the amount of disk space.

III. THE SPACE PARAMETER

The usual method of requesting space is to ask for a quantity of space and let the system select the appropriate tracks. In multiprogramming environments where several jobs may request space concurrently, the system is in a much better position to know what space is available. Space may be requested in units of block size, tracks, or cylinders.

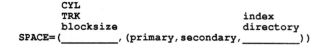

```
        CYL
        TRK                          index
        blocksize                    directory
SPACE=(_____, (primary,secondary,_____))
```

- Block size, TRK, or CYL requests that space be allocated in units of number of bytes per block, tracks, or cylinders. (The average record length cannot exceed 65,535 bytes.)
- *primary* is the number of units (blocks, tracks, or cylinders) to allocate. This space is called *primary allocation* and is always allocated on a single volume. For example, SPACE = (80,2000) requests 2000 blocks of 80 bytes each, and SPACE = (CYL,20) requests 20 cylinders.
- *secondary* is the number of units to allocate if the primary allocation is exceeded. This space is called the *secondary allocation*. Fifteen secondary allocations can be given on the first volume and 16 on each of any subsequent

volumes. Both the primary and secondary must be large enough to contain the largest block written, or space is allocated and erased as the system tries to find a space large enough for the record. The secondary amount is optional, and if omitted, no secondary allocation is given.

- *directory* reserves space for the names of members of partitioned data sets. It is coded only for partitioned data sets.
- Index reserves index space for ISAM data sets.

The SPACE parameter is ignored for nondirect-access volumes such as tapes.

If you write a SPACE parameter as SPACE = (TRK,(10,2)), space is allocated as shown in Figure 42.

Primary	1st secondary	2nd secondary		15th secondary
10 tracks	2 tracks	2 tracks	. . .	2 tracks

Figure 42. Space allocation for SPACE = (TRK,(10,2))

A. Space Units

1. Block size: requesting blocks of space

The block size is often used to request space because a block corresponds to your data. The block size is also device-independent so that the same amount of space is allocated regardless of the device type.

The system computes the actual number of tracks to allocate based on the number of blocks that completely fit on a track. (Table 3 describes the capacity of the direct-access volumes.) For example, SPACE = (1000,100) allocates four 3380 tracks because 31 1000-byte blocks fit on a track. Although SPACE = (10000,10) requests the same total storage (100,000 bytes), three 3380 tracks are allocated because four 10,000-byte blocks fit on a track. Space is always rounded up to a whole number of tracks.

The block size should equal the DCB = BLKSIZE subparameter so that the system can include the interblock gaps in its calculation. If secondary allocation is required, the system computes the amount of secondary space to allocate by multiplying the increment times the BLKSIZE subparameter rather than the block size in the SPACE parameter.

If the blocks have keys, KEYLEN = *keysize* should be coded as a DCB subparameter so that the system can include space for the keys in its calculation. The block size should be an average for variable or undefined format records. The system does not account for the space saved when track overflow is required. The CONTIG and ROUND subparameters explained later are used to allocate contiguous space.

Table 3.   Direct-Access Storage Device Capacities

Device	Bytes Required to Store Block		Track Capacity in Bytes	Maximum Block Size
	Blocks without Keys Bi,Bn	Blocks with Keys Bi,Bn		
3330/MSS	135 + DL	191 + KL + DL	13,165	13,030
3340/3344	167 + DL	242 + KL + DL	8,535	8,368
3350	185 + DL	267 + KL + DL	19,254	19,069
3375	224 + ((DL + 191)/32)(32)[1]	224 + ((KL + 191)/32)(32)[1] + ((DL + 191)/32)(32)	36,000	32,760[2]
3380	256 + ((DL + 267)/32)(32)[1]	256 + ((KL + 267)/32)(32)[1] + ((DL + 267)/32)(32)	47,968	32,760[2]

Bi—The actual space required to store all but the last block on the track.
Bn—The actual space required to store the last block on the track.
DL—The data length (BLKSIZE) in bytes.
KL—The key length (KEYLEN) in bytes.

$$\text{blocks/track} = 1 + \frac{\text{track capacity} - \text{Bn}}{\text{Bi}} \quad \text{truncated to integer.}$$

[1]Multiply by 32, truncate to integer, and divide by 32.
[2]In theory, the 3375 can contain a 35,616-byte block and the 3380 a 47,476-byte block. But the system can only write 32,760-byte blocks.

2.   TRK: requesting tracks

Since space is always allocated in units of whole tracks, TRK allows you to request an exact amount of space. TRK is device-dependent; SPACE = (TRK,1) results in 47,968 bytes on a 3380 disk and 19,069 bytes on a 3350 disk.

TRK is used often. After you have allocated a few data sets, you'll become accustomed to estimating size in tracks. It is rather like determining how long it will take you to drive to some place in a city. With experience, you usually do this by feel rather than by calculating the distance divided by speed. The problem with allocating space in units of tracks is that the number of records that can fit on a track depends upon the BLKSIZE, the LRECL, and the type of disk unit. In other words, you need to know what your DCB subparameters are, what the track size of your disk pack is, and how many records you have to store. If you don't have a feel for how many tracks to allocate, then you must do arithmetic. In any case, you may not know how many records you are going to store.

3.   CYL: requesting cylinders

CYL requests complete cylinders, resulting in faster access by eliminating the need for access arm movement. CYL is also device-dependent: SPACE = (CYL,1) obtains

719,520 bytes on a 3380 disk and 572,070 bytes on a 3350 disk. CYL must be coded for ISAM data sets. CYL is not often used. You'll need to use it only when:

- You want a large amount of space.
- You are concerned about fast access. Since all the tracks in a cylinder lie in the same plane, the read/write head does not need to be moved to access any tracks in a cylinder.

You must compute (or estimate) the amount of space required if TRK or CYL is used. See the following section on computing storage space.

The UNIT parameter should not request a group name defining more than one type of device. For example, if SYSDA defines both 3380 and 3350 disks, UNIT = SYSDA, SPACE = (TRK,1) yields 47,968 bytes if a 3380 is selected and 19,069 bytes if a 3350 is selected; you would not know which.

B. Secondary: Secondary Allocation

If a secondary is coded and the primary space allocation is exceeded, a secondary allocation is made based on the increment times the units. The system will allocate a maximum of 15 secondary amounts on the first volume and 16 secondary amounts on any additional volumes specified; if more extents are needed, the step is terminated. For example, SPACE = (800,(10,20)) results in a primary allocation of 10 blocks of 800 bytes each, and each extent is allocated 20 blocks of 800 bytes. The maximum space that could be allocated on a single volume is then 10 + 20(15) = 310 blocks of 800 bytes.

Extents are usually not contiguous, and so the access time increases as extents are allocated. High-usage data sets should usually not have secondary extents. The MXIG and ALX subparameters described later provide an alternative to secondary extents.

If the data set was created without an increment specified in the SPACE parameter, another SPACE parameter may later specify an increment. If the data set was created with an increment, the SPACE parameter can also override it with a different increment. In both cases the new increment is effective only for the duration of the step and does not change the original increment or the 15-extent limit. For example, a data set might be created by:

```
//A DD DSN=HOLDIT,DISP=(NEW,CATLG),UNIT=SYSDA,SPACE=(100,(10,20))
```

Later you might add to it and wish to increase the size of the extents.

```
//ADD DD DSN=HOLDIT,DISP=(MOD,KEEP),SPACE=(100,(0,200))
      [ Each extent allocated during this step is given 200 blocks
      of 100 bytes.  Later runs will revert to an extent size of 20
      blocks of 100 bytes. ]
```

Be careful when you override a DD statement in a cataloged procedure containing a SPACE parameter. If the overriding statement describes an existing data set, you would usually not code a SPACE parameter. However, if a secondary allocation is required, the SPACE parameter on the overridden statement specifies the increment not the increment specified when the data set was created. Code SPACE= on the overriding DD statement to nullify the SPACE parameter to avoid this problem.

In computing the amount of space required, you must consider the device type, track capacity, tracks per cylinder, cylinders per volume, block size, key length, and device overhead. Table 3 lists the capacity of direct-access volumes.

Device overhead refers to the space required on each track for hardware data, such as address markers and interblock gaps. Device overhead varies with each device and also depends on whether the blocks are written with keys. To compute the actual space needed for each block, use the formulas in Table 3.

For example, if a data set without keys containing 100 blocks is blocked at 800 bytes, you can use Table 3 to compute the number of blocks per track on a 3380 disk. The formula is:

```
Bi = 256 + ((DL+267)/32)(32) = 256 + ((800+267)/32)(32) = 1,312

      47,968 - 1,312             46,656
1 +   ---------------   = 1 +   ------ = 36 blocks per track
          1,312                  1,312
```

Since 100 blocks must be stored, three tracks are required. At this point you might well consider requesting space in blocks and letting the computer do these calculations. SPACE=(800,100) and SPACE=(TRK,3) are equivalent for a 3380 disk.

The following system completion codes are given for common errors in space allocation.

- B37 indicates that not enough space was allocated on the volume. The step is abnormally terminated.

- E37 indicates that all 16 extents have been allocated on the volume but more space is required. The step is abnormally terminated.

C. Directory, Index: Directory or Index Space

Partitioned data sets must have space allocated for a directory containing the names, aliases, and locations of each member. The directory is allocated in units of 256-byte blocks and each block can contain about five member names. To estimate the number of directory blocks, sum the member names, divide by 5, and round up to the nearest integer. For example, if a partitioned data set has 32 members, allocate 32/5 or 7 directory blocks: SPACE=(800,(20,100,7)).

Allow a liberal margin for adding new members when creating the data set because the directory cannot be extended later. If it fills up, the data set must be recreated. (Chapter 15 describes how to recreate a partitioned data set.) Space for the directory is also allocated in full track units, and any unused space on the track is wasted unless there is enough room to contain a block of the first member. The directory space is obtained from the primary allocation and must be considered in estimating the total space required.

ISAM data sets may be allocated space for the index in the SPACE parameter. Chapter 18 describes ISAM data sets in detail.

D. Special Space Options

Several positional subparameters may be coded with the SPACE parameter to release unused space and allocate space for faster access. (Only CONTIG is permitted for ISAM data sets.)

```
        CYL                                        ALX
        TRK                        index           MXIG
        blocksize                  directory       CONTIG
SPACE=(_____, (primary, secondary,_____)),RLSE,_____,ROUND)
```

1. RLSE: releasing space

RLSE releases all unused space when the data set is closed. It permits you to allocate more space than perhaps is needed without wasting space. For example, if SPACE = (800,20,RLSE) is coded and only four blocks are written, the space for the remaining 16 blocks is released. If an extent is allocated and is only partially used, the remainder of the extent is also released. If space is requested in cylinders, only excess cylinders are released; otherwise excess tracks are released.

Space is released only if the data set is not empty and if the data set is closed after being opened for output. RLSE can also be used to release space in an existing data set. Code SPACE=(,,RLSE) on a DD statement referring to the data set to release any excess space when the data set is closed. [Code SPACE = (units, (,secondary),RLSE) if the existing data set may require secondary allocation.]

At first glance it appears that RLSE should always be used, but there are some drawbacks. RLSE requires I/O time to release the space. Then any added data in a subsequent step must be placed in an extent, with the resultant slower processing time. Also RLSE should not be coded if you plan to add later to the data set and wish to reserve space.

If you override a DD statement in a cataloged procedure with a DD statement defining an existing data set, be sure to code SPACE= to nullify any SPACE parameter on the overridden DD statement. If you do not, and the SPACE parameter on the overridden statement contains the RLSE subparameter, excess space in the data set is released when it is closed.

2. CONTIG, MXIG, ALX: minimizing access time

CONTIG, MXIG, and ALX are mutually exclusive positional parameters used to allocate contiguous space. Since contiguous space minimizes access arm movement, the access time is decreased. CONTIG requests that the primary space be allocated only on contiguous tracks and cylinders; that is, all tracks on a cylinder are contiguous, and if more than one cylinder is needed, the cylinders are also contiguous. Always code CONTIG if track overflow is used.

MXIG allocates the primary space as the largest contiguous free area on a volume, but only if that area is as large or larger than the amount requested. This may result in considerably more space being allocated than was requested (anywhere from the amount requested to the entire volume), and it should be used only for large data sets as an alternative to requesting secondary allocation. RLSE can release excess space.

ALX allocates the primary area by building up a list of the five largest contiguous free areas on the volume and allocates all of these areas that are as large or larger than the space requested. You might obtain a single area as large as the entire volume or five areas all much larger than requested. Since ALX can also allocate much more space than was requested, it should be used only for very large data sets as an alternative to requesting secondary allocation. RLSE can release excess space.

```
SPACE=(100,(20,10),,CONTIG)
     [ Space is allocated only if it is contiguous. ]

SPACE=(100,(1000,5),RLSE,ALX)
     [ Somewhere between 100,000 bytes and the entire volume are
     allocated in up to five areas whose minimum size is 100,000
     bytes.  Excess space is released. ]

SPACE=(100,(1000,10),,MXIG)
     [ Anywhere between 100,000 bytes and the entire volume could
     be allocated with all space being contiguous. ]
```

3. ROUND: rounding up to cylinders

Space requested by block size can be allocated on cylinder boundaries by coding ROUND. The system computes the space needed, rounds up to the nearest cylinder, and allocates complete cylinders so that the space begins on the first track of a cylinder and ends on the last track of a cylinder. CONTIG must be coded if contiguous cylinders are wanted. ROUND ensures that the data is placed on the minimum number of cylinders possible by starting on a cylinder boundary. This decreases access time because the access arm movement is minimized.

```
SPACE=(1000,800,,,ROUND),UNIT=3380
     [ Two 3380 cylinders would be allocated.  The cylinders might
     not be contiguous. ]

SPACE=(1000,(800,10),RLSE,CONTIG,ROUND),UNIT=3380
     [ Two 3380 cylinders would be allocated.  The cylinders are
     contiguous, secondary allocation is permitted, and excess
     cylinders are released. ]
```

IV. DCB PARAMETER

The RECFM, LRECL, and BLKSIZE parameters are required for new data sets on direct-access volumes unless these parameters are coded in the program. The block size should not exceed the track size or the 32,760-byte limitation of the standard access methods. If the logical record length exceeds the track size, spanned records must be requested (RECFM = VS or VBS).

The most efficient block size in terms of I/O count, storage space, and CPU time is a full track or some even fraction of a full track. These efficiencies are at the expense of region size. Buffers are allocated within a region to contain the blocks as they are read or written. Table 4 illustrates the efficiency of an unblocked data set, an inefficient block size, and half-track blocking. The buffer size assumes double buffering.

Table 4.   Efficiency of Block Sizes on a 3380

Blocking	BLKSIZE	I/O Count to read 10,000-record Data Set	3380 Disk Storage Required in Tracks	Bytes for Buffer Space Required in Real Storage
Unblocked	80	10,000	121	160
Normal	6,160	130	19	12,320
Half track	23,440	35	18	46,880
Inefficient	23,520	35	35	47,040

The CPU times are not shown because they vary with the computer model and system versions. Each I/O requires some CPU time, and the fewer I/Os, the less CPU time used. Table 4 shows that it is not enough just to block, you must block to an even fraction of the track size to avoid wasting space. Increasing the block size from 23,440 to 23,520 increased the 3380 disk storage required from 18 to 35 tracks.

As mentioned in Chapter 8, a simple rule of thumb is to choose a block size of 6,233 bytes or as close as you can get under this. Table 4 illustrates that a block size of 6,160 rather than of 23,440 only increased the tracks required from 18 to 19. The suggested record lengths for data and text are:

- Data records: DCB = (RECFM = FB,LRECL = 80,BLKSIZE = 6160) If the LRECL isn't 80, choose some multiple of it that results in a block size close to 6200.
- Text records: DCB = (RECFM = VB,LRECL = 255,BLKSIZE = 6233)

V. PARTITIONED DATA SETS

You generally use a partitioned data set when you want to keep several sequential data sets together. You also use partitioned data sets as program libraries, to contain programs in load module form. A partitioned data set consists of several members (actually, sequential data sets) stored in the same data set as shown in Figure 43.

Each partitioned data set has a directory—an area where the member names are kept as shown in Figure 44.

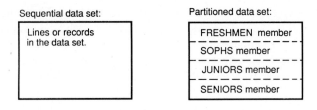

Figure 43. Sequential and partitioned data sets

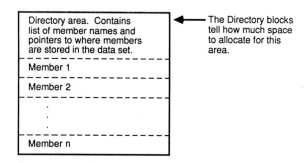

Figure 44. Directory of a partitioned data set

When you allocate a partitioned data set, you must tell the system the number of directory blocks to set aside within the primary area.

```
SPACE=(units,(primary,secondary,directory))
```

As a rule of thumb:

```
Directory blocks = estimated members/5
```

VI. ESTIMATING SPACE

When you allocate disk space, it is better to allocate a bit too much than too little. If you allocate too little, the data set is written and you incur most of the run cost before you overflow the data set, wasting the entire run. If you allocate too much, you waste only some disk space.

There are two basic ways to allocate space for a disk data set.

- By calculating the amount of space. Usually you allocate space in blocks when you do this.
- By feel, experience, judgement, or seat of the pants. You usually allocate space in tracks when you do it this way.

A. Estimating Blocks

The advantage of allocating space in units of blocks is that it is based on the number of records in your data set, and doesn't depend on the track size of the disk. You can estimate the number of records in your data set, calculate the number of records per block, and then calculate the number of blocks needed. You don't have to take into consideration the track size.

To compute the records per block, you use the LRECL for FB records and an average record length for VB records. The formulas are:

```
records per block = BLKSIZE/LRECL   (for FB records)

records per block:  BLKSIZE/average record length (for VB records)

# of blocks needed = estimated # of records/records per block
```

For 1,000 fixed blocked records with BLKSIZE = 3200, LRECL = 80:

```
records per block = 3200/80 = 40

number of blocks needed = 1000/40 = 25
```

Calculating the number of blocks for variable-length blocked records is slightly different. For a typical data set with fixed-length blocked records:

```
DCB=(RECFM=FB,LRECL=80,BLKSIZE=3200)
```

To store 1,000 records, we calculate the number of blocks as:

```
records per block = 3200/80 = 40
number of blocks needed = 1000/40 = 25
```

For a typical data set with variable-length blocked records:

```
DCB=(RECFM=VB,LRECL=255,BLKSIZE=3120)
```

You must estimate the average record length. If we assume it is 50, to store 1,000 records, we calculate the number of blocks as:

```
blocks = number of records needed /number of records per block
records per block = 3120/50 = 62.4, rounded up to 63
number of blocks needed = 1000/63 = 15.9, rounded up to 16
```

There are several problems with allocating space in units of blocks:

- You may not be able to estimate the number of records you are going to store. Even if you could count them, it might take hours. It's like guessing the length of a book. You can tell at a glance whether a book is big or small, but you would probably have no idea how many lines there are in it because you're not used to quantifying a book's size by the number of lines.

- For variable blocked records, you must estimate the average record length to estimate the number of records per block.
- You must still do some arithmetic (when the computer is supposed to be the one doing the math).

B. Estimating Tracks

Now let's review how you can determine how many tracks your data set would take on a 3380 disk. Assume you have 10,000 records 100 bytes long blocked 64 records per block. A 3380 track is 47,476 bytes long with an inter-block gap of 523 bytes. Here is how the records and blocks are stored on a track. First, a block contains 64 records as show in Figure 45.

100 bytes-per-record * 64 = 6400 bytes				
1	2	3	...	64

64 records\block

Figure 45. A block containing 64 records

Then, with an inter-block gap of 523 bytes, six blocks fit on a track as shown in Figure 46.

6400 bytes	523 bytes	6400 bytes	523 bytes	•	6400 bytes	523 bytes	5938 bytes
block 1	gap	block 2	gap	•	block 6	gap	unused

Figure 46. Six blocks fit on a track

```
Bi = 256 + ((DL+267)/32)(32) = 256 + ((6400+267)/32)(32) = 6,912

     47,968 - 6,912               41,056
1 +  --------------  =  1 +       ------ = 6.9
         6,912                     6,912

     6.9 truncates to 6 blocks per track.
```

Calculating the blocks per track is only the first step. The next step is to calculate the number of tracks needed. There are six blocks per track, 64 records per block, and 10,000 records.

```
10,000/(64*6) = 26.04, rounded up to 27
```

You round up because the system allocates in units of full tracks. If you truncate, the remainder of your data set cannot be stored.

It's a lot easier to calculate the necessary blocks than to calculate the number of tracks required. And, of course, track size is device-dependent. If you had allocated your data set on a 3350 disk rather than a 3380 disk, the data set would have required 79 tracks rather than the 27 tracks we calculated for the 3380.

But you usually don't allocate space in tracks by calculating it. After gaining some experience, you will get a feel for how many tracks it takes to store your data sets. You can use a system utility to examine your data sets and see how many tracks are allocated and how many are used.

If you don't know how many records you have, this is the most painless method. And the reason you usually estimate in units of tracks is that the statistics your installation provides about your data sets are usually in units of tracks.

VII. THE LABEL PARAMETER: DATA SET LABELS

The LABEL parameter must be coded if the data set on a direct-access volume has user labels in addition to the standard labels. To specify user labels, code LABEL = (,SUL). The LABEL parameter is more commonly used for data set protection (see Chapter 17) and for magnetic tape labels (see Chapter 12). Since user labels are seldom used, a full description of LABEL is deferred until these chapters.

VIII. MULTIVOLUME DATA SETS

Data sets on direct-access volumes may be spanned over several volumes by specifying the volumes in the VOL parameter. VOL = (,,,2) would request two nonspecific volumes, and VOL = SER = (PACK02,PACK03) would request two specific volumes. The UNIT may mount volumes in parallel or defer mounting until the volumes are needed. If there are more volumes than units available, mounting must be deferred.

The primary space allocation is always made on the first volume, and 15 extents can also be allocated on it. The second and subsequent volumes can each contain 16 secondary amounts. A disposition of MOD will allow you to extend a data set in a subsequent job step. Code DISP = (MOD,CATLG) when extending multivolume cataloged data sets, even if the data set is already cataloged. CATLG records new volume serial numbers in the catalog as the data set is extended.

Volume switching during writing occurs when space is exceeded on the volume. During reading, volume switching occurs when an extent is read that resides on another volume. The next example illustrates the creation, extension, and retrieval of a multivolume data set.

```
//STEP1 EXEC PGM=CREATE
//A DD DSN=MULTI,DISP=(NEW,CATLG),
//     UNIT=SYSDA,VOL=(,,,3),SPACE=(TRK,(4000,1000))
     [ The data set is created and may be written onto three
     nonspecific volumes. ]
//STEP2 EXEC PGM=EXTEND
//B DD DSN=MULTI,DISP=(MOD,CATLG)
     [ The data set is extended onto volumes as needed. ]
//STEP3 EXEC PGM=RETRIEVE
//C DD DSN=MULTI,DISP=OLD
     [ The data set is read. ]
```

IX. USING DATA SETS ON DIRECT-ACCESS VOLUMES

To create a data set on a direct-access volume, allocate space with the SPACE parameter. Always code the UNIT, DSN, and DISP parameters, except in the rare circumstances when it is apparent that they are not needed; for example, UNIT is not needed if VOL = REF is coded. The VOL parameter is needed if the data set is to be placed on a specific volume or on several nonspecific volumes, or if a private volume is mounted. DCB subparameters are coded as required: RECFM, LRECL, and BLKSIZE are the most common.

To retrieve an existing data set, code UNIT, VOL, DSN, and DISP. (Omit UNIT and VOL if the data set is cataloged or passed.) The RECFM, LRECL, and BLKSIZE DCB subparameters are not required. The following examples show the creation and retrieval of temporary and nontemporary data sets.

```
//STEP1 EXEC PGM=WON
//DD1 DD DSN=&&PASSIT,DISP=(NEW,PASS),
//       UNIT=SYSDA,SPACE=(4200,(10,5)),
//       DCB=(RECFM=FB,LRECL=100,BLKSIZE=4200)
     [ A temporary data set is created and passed to a subsequent
     step. ]
//DD2 DD DSN=SAVIT,DISP=(NEW,CATLG),
//       UNIT=SYSDA=SPACE=(4200,20,10),RLSE),
//       DCB=(RECFM=FB,LRECL=100,BLKSIZE=4200)
     [ A nontemporary data set is created and cataloged for later
     use. ]
//DD3 DD DSN=KEEPIT,DISP=(NEW,KEEP),
//       UNIT=SYSDA,VOL=SER=PACK01,SPACE=(TRK,100),
//       DCB=(RECFM=U,BLKSIZE=13030)
     [ A nontemporary data set is created but not cataloged. ]
//STEP2 EXEC PGM=DOS
//DD4 DD DSN=&&PASSIT,DISP=(OLD,DELETE)
     [ The passed data set is retrieved. ]
//DD5 DD DSN=SAVIT,DISP=SHR
     [ The cataloged data set is retrieved. ]
//DD6 DD DSN=KEEPIT,DISP=OLD,UNIT=SYSDA,VOL=SER=PACK01
     [ The kept data set is retrieved. ]
```

In the next example, suppose that a data set containing 575,000 records is to be stored on a 3380 volume. Each record is 1,500 bytes. Since you expect the data set will be used often, you should try to minimize access time by making the space contiguous.

First select a block size. For efficiency, let's select half-track blocking. The blocking factor is (47,968/2)/1500, which truncates to 15. The block size is 15 × 1,500 = 22,500. The DCB parameters are then:

```
RECFM=FB,LRECL=1500,BLKSIZE=22500
```

The next question is whether the data set will fit on a single volume. Each track contains two blocks or 30 records, so you will need 575,000/30 = 19,167 tracks. A single 3380 volume contains 13,275 tracks, so you will need at least two volumes. You should allocate roughly half the tracks in the primary allocation and allocate the remaining tracks in two secondary allocations. The DD statement is coded as:

```
//ddname DD DSN=dsname,DISP=(NEW,CATLG),
//          UNIT=3380,VOL=SER=(PACK12,PACK13),
//          SPACE=(22500,(9500,4834),RLSE,CONTIG,ROUND),
//          DCB=(RECFM=FB,LRECL=1500,BLKSIZE=22500)
```

Take special care in production jobs to set up the JCL to reduce the risk of terminating because disk storage is not available. Make sure you can restart the job if it does terminate. If a job creates temporary data sets in one step and terminates in a subsequent step, the temporary data sets are deleted. The job must then be restarted from the step that created the temporary data sets. This can be expensive. Make such temporary data sets nontemporary and delete them when they are no longer needed for restart.

The system does not reserve space for secondary allocations before they are needed, so that if a volume reaches capacity and an extent is required, the step must be terminated because space is unavailable. This problem is common in multi-programming systems where several jobs may request space concurrently on a public volume and available space cannot be guaranteed. One solution is to allow the data set to extend onto other volumes by making it a multivolume data set with the VOL parameter.

```
//DD1 DD UNIT=3380,SPACE=(22000,(9500,4834)),VOL=(,,,2)
```

To ensure that there is enough space for all steps within a job, allocate all the space in the first step. Use the IEFBR14 null program to allocate space as follows:

```
//stepname EXEC PGM=IEFBR14
//any-ddname DD all-parameters-to-create-the-file
```

Include a DD statement for each data set for which space is to be allocated. The following example allocates space for a PAYROLL data set.

```
//TEST#9 JOB (5542,30),'PAYROLL RUN',CLASS=A
//STEP1 EXEC PGM=IEFBR14
//A DD DSN=PAYROLL,DISP=(NEW,CATLG),
//      UNIT=SYSDA,VOL=SER=PACK12,SPACE=(1600,(200,50)),
//      DCB=(RECFM=FB,LRECL=80,BLKSIZE=1600)
```

Subsequent steps can now write the PAYROLL data set by coding a DD statement as follows:

```
//ddname DD DSN=PAYROLL,DISP=OLD
```

Delete all nonpermanent direct-access data sets in the last step in which they are needed to free up space for subsequent steps and for other jobs. If a production job has difficulty obtaining space, you might permanently allocate space for all the data sets, even temporary ones. Although this reduces the disk space available to the installation, it guarantees that this job will not be terminated for lack of direct-access space.

Data sets on direct-access volumes also cause problems when jobs are rerun if data sets to be created already exist in the job. For example, assume the previous job was run creating the PAYROLL data set. Suppose that for some reason the job must be rerun. If the job is rerun without JCL changes, it will terminate in STEP1 because a data set cannot be created if it already exists on the same direct-access volume. (There is no DISP parameter to tell the system to create a new data set, wiping out the old data set if it should exist.) You can make the appropriate JCL changes (DISP =NEW to DISP=OLD), but this is error prone and leads to frustration. You might include the following IEFBR14 null program step to delete the data set.

```
//STEP1 EXEC PGM=IEFBR14
//A DD DSN=dsname,DISP=(OLD,DELETE)
```

However, if the data set is not there to delete, the job will be terminated with a JCL error. Instead you can execute the IBM-supplied utility program IEHPROGM described in Chapter 15 as the first step in the job to scratch any unwanted data sets. IEHPROGM scratches the data sets if they exist, and continues execution if they do not exist. Unfortunately, it does issue a return code of 8 if the data set does not exist to delete, and you may have to change your COND parameters on subsequent job steps. By using IEHPROGM as the first step to delete any unwanted data sets, the job can always be rerun without any JCL changes.

X.   OTHER SPACE PARAMETERS

A.   ABSTR: Requesting Specific Tracks

Space can be allocated by giving the starting track address and the number of tracks to allocate. This always gives contiguous space, but should be used only for location-dependent data sets. It is sometimes used for very high usage data sets to place them near the VTOC or to place them under the fixed-head portion of 3344 or 3350 disks. Space is allocated only if all the tracks are available. To request absolute tracks, code:

```
                                    index
                                    directory
  SPACE=(ABSTR,(quantity,address,_____))
```

The quantity is the number of tracks desired and the address is the relative track address of the first track wanted. (The address of the first track on a volume is 0, but it cannot be allocated because it contains a pointer to the table of contents.) The directory requests directory space for partitioned data sets, and index requests index space for ISAM data sets.

```
  SPACE=(ABSTR,(200,2400))
      [ Two hundred tracks are requested, starting at relative track
      address 2400. ]
```

B. SPLIT: Splitting Cylinders between Data Sets (VS1 Only)

SPLIT splits the tracks on a cylinder between several data sets to reduce the processing time of data sets that have corresponding records. For example, a personnel file might be divided into several data sets, one containing names, another salary, and another work experience. For each name there is a record in corresponding data sets containing salary and work experience. If cylinders are split among the data sets, the corresponding records in each data set can be read without access arm movement.

To split cylinders, place the associated DD statements in sequence, and specify the space required for the first data set and the total space required for all data sets on the first DD statement. Each subsequent DD statement then requests its portion of the total space. To request space in units of cylinders, code the following on the first DD statement:

```
  SPLIT=(number,CYL,(total,increment))
```

The *total* is the total cylinders to allocate for all data sets, the *number* is the number of tracks on each cylinder to allocate to the first data set, and the *increment* specifies the number of cylinders of secondary allocation. The secondary allocation is given only to the data set exhausting its allocated space—it is not split with other data sets. Each succeeding DD statement must contain SPLIT = *number*, giving the number of tracks per cylinder to allocate to its data set.

```
  //DD1 DD DSN=ONE,DISP=(NEW,CATLG),UNIT=SYSDA,SPLIT=(5,CYL,1)
      [ One cylinder is allocated for all data sets.  Data set ONE
      is allotted 5 tracks on the cylinder. ]
  //DD2 DD DSN=TWO,DISP=(NEW,CATLG),SPLIT=15
      [ Data set TWO is allocated 15 tracks on the cylinder. ]
```

To request space in units of blocks, code the following on the first DD statement.

```
SPLIT=(percent,block size,(total,increment))
```

The *block size* is the average block size, the *total* is the total number of blocks for all data sets, and the *percent* is an integer from 1 to 99 specifying the percentage of tracks per cylinder to allot to the first data set. The *increment* is the number of blocks of secondary allocation. The system rounds up to an integral number of cylinders for both primary and secondary allocation. Each succeeding DD statement must contain SPLIT = *percent*, giving the percentage of tracks on each cylinder to allot to it. (KEYLEN = *length* must be coded if the blocks have keys.)

```
//DD1 DD DSN=ONE,DISP=(NEW,CATLG),
//       UNIT=SYSDA,SPLIT=(20,800,(30,10))
     [ Thirty 800-byte blocks are allocated to all data sets, and
     ten 800-byte blocks of secondary allocation are permitted.
     Data set ONE is allocated 20 percent of the tracks on each
     cylinder. ]
//DD2 DD DSN=TWO,DISP=(NEW,CATLG),SPLIT=80
     [ Data set TWO is allotted the remaining 80 percent of the
     tracks on each cylinder. ]
```

The average block length for split data sets cannot exceed 65,535 bytes. SPLIT cannot be used for ISAM, partitioned or direct organization, or for data sets residing on drums. The space allocated to split data sets is not released until all data sets sharing the cylinders are deleted.

C. SUBALLOC: Suballocating Space among Data Sets (VS1 Only)

SUBALLOC allows space to be reserved and suballocated in contiguous order to several data sets. For example, an installation may control space on direct-access volumes by allotting a fixed amount of space to each user who then suballocates this space for his or her data sets.

A data set must first be created to reserve the space for suballocation. Space can be reserved by any of the three previous methods: SPACE, ABSTR, or SPLIT. This data set can be used only for suballocation because space is removed from the front of it. It is effectively deleted when all its space is suballocated. To suballocate space, code the following on a subsequent DD statement.

```
             CYL
             TRK
             blocksize
SUBALLOC=(_____, (primary,secondary,directory),referback)
```

The *block size*, TRK, CYL, *primary*, *secondary*, and *directory* are the same as in the SPACE parameter. The *secondary* applies only to the suballocated data set, not to the original data set. The *referback* points to a previous DD statement describing the data set from which to suballocate. The system suballocates space only if it is contiguous, and space obtained by suballocation cannot be further suballocated. Suballocated space can be released individually for each data set, without all suballocated space being released.

```
//STEP1 EXEC PGM=ONE
//DD1 DD DSN=ALL,DISP=(NEW,KEEP),
//        UNIT=SYSDA,SPACE=(800,100,,CONTIG)
        [ Space is reserved for suballocation. ]
//DD2 DD DSN=DATA1,DISP=(NEW,CATLG),
//        SUBALLOC=(800,20,DD1)
        [ Twenty 800-byte blocks are suballocated from ALL for DATA1.
        The UNIT parameter is not required. ]
//STEP2 EXEC PGM=TWO
//DD3 DD DSN=DATA2,DISP=(NEW,CATLG),
//        SUBALLOC=(800,(30,20),STEP1.DD1)
        [ Thirty 800-byte blocks are suballocated from ALL for DATA2,
        and a secondary allocation of twenty 800-byte blocks is
        permitted. ]
```

XI. MSVGP: MASS STORAGE VIRTUAL GROUP

Each mass storage system can contain up to 4,720 mass storage volumes, and each volume is equivalent in storage to a 3330 Model 1 disk volume. The MSS volumes appear to the user as 3330 disk volumes. One main advantage they have over tapes or mountable disk packs is that they are "mounted" automatically. In fact, they are not mounted but copied to a 3330 disk volume. Data sets on MSS volumes are usually cataloged.

The device name for MSS is 3330V. A specific volume request is made with the VOL parameter. For nonspecific requests, the MSVGP = *group* parameter specifies an installation-defined name for a group of MSS volumes. One group name, SYS-GROUP, is standard on all systems. When MSVGP is coded, the volume is assumed to be private. Along with the group name, the installation defines a default space allocation. The SPACE parameter may be omitted when MSVGP is coded and the default space allocation is made; MSVGP is ignored for specific volume requests when VOL = SER is coded.

If you don't want the data set to be placed on a volume different from that of some data set referred to in a prior step, you can code:

```
MSVGP=(group,ddname)
        [ The ddname must appear in a prior job step.  The
        system will place the data set on a different MSS volume from
        that used by the data set referenced by the ddname. ]
```

EXERCISES

1. Use the program in Chapter 5, but modify the GO.OUT DD statement to write the lines into a data set named THING on disk. Make THING a cataloged data set.

2. Now rerun the same program, but modify the JCL to add the following three lines to the end of THING.

```
CARD 3
CARD 4
CARD 5
```

3. Run the job again to read THING and print the lines, verifying that the three lines were added.

4. Again change the JCL to place only the following lines in THING.

```
CARD 6
CARD 7
CARD 8
```

Do this twice, once by overriding THING, and once by deleting THING and recreating it.

5. Suppose that you pick up an old job that contains the following DD statement:

```
//ONE DD DSN=THING,DISP=(,CATLG),
//       UNIT=3330,SPACE=(80,100000),
//       DCB=(RECFM=FB,BLKSIZE=80,LRECL=80)
```

Suppose that you also know that the program writes 100,000 records, runs in 120K of storage, consumes 100 CPU seconds, and is run during the prime shift. Using your installation's cost equation and assuming that the CPU time and region size remain constant, how much could be saved for a run with full-track blocking? How much could be saved in disk storage costs using full-track blocking if the data set were stored a year? If your installation does not charge for disk storage, assume a charge of one cent per track per day.

Chapter 12

MAGNETIC TAPES

I. DESCRIPTION OF TAPE

A. Tape Hardware

Disk packs on mainframe computers are large, expensive, and fragile. By contrast, tape reels cost as little as $15, can hold vast amounts of data, survive the postal service, and be carried around in a briefcase. Tape can contain only sequential data sets. Tape is an inherently sequential I/O device.

Tapes used for storing computer data consist of a reel of half-inch wide magnetic tape similar to those used in cassette tapes, although the recording method and content are different. A typical tape reel might contain 138 million bytes. (A 3480 tape cartridge can contain approximately 200 million bytes.) A 3380 disk pack comparably blocked contains 572 million bytes.

A byte of data is stored in a row across the width of the tape; the position of each bit across the width is called a *track*. The *density* is the distance between successive bits along the length of the tape. A density of 6250 bits per inch (*bpi*) is dominant today. (In the past, tape drives with 200, 556, 800, and 1600 bpi were manufactured.)

Long ago, computers had six-bit bytes, and the data was recorded on seven tracks (one bit added for parity). System/370 computers have eight-bit bytes, and for them data are recorded on nine tracks (one bit added for parity). The parity bit is added to make the number of bits in a column odd. This enables the tape drive to detect when a bit is lost. Newer tape drives have additional parity checks that enable them to detect and correct all single-bit errors and most double-bit errors.

Data can be recorded on the same tape reel at any density as long as it is the same density on the entire tape. Dual-density 9-track tape drives are available to process either 800/1600- or 1600/6250-bpi densities. The 6250-bpi tape drives were the standard, but they are now being replaced by tape cartridge drives.

The 3480 tape drives use tape cartridges rather than tape reels. A tape cartridge is about one fourth the size and weight of a tape reel. Tape cartridges are more reliable and they are automatically mounted. The 3480 tape drives are 16-track and the density is approximately 38,000 bpi. Although the 3480 tape unit is considerably different in design from older tape drives, they are the same from the programming standpoint.

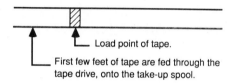

Load point of tape.

First few feet of tape are fed through the tape drive, onto the take-up spool.

Figure 47. Tape load point

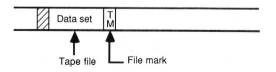

Tape file   File mark

Figure 48. Tape file mark

The usable portion of a tape reel is marked by two small aluminum strips: one pasted about 10 feet from the start of the tape to mark the load point as shown in Figure 47 and allow a leader for threading; and the other about 14 feet from the end of the reel to mark the end-of-volume with enough room to allow unfinished blocks to be completely transmitted. The VOL = SER parameter can specify that other tape reels can be mounted when the end-of-volume is reached.

Any old data on a tape reel is erased as the tape is written. The computer operator must insert a small *write-enable ring* (also termed the *file protect ring*) into the circular groove provided for it on the tape reel before the tape can be written on. If the ring is removed, the tape can be read, but it is fully protected against being written on accidentally. (To remember the function of the file protect ring, think: "No ring-ee, no write-ee.") The operator must be told whether to write-enable a tape or not; it cannot be specified by JCL.

Blocks written on a tape are separated by an interblock gap, a length of blank tape. The end of a data set or file is marked by a 3.6-inch gap followed by a special block written by the hardware called a *file* or *tape mark* as shown in Figure 48. Several data sets can be contained on a single reel of tape. The last file on tape is marked with an end-of-volume marker that consists of two tape marks as shown in Figure 49.

Tapes are read by moving the tape past the read head to transmit the data into contiguous ascending storage locations. If an error is detected, the system attempts to reread the block several times before pronouncing an I/O error. Your program can be notified if the file mark is read. Tapes can also be read backwards by moving the tape in the opposite direction, placing the data in descending order of addresses in storage. (This sounds intriguing, but uses for it are rare.)

A tape is written by transmitting data in storage in increasing order of addresses onto the tape as it passes the write head. The data is immediately read back as it passes the read head to ensure that it is recorded correctly. Tapes can also be backspaced and forward spaced over blocks or files, rewound to the load point, and unloaded.

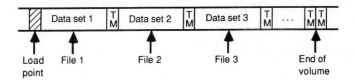

Figure 49. Several files stored on tape

B. Using Tape Storage

Tapes are usually stored in a fireproof vault, and a computer operator must retrieve the tape reel and mount it on a tape drive when you want to use it. Tape storage is ideal for:

- Storing large amounts of sequential data.
- Long-term storage of inactive data sets. If you aren't going to use data sets for some time, you can copy them to tape and free up scarce disk storage.
- Sending data sets from one installation to another. You can copy the data sets to tape and mail or carry the tape.
- Critical data sets. You can make backup copies of the data sets on tape. (Your installation may also back up the disk packs onto tape on a regular basis.)

To use a tape, you must tell the computer operator which tape reel you want. The system will then select an available tape drive and tell the operator to mount the tape on it. When the job is finished with the tape, the system notifies the operator to dismount the tape reel so that other users can mount their tapes on the tape drive. No one else can use a tape device while it is assigned to you.

Tape reels are usually assigned in one of two ways at an installation. At some installations, you request a tape before you run your job. The operators will give you the volume serial number of the tape, which you then specify in your JCL with the VOL parameter. At other installations, you request a tape when you submit your job, leaving off the VOL parameter and specifying a DISP of CATLG. When the operator assigns a tape to your job, the volume serial number is saved in the catalog, along with the data set name.

II. LABEL: TAPE LABELS

The LABEL parameter tells the type of label, the relative file number on the tape, and whether the data set is to be protected for input or output. The complete LABEL parameter is coded as:

```
                    NOPWREAD  IN   RETPD=nnnn
                    PASSWORD  OUT  EXPDT=yyddd
    LABEL=(file,type,_____,___ _____)
```

PASSWORD, NOPWREAD, EXPDT, and RETPD specify data set protection and are explained in Chapter 17. The usual form of the LABEL parameter for tape is:

```
LABEL=(file,type)
```

A.   FILE: Relative File Number

Data sets are stored on tape in what are termed files. The data are written sequentially onto tape, followed by a file mark that marks the end of the file or data set. Several data sets can be placed on the same tape reel.

Unless the data set is the first file on the tape, *file* must give the relative file number to position the tape properly. The *file* is a one- to four-digit sequence number describing the data set's position relative to other data sets on the volume. (The first file on the tape is number one.) If the file is omitted or zero is coded, one is assumed. (The tape is spaced to the end-of-volume if the file is higher than the number of data sets on the volume.) The file can be the relative sequence number over several labeled tape volumes, but it must be the relative sequence number for each unlabeled volume. That is, the relative sequence number starts with one with each unlabeled tape reel. The relative sequence number starts with one with just the first reel if the reels are labeled.

The file is recorded in the catalog if the data set is cataloged. It is also passed with the data set, so that if a DD statement refers to a passed data set, the file number need not be supplied. Here's an example of a passed data set on tape.

```
//STEP1 EXEC PGM=WON
//DD1 DD DSN=ALL,DISP=(OLD,PASS),
//        UNIT=TAPE9,VOL=SER=000421,LABEL=2
//STEP2 EXEC PGM=TOO
//DD2 DD DSN=*.STEP1.DD1,DISP=(OLD,KEEP)
```

B.   TYPE: Label Type

Tapes may be labeled to contain both volume and data set labels, either standard as provided by IBM, nonstandard as devised by the installation, a combination of both, or they can contain ASCII labels.

A tape volume label is a block written on the tape by the installation using the IBM-supplied utility program IEHINITT, before the tape is used. (The one- to six-character label is usually pasted on the tape reel to help the operator locate the tape.) The volume label is not separated from the first data set on the tape by a tape mark. Table 5 describes the volume label.

Data sets on standard labeled tapes are illustrated in Figure 50 and consist of a header block, a tape mark, the data set itself, another tape mark, and a trailer block. The last file on the tape is followed by two tape marks denoting the end-of-volume. The header block contains the description of the data set: record format, record size, block size, and data set name. The trailer block contains the same information as the

Table 5.   VOL1 Record Format

Byte Position	No. Bytes	Contents (80-byte record)
1	4	Characters 'VOL1'
5	6	Volume serial number. Left justified, padded on right with blanks.
11	70	Unused characters.

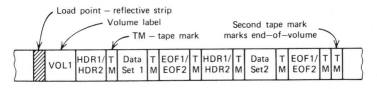

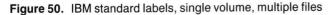

Figure 50. IBM standard labels, single volume, multiple files

header block so that the tape can be read backward. Table 6 illustrates the header block format and Table 7 the trailer block. Figure 51 illustrates a multivolume file.

Data set labels are created by the system when the data set is created and standard labels are requested. If you request no label, neither volume nor data set labels are created. The tape would then contain the first data set, a tape mark, the next data set, a tape mark, etc., as shown in Figure 52. The last data set on the tape is followed by two tape marks. The label type is not retained in the catalog, but it is passed with a data set.

You may specify the following types of labels.

SL	Standard Labels (assumed if *type* is omitted)
BLP	Bypass Label Processing
NL	No Labels
NSL	NonStandard Labels
SUL	Both Standard and User Labels
LTM	Leading Tape Mark on an unlabeled tape
AL	American National Standard Labels
AUL	Both American National Standard and User Labels

The only label types you are likely to use are SL, BLP, and NL.

1. SL: standard labels

If SL is coded or the type is omitted, the system assumes standard labels and reads in the first file to see whether it contains a valid label. It then checks the volume serial

Table 6.   HDR1/EOF1/EOV1 Record Formats

Byte Position	No. Bytes	Contents (80-byte records)
1	4	Characters 'HDR1' or 'EOV1' or 'EOF1'
5	17	Data set name. Rightmost 17 characters, left justified, padded on right with blanks.
22	6	Volume serial number. Right justified, padded on left with blanks. For multivolume file, serial number of first file.
28	4	Volume sequence number (0001–9999). Sequence number of a multivolume file; 0001 for single volume file.
32	4	File number (0001–9999). Number of file on tape.
36	4	Generation number (0001–9999) for generation data group.
40	2	Version number (00–99) for generation data group.
42	6	Creation date. 'byyddd'
48	6	Expiration date. 'byyddd'
54	1	Data set security. 0-no protection, 1-PASSWORD protection, 2-NOPWREAD protection.
55	6	Block count of blocks in file. Zero in HDR1.
61	27	Special codes.

Table 7.   HDR2/EOF2/EOV2 Record Formats

Byte Position	No. Bytes	Contents (80-byte records)
1	4	Characters 'HDR2' or 'EOF2' or 'EOV2'
5	1	Record format. F-fixed length, V-variable length, U-undefined length.
6	5	BLKSIZE
11	5	LRECL
16	1	DEN
17	1	Data set position. 1-volume switch has occured; otherwise 0.
18	17	'job-name/job-step' that created file.
35	2	TRTCH (7-track tape only).
37	1	Control character. A-ASCII, M-machine, b-no control characters.
38	1	Reserved
39	1	Block attribute. B-blocked, S-spanned, R-blocked and spanned, b-unblocked records.
40	8	Reserved
48	1	MVS only. Contains 'C' if file contains checkpoint data set.
49	32	Reserved

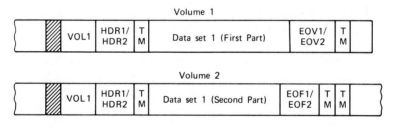

Figure 51. IBM standard labels, multivolume file

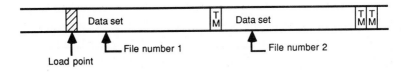

Figure 52. Tape with no labels

number in the label with that supplied in the VOL = SER parameter. If they do not check, the system tells the operator to mount the proper volume.

Most installations require you to use tapes with standard labels. If the tape does not have a standard label and a specific volume is not requested with VOL = SER, the operator is requested to supply label information, and a volume label is then written on the tape. If the label being read is of a different density from that specified or assumed on the DD statement, and if the tape is mounted on a multiple-density drive, the density is changed and the system attempts to read the label again.

When the serial number checks, the system positions the tape to the proper file. If the tape is being written, the data set name given by DSN is written into a data set label. (Only the 17 rightmost characters are written.) If the tape is being read, the DSN parameter is checked against the name in the data set label, and the program is terminated if the names do not check. You must supply the volume serial number, file number, and data set name for each nontemporary data set created.

A trailer label is written on the current volume if an end-of-volume condition is encountered while writing a tape, and processing continues on the next volume. Standard labels are created by the IBM-supplied IEHINITT utility program before the tape is used and are not changed thereafter.

2.   BLP: bypass label processing

BLP positions the tape to the specified file without checking for volume or data set labels. Data set labels are not created when a data set is written. As a consequence, no DCB parameters can be obtained from the label when the data set is read; they must be coded in the program or in the DCB parameter on the DD statement. BLP is normally used to write on blank tapes or on tapes containing files having a different parity, density, or number of tracks. BLP is also used when the file type or data set name is unknown.

If a tape containing standard labels is written on with BLP, the volume label is overwritten and destroyed. If a tape with standard labels is read with BLP, the first file contains the volume label and the header block for the first data set, the second file contains the data set, and the third file contains the trailer block. The formula for computing the BLP file number for a standard labeled tape is given by:

$$\text{BLP file number} = (\text{SL file number} - 1) \times 3 + 2$$

BLP is especially useful when the file type or data set name is unknown. For example, LABEL = (1,BLP) would let you read the tape label and data set name of the first file of a tape having standard labels. LABEL = (2,BLP) would let you read the first file of a tape having standard labels in which you did not know the data set name. Remember that to read a nonlabeled tape, you must supply all the necessary DCB information because the system cannot obtain it from the data set label.

Unlabeled tapes should be dismounted at the end of the last step in which they are needed by using DISP = (..,KEEP) so that the system will not use them for scratch. BLP is an option that must be specified in the cataloged reader procedure. If the BLP option is not specified and BLP is coded, it is treated as NL.

3. NL: no labels

NL is like BLP except that NL reads in the first file on the tape to ensure that it does not contain a volume label. Nonlabeled tapes are often used for sending tapes to another installation. That way you don't have to worry about the tape label corresponding to the standards at the other installation or about accidentally matching the volume serial number of an existing tape at that installation.

NL can produce some unexpected results. Blank tapes, because they do not contain a tape mark, are read to the end-of-volume. If the tape contains previous data of a different parity, track, or density, an I/O error results and the program is abnormally terminated. You must know what is on a tape to use NL—if you do not know, use BLP. If the tape does not have the proper label and a specific volume is not requested with VOL = SER, the operator is requested to supply label information, and a volume label is then written on the tape. If the tape originally contained a standard label, a new label is written only if any retention data has expired and if the tape does not contain password protected data sets.

To process ASCII data sets on unlabeled (NL) tapes, you must code the DCB = OPTCD = Q parameter.

4. NSL: nonstandard labels

NSL gives control to installation-written routines for label processing.

5.   SUL: standard and user labels

SUL is identical to SL except that the user data set labels are additionally processed by installation-provided routines.

6.   LTM: leading tape mark

LTM is identical to BLP except that if the tape has a leading tape mark, it is ignored. LTM is used to read Disk Operating System (DOS) files.

7.   AL: American National Standard Labels

American National Standard (ANS) labels are defined by the American National Standards Institute in the *American National Standard Magnetic Tape Labels for Information Interchange*, ANS X3.27-1969.

8.   AUL: ANS and user labels

AUL is identical to AL, except that user data set labels are additionally processed by installation-provided routines.

9.   Specifying label types

The following examples illustrate ways to code the LABEL parameter to specify labels.

```
//A DD UNIT=TAPE,LABEL=(,BLP)
      [ The tape is positioned to file 1 without label checking. ]
//B DD DSN=MYDATA,DISP=OLD,UNIT=2400,VOL=SER=000300,LABEL=2
      [ The tape is positioned to file 2, and standard labels are
      assumed. ]
//C DD UNIT=TAPE,LABEL=(3,NL)
      [ The tape is positioned to file 3.  The tape must not have a
      label. ]
//D DD DSN=IT,UNIT=TAPE,LABEL=(1,SL)
//E DD DSN=IT,UNIT=TAPE
      [ D and E are equivalent since the LABEL parameters in D are
      assumed if LABEL is omitted. ]
```

C.   IN/OUT: Input or Output Protection

Coding IN protects the file from being opened for output, and OUT protects it from being opened for input. The step is abnormally terminated if the data set is opened incorrectly.

The IN and OUT LABEL subparameters are primarily for FORTRAN programs. FORTRAN opens data sets for INOUT or OUTIN, depending on whether the first use of the data set is a READ or WRITE. Since this opens data sets for both output and input, the write-enable ring must always be inserted even if the tape is only read, negating the protection afforded by file protecting a tape. Likewise, operator intervention is required for reading data sets that have retention checks. Coding LABEL = (,,,IN) opens the data set for input only, allowing the write-enable ring to be removed and retention protected data sets to be read without operator intervention.

```
//A DD LABEL=(2,SL,,IN),...
     [ The data set can only be read. ]
```

III. TAPE STORAGE CAPACITY

The following equation calculates the length of tape in feet required for tape storage:

```
                              (BLKSIZE/density) + k
length-in-feet = records   --------------------
                              12 (blocking factor)
```

Length-in-feet	Length of tape in feet required to store the records. A standard tape reel is 2400 feet; a 3480 tape cartridge is approximately 500 feet.
Records	Number of records in the data set.
BLKSIZE	Length of the block in bytes.
Density	Bits per inch: 200, 556, 800, 1600, 6250, or 38,000 bpi.
k	Interblock gap in inches: 0.75 for 7-track, 0.6 for 800/1600 bpi 9-track, 0.3 for 6250 bpi, and 0.08 for 38,000 bpi (3480) tapes.
Blocking-factor	Number of records per block: BLKSIZE/LRECL. For variable-length records, it is the average block length divided by the average record length.

For example, if 400-byte records with 10 records per block are stored on a 9-track, 6250 bpi tape, the length required to store 400,000 records is computed as:

```
                      (4000/6250 + 0.3)
length = 400,000   -----------------   = 3,133.3 feet
                      12 x 10
```

Since a single tape reel contains 2,400 feet, two tape reels would be required to contain this file. If 50 records were contained in a block for a block size of 20,000, the length would be:

```
                      (20,000/6250 + 0.3)
length = 400,000   -------------------   = 2,133.3 feet
                      12 x 50
```

The data could then be placed on a single tape reel.

IV. ACCODE: ACCESS CODE

For an ISO/ANSI/FIPS Version 3 tape output data set, you can specify the access code by:

```
//ddname DD ACCODE=code,...
```

The *code* can be from one to eight characters, first character A–Z.

V. DCB SUBPARAMETERS

The usual DCB subparameters RECFM, LRECL, and BLKSIZE are specified as needed for tapes. Fixed, variable, and undefined record formats are all permitted. The block size should be at least 18 bytes long to eliminate mistaking blocks for noise. The maximum block size is 32,767 bytes. A DEN subparameter may be required to specify density, and TRTCH is needed for 7-track tapes.

A. DEN: Tape Density

You rarely need to write the DEN parameter because the default is usually what you want. Omit the DEN for 3480 tape cartridges. The following list gives the various values of DEN.

DEN	7-Track Density	9-Track Density
0	200 bpi default	—
1	556 bpi	—
2	800 bpi	800 bpi (default for 800-bpi drives)
3	—	1600 bpi default for 1600 and 800/1600 dual-density drives)
4	—	6250 bpi (default for 6250 and 1600/6250 dual-density drives)

DEN is required for 7-track tape drives unless the tapes are 200-bpi density (and few are). DEN is required for 9-track drives only if an 800- or 1600-bpi tape is to be written on a dual-density drive having a higher density.

On 9-track dual-density tape drives, the DEN parameter is ignored for input. The system reads the tape label to determine the density. For output, the system writes the tape at the density you specify. If you omit the DEN parameter, the system writes the tape at the highest density of the tape drive. If you are writing the first file of a tape with standard labels and the tape label is of a different density, the system will rewrite the label to agree with the density of the data set being written.

B.   TRTCH: 7-track Tape Recording Technique

TRTCH is used for the obsolete 7-track drives to specify parity, data conversion, and translation. Parity can be even or odd, *data conversion* permits binary data to be recorded by 7-track drives, and *translation* is used to read or write BCD tapes. The following options are possible:

- TRTCH omitted specifies odd parity, translation off, conversion off. (This mode of processing tapes is used to process data from second-generation computers.) For a write, only the rightmost six bits are written onto tape; the two high-order bits are ignored. For a read, each character on the tape is read into the six rightmost bits of each byte; the two high-order bits are set to zero.
- TRTCH = E is the same as omitting TRTCH except parity is even.
- TRTCH = T specifies odd parity, translation on, conversion off. (BCD/EBCDIC translation.) For a write, each 8-bit EBCDIC character is converted to a 6-bit BCD character. For a read, each 6-bit character is converted to an 8-bit EBCDIC character.
- TRTCH = ET is the same as TRTCH = T except parity is even.
- TRTCH = C specifies odd parity, translation off, conversion on. (This mode is used to record binary data on 7-track tapes.) Read backwards forces conversion off. For a write, three 8-bit bytes (24 bits) are written as for 6-bit characters (24 bits). If storage data is not a multiple of three bytes, two or three characters are written as needed, and unused bit position of the last character are set to zero. For a read, four 6-bit characters are read as three 8-bit bytes. If the data is not a multiple of four characters, the last one, two, or three characters are read into storage, and the remaining bits of the unfilled bytes are set to zero.

The TRTCH parameter is stored in the label of a data set with standard labels. Thus TRTCH does not need to be coded to read a tape with standard labels.

VI. USING TAPES

The system needs to know the following things to write a tape:

- RECFM—Record Format. It is usually F or FB (Fixed-length or Fixed-length Blocked), V or VB (Variable-length or Variable-length Blocked), or U (Undefined).
- LRECL—Logical Record Length in bytes.
- BLKSIZE—Block Size in bytes.
- Label type—SL is the usual, with BLP and NL occasionally used.
- File number—Number of the file that contains the data set.

For a labeled tape, all these except the file number are stored in the data set label on the tape itself. Here is a typical DD statement to write a data set onto tape:

```
//OUT DD DSN=TEST.DATA,DISP=(NEW,KEEP),
//       UNIT=TAPE,VOL=SER=970216,
//       DCB=(RECFM=FB,LRECL=80,BLKSIZE=6400)
```

A single data set can be stored across several tape reels so that an unlimited amount of information can actually be stored. Tapes can contain only sequential data sets. Several data sets can be stored on a single tape reel by separating them with tape marks. The following example writes onto file 3 of a tape. This requires that files 1 and 2 already exist on the tape, and is illustrated in Figure 53.

```
//INFILE DD DSN=PAYROLL,DISP=(NEW,KEEP),
//           UNIT=TAPE,VOL=SER=004435,LABEL=3
```

If any file is rewritten, all subsequent files on that tape reel are destroyed and must be rewritten. Thus if a tape contains three files and the second file is rewritten, the first file is unchanged, but the third file is destroyed.

Tapes may be rewritten many times, and any old data on a tape is erased as the tape is written. Tapes are updated by reading the old master file and applying the transactions to produce a new tape. An automatic backup is obtained by keeping the old tape and the transactions.

Although new tapes are 2,400 feet long, only the first few feet of a tape are usually read or written. As this portion of the tape becomes worn, computer operators may strip the tape by clipping off a few yards. Thus old tape reels may become shorter as they are recycled over their lives.

Tape makes excellent long-term storage because a reel of tape is inexpensive and can contain a great deal of information in a small storage space. Tapes may be faster or slower than direct-access storage devices depending on the particular device. Tapes must be mounted by an operator, and this may increase the turnaround time of the job.

When a tape is first mounted by the operator, it is positioned to the load point. Some programming languages also have a REWIND command to rewind the tape. This also positions it to the load point as illustrated in Figure 54.

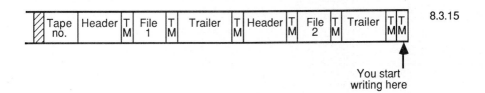

8.3.15

You start
writing here

Figure 53. Writing onto a tape

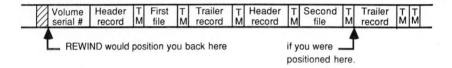

Figure 54. Rewinding a tape

A disposition of NEW in a DD statement for a tape data set positions the tape to the start of a file. A disposition of MOD positions the tape to the beginning (if the data set doesn't already exist on tape) or the end of a tape file (if it already exists). Figure 55 shows this for a labeled tape.

A disposition of KEEP rewinds the tape to the load point and unloads it. A disposition of PASS rewinds the tape to the start of the data set and keeps the tape mounted. Coding VOL=(,RETAIN,..) also keeps the tape mounted between job steps. Minimize operator intervention by not unloading tapes between job steps if they are to be used again within the job.

To create a data set on tape, always code the UNIT, DSN, DISP, and VOL parameters, except in those rare circumstances when it is apparent that they are not required; for example, DSN is not required for temporary data sets. Code DCB subparameters as needed. RECFM, LRECL, and BLKSIZE are the most common. LABEL is needed unless the data set is on the first file of a standard-labeled tape. DEN is required if you don't want the default density for the tape drive.

To access an old data set on tape, code UNIT, VOL, DSN, DISP, LABEL, and DCB as needed. DCB subparameters can be obtained from the data set label only if the tape has standard labels. Omit UNIT and VOL if the data set is cataloged or passed. If the data set is not cataloged or passed or is not on the first file, LABEL must give the file number. The following example shows several uses of tapes.

```
//STEP1 EXEC PGM=ENA
//A DD UNIT=TAPE9
     [ A scratch data set is placed on file 1 of a standard-labeled
     9-track tape. ]
//B DD DSN=SALARY,DISP=(NEW,PASS),
//     UNIT=TAPE7,VOL=SER=000250,LABEL=(2,BLP),
//     DCB=(DEN=2,TRTCH=C)
     [ A data set created on file 2 of an unlabeled 7-track tape is
     passed.  The tape is written at 800 bpi. ]
//C DD DSN=TENURE,DISP=(NEW,CATLG),
//     UNIT=TAPE9,VOL=(,RETAIN,SER=000451),LABEL=2
     [ A data set created on file 2 of a 9-track tape is cataloged.
     The tape is kept mounted at the end of the step. ]
//STEP2 EXEC PGM=DIA
//D DD DSN=*.STEP1.B,DISP=(MOD,KEEP),
//     LABEL=(2,BLP),DCB=(DEN=2,TRTCH=C)
     [ The data set on the 7-track tape is retrieved. ]
//E DD DSN=TENURE,DISP=OLD
     [ The data set on the 9-track tape is retrieved. ]
```

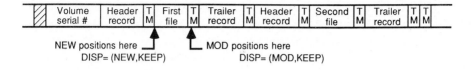

| Volume serial # | Header record | T M | First file | T M | Trailer record | T M | Header record | T M | Second file | T M | Trailer record | T M | T M |

NEW positions here   MOD positions here
     DISP= (NEW,KEEP)   DISP= (MOD,KEEP)

Figure 55. DISP = MOD for a labeled tape

VII. MULTIVOLUME DATA SETS

Data sets too large to be contained on one tape volume can be extended onto several volumes. The VOL parameter may request specific volumes or a maximum number of nonspecific volumes. The UNIT parameter may mount volumes in parallel or defer mounting until the volumes are needed. Use parallel mounting only if there are few volumes and if the volumes are processed quickly. Mounting is deferred so as not to monopolize the tape units, especially if volume processing is slow. If there are more volumes than tape units, mounting must be deferred.

Use a disposition of DISP = (MOD,CATLG) when extending multivolume cataloged data sets, even if the data set is already cataloged. CATLG records new volume serial numbers in the catalog as the data set is extended.

Volume switching during writing occurs when the end-of-volume marker is reached on tape volumes. During reading, volume switching occurs when an end-of-volume is encountered on tape. The following example shows the creation, extension, and retrieval of multivolume tape data sets.

```
//STEP1 EXEC PGM=CREATE
//A DD DSN=MULTI,DISP=(NEW,CATLG),UNIT=TAPE,VOL=SER=(000100,000200)
     [ A tape data set is created on volumes 100 and 200.  All
     volumes are recorded in the catalog. ]
//STEP2 EXEC PGM=EXTEND
//C DD DSN=MULTI,DISP=(MOD.CATLG),UNIT=(,.DEFER),VOL=(,,,4)
     [ If more volumes are required, the operator must assign and
     mount them.  Any new volume serial numbers are entered into
     the catalog. ]
//STEP3 EXEC PGM=RETRIEVE
//E DD DSN=MULTI,DISP=OLD,UNIT=(,,DEFER)
     [ The volumes are mounted one at a time as required. ]
```

EXERCISES

1. Modify the GO.OUT DD statement in the program from Chapter 5 to write the lines onto a tape file. Write them as file 1 of a standard labeled tape at the highest density available.

2. The tape generated by Exercise 1 now contains three physical files, a volume label and header label, the data set, and a trailer label. Modify the JCL in the program from Chapter 5 to read the tape records and print them. Read each of the three physical files on the tape. (Since they all have 80-byte records, the program can read them.) Verify that the volume label, header label, data set, and trailer label contain the correct information.

Chapter 13

CATALOGED AND IN-STREAM PROCEDURES

Coding the numerous JCL statements required for a job is difficult and error prone. As a result, JCL statements that have potential use by several users are often placed in a cataloged procedure. You may invoke the JCL in the cataloged procedure with a single EXEC statement. Cataloged procedures are stored as members in partitioned data sets established by the installation.

In-stream procedures are identical to cataloged procedures except that they are placed right along with the job in the input stream, immediately after the JOB statement rather than as members of partitioned data sets. In-stream procedures are used to test JCL before placing it in a cataloged procedure. They are also used for procedures of limited use.

Cataloged and in-stream procedures may also have symbolic parameters coded in the JCL statements. The symbolic parameters can be given default values, and you may assign a value on the EXEC statement. For example, a procedure to copy a disk data set onto tape might have the disk data set name and the tape volume serial number coded as symbolic parameters because they would likely change each time the procedure is invoked. Symbolic parameters provide a means of generalizing JCL, another reason for creating procedures.

A procedure may consist of several job steps. Procedures can contain all but the following JCL statements:

- EXEC statements invoking procedures. (A procedure cannot invoke another procedure.)
- JOB, delimiter (/*), or null (//) statements.
- JOBLIB DD statements.
- DD * or DATA statements.
- Any JES2 or JES3 control statements.

I.   CATALOGED PROCEDURES

Cataloged procedures are normally kept in a system library named SYS1.PROCLIB, but other libraries may be concatenated to it. The libraries are searched in the order they are concatenated. The IBM-supplied utility program IEBUPDTE described in Chapter 14 adds and replaces procedures in the partitioned data set.

A cataloged procedure begins with a PROC statement and is followed by the JCL statements that constitute the procedure. The PROC statement is optional if symbolic parameters are not assigned default values. The PROC statement is coded as:

```
//procedure-name PROC symbolic-parameters comments
```

The *procedure-name* must be unique within the procedure library. The procedure-name is one to eight alphanumeric (A to Z, 0 to 9) or national (@ $ #) characters. The first character must be alphabetic (A to Z) or national. The symbolic parameters are described later in this chapter.

The following JCL illustrates a cataloged procedure.

```
//ADDPROC PROC
//GO EXEC PGM=IEBUPDTE
//SYSPRINT DD SYSOUT=A
//SYSUT1    DD DSN=SYS1.PROCLIB,DISP=OLD
//SYSUT2    DD DSN=*.SYSUT1,DISP=OLD
```

This particular procedure executes the IEBUPDTE utility described in Chapter 15 to add procedures to the SYS1.PROCLIB library. To invoke the procedure, you need only code the following:

```
// EXEC ADDPROC
//GO.SYSIN DD DATA
    [ ADD and REPL statements followed by the JCL statements as
    required. ]
/*
```

Often a program must read lines of data that seldom change from run to run. The following example illustrates such a program.

```
//GO EXEC PGM=ONE
//SYSIN DD *
    [ lines of data ]
/*
```

We might wish to store the above step as a cataloged procedure, and since the lines of data seldom change, we would like to make it a part of the cataloged procedure as well. The procedure library contains 80-column lines of data, and any data, not just JCL, can be added as a member. The SYSIN DD statement must then point to the member containing the lines of data. The following example shows how the two members might appear if added to SYS1.PROCLIB.

```
Member RUN
  //RUN PROC
  //GO EXEC PGM=ONE
  //SYSIN DD DSN=SYS1.PROCLIB(CARDS),DISP=OLD


Member CARDS
     [ lines of data ]
```

The procedure is named RUN and the lines of data are placed in a member named CARDS. (The lines could have been placed in some other data set if desired.) The program is now executed with a single // EXEC RUN statement.

II. IN-STREAM PROCEDURES

In-stream procedures begin with a PROC statement and must be terminated by a PEND statement. The PEND statement is coded as:

```
//optional-name PEND comments
```

The in-stream procedure is placed following the JOB statement but before the first EXEC statement of the JOB. Up to 15 in-stream procedures can be included in a single job. Each in-stream procedure may be invoked several times within the job.

The following sample illustrates an in-stream procedure named RUN.

```
//MYJOB JOB (2216,82),'TEST RUN',CLASS=A
//RUN PROC              <------
//GO EXEC PGM=ONE              |    This is the
//SYSOUT DD SYSOUT=A           |    in-stream procedure
// PEND                 <------
//STEP1 EXEC RUN        <==  This executes the in-stream procedure
```

III. SYMBOLIC PARAMETERS

Procedures may be modified for execution by overriding parameters on DD statements. This is often inconvenient because you must know the parameters that can be overridden, the stepnames within the procedure, the ddnames of the statements overridden, and the order of the DD statements. *Symbolic parameters* provide an alternative means of modifying procedures for execution. The following example illustrates symbolic parameters.

```
//RUN PROC PROGRAM=ONE,UNIT=SYSDA
//GO EXEC PGM=&PROGRAM
//A DD UNIT=&UNIT,SPACE=(TRK,20)
```

The ampersands preceding PROGRAM and UNIT mark them as symbolic parameters. The PROC statement allows default values to be assigned to symbolic parameters. The RUN procedure can be invoked by a // EXEC RUN statement and the procedure is interpreted as:

```
//GO EXEC PGM=ONE
//A DD UNIT=SYSDA,SPACE=(TRK,20)
```

Values can also be assigned to symbolic parameters on the EXEC statement. Any values coded on the EXEC statement override the values on the PROC statement for the duration of the run.

```
// EXEC RUN,UNIT=TEMP,PROGRAM=TWO
```

The procedure is now interpreted as:

```
//GO EXEC PGM=TWO
//A DD UNIT=TEMP,SPACE=(TRK,20)
```

A. Coding Symbolic Parameters

A symbolic parameter is preceded by an ampersand and may be one to seven alphanumeric (A to Z, 0 to 9) or national (# @ $) characters, the first of which must be alphabetic (A to Z) or national. Symbolic parameters can be coded only in the operand field of JCL statements; they cannot appear in the name or operation field. Keywords for the EXEC statement such as PGM, COND, and PARM, cannot be used as symbolic parameter names. If more than one value is assigned to a symbolic parameter on a PROC or EXEC statement, only the first is used.

```
//RUN PROC NAME=LIB1,NAME=LIB2
//STEP1 EXEC PGM=ONE
//A DD DSN=&NAME, ...
//STEP2 EXEC PGM=TWO
//B DD DSN=&NAME, ...
```

Each appearance of the symbolic parameter &NAME in this procedure is assigned a default value of LIB1. You might override this default for a run, and each appearance of &NAME in the procedure is changed. If symbolic parameters had not been used, each DD statement would have to be overridden.

Symbolic parameters may be coded in any order on PROC or EXEC statements. If &NAME and &VOLS are symbolic parameters defined in a FORTRAN compile, link edit, and GO procedure, the following could be coded.

```
//EXEC FORTGCLG,NAME='SYS1.FORTERR',
//     REGION.FORT=104K,VOLS=003345,COND.GO=EVEN
```

B. Assigning Values to Symbolic Parameters

Values containing special characters other than [blank , . / ') (* & + − =] must be enclosed in apostrophes. Code a legitimate apostrophe as two consecutive apostrophes.

```
//RUN PROC NAME='SYS1.PROCLIB',TAPE='2400-6'
```

The value assigned to a symbolic parameter can be of any length, but it cannot be continued onto another line. The following statement is in error.

```
//RUN PROC NAME='SYS1.,
//         PROCLIB',TAPE='2400-6'
```

It should be coded as:

```
//RUN PROC NAME='SYS1.PROCLIB',
//         TAPE='2400-6'
```

Symbolic parameters can be concatenated with other symbolic parameters (PARM = &LEFT&RIGHT), with regular parameters (SPACE = &SPACE), or with portions of regular parameters [SPACE = (TRK,&PRIMARY)]. The combined text produced by such a concatenation must not exceed 120 characters. (The entire DD statement may, of course, contain many more characters.)

```
//RUN PROC VOLS=',3,4',NAME=A,IN='NEW,',OUT=KEEP
//A DD VOL=SER=(2&VOLS),DSN=SYS1.&NAME,DISP=(&IN&OUT)
```

The DD statement is interpreted as:

```
//A DD VOL=SER=(2,3,4),DSN=SYS1.A,DISP=(NEW,KEEP)
```

Nullify symbolic parameters by coding the keyword and equal sign without a value, either on the PROC or EXEC statement.

```
//RUN PROC VOLS=,NAME=PROCLIB
//A DD VOL=SER=(2&VOLS),DSN=SYS1.&NAME
```

The DD statement is interpreted as:

```
//A DD VOL=SER=(2),DSN=SYS1.PROCLIB
```

A delimiter, such as a leading or trailing comma, next to a symbolic parameter is not removed when the parameter is nullified.

```
//RUN PROC VOLS=
//A DD VOL=SER=(2,&VOLS)
```

The DD statement is interpreted as follows, but the system considers this a syntax error and fails the job.

```
//A DD VOL=SER=(2,)
```

To solve this problem, omit the comma preceding the symbolic parameter and include the comma as part of the symbolic parameter. The following example corrects the previous error.

```
//RUN PROC VOLS=
//A DD VOL=SER=(2&VOLS)
```

The procedure could be invoked as:

```
//EXEC RUN,VOLS=',3'
```

The DD statement would be interpreted as:

```
//A DD VOL=SER=(2,3)
```

If the symbolic parameter is not followed by a special character other than a period or left parenthesis [, / ') * & + − =], the symbolic parameter must be followed by a period to separate it from the text.

```
//RUN PROC TAPE=2400,NAME=SYS1
//A DD UNIT=&TAPE-2,DSN=&NAME..P
```

The DD statement is interpreted as:

```
//A DD UNIT=2400-2,DSN=SYS1.P
```

Positional parameters as symbolic parameters should be separated from any following parameters with a period rather than a comma. This is so that if the positional parameter is nullified, a leading comma will not result. The following example illustrates the correct way to code a positional parameter as a symbolic parameter.

```
//RUN PROC TYPE='DUMMY,'
//GO EXEC PGM=ONE
//A DD &TYPE.DSN=THING
```

The DD statement is interpreted as:

```
//A DD DUMMY,DSN=THING
```

Symbolic parameters must always be given values, either on the PROC statement as a part of the procedure or on the EXEC statement invoking the procedure. Otherwise the system considers it a JCL error. The one exception to this is the DSN parameter. If DSN = &*name* is coded and no value is assigned to the name on the PROC or EXEC statement, the system interprets &*name* to mean a temporary data set.

All symbolic parameters given a value on a PROC or EXEC statement must appear as symbolic parameters in the procedure. The following procedure is in error because DISK does not appear as a symbolic parameter in the procedure.

```
//RUN PROC DISK=3380
//GO EXEC PGM=ONE
//A DD UNIT=3380,SPACE=(TRK,20)
```

This error can be corrected by recoding the DD statement in the procedure.

```
//A DD UNIT=&DISK,SPACE=(TRK,20)
```

It can also be corrected by overriding the UNIT parameter with a DD statement.

```
// EXEC RUN
//GO.A DD UNIT=&DISK
```

The preceding example shows that symbolic parameters can be coded on overriding DD statements. DD statements containing symbolic parameters can also be overridden if you are careful not to override a symbolic parameter assigned a value. If the UNIT = &DISK correction is made to the above procedure, the following step is in error because &DISK is given a value on the PROC statement but does not now appear in the procedure.

```
// EXEC RUN
//GO.A DD UNIT=3380
```

C. Use of Symbolic Parameters

One final example should serve to show the usefulness of symbolic parameters. The linkage editor step usually contains a DD statement named SYSLIB to describe the libraries that the linkage editor is to search for subroutines. SYSLIB is often concatenated to describe several subroutine libraries.

```
//LKED EXEC PGM=LINKEDIT
//SYSLIB DD DSN=SYS1.FORTLIB,DISP=SHR
//       DD DSN=SYS1.SSPLIB,DISP=SHR
```

The linkage editor searches both SYS1.FORTLIB and SYS1.SSPLIB to find needed subroutines. Now suppose that the above LKED step is part of a FORTRAN compile, link edit, and GO procedure named FORTGCLG. You might wish to concatenate your own private library to SYSLIB.

```
// EXEC FORTGCLG
     .        .      .      .     .
//LKED.SYSLIB DD
//           DD
//           DD DSN=PRIVLIB,DISP=SHR
```

PRIVLIB is concatenated to SYS1.FORTLIB and SYS1.SSPLIB. Now consider what happens if the installation changes the FORTGCLG procedure by adding a subroutine library. SYSLIB might be changed to:

```
//SYSLIB DD DSN=SYS1.NEWFORT.DISP=SHR
//       DD DSN=SYS1.FORTLIB,DISP=SHR
//       DD DSN=SYS1.SSPLIB,DISP=SHR
```

The PRIVLIB DD statement now overrides the SYS1.SSPLIB DD statement. If the job uses subroutines in SYS1.SSPLIB, it will fail because SYS1.SSPLIB is no longer searched. The JCL must be changed by adding another // DD statement. Symbolic parameters solve this problem very nicely. Suppose the procedure had originally been coded to allow the user to specify a private library as a symbolic parameter.

```
//FORTGCLG PROC LIB='SYS1.FORTLIB'
     .      .      .       .      .
//        DD DSN=SYS1.FORTLIB,DISP=SHR
//        DD DSN=SYS1.SSPLIB,DISP=SHR
//        DD DSN=&LIB,DISP=SHR
```

A private library is concatenated by coding the following:

```
// EXEC FORTGCLG,LIB=PRIVLIB
```

Not only is this method simpler to code with less chance of error, but, equally important, the installation can freely add libraries to the SYSLIB DD statement without disturbing anyone's JCL.

A cataloged procedure is not the only way of generalizing JCL. You can also use a text editor, with its ability to make global changes, to help generalize JCL. Rather than writing a cataloged procedure, you can use a text editor to copy in JCL statements from a file to wherever they are needed. Then you can make global changes as needed. For example, if the volume serial number changes each time you run some JCL, you could store the JCL statements as a cataloged procedure with the volume serial number as a symbolic parameter. Alternatively, you could just write the JCL with the volume serial number as some unique characters, such as the following:

```
//INPUT DD DSN=X0225.TEST.DATA,DISP=(NEW,CATLG),
//          UNIT=TAPE9,VOL=SER=VOLUME
```

With a text editor, you could make a global change of VOLUME to whatever volume serial number you wanted. This gives you much of the flexibility of symbolic parameters without the bother of writing a cataloged procedure.

EXERCISES

Write an in-stream procedure to allocate some number of tracks on a specified pack for a data set and write lines of data into the data set. The procedure is to be invoked as follows:

```
//EXEC BLOPPO,PACK=volume,TRACKS=number
//PGM.SYSIN DD*
     [ PL/I program from Chapter 5 ]
/*
//CARD.IN DD *
     [ lines of input ]
/*
```

The procedure is to have three steps. The first step is to execute the IEFBR14 null program to allocate the specified number of tracks on the pack selected. The second and third steps are to be the PLIXCG procedure. You will need one of your old run listings to determine the JCL statement required for the procedure.

Chapter 14

THE LINKAGE EDITOR AND LOADER

The linkage editor and loader, although not a part of JCL proper, are invoked by JCL and are used for many JCL applications. An understanding of their function is necessary to use System/370 facilities. This chapter also illustrates the use of partitioned data sets.

I. THE LINKAGE EDITOR

The linkage editor program processes object modules, linkage editor control statements, and other load modules to produce load modules that can be executed. A single linkage editor step can process several object and load modules to produce either single or multiple load modules.

An *object module* is a sequential data set containing relocateable machine instructions and data produced by a language compiler. Object modules are usually placed in a temporary data set to be passed to a subsequent linkage editor step. Object modules can also be saved for later processing by writing them as a nontemporary data set or by punching them onto cards. However, there is almost no need for this because load modules are more convenient and efficient to save.

The linkage editor processes the object modules to form a load module suitable for execution. A load module must be made a member of a partitioned data set on a direct-access volume. The load module is placed into a temporary data set if it is not to be used again. You may elect to place it in a nontemporary data set so that the program can be loaded into storage later and executed without the cost of the compilation or linkage editor steps. This is often done for computer programs when they go into production and are changed only infrequently. Replacement subroutines can be link edited with an old load module to produce a new load module.

The basic unit processed by the linkage editor is a *control section*, a unit of program (instructions and data) that is itself an entity. A control section, the smallest separately relocateable unit of a program, is usually the main program or a subroutine.

Several sources of input can be supplied to the linkage editor with DD statements. A primary input, defined by a DD statement whose ddname is SYSLIN, is always required. It often describes a temporary data set passed from a compile step and is concatenated with the input stream, allowing both newly compiled subroutines and control statements in the input stream to be included.

Several additional sources of input can, if needed, be included with linkage editor control statements. For example, when replacement subroutines are compiled and link edited, the old load module is made an additional input source so that those subroutines not recompiled can be included.

Finally, subroutine libraries can be searched for required subroutines. For example, subroutines used by a FORTRAN program can be automatically looked up in a library. Subroutine libraries are described by a DD statement whose ddname is SYSLIB, and several libraries can be concatenated together.

The linkage editor processes the primary input first and any additional input next. It searches the subroutine libraries last if any unresolved references remain. If two modules with the same name are encountered in a library, only the first is used.

A. JCL for the Linkage Editor

The linkage editor, an IBM-supplied program usually named HEWL, is contained in SYS1.LINKLIB. (An installation can create several linkage editor programs and assign them other names.)

```
//LKED EXEC PGM=HEWL,REGION=96K,PARM=(option,option,...,option)
```

The linkage editor step is traditionally named LKED. The PARM options, which can be coded in any order, request various options.

- LIST lists the linkage editor control statements and is usually specified.
- MAP produces a storage map showing the relative locations of control sections and helps you estimate the region size needed for the program.
- XREF includes MAP plus a cross-reference table of the load module. (MAP and XREF are mutually exclusive.)
- NCAL cancels the automatic library call mechanism and is often used for creating subroutine libraries so that the load module contains a single subroutine.
- LET marks load modules as executable even if minor errors are found; for example, external references left unresolved by NCAL.
- ALIGN2 (VS1 only) aligns the control sections on 2K page boundaries.
- OVLY permits an overlay structure. Overlay structures are described later in this chapter.

There are more options, but they are seldom used. The following parameters are coded for most linkage editor steps.

```
//LKED EXEC PGM=HEWL,PARM=(LIST,XREF)
```

The HEWL program also requires a SYSPRINT DD statement to describe a print data set, a SYSUT1 DD statement to allocate a scratch data set, and a SYSLIN DD statement to describe the primary input. A SYLMOD DD statement is required to describe the data set that is to contain the load module, a SYSLIB DD statement is needed for automatic call lookup, and other DD statements may be included to describe additional sources of input. The following example illustrates the use of the linkage editor in a COBOL compile, link edit, and GO cataloged procedure.

```
//COBUCLG PROC
//COB EXEC PGM=IKFCBL00,REGION=128K
        [ The OS/VS COBOL compiler is named IKFCBL00 and is contained
        in SYS1.LINKLIB. ]
//SYSPRINT DD SYSOUT=A
        [ SYSPRINT describes a print data set. ]
//SYSUT1    DD UNIT=SYSDA,SPACE=(460,(700,100))
//SYSUT2    DD UNIT=SYSDA,SPACE=(460,(700,100))
//SYSUT3    DD UNIT=SYSDA,SPACE=(460,(700,100))
//SYSUT4    DD UNIT=SYSDA,SPACE=(460,(700,100))
        [ The SYSUTn DD statements are work data sets used by
        the compiler.]
//SYSLIN    DD DSN=&&LOADSET,DISP=(MOD,PASS),
//             UNIT=SYSDA,SPACE=(80,(500,100))
        [ SYSLIN describes the data set that is to contain the object
        module produced by the compiler.  A disposition of MOD is
        used so that if there are several compile steps, the object
        modules are all placed in one sequential data set. ]
//LKED EXEC PGM=HEWL,PARM=(LIST,XREF,LET),
//          COND=(5,LT,COB),REGION=96K
        [ COND bypasses the link edit step unless the compile step
        returns a completion code of 5 or less.  By convention,
        condition codes greater than 5 represent severe errors. ]
//SYSLIN DD DSN=&&LOADSET,DISP=(OLD,DELETE)
//       DD DDNAME=SYSIN
        [ SYSLIN describes the primary input--the output from the
        compiler concatenated with the input stream.  The DCB
        attributes are built-in as RECFM=FB,LRECL=80. ]
//SYSLMOD DD DSN=&&GOSET(GO),DISP=(NEW,PASS),
//           UNIT=SYSDA,SPACE=(1024,(50,20,1))
        [ SYSLMOD defines the data set to contain the load module
        produced.  The DCB attributes are built-in as
        RECFM=U,BLKSIZE=track-size. ]
//SYSLIB DD DSN=SYS1.COBLIB,DISP=SHR
        [ SYSLIB points to the library used for the automatic call
        lookup.  The DCB attributes are built-in as
        RECFM=FB,LRECL=80. ]
//SYSUT1 DD UNIT=(SYSDA,SEP=(SYSLIN,SYSLMOD)),SPACE=(1024,(50,20))
        [ SYSUT1 defines a scratch data set used by the linkage
        editor. ]
//SYSPRINT DD SYSOUT=A
        [ SYSPRINT defines a print data set.  The DCB attributes are
        built in as RECFM=FBA,LRECL=121. ]
//GO EXEC PGM=*.LKED.SYSLMOD,COND=((5,LT,COB),(5,LT,LKED))
        [ GO executes the program created by the linkage editor.  COND
        bypasses the step unless both the compiler and linkage
        editors return completions codes of 5 or less. ]
```

The entire procedure is now executed as follows:

```
// EXEC COBUCLG
//COB.SYSIN DD *
    [ COBOL source statements ]
/*
//LKED.SYSIN DD *
    [ any linkage editor control statements ]
/*
//GO.ddname DD ...
    [ Any DD statements required by the program are placed here. ]
```

B. Linkage Editor Messages

The linkage editor issues one of the following messages when it has completed.

- member-name NOW ADDED TO DATA SET.
- member-name NOW REPLACED in DATA SET. The *member-name* was already in the SYSLMOD data set, and it is replaced with the new member.
- member-name DOES NOT EXIST BUT HAS BEEN ADDED TO THE DATA SET. This nihilistic message means that you asked to replace a load module in the SYSLMOD data set, the load module was not there to replace, and so the load module was added rather than replaced. The DISP parameter on the SYSLMOD DD statement tells whether to add or replace. DISP = MOD or NEW is a request to add, and DISP = OLD is a request to replace.
- MODULE HAS BEEN MARKED NOT EXECUTABLE. Although the module is not executable, you may be able to recover by link editing the control section causing the problem and replacing it in the load module. An unresolved external reference often causes this error.

If the *member-name* in any of the messages is TEMPNAME, it also means something went wrong. When you add a load module to a library (DISP = MOD on the SYLMOD DD statement), and one already exists in the library with the same name, the linkage editor adds the new member under the name TEMPNAME.

C. Batch Compilation

Compilation is not a function of the linkage editor. However, batch compilation requires special control statements in some language processors, and this is a natural place to describe them. With batch compilation, a single compilation step can compile a main program and several subroutines. Batch compilation is requested as follows.

- Assembler Language. The assembler does not do batch compilation. Each program or subroutine must be assembled in a separate step.
- COBOL. The BATCH option must be specified as a PARM of the compile step and a CBL statement must precede each program or subroutine.

```
// EXEC COBUCLG,PARM.COB=BATCH
//COB.SYSIN DD *
CBL                          (Begins in column 1)
    [ main program ]
CBL
    [ subroutine ]
   . . .
```

- FORTRAN. Batch compilation does not require any special control statements. Simply place all the FORTRAN programs, functions, or subroutines together to compile.
- PL/I. A PROCESS statement must follow each program or external procedure.

```
// EXEC PLIXCLG
//PLI.SYSIN DD *
    [ main program ]
* PROCESS                    (Begins in column 1)
    [ external procedure ]
* PROCESS
   . . .
```

D. Linkage Editor Control Statements

Several linkage editor control statements may be included for special processing. (Some statements that are rarely used have been omitted.) The linkage editor control statements can be placed before or after any object modules or other control statements. The control statements are used to combine, delete, replace, rearrange, and order control sections.

The linkage editor control statements are coded in columns 2 to 71. To continue a linkage editor control statement, interrupt the statement after a comma anywhere before column 72, code a nonblank character in column 72, and continue in column 16 of the next line. The following example illustrates a continued statement.

```
    INCLUDE INPUT,                                          X
            DD2 (ONE, TWO)
```

1. ENTRY statement

The ENTRY statement specifies the first instruction to be executed in a load module. It can be a control section name or entry name within a control section. Each load module must have an entry point. If the ENTRY statement is omitted, the system assumes the first byte of the first control section is the entry point—unless an assembler-produced END statement specifies an entry point. The ENTRY statement is coded as:

```
ENTRY name
    [ The name must be the name of an instruction, not data. ENTRY
    must begin in column 2 or beyond. ]
ENTRY SUB1
    [ Execution begins at SUB1. ]
```

The entry names for the various language processors are:

Assembler	CSECT name
COBOL	PROGRAM-ID name
FORTRAN	MAIN
PL/I	PLISTART

The entry point is not retained if the load module is link edited again. If the main routine is not the first routine in the load module, the ENTRY statement must be included each time the load module is link edited.

2. INCLUDE statement

The INCLUDE statement specifies additional sources of linkage editor input to be included. The included data can also contain an INCLUDE statement, but no data following the INCLUDE statement in the inserted data set is processed.

INCLUDE is most often used to include an old load module when subroutines within it must be recompiled and link edited. The linkage editor first processes the new subroutine and then includes all the old load module except the replaced subroutines. The INCLUDE can be coded in two ways.

- For a sequential data set:

```
INCLUDE ddname,ddname,...,ddname
```

- For a partitioned data set:

```
INCLUDE ddname(member,...,member),ddname(...),...
```

The *ddname* is the name of a DD statement describing the data to include. It can be either a partitioned or sequential data set containing both object modules and control statements, or a partitioned data set containing just load modules. Many INCLUDE statements are permitted. A member name must be coded for all members to be included from a library. Code just the ddname for sequential data sets.

```
INCLUDE INPUT1,DD1
INCLUDE INPUT2,DD2(ONE,TWO),DD3(SQRT)
        [ Three sequential data sets described by the INPUT1, DD1, and
        INPUT2 DD statements are included.  Members ONE and TWO are
        also included from the library described by the DD2
        statement, and member SQRT is included from the library
        described by DD3. ]
```

The sequence of data sets and modules in the load module that is created does not necessarily follow the order of the INCLUDE statements. The ORDER statement described later can specify the order.

3.   LIBRARY statement

The LIBRARY statement names control sections to be looked up in libraries other than the libraries described by the SYSLIB DD statement. LIBRARY also allows external references to go unresolved for a particular run or for the life of the load module. (The NCAL option on the EXEC statement cancels all automatic call lookups.) The LIBRARY statement can be coded in the following ways.

```
LIBRARY ddname(member,...,member),ddname(..),...
        [ A DD statement with the given ddname must be included
        to describe the library.  The member names of each control
        section to look up in the library must be given. ]

LIBRARY (name,...,name)
        [ The control sections named are left unresolved for the run--
        no automatic call lookup takes place for the named control
        sections.  For example, a subroutine in a library might be
        referred to in a program but might not be called during a
        particular run.  Since the subroutine will not be called, the
        reference can be left unresolved to save storage by not
        loading the subroutine.  (LET should also be coded on the
        EXEC statement.) ]

LIBRARY *(name,...,name)
        [ The asterisk appended to the names causes the external
        references to go unresolved for the entire life of the load
        module. ]
```

The above parameters can all be coded on one or several LIBRARY statements.

```
LIBRARY DD1(SUB1,SUB2),(HALT),*(ALTO)
        [ SUB1 and SUB2 are looked up in the library described by the
        DD1 DD statement.  No automatic subroutine lookup is made for
        HALT or ALTO.  Furthermore, ALTO is left unresolved for the
        life of the load module. ]
```

4.   NAME statement

The NAME statement marks the end of a load module, names it, and permits several load modules to be produced by a single link edit step. NAME is often used to create a subroutine library. Several subroutines can be compiled together, with each subroutine added to the library as a separate load module. Place the NAME statement after the last object module that is to be included in the load module. Any ENTRY statements must precede the NAME statement. The NAME statement is coded as:

```
NAME name     or    NAME name(R)
```

Any name can be selected for the load module, but since that name is the one matched in the library lookup, use the subroutine name. The (R) is coded if the subroutine replaces an existing subroutine in the load module. If (R) is omitted for a replacement module, the new module is added and renamed TEMPNAME.

```
NAME SUB1
     [ SUB1 is added. ]
NAME SUB2(R)
     [ SUB2 is replaced. ]
```

5. REPLACE statement

The REPLACE statement replaces one control section with another, or deletes a control section. Control sections are automatically replaced if the new control section has the same name as the old control section. REPLACE can replace an old control section with one having a different name. To replace a control section, place the REPLACE statement immediately before the module or INCLUDE statement containing the old control section. Name the old and new control sections with the REPLACE statement as follows:

```
REPLACE old-name(new-name)
     [ The old-name is replaced by the control section
     following it. The control section is assigned the new-name. ]
```

To delete a control section, code REPLACE as follows:

```
REPLACE name
```

6. PAGE statement (MVS only)

The PAGE statement aligns a control section on a 4K page boundary. PAGE is coded as follows:

```
PAGE name,name, ... ,name
```

7. ORDER statement

The ORDER statement reorders the control sections in a load module. Normally the control sections are left in the order in which they are encountered. Paging is more efficient if the control sections are ordered to minimize paging. The ORDER statement orders the control sections in the order in which the names are listed on the statement. Any names not appearing on the ORDER statement are placed last. There may be multiple ORDER statements. The general form is:

```
ORDER name,name, ... ,name
```

To align a control section on a 4K page boundary, code the names as follows:

```
ORDER name(P),name(P),...,name(P)
```

Two other control statements, the INSERT and OVERLAY, are used for overlay structures and are described in the following section.

E.   Creating Program Libraries

Suppose now that a COBOL program is to be compiled and retained in a data set named PROGRAM. A member name must be selected with from one to eight alphanumeric (A to Z, 0 to 9) or national (@ $ #) characters, beginning with an alphabetic (A to Z) or national character. Perhaps THING is an appropriate name. The COBUCLG cataloged procedure can be used, but we must override the SYS-LMOD DD statement to create the nontemporary data set.

```
// EXEC COBUCLG,PARM.COB=BATCH
//COB.SYSIN DD *
CBL
     [ MAIN source statements ]
CBL
     [ SUB1 source statements ]
CBL
     [ SUB2 source statements ]
/*
//LKED.SYSLMOD DD DSN=PROGRAM(THING),DISP=(NEW,CATLG),UNIT=SYSDA,
//              VOL=SER=PACK12,SPACE=(1024,(100,30,10))
     [ The PROGRAM data set is created. and the load module is
     added as a member named THING.  The SPACE parameter is also
     overridden to allocate a more precise amount of space and to
     enlarge the directory space. ]
//GO.IN DD DSN=JUNK,DISP=SHR
     [ Any DD statements for the GO step are placed here. ]
```

Three routines, MAIN, SUB1, and SUB2 are combined into a load module named THING in the PROGRAM data set. Several other programs could be placed in PROGRAM as long as they are given different member names. The program can now be executed in a single step.

```
//GO EXEC PGM=THING
//STEPLIB DD DSN=PROGRAM,DISP=SHR
     [ The STEPLIB DD statement describes the data set containing
     the program to execute.  The JOBLIB DD statement could have
     been used as well. ]
//IN DD DSN=JUNK,DISP=SHR
```

Now suppose that SUB1 contains an error and must be replaced. We can replace SUB1 as follows:

```
// EXEC COBUCLG
//COB.SYSIN DD *
     [ SUB1 source statements ]
/*
//LKED.SYSLMOD DD DSN=PROGRAM(THING),DISP=SHR,SPACE=,UNIT=
     [ SYLMOD is again overridden to describe the data set that is
     to contain the new load module.  Since THING is already a
     member of PROGRAM, it is replaced by the new load module.  By
     selecting a different name, the new load module would be
     added rather than replace the old load module.  The SPACE=
     parameter is coded to nullify the SPACE parameter on the
     overridden SYSLMOD statement so that it does not change the
     secondary allocation specified when PROGRAM was created.  The
     UNIT= is written because we want the system to locate the
     data set from the catalog. ]
//LKED.DD1 DD DSN=PROGRAM,DISP=SHR
     [ The DD1 statement describes the library containing the old
     load module. ]
//LKED.SYSIN DD *
  ENTRY THING
     [ The main routine is no longer loaded first, and so we must
     tell the linkage editor that THING is the entry point. ]
  INCLUDE DD1(THING)
     [ The old load module is included as additional input. ]
/*
//GO.IN DD DSN=JUNK,DISP=SHR
```

F. Overlay Structures

If a program is too large to fit into storage (which should rarely occur with virtual storage), the linkage editor can separate the program into several segments, each small enough to fit. Each segment is then loaded into storage as needed, overlaying the previous segment. Don't do overlays unless you absolutely must.

1. Segmenting the program

A *segment* is the smallest unit of a program (one or more control sections) that can be loaded as one logical entity during program execution. The *root segment* (first segment) is that portion of the program which must remain in storage throughout execution. If your entire program must be in storage during execution, it cannot be segmented or overlaid.

A program is segmented by following the flow of control within the program to determine the dependencies among the subroutines. For example, suppose that a program reads some input, performs some processing, and finally prints the results. We can break this program into the following four segments.

1. A root segment containing the program's main routine.
2. A segment containing subroutines that read the input.
3. A segment containing subroutines that perform the processing.
4. A segment containing subroutines that print the results.

The following diagram, called an *overlay tree structure*, illustrates the program's structure. (Multiple structures are possible but are rarely needed.) The main routine calls the read routines, causing the first segment to be loaded. When the main routine calls the processing subroutines, they overlay the read routines. The output subroutines will in turn overlay the processing subroutines as shown in Figure 56.

Each vertical line in the diagram represents a segment. Figure 57 illustrates a more complex program with nine segments.

S1 through S11 represent subroutines (S1 would be the main routine), and the tree structure shows the segmentation. If we follow down the tree structure, say from S1 to S2 to S5, without backtracking, we establish a *path*. Segments in a path can all be in storage at the same time, and a subroutine can call only other subroutines in its path; that is, S3 can call S4, but not S5; whereas S2 can call S3, S4, or S5.

2. OVERLAY statement

The OVERLAY statement describes the overlay structure to the linkage editor. Begin by naming the origin of each segment (the horizontal lines on the tree structure). The names are arbitrary from one to eight alphanumeric (A to Z, 0 to 9) characters, the first of which must be alphabetic (A to Z). The names FIRST, SECOND, THIRD, and FOURTH are chosen for the example as shown in Figure 58.

The OVERLAY statement is coded as:

```
OVERLAY name
```

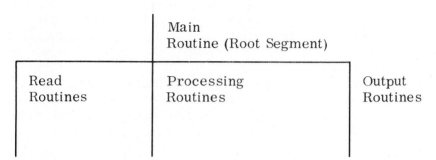

Figure 56. Simple overlay structure

The *name* is the name of the segment origin, that is, FIRST, SECOND, THIRD, or FOURTH in our example. The normal JCL for an OVERLAY consists of the following:

```
// EXEC procedure,PARM.LKED=OVLY
     [ The procedure is any cataloged procedure with a link edit
     step. ]
     .      .     .      .     .
//LKED.SYSIN DD *
     [ OVERLAY statements, object decks, or other linkage editor
     control statements. ]
/*
     .      .     .      .     .
```

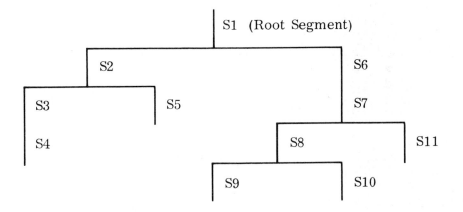

Figure 57. Overlay structure with nine segments

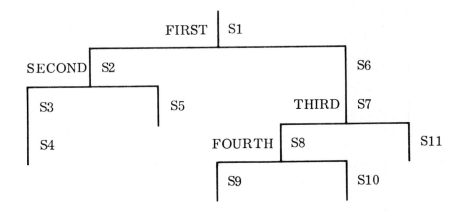

Figure 58. Sample overlay structure

The PARM.LKED = OVLY parameter tells the linkage editor that OVERLAY statements follow. To arrange the object modules and OVERLAY statements, follow down the paths of the tree structure and describe each segment by an OVERLAY statement, followed by the appropriate object module or INCLUDE statement. Work from top to bottom and left to right. An example of the above tree structure can clarify this simple process.

```
//LKED.SYSIN DD *
   INCLUDE S1
   OVERLAY FIRST
   INCLUDE S2
   OVERLAY SECOND
   INCLUDE S3, S4
   OVERLAY SECOND
   INCLUDE S5
   OVERLAY FIRST
   INCLUDE S6,S7
   OVERLAY THIRD
   INCLUDE S8
   OVERLAY FOURTH
   INCLUDE S9
   OVERLAY FOURTH
   INCLUDE S10
   OVERLAY THIRD
   INCLUDE S11
/*
```

3.   INSERT statement

It is often inconvenient to insert control sections physically after the appropriate OVERLAY statements. Rather than rearranging the control sections themselves, you can put the control sections anywhere in the primary input and then use the INSERT statement to tell the linkage editor how to arrange them.

Place an INSERT statement naming the control sections after the OVERLAY statement defining the segment in which they are to appear. Place the INSERT statement before any OVERLAY statements if the control section belongs in the root segment. INSERT is coded as:

```
INSERT name,name,...,name
```

The control sections named are inserted wherever the INSERT statement is placed. The control sections can be object modules passed from a previous compilation step, object decks, or object and load modules brought in by an INCLUDE statement. The control sections themselves can appear anywhere in the primary input— before or after the INSERT statement. If the control sections named on the INSERT statement are not found in the primary input, the automatic library search mechanism is used.

The following example illustrates the use of INSERT and INCLUDE statements in segmenting the program in the preceding example. Assume S6 is contained in a sequential data set named SUBS, that S3 and S8 are passed from a compilation step, and the remaining control sections are contained in a partitioned data set MORSUBS.

```
// EXEC COBUCLG,PARM.COB=BATCH,PARM.LKED=OVLY
     [ The COBOL compile, link edit, and go procedure is invoked. ]
//COB.SYSIN DD *
CBL
     [ S3 source statements ]
CBL
     [ S8 source statements ]
/*
//LKED.DD1 DD DSN=SUBS,DISP=SHR
     [ A DD statement is included for SUBS. ]
//LKED.DD2 DD DSN=MORSUBS,DISP=SHR
     [ MORSUBS must also be defined. ]
//LKED.SYSIN DD *
  INCLUDE S1,S2,S4,S5,S7,S9,DD2(S10,S11)
     [ Include the primary input. ]
  INSERT S1
  OVERLAY FIRST
  INSERT S2
  OVERLAY SECOND
  INSERT S3,S4
  OVERLAY SECOND
  INSERT S5
  OVERLAY FIRST
  INCLUDE DD1      <== SUBS is included here.
  INSERT S7
  OVERLAY THIRD
  INSERT S8
  OVERLAY FOURTH
  INSERT S9
  OVERLAY FOURTH
  INSERT S10
  OVERLAY THIRD
  INSERT S11
/*
```

The overlay structure is not retained when the load module is link edited again. Consequently, the OVERLAY and INSERT statements must be included each time the load module is link edited.

G. *Compressing Partitioned Data Sets*

Partitioned data sets tend to grow as new members are added and old members replaced. Both new and replacement members are added to the end of the data set, and the name is entered into the directory along with the location where the member was stored. Remember that a replacement member does not occupy the same space as the old member—the space occupied by the old member is unavailable for allocation until the set is recreated or compressed. As members are added and replaced, the data set may become full. The IBM-supplied utility IEBCOPY compresses data sets to reclaim space occupied by replaced members. See Chapter 15 for a description of how to compress a partitioned data set.

II. THE LOADER

The loader performs all the functions of the linkage editor except for producing a load module. It combines the link edit and go steps into a single load and go step. The advantage of the loader is that it saves roughly half the cost of the linkage editor step. The loader does not create an object module, but builds the executable program in real storage. Consequently, the loader has no SYSLMOD DD statement, and any linkage editor control statements are ignored.

The JCL to execute the loader is illustrated in the following COBOL compile and GO procedure.

```
//COBUCG PROC
//COB EXEC PGM=IKFCBL00,REGION=128K
//SYSPRINT DD SYSOUT=A
//SYSLIN DD DSN=&&LOADSET,DISP=(MOD,PASS),
//          UNIT=SYSDA,SPACE=(80,(500,100))
//GO EXEC PGM=LOADER,PARM=(loader-options/program-options)
        [ The MAP, NCAL, and LET loader-options are identical to those
        of the linkage editor.  EP=name may be coded to
        specify the entry point.  Notice that the loader parameters
        are separated from the GO step parameters by the slash. ]
//SYSLIN   DD DSN=&&LOADSET,DISP=(OLD,DELETE)
//SYSLOUT DD SYSOUT=A
        [ SYSLOUT is used for error and warning messages. ]
//SYSLIB   DD DSN=SYS1.COBLIB,DISP=SHR
        [ Other libraries may be concatenated for automatic library
        search. ]
```

This procedure might be executed as follows:

```
// EXEC COBUCLG,PARM=MAP
        [ The slash may be omitted if no parameters are passed to the
        GO step. ]
//GO.ddname DD ...
        [ Any DD statement required by the program are placed here. ]
```

EXERCISES

1. Compile the program from Chapter 5 using the PLIXCLG procedure and create a partitioned data set named PGMS, adding the program as a member named COPY.

2. Make up an in-stream procedure to execute the COPY program. Execute the in-stream procedure to ensure that the program works correctly.

3. Add the following subroutine to PGMS as a member named SUB. Use the PLIXCL procedure.

```
SUB: PROC;
 PUT SKIP LIST('I HAVE BEGUN');
 END SUB;
```

4. Modify the program from Chapter 5 to add one statement calling the subroutine SUB as shown:

```
TEST: PROC OPTIONS(MAIN);
 CALL SUB;
```

Recompile the modified program and replace member COPY in PGMS with it. Include the member SUBS. Execute this new program with the in-stream procedure to make sure that it works correctly.

Chapter 15

IBM UTILITY PROGRAMS

The IBM-supplied utility programs provide a variety of useful functions, such as copying data sets, listing them, and maintaining source libraries. Although not a part of JCL, they are an important part of System/370, and a knowledge of them is important to all programmers.

The utility programs described in this chapter are not used for VSAM files. The Access Method Services (AMS) programs described in Chapter 18 must be used for VSAM files. The AMS programs may also be used for non-VSAM files and perform many of the same functions as the utility programs in this chapter.

When they were written a quarter of a century ago, the utility programs were anything but user friendly and they have gone virtually unchanged since then. Because they are so difficult to use, most people use an alternative when it is available, such as DYL-280 (DYL-280 is a product of Stirling Software, Dylakor Division, Chattsworth, CA.), the utility feature of ISPF/PDF, or TSO. The utility programs are used when there is no alternative and when it is necessary to perform a function that will run on all OS installations. For example, most data sets and applications mailed from one installation to another use the IBM utility programs for their installation because the utility programs are a part of the operating system and all installations have them.

Some of the utility programs perform limited functions for the operators or systems programmers and these are omitted. Some features of the utility programs in VS1 are not supported in MVS and they are also omitted. The following utility programs are described:

IEHPROGM	Data set maintenance.
IEBGENER	Copy sequential data sets.
IEBCOPY	Copy and compress partitioned data sets.
IEHMOVE	Copy or move sequential, partitioned, or direct data sets.
IEBPTPCH	Print or punch data sets.
IEBUPDTE	Maintain source libraries.
IEHLIST	List direct-access volume information.

The utility programs are executed by the same general JCL statements.

```
//stepname EXEC PGM=program-name
//SYSPRINT DD SYSOUT=A
     [ Prints the utility messages. ]
//SYSUT1    DD ...
     [ If needed, describes an input data set. ]
//SYSUT2    DD ...
     [ If needed, describes an output data set. ]
//SYSIN DD *
     [ control statements ]
/*
```

The control statements must be coded in columns 2 to 71. To continue a control statement, break the statement at a comma, code a nonblank character in column 72, and continue the statement in column 16 of the following line. The following example illustrates a continued statement:

```
PRINT TYPORG=PO,STOPAFT=100,                                          X
                 SKIP=3
```

I. IEHPROGM: DATA SET MAINTENANCE

IEHPROGM performs the following functions:

- Scratches data sets residing on direct-access volumes. Also scratches members of partitioned data sets.
- Renames a data set residing on a direct-access volume, or a member of a partitioned data set.
- Catalogs or uncatalogs a data set.
- Builds or deletes a catalog index.
- Builds or deletes a generation index.

The ISPF/PDF utilities can do most of what IEHPROGM does and are much easier to use. Generally, you should need to use IEHPROGM only for performing the utility functions with a batch job. IEHPROGM has the following general form:

```
//stepname EXEC PGM=IEHPROGM
//SYSPRINT DD SYSOUT=A
//ddname    DD VOL=REF=SYS1.SVCLIB,DISP=OLD
     [ One DD statement must be included to point to a permanently
     mounted direct-access volume.  Since SYS1.SVCLIB resides on
     the system residence volume and must be permanently mounted,
     the DD statement refers to it. ]
//ddname DD UNIT=device,VOL=SER=volume,DISP=OLD
     [ A DD statement must be included to point to each volume
     referenced in the control statements. ]
//SYSIN DD *
     [ control statements ]
/*
```

Several control statements may be included:

```
SCRATCH DSNAME=dsname,VOL=device=volume,PURGE
     [ Scratches a data set on a direct-access volume.  PURGE is
     required only for data sets whose retention date has not
     expired.  The data set is not uncataloged.  The device is the
     same as the UNIT=device, and the volume is the same as
     the VOL=SER=volume.  Thus you could code
     VOL=SYSDA=PACK12. ]
SCRATCH DSNAME=dsname,VOL=device=volume,PURGE,MEMBER=member
     [ Scratch a member of a partitioned data set.  PURGE is
     required only for data sets whose retention date has not
     expired. ]
RENAME DSNAME=old-dsname,VOL=device=volume,NEWNAME=new-dsname
     [ Rename a direct-access data set.  Note that the catalog
     entry is not changed. ]
RENAME DSNAME=old-dsname,VOL=device=volume,                      X
                MEMBER=old-member,                               X
                NEWNAME=new-member
     [ Renames a member of a partitioned data set. ]
CATLG DSNAME=dsname,VOL=device=volume
     [ Catalogs a data set. ]
UNCATLG DSNAME=dsname
     [ Uncatalogs a data set. ]
```

The BLDX, DLTX, and BLDL statements that follow cannot be coded in MVS. For MVS, use the AMS program described in Chapter 18.

```
BLDX INDEX=index
     [ Build a new index in the catalog.  (Not in MVS.)  If
     higher-level indexes are required, they are created.  The
     index is the fully qualified name of the index to
     create, and cannot exceed 44 characters. ]

DLTX INDEX=index
     [ Removes an index from the catalog.  (Not in MVS.)  Only an
     index that has no catalog entries can be removed.  The
     index is the fully-qualified index name. ]

BLDG INDEX=index,ENTRIES=n,EMPTY,DELETE
     [ Build a generation index.  (Not in MVS.)  The index is
     a 1- to 35-character qualified name of the generation index.
     ENTRIES=n specifies the number of entries (1 to 255) to
     be contained in the generation index.  EMPTY is an option to
     specify that all entries are to be removed from the
     generation index when it overflows.  If EMPTY is omitted, the
     entries with the largest generation numbers will be
     maintained in the catalog when the generation index
     overflows.  DELETE is an option to scratch generation data
     sets after their entries are removed from the index.  If
     DELETE is omitted, the data sets are not scratched. ]
```

The following example scratches a data set named JUNK residing on PACK12, and member MONTANA from a partitioned data set named STATE residing on PACK14.

```
//STEP1 EXEC PGM=IEHPROGM
//SYSPRINT DD SYSOUT=A
//DDA      DD VOL=REF=SYS1.SVCLIB,DISP=OLD
//DDB      DD UNIT=SYSDA,VOL=SER=PACK12,DISP=OLD
//DDC      DD UNIT=SYSDA,VOL=SER=PACK14,DISP=OLD
```

```
//SYSIN    DD *
  SCRATCH DSNAME=JUNK,VOL=SYSDA=PACK12
  SCRATCH DSNAME=STATE,VOL=SYSDA=PACK14,MEMBER=MONTANA
/*
```

The next example renames a cataloged data set named JUNK to STUFF.

```
//STEP1 EXEC PGM=IEHPROGM
//SYSPRINT DD SYSOUT=A
//DDA       DD VOL=REF=SYS1.SVCLIB,DISP=OLD
//DDB       DD UNIT=SYSDA,VOL=SER=PACK12,DISP=OLD
//SYSIN     DD *
  RENAME DSNAME=JUNK,VOL=SYSDA=PACK12,NEWNAME=STUFF
  UNCATLG DSNAME=JUNK
  CATLG DSNAME=STUFF,VOL=SYSDA=PACK12
/*
```

II. IEBGENER: COPY SEQUENTIAL DATA SETS

IEBGENER performs the following functions:

- Copies a sequential data set from any device to any device.
- May reblock the data set.

One weakness with IEBGENER is that it does not produce an audit trail. Since it does not tell you how many records it copied, you must trust that the data set was copied. DYL280 performs many of the functions of IEBGENER and produces an audit trail. If DYL280 is available, you should consider using it. IEBGENER has the following general form:

```
//stepname EXEC PGM=IEBGENER
//SYSPRINT DD SYSOUT=A
//SYSUT1    DD ...
     [ SYSUT1 describes the input data set.  It may be
     concatenated. ]
//SYSUT2    DD ...
     [ SYSUT2 describes the output data set.  The DCB parameters
     are copied from the SYSUT1 data set if the DCB parameter is
     not coded. ]
//SYSIN     DD DUMMY
     [ Since there are no control statements, SYSIN is made a dummy
     data set. ]
```

The following example copies a disk data set named JUNK to tape number 2345, reblocking the output.

```
//STEP1 EXEC PGM=IEBGENER
//SYSPRINT DD SYSOUT=A
//SYSUT1    DD DSN=JUNK,DISP=SHR
//SYSUT2    DD DSN=JUNK,DISP=(NEW,KEEP),UNIT=TAPE9,VOL=SER=002345,
//             DCB=(RECFM=FB,LRECL=80,BLKSIZE=8000)
```

The following DD statements may be coded for input and output.

```
Control statement:     //SYSUT1 DD *
Card output:           //SYSUT2 DD SYSOUT=B,DCB=BLKSIZE=80
Printed output:        //SYSUT2 DD SYSOUT=A,DCB=BLKSIZE=n
    [ The n may be 1 to the printer's maximum line width. ]
```

- Member of a partitioned data set input:

```
//SYSUT1 DD DSN=PGM(TEST),DISP=SHR
```

- Add a member to a partitioned data set for output:

```
//SYSUT2 DD DSN=LIB(THING),DISP=OLD
```

III. IEBCOPY: COPY PARTITIONED DATA SETS

IEBCOPY performs the following functions:

- Copies a partitioned data set to a direct-access volume. Often used to expand the space allocation or change the directory space.
- Copies a partitioned data set, converting it to a sequential data set (termed *unloading*). Used to save a partitioned data set on tape or to create a backup copy.
- Copies an unloaded partitioned data set to a direct-access volume (termed *loading*). Used to restore a partitioned data set from tape.
- Copies a partitioned data set in place to reclaim the space occupied by deleted members. (This is called compressing the data set.)

ISPF/PDF performs many of the functions of IEBCOPY and is much easier to use. If it is available, you are usually better off using it than IEBCOPY. IEBCOPY has the following general form:

```
//stepname EXEC PGM=IEBCOPY
//SYSPRINT   DD SYSOUT=A
//SYSUT3     DD UNIT=device,SPACE=(TRK,(1,1))
//SYSUT4     DD UNIT=device,SPACE=(TRK,(1,1))
    [ SYSUT3 and SYSUT4 are work data sets. ]
//in-ddname  DD DSN=old-dsname,DISP=SHR
    [ Points to the input data set.  Cannot be concatenated. ]
//out-ddname DD DSN=new-dsname,DISP=(..),
```

```
//                    UNIT=device,VOL=SER=volume,SPACE=(..)
       [ Describes the output data set. ]
//SYSIN      DD *
  COPY INDD=in-ddname,OUTDD=out-ddname
/*
```

For all but the compress operation, you can increase the space allocated to the output data set or reblock it. If the DCB parameter is not coded on the *out-ddname* DD statement, the blocking is unchanged. The data set is reblocked by specifying the BLKSIZE subparameter.

A. Unload a Partitioned Data Set

The following example assumes that a cataloged partitioned data set named TEST is to be unloaded to tape number 2345.

```
//STEP1 EXEC PGM=IEBCOPY
//SYSPRINT DD SYSOUT=A
//SYSUT3    DD UNIT=SYSDA,SPACE=(TRK,(2,2))
//SYSUT4    DD UNIT=SYSDA,SPACE=(TRK,(2,2))
//IN        DD DSN=TEST,DISP=SHR
//OUT       DD DSN=TEST,DISP=(NEW,KEEP),UNIT=TAPE9,VOL=SER=002345
//SYSIN     DD *
  COPY INDD=IN,OUTDD=OUT
/*
```

B. Load a Partitioned Data Set

The following example loads the TEST data set from tape to disk volume PACK12. Assume that TEST does not already exist on PACK12.

```
//STEP1 EXEC PGM=IEBCOPY
//SYSPRINT DD SYSOUT=A
//SYSUT3    DD UNIT=SYSDA,SPACE=(TRK,(2,2))
//SYSUT4    DD UNIT=SYSDA,SPACE=(TRK,(2,2))
//IN        DD DSN=TEST,DISP=OLD,UNIT=TAPE9,VOL=SER=002345
//OUT       DD DSN=TEST,DISP=(NEW,CATLG),
//             UNIT=SYSDA,VOL=SER=PACK12,SPACE=(TRK,(10,5,10))
//SYSIN     DD *
  COPY INDD=IN,OUTDD=OUT
/*
```

C. Copy a Partitioned Data Set as a Partitioned Data Set

The following example copies the TEST data set from PACK12 to PACK10, expanding the directory space.

```
//STEP1 EXEC PGM=IEBCOPY
//SYSPRINT DD SYSOUT=A
//SYSUT3   DD UNIT=SYSDA,SPACE=(TRK,(1,1))
//SYSUT4   DD UNIT=SYSDA,SPACE=(TRK,(1,1))
//IN       DD DSN=TEST,DISP=SHR
//OUT      DD DSN=$$$$$$$$,DISP=(NEW,KEEP),
     [ The copy of TEST is given a unique name. ]
//            UNIT=SYSDA,VOL=SER=PACK10,SPACE=(TRK,(10,5,20),RLSE)
//SYSIN    DD *
   COPY INDD=IN,OUTDD=OUT
/*
```

The next step scratches TEST and renames the copy.

```
//STEP2 EXEC PGM=IEHPROGM,COND=(0,NE,STEP1)
//SYSPRINT DD SYSOUT=A
//DD1      DD DSN=*.STEP1.IN,DISP=OLD,VOL=REF=*.STEP1.IN
//DD2      DD DSN=*.STEP1.OUT,DISP=OLD,VOL=REF=*.STEP1.OUT
//SYSIN    DD *
   UNCATLG DSNAME=TEST
   SCRATCH DSNAME,TEST,VOL=SYSDA=PACK12
   RENAME DSNAME=$$$$$$$$,VOL=SYSDA=PACK10,NEWNAME=TEST
   CATLG DSNAME=TEST,VOL=SYSDA=PACK10
/*
```

D. Select and Exclude Members in a Copy

In all of the previous copy operations, the SELECT statement can select specific members to copy, or the EXCLUDE statement can select specific members to exclude from a copy. SELECT and EXCLUDE are mutually exclusive. SELECT or EXCLUDE is placed immediately after the COPY statement.

```
COPY INDD=...
SELECT MEMBER=(member,member,...,member)
     [ Only the named members are copied. ]

SELECT MEMBER=((member,newname),...)
     [ The member is copied and assigned a new name. ]

SELECT MEMBER=((member,,R),...)
     [ The copied member replaces an identically named member in
     the output data set. ]


EXCLUDE MEMBER=(member,member,...,member)
     [ All members except those named are copied. ]
```

E. Compress a Partitioned Data Set

SELECT and EXCLUDE cannot be coded for a compress operation. The following example compresses the TEST data set. The input and output data sets are the same.

```
//STEP1 EXEC PGM=IEBCOPY
//SYSPRINT DD SYSOUT=A
//SYSUT3    DD UNIT=SYSDA,SPACE=(TRK,(1,1))
//SYSUT4    DD UNIT=SYSDA,SPACE=(TRK,(1,1))
//INOUT     DD DSN=TEST,DISP=OLD
//SYSIN     DD *
  COPY INDD=INOUT,OUTDD=INOUT
/*
```

To release any excess space, code the INOUT DD statement as:

```
//INOUT DD DSN=TEST,DISP=OLD,SPACE=(,,RLSE)
```

IV. IEHMOVE: COPY OR MOVE DATA SETS

IEHMOVE performs the following functions:

- Copies or moves data sets. It can copy or move from one type of I/O device to another. A move differs from a copy in that the move scratches the original data set after the copy, and any catalog entry is updated to point to the new copy.
- Copies or moves sequential, partitioned, or direct data sets.
- Automatically allocates space for the new data set.
- Reblocks the copied or moved data set if requested.
- Copies or moves groups of data sets that have the same qualified names.

In some ways IEHMOVE is redundant to IEBCOPY and IEBGENER, but is more powerful than either. Its main advantage is that you need not specify the space allocation of the copied or moved data set because IEHMOVE allocates space based on the size of the old data set. IEHMOVE can also copy data set groups, which, if you follow a naming convention, permits all related data sets to be copied or moved together. IEHMOVE has the following general form:

```
//stepname EXEC PGM=IEHMOVE
//SYSPRINT DD SYSOUT=A
//SYSUT1    DD UNIT=device,VOL=SER=volume,DISP=OLD
     [ Points to a direct-access volume that must contain about 50
     tracks of work space. ]
//ddname    DD VOL=REF=SYS1.SVCLIB,DISP=OLD
     [ One DD statement must point to a permanently mounted volume.
     Since SYS1.SVCLIB resides on the system residence volume
     which must be permanently mounted, referring to it
     accomplishes this. ]
//tape      DD DSN=dsname,DISP=(..,KEEP),UNIT=device,VOL=SER=volume,
//          L LABEL=(file,type),DCB=(..)
     [ If a data set is copied to or from a tape volume, include a
     DD statement for each tape volume to supply the DCB
     parameters.  For an unloaded data set, code DCB=LRECL=80. ]
```

```
//ddname    DD UNIT=device,VOL=SER=volume,DISP=OLD
     [ One or more DD statements pointing to direct-access volumes
       referred to by the subsequent control statements. ]
//SYSIN     DD *
     [ control statements ]
/*
```

If IEHMOVE copies or moves data sets to a direct-access volume, it determines the amount of space required from the original data set, taking into consideration the different track capacities of the devices. When data sets are copied or moved to tape, the space requirement is also saved on tape so that if the tape data set is copied or moved back to a direct-access volume, IEHMOVE can still allocate the space.

Alternatively, space can be preallocated. IEHMOVE will use this space rather than allocating the space. Preallocate the space with the IEFBR14 null program. To change the blocking of a partitioned data set, preallocate the space with the new DCB parameters. For a tape data set, an existing data set must be rewritten with DISP =OLD.

To move or copy multiple volume data sets, list all the volumes on the DD statement. The following DD statement indicates that the data set is contained on two tape volumes.

```
//DD1 DD UNIT=TAPE9,VOL=SER=(003322,003323),...
```

To specify the file number of a tape volume, code the FROM or TO options on the control statements as follows:

```
FROM=device=(volume,file#)
TO=device=(volume,file#)
TO=TAPE9=(003322,3)
     [ Specifies file 3 on tape 003322. ]
```

A. COPY/MOVE DSNAME

The COPY/MOVE DSNAME statements copy or move sequential data sets. They are coded as follows:

```
COPY DSNAME=dsname,FROM=device=volume,TO=device=volume
```

```
MOVE DSNAME=dsname,FROM=device=volume,TO=device=volume
```

- DSNAME=*dsname* specifies the name of the data set to move or copy.
- FROM=*device*=*volume* specifies the device type and volume serial number upon which the original data set resides. Omit the FROM option if the data set is cataloged.
- TO=*device*=*volume* specifies the device type and volume serial number to which the data set is moved or copied.

The following options may also be coded on the COPY or MOVE statements:

- FROMDD = *tape* is coded for tape input volumes. It names a DD statement from which to copy the DCB and LABEL information.
- TODD = *tape* is coded for tape output volumes. It names a DD statement from which to copy the DCB and LABEL information.
- UNCATLG uncatalogs the original data set. UNCATLG is ignored if the FROM option is coded.
- CATLG catalogs the new data set and can only be used with a copy.
- RENAME = *new-dsname* renames the new data set.

The following example copies the SEQT disk data set residing on PACK15 to file 2 of tape 003322.

```
//STEP1 EXEC PGM=IEHMOVE
//SYSPRINT DD SYSOUT=A
//SYSUT1    DD UNIT=SYSDA,VOL=SER=PACK12,DISP=OLD
//DDA       DD VOL=REF=SYS1.SVCLIB,DISP=OLD
//DDB       DD UNIT=SYSDA,VOL=SER=PACK15,DISP=OLD
//DDC       DD DSN=SEQT,DISP=(NEW,KEEP),
//             UNIT=TAPE9,VOL=SER=003322,LABEL=2,DCB=(SEQT,DEN=3)
//SYSIN     DD *
   COPY DSNAME=SEQT,TO=TAPE9=(003322,2),TODD=DDC
/*
```

B. COPY/MOVE DSGROUP

A DSGROUP consists of all cataloged data sets that reside on the same direct-access volume and have the same name qualifications. For example, if cataloged data sets are named A.B.X, A.B.Y.Z, and A.C.W, DSGROUP = A would specify all three, and DSGROUP = A.B would specify the first two.

```
COPY DSGROUP=index,TO=device=volume
MOVE DSGROUP=index,TO=device=volume
```

- DSGROUP = *index* specifies the qualifier.
- TO = *device* = *volume* specifies the device type and volume to which the dsgroup is to be moved.

UNCATLG may also be coded to uncatalog the original data set, and CATLG can be specified for COPY to catalog the new data set. TODD = *tape* must be coded to copy or move to a tape volume. Each data set is copied onto a separate file. The DCB subparameters RECFM, LRECL, and BLKSIZE are ignored on the tape DD statement if they are coded. The DCB information is obtained from the copied data set.

The following example copies all data sets cataloged on PACK15 qualified by A.A0000 to tape 003322 and 003323. (Perhaps they will not fit on a single tape reel.)

```
//STEP1 EXEC PGM=IEHMOVE
//SYSPRINT DD SYSOUT=A
//SYSUT1   DD UNIT=SYSDA,VOL=SER=PACK12,DISP=OLD
//DDA      DD VOL=REF=SYS1.SVCLIB,DISP=OLD
//DDB      DD UNIT=SYSDA,VOL=SER=PACK15,DISP=OLD
//DDC      DD DSN=A.A0000,DISP=(NEW,KEEP),
//            UNIT=TAPE9,VOL=SER=(003322,003323),LABEL=1
//SYSIN    DD *
  COPY DSGROUP=A.A0000,TO=TAPE=003322
/*
```

If there are three data sets in the group, the first is copied into file one of the tape, the second into file two, and the third into file three.

C. COPY/MOVE PDS

The COPY/MOVE PDS statement copies or moves a partitioned data set. The partitioned data set is unloaded if moved or copied to a tape. Unloading converts the partitioned data set to 80-byte blocked records, enabling it to be stored as a sequential data set. When an unloaded partitioned data set is moved back to a direct-access volume by IEHMOVE, it is reconstituted as a partitioned data set. An unloaded partitioned data set must be loaded onto the same device type from which it was unloaded. The statements are coded as follows:

```
COPY PDS=dsname,FROM=device=volume,TO=device=volume
MOVE PDS=dsname,FROM=device=volume,TO=device=volume
```

- PDS = *dsname* names the partitioned data set to move or copy.
- FROM = *device* = *volume* describes the device and volume upon which the data set resides. Omit the FROM if the data set is cataloged.
- TO = *device* = *volume* describes the device and volume where the data set is moved.

The following options may also be coded:

- FROMDD = *tape* is coded for a tape input volume. It must contain an unloaded partitioned data set, and the DCB subparameters on the tape DD statement must be (RECFM = FB,LRECL = 80,BLKSIZE = ..).
- TODD = *tape* is coded for a tape output volume. The partitioned data set is unloaded onto it, and the DCB subparameters on the tape DD statement must be (RECFM = FB,LRECL = 80,BLKSIZE = ..).

- EXPAND = *nn* expands the partitioned data set directory to the number of directory blocks indicated by *nn*. You can also preallocate the space for the new copy and specify the directory space. EXPAND is ignored if the space is preallocated.
- UNCATLG uncatalogs the original data set. UNCATLG is ignored if the FROM option is coded.
- CATLG catalogs the new data set and can only be used for a COPY.
- RENAME = *new-dsname* renames the new data set.

The COPY/MOVE PDS statements may be followed by statements to include members from another partitioned data set, exclude or include selected members from the data set, or replace members of the original data set with members from another data set as they are copied.

1.   INCLUDE statement

The INCLUDE statement copies selected members from another partitioned data set or the entire data set. Several INCLUDE statements may be placed after the COPY/MOVE, and they are coded as follows:

```
INCLUDE DSNAME=dsname,MEMBER=member,FROM=device=volume
```

- DSNAME = *dsname* names the partitioned data set from which to copy the additional members. You must include a DD statement pointing to the volume containing the data set. Even if the operation is a MOVE, members of this data set are not scratched.
- MEMBER = *member* names the member to include. If omitted, all members are included.
- FROM = *device* = *volume* specifies the device type and volume containing the DSNAME data set. Omit the FROM option if the DSNAME data set is cataloged.

2.   EXCLUDE statement

The EXCLUDE statement excludes selected members from the copy or move. For a move, even the excluded members are scratched. There may be several EXCLUDE statements following the COPY/MOVE. They are coded as:

```
EXCLUDE MEMBER=member
      [ Names the members to exclude. ]
```

3.   SELECT statement

The SELECT statement selects specific members to copy. The members may also be renamed as they are copied. SELECT cannot be used with either the EXCLUDE or

REPLACE statements, and it cannot be used when a data set is unloaded or loaded. SELECT is coded as:

```
SELECT MEMBER=(member,member,...,member)
SELECT MEMBER=((member,new-name),..)
```

MEMBER names the members to copy. Only the named members are copied. If the *new-name* is coded, the copied member is renamed to this.

4.   REPLACE statement

The REPLACE statement excludes members from the copy and replaces the members with a member from another data set. The old and new members must have the same names. There can be several REPLACE statements, and REPLACE cannot be used for unloading or loading data sets. REPLACE is coded as:

```
REPLACE DSNAME=dsname,MEMBER=member,FROM=device=volume
```

- DSNAME = *dsname* names the partitioned data set containing the replacement member. Include a DD statement to point to the volume containing the data set.
- MEMBER = *member* names the member to replace.
- FROM = *device* = *volume* specifies the device type and volume containing the DSNAME data set. Omit the FROM option if the data set is cataloged.

The following example copies a data set named PDS from PACK12 to PACK14 and names it NEW.PDS. Members of ONE and TWO are replaced from a data set named OLD.PDS residing on PACK12.

```
//STEP1 EXEC PGM=IEHMOVE
//SYSPRINT DD SYSOUT=A
//SYSUT1   DD UNIT=SYSDA,VOL=SER=PACK12,DISP=OLD
//DDA      DD VOL=REF=SYS1.SVCLIB,DISP=OLD
//DDB      DD UNIT=SYSDA,VOL=SER=PACK10,DISP=OLD
//DDC      DD UNIT=SYSDA,VOL=SER=PACK12,DISP=OLD
//DDD      DD UNIT=SYSDA,VOL=SER=PACK14,DISP=OLD
//SYSIN    DD *
  COPY PDS=PDS,TO=SYSDA=PACK14,CATLG
   REPLACE DSNAME=OLD.PDS,MEMBER=ONE
   REPLACE DSNAME=OLD.PDS,MEMBER=TWO
  /*
```

V. *IEBPTPCH: PRINT OR PUNCH DATA SETS*

IEBPTPCH performs the following functions:

- Prints or punches a sequential data set.
- Prints or punches an entire partitioned data set or only selected members.
- Allows some formatting of the printed or punched output.
- Allows some selection of records for printing or punching.
- Prints or punches the directory of a partitioned data set.

IEBPTPCH has the following general form:

```
//stepname EXEC PGM=IEBPTPCH
//SYSPRINT DD SYSOUT=A
//SYSUT1   DD ...
      [ Describes the input data set. ]
//SYSUT2 DD SYSOUT=A,DCB=LRECL=record-length
      [ Describes the output data set, usually the printer.  Code
      SYSOUT=B for the card punch.  The RECFM is either FBA or FMA.
      For the printer, the LRECL must include the print control
      character.  For a 132-character line printer, LRECL=133
      should be coded.  BLKSIZE can be coded to block the output. ]
//SYSIN DD *
      [ control statements ]
/*
```

A. *PRINT Statement*

The PRINT statement prints the input data set in groups of eight characters, each group separated by two blanks. Twelve groups are printed per line for a total of 96 characters. An asterisk is printed after each logical record, and two asterisks are printed after the last record in a block. This format is good for the hexadecimal format, but poor for character data. The blanks separating the fields make it difficult to tell the field locations of the character data, and blank characters are easily mistaken for the blanks separating the fields.

If the LRECL of the input data set is longer than a single line, the record is printed on successive lines. The RECORD statement described later allows individual fields within the record to be formatted and the fields printed in specific columns on the line. However, only a single line per input record can then be printed.

A single PRINT statement is placed after the SYSIN DD statement, coded as follows:

```
PRINT option,option,...,option
```

The following options may be coded:

- PREFORM = A or M specifies that a control character is the first character of each record. The control character is not printed, but controls the printer. When PREFORM is coded, any other print options are ignored. The A specifies ASA control characters, and the M specifies machine code control characters. If the input record is longer than the print line, the record is printed on successive lines, single spacing all but the last. The last line is controlled by the control characters.

- TYPORG = PO or PS specifies the data set organization; PO for partitioned and PS for sequential. Omitting TYPORG also indicates a sequential data set.

- TOTCONV = XE or PZ specifies the conversions to be performed for printing. TOTCONV is overridden by any subsequent RECORD statements. If omitted, each byte of the input data is printed as a character. XE specifies that each byte of data is to be printed in two-character hexadecimal representation. The input data characters 'THE' would print as 'E3C8C5'. PZ specifies that the input data is packed decimal and each byte of data is to be printed as two numeric characters.

- CNTRL = 1, 2, or 3 specifies the printer spacing. Single spacing is assumed if CNTRL is omitted. CNTRL = 1 specifies single spacing, 2 double spacing, and 3 triple spacing.

- STRTAFT = n specifies the number of logical records to be skipped before printing. STRTAFT defaults to zero if omitted, and n cannot exceed 32,767. For a partitioned data set, STRTAFT applies to each member rather than to the entire data set.

- STOPAFT = n specifies the number of logical records to print. STOPAFT defaults to the entire data set if omitted, and n cannot exceed 32,767. For a partitioned data set, STOPAFT applies to each member.

- SKIP = n specifies that every nth record is to be printed. Each successive record is printed if SKIP is omitted. SKIP = 3 prints the 3rd, 6th, 9th, etc., records.

- INITPG = n specifies the initial page number. INITPG defaults to 1 if omitted, and n cannot exceed 9999.

- MAXLINE = n specifies the maximum lines per page, including blank lines and titles. MAXLINE defaults to 60 if omitted. Several other options are required when the MEMBER or RECORD statements are coded. These options are described with the appropriate statements.

The following PRINT statement prints a partitioned data set, double spaced with 50 lines per page. Records 110, 120, 130, and 140 are printed for each member.

```
PRINT TYPORG=PO,CNTRL=2,STRTAFT=100,STOPAFT=4,SKIP=10,MAXLINE=50
```

The next example prints each record of a sequential data set, single spaced, with 60 lines per page.

```
PRINT
```

B. MEMBER Statement

Several MEMBER statements may be placed after the PRINT statement to select partitioned data set members to print. Without MEMBER statements, every member of the partitioned data set is printed. A MAXNAME=n option must be coded in the PRINT statement to specify the number of MEMBER statements. The MEMBER statement is coded as:

```
MEMBER NAME=member
```

The following example prints member ONE and TWO of a partitioned data set.

```
PRINT TYPORG=PO,MAXNAME=2
MEMBER NAME=ONE
MEMBER NAME=TWO
```

C. RECORD Statement

The RECORD statement specifies the format in which to print the records. If it is omitted, every field in the record is printed as character data or as specified by the TYPCONV option on the PRINT statement. The RECORD statement also specifies the columns in which to print the data. Only a single line can be printed per input record. Several RECORD statements may be placed after the PRINT statement. The RECORD statement is coded as:

```
RECORD FIELD=(length,position,conversion,column),...
```

- *length* specifies the length in bytes of the field to print.
- *position* specifies the starting byte position of the field. (The first byte position is 1.)
- *conversion* specifies the conversion (PZ or XE) to be done on the field. PZ specifies packed decimal so that the *length* characters print in [*length(2)-1*] columns. XE specifies that the data is to be printed as hexadecimal so that *length* characters print in [length(2)] columns. Coding two consecutive commas to omit the conversion results in printing each byte of data as a character.
- *column* specifies the starting column number in which the field is to be printed. (The first column is 1.)

The number of FIELD subparameters must be specified in the MAXFLDS=n option of the PRINT statement. In the following example, fields 1 to 20 are printed in columns 1 to 20 as character data, fields 73 to 80 are printed in columns 30 to 44 as packed decimal, and fields 60 to 69 are printed in columns 50 to 69 as hexadecimal.

```
PRINT MAXFLDS=3
RECORD FIELD=(20,1,,1),FIELD=(8,73,PZ,30),FIELD=(10,60,XE,50)
```

The IDENT option permits records with different formats to be printed under the control of different RECORD statements. IDENT does not work as you might wish, and is of limited usefulness. Usually in a data set containing records of different formats, a fixed field in each record denotes the record type, and you would like to select records based on such a field and print the record with the appropriate formats. Unfortunately, IDENT expects records having the same format to be grouped together, with each group separated by a special record that denotes the end of the record group.

There may be several RECORD statements, each containing a single IDENT option coded as follows:

```
RECORD IDENT=(length,'text',location),FIELD=...
```

- *length* specifies the length of the 'text' that identifies the last record to be printed under that format. After this record is printed, the next RECORD statement is activated. The length cannot exceed eight bytes.
- *'text'* is from one to eight literal characters that identify the record.
- *location* specifies the starting location of the field in the record containing the identifying characters. (The first position is 1.)

The MAXGPS $=n$ option on the PRINT statement must specify the total number of IDENT parameters appearing in RECORD statements. In addition, the MAXLITS $=n$ option must also specify the sum of the characters contained in the IDENT literals. The following example illustrates the workings of IDENT.

```
PRINT MAXFLDS=2,MAXGPS=2,MAXLITS=2
RECORD IDENT=(1,'1',80),FIELD=(20,1,,1)
RECORD IDENT=(1,'2',80),FIELD=(10,1,,1)
```

- The input records are read and printed according to the FIELD option of the first RECORD statement.
- When a record is encountered with a '1' in position 80, it too is printed in this same format.
- The next RECORD statement is activated, and the input records are read and printed according to the RECORD statement's FIELD format.
- When a record is encountered with a '2' in position 80, it too is printed in this same format.
- Since there are no more RECORD statements to be activated, the printing is terminated.

D. TITLE Statement

The TITLE statement is placed after a PRINT statement to print a title at the start of each new page. TITLE is coded as:

```
TITLE ITEM=('title',column),ITEM=...
```

- *'title'* is 1 to 40 characters to print as the title.
- *column* is the starting column in which to print the title. (The first position is 1.)

One or two TITLE statements may be placed after the PRINT statement to print one or two title lines.

```
TITLE ITEM=('COLUMNS AS SHOWN',1)
TITLE ITEM=('10',10),ITEM=('20',20),ITEM=('30',30),ITEM=('40,40)
```

These two statements would print the following titles:

```
COLUMNS AS SHOWN
              10    20    30    40
```

E. Partitioned Data Set Directory

To print a partitioned data set directory, SYSUT1 must point to the partitioned data set, the DCB must be coded with RECFM = U and BLKSIZE = 256, and the PRINT statement must include TYPORG = PS. The following example prints the directory of a partitioned data set named TEST.

```
//STEP1 EXEC PGM=IEBPTPCH
//SYSPRINT DD SYSOUT=A
//SYSUT1    DD DSN=TEST,DISP=SHR,DCB=(RECFM=U,BLKSIZE=256)
//SYSUT2    DD SYSOUT=A,DCB=LRECL=133
//SYSIN     DD *
  PRINT TYPORG=PS
/*
```

F. PUNCH Statement

The PUNCH statement punches the input data in columns 1 to 80 of the punched cards. The PREFORM, TYPORG, TOTCONV, CNTRL, STRTAFT, STOPAFT, SKIP, MAXNAME, MAXFLDS, MAXGPS, and MAXLITS options described for the PRINT statement may be included on the PUNCH statement.

```
PUNCH option,option,...,option
```

- CDSEQ = n specifies the initial sequence number n to be punched in columns 73 to 80 of each card. CDSEQ starts over again for each member of a partitioned data set. If CDSEQ is omitted, the cards are not sequenced.
- CDINCR = n specifies the increment n of the sequence numbers. The increment defaults to 10 if CDINCR is omitted.

The following example punches two members of a partitioned data set, ONE and TWO.

```
//STEP1 EXEC PGM=IEBPTPCH
//SYSPRINT DD SYSOUT=A
//SYSUT1    DD DSN=TEST,DISP=SHR
//SYSUT2    DD SYSOUT=B,DCB=LRECL=80
//SYSIN     DD *
  PUNCH TYPORG=PO,MAXNAME=2
  MEMBER NAME=ONE
  MEMBER NAME=TWO
/*
```

VI. IEBUPDTE: MAINTAIN SOURCE LIBRARY

IEBUPDTE is used to create and update a sequential or partitioned data set containing source data. The functions of IEBUPDTE are usually done by using a text editor, such as ISPF/PDF. The main use for IEBUPDTE today is to distribute source libraries to different installations. It also updates IBM source libraries such as the cataloged procedure libraries. The source libraries normally contain 80-character lines in which columns 73 to 80 contain sequential numbers. IEBUPDTE has the following general form:

```
//stepname EXEC PGM=IEBUPDTE,PARM=NEW or MOD
     [ NEW specifies that a new data set is to be created.  MOD,
     the default if the PARM is omitted, indicates that the output
     data set exists and is to be updated. ]
//SYSPRINT DD SYSOUT=A
//SYSUT1    DD ...
     [ Specifies the input data set.  Not required for creating a
     new library. ]
//SYSUT2 DD ...
     [ Specifies the output data set.  Not required for updating in
     place. ]
//SYSIN DD *
     [ control statements ]
/*
```

The control statements are the following. (The ./ begins in column 1.)

- ./ ADD NAME = member,LIST = ALL

Precedes and names a member or a data set to be added to the SYSUT2 data set. The *member* must not already exist in the output partitioned data set. There can be only one ADD for a sequential data set, the NAME options should be omitted, and PARM = NEW must be coded on the EXEC statement. The LIST = ALL is an option to list the entire member on SYSPRINT.

- ./ REPL NAME = member,LIST = ALL

Precedes a member to replace an existing member in the SYSUT2 partitioned data set.

- ./ NUMBER NEW1 = first,INCR = increment

A single NUMBER statement may follow an ADD or REPL statement to number the new member of a data set. NEW1 specifies the first sequence number and INCR the increment. The source statements are numbered in columns 73 to 80.

- ./ REPRO NAME = member,LIST = ALL

Copies the member or data set from the SYSUT1 DD data set.

- ./ REPRO NEW = PO,MEMBER = member,LIST = ALL

Copies the SYSUT1 sequential data set specified by the SYSUT1 DD statement into the SYSUT2 partitioned data set under the member name specified.

- ./ REPRO NEW = PS,NAME = member,LIST = ALL

Copies the member of the SYSUT1 partitioned data set into the SYSUT2 sequential data set.

- ./ CHANGE NAME = member-name,LIST = ALL

The CHANGE statement precedes the DELETE, NUMBER, or data statements that update the member or data set. Omit the NAME option to update a sequential data set.

- ./ DELETE SEQ1 = n,SEQ2 = n

The DELETE statement follows a CHANGE statement and deletes all records SEQ1 through SEQ2.

- ./ NUMBER SEQ1 = start,SEQ2 = late,NEW1 = first,INCR = increment

One or more NUMBER statements may follow a CHANGE statement to renumber a portion of a member. The source statements from SEQ1 through SEQ2 are renumbered as specified by NEW1 and INCR.

- ./ NUMBER SEQ1 = ALL,NEW1 = start,INCR = increment

A single NUMBER statement with SEQ1 = ALL may follow a CHANGE statement to renumber the entire member.

- DATA STATEMENTS

Data lines placed after the CHANGE statements must contain sequence numbers in columns 73 to 80 with leading zeros. If the sequence number matches a record in the member, the data replaces it. Otherwise the data line is inserted in the order of its sequence number.

- ./ ENDUP Marks the end of all the control statements.

The following options may also be coded on the ADD, REPL, CHANGE, and REPRO statements.

- SEQFLD = ddl specifies the starting column dd and the length l to contain the sequence numbers. The dd cannot exceed 80, and l cannot exceed 8. The default is 738 if SEQFLD is omitted.
- LEVEL = hh specifies the update level in hexadecimal (00-FF). This level number is recorded in the directory of the output member, and can be used to keep track of the update levels.

A. Partitioned Data Sets

1. Creating a library

Code the following control statements to create a library.

- ./ ADD NAME = member,LIST = ALL

The SYSUT1 statement is omitted. Each ADD statement is followed by the member to add.

- ./ REPRO NAME = member,LIST = ALL

The named members are copied from the SYSUT1 DD data set into the SYSUT2 data set. Code the NEW = PO option if SYSUT1 is a sequential data set.

The following example creates a partitioned data set named PDS to contain 80 column lines. Two members are added, ONE and TWO.

```
//STEP1EXEC PGM=IEBUPDTE,PARM=NEW
//SYSPRINT DD SYSOUT=A
//SYSUT2   DD DSN=PDS,DISP=(NEW,CATLG),
//            UNIT=SYSDA,VOL=SER=PACK12,
//            DCB=(RECFM=FB,LRECL=80,BLKSIZE=12960),
//            SPACE=(12960,(10,5,10))
//SYSIN    DD *
./ ADD NAME=ONE,LIST=ALL
    [ Place member ONE data here ]
./ ADD NAME=TWO,LIST=ALL
    [ Place member TWO data here ]
./ENDUP
/*
```

2. Updating

The next example replaces member ONE, adds member TWO, and deletes records 12 to 15 in member THREE.

```
//STEP1EXEC PGM=IEBUPDTE
//SYSPRINT DD SYSOUT=A
//SYSUT1    DD DSN=PDS,DISP=OLD
    [ DISP must be OLD. ]
//SYSUT2    DD DSN=PDS,DISP=MOD
    [ DISP must be MOD. The input and output data sets
    are the same. ]
SYSIN       DD *
./ REPL NAME=ONE,LIST=ALL
    [ New member ONE placed here. ]
./ ADD NAME=TWO,LIST=ALL
    [ New member TWO placed here. ]
./ CHANGE NAME=THREE,LIST=ALL
./ DELETE SEQ1=12,SEQ2=15
./ ENDUP
/*
```

Specific columns can be updated by coding the COLUMN option on the CHANGE statement.

- ./ CHANGE NAME = member,LIST = ALL,COLUMN = dd

For any data records that follow and whose sequence numbers match existing records in the data set, columns *dd* through 80 of the data record replace the same columns of the existing record.

3. Inserting records

There are two ways to insert records.

- Place the data lines after the CHANGE statement. The data must contain a sequence number in columns 73 to 80, with leading zeros. The data lines are inserted in place based on this sequence number. (A line replaces a record if the data set already contains a record having this sequence number; otherwise it inserts the record.)
- Use the NUMBER statement to denote where the data records are to be inserted. There can be several NUMBER statements to insert the records.

```
./CHANGE NAME=member,LIST=ALL
./NUMBER SEQ1=after,NEW1=start,INCR=incr,INSERT=YES
```

The records are inserted following the *after* record. They are numbered beginning with *start*, and each succeeding record is incremented by *incr*. If the last inserted record is numbered such that it is greater than the following existing record, all the following existing records are renumbered using *incr*.

4. Updating in place

The data set can also be updated in place. Records can only be replaced or renumbered, and there can be only one CHANGE statement per job step. With the previous changes, the entire member is copied and changed and replaces the old member. In a partitioned data set, the new member is added to the end of the data set, and the space occupied by the original member becomes unusable. The following example illustrates the update in place.

```
//STEP1EXEC PGM=IEBUPDTE
//SYSPRINT DD SYSOUT=A
//SYSUT1   DD DSN=PDS,DISP=OLD
     [ Note that SYSUT2 is not required. ]
//SYSIN    DD *
./CHANGE NAME=THREE,LIST=ALL,UPDATE=INPLACE
THIS DATA LINE REPLACES RECORD 10                      00000010
./NUMBER SEQ=ALL,NEW1=10,INCR=10
./ENDUP
/*
```

B. Sequential Data Sets

1. Creating a sequential data set

Code the following control statements to create a sequential data set.

- ./ ADD LIST = ALL

  A single ADD statement may be followed by the lines of data to be placed in the data set. SYSUT1 is omitted.

- ./ REPRO NEW = PS,NAME = member,LIST = ALL

A single REPRO statement copies the named member of the SYSUT1 data set into the SYSUT2 sequential data set. Omit the NEW = PS if SYSUT1 is a sequential data set to be copied in its entirety.

The following example copies the member named ONE from the PDS data set to create a sequential data set on tape.

```
//STEP1 EXEC PGM=IEBUPDTE,PARM=NEW
//SYSPRINT DD SYSOUT=A
//SYSUT1    DD DSN=PDS,DISP=SHR
//SYSUT2    DD DSN=SEQT,DISP=(NEW,KEEP),
//             UNIT=TAPE9,VOL=SER=003322,
//             DCB=(RECFM=FB,LRECL=80,BLKSIZE=8000)
//SYSIN     DD *
./REPRO NEW=PS,NAME=ONE,LIST=ALL
/*
```

2.   Updating

Sequential data sets are updated like partitioned data sets with the REPL and CHANGE statements. The NAME option is omitted from the statements. A single REPL statement replaces the entire sequential data set. The CHANGE statement is identical to that for partitioned data sets, except for omitting the NAME option. The following example updates an existing sequential data set in place. With the update in place, you can only replace or renumber records, and the data set must reside on a direct-access volume.

```
//STEP1EXEC PGM=IEBUPDTE
//SYSPRINT DD SYSOUT=A
//SYSUT1    DD DSN=SEQT,DISP=OLD
//SYSUT2    DD DSN=SEQT,DISP=MOD
//SYSIN     DD *
./CHANGE LIST=ALL,UPDATE=INPLACE
THIS DATA LINE REPLACES RECORD 10          00000010
./NUMBER SEQ1=ALL,NEW1=10,INCR=10
/*
```

VII. IEHLIST: LIST DIRECT-ACCESS VOLUME INFORMATION

IEHLIST performs the following functions:

- Lists the entries in the directory of a partitioned data set created by the linkage editor.
- Lists the Volume Table of Contents (VTOC) of direct-access volumes.

IEHLIST has the following general form:

```
//stepname EXEC PGM=IEHLIST
//SYSPRINT DD SYSOUT=A
//ddname   DD UNIT=device,VOL=SER=volume,DISP=OLD
    [ A DD statement must describe each volume referred to by the
    control statements. ]
//SYSIN DD *
    [ control statements ]
/*
```

The following two control statements are provided.

A. LISTPDS Statement

The LISTPDS statement lists the directory of partitioned data sets such as those created by the linkage editor. From the listing, you can see what members the data set contains, their size, and various attributes for each. There may be several LISTPDS statements coded as follows:

```
                                                  DUMP
                                                  FORMAT
LISTPDS=DSNAME=(dsname, ...)VOL=device=volume,_____
```

- DSNAME = (*dsname*,...) lists 1 to 10 partitioned data set names.
- VOL = *device* = *volume* specifies the device type and volume serial number upon which the data sets reside.
- FORMAT edits the listing.
- DUMP lists the output in unedited hexadecimal form.

B. LISTVTOC Statement

The LISTVTOC statement lists the VTOC for direct-access volumes. From this, you can tell what data sets reside on the volume, their DCB attributes, the amount of space they occupy, the number of extents allocated, and the amount of free space on the volume. There may be several LISTVTOC statements in a job step, coded as follows:

```
LISTVTOC VOL=device=volume,option,option,...,option
    [ VOL=device=volume specifies the device type and volume whose
    VTOC is to be listed. ]
```

The following options may be coded:

- DUMP lists the VTOC in unedited, hexadecimal form. If neither DUMP nor FORMAT are coded, an abbreviated edited format is printed.
- FORMAT lists the VTOC in comprehensive, edited form. DUMP cannot be coded with FORMAT.

- DATE = *dddyy* flags each entry in the listing with an asterisk whose retention date is less than this date. The *ddd* is the Julian day of the year, and *yy* is the year. No asterisks are printed if DATE is omitted.
- DSNAME = (*dsname*,...,*dsname*) specifies 1 to 10 data set names to be listed. If DSNAME is omitted, all data sets residing on the volume are listed.

The following example lists the directory of a data set named PDS residing on PACK10 and lists the VTOC of PACK14.

```
//STEP1 EXEC PGM=IEHLIST
//SYSPRINT DD SYSOUT=A
//DD1      DD UNIT=SYSDA,VOL=SER=PACK10,DISP=OLD
//DD2      DD UNIT=SYSDA,VOL=SER=PACK14,DISP=OLD
//SYSIN    DD *
  LISTPDS DSNAME=PDS,VOL=SYSDA=PACK10,FORMAT
  LISTVTOC VOL=SYSDA=PACK14,FORMAT
/*
```

EXERCISES

In these exercises, place both data sets on the same disk volume. You will also need a scratch tape. You may run the exercises as separate jobs or combine several steps into a single job.

- Using IEBGENER, create a partitioned data set named ORIGINAL, containing 80-byte lines. Place two members in it.

  Member ONE: CARD 1
                    CARD 2
  Member TWO: CARD 3
                    CARD 4
                    CARD 5

- Use IEHMOVE or IEBCOPY to unload ORIGINAL to the scratch tape. Then load it back into the same disk volume, renaming it COPY.
- Use IEHPROGM to delete COPY(TWO).
- Use IEBCOPY or IEHMOVE to copy ORIGINAL(TWO) to COPY as member THREE.
- Use IEBGENER to replace COPY(ONE) with the following lines:

  ```
  CARD 6
  CARD 7
  ```

- Use IEBCOPY to compress COPY.

- Use IEBPTPCH to print the directory and each of the members in copy.
- Use IEHLIST to list the VTOC of the disk volume and the member names in COPY.
- Use IEBUPDTE to copy members ONE and THREE from COPY into a sequential data set named SOURCE. Number the lines in SOURCE by increments of 20, and use IEBPTPCH to list it.
- Use IEHPROGM to delete and uncatalog ORIGINAL, COPY, and SOURCE.

Chapter 16

SORT/MERGE

I. SORTING CONCEPTS

Sorting consists of arranging records in ascending or descending sequence. The sort order of alphanumeric data is termed its *collating sequence*, which specifies the sort order of each alphanumeric character in the character set. The two popular collating sequences are EBCDIC and ASCII. You will likely use only EBCDIC on IBM mainframe computers. ASCII is the standard for personal computers. The collating sequences, from low to high, are:

```
EBCDIC:            ASCII:
--------           ------
blank              blank
.<(+$*);-/,>'="     0 through 9
a through z        ; < = >
A through Z        A through Z
0 through 9        a through z
```

In sorting character fields, the characters are compared from left to right to determine the sequence of the fields. Thus, NORTH would sort before NORTHERN because while the first five characters are identical, the sixth character in NORTH is a blank, which places it before the E in NORTHERN.

Numeric fields sort according to their numeric values, taking into consideration the signs. That is, 100 is greater than 50; 50 is greater than -100. The main problem with numeric data lies in confusing it with character data that happens to contain only numbers. Character data is compared one character at a time, from left to right. With numeric data, it is the numeric value that is compared. The following example shows the difference. The fields are listed in ascending sequence for both character and numeric data.

```
AS CHARACTER DATA:      AS NUMERIC DATA:

b999   (blank comes        9  (9 is less
0009    before zero)     999   than 999)

  +9   (+ comes          -9  (-9 is less
  -9    before -)        +9   than +9)

  b9   (blank comes      -9  (-9 is less
  -9    before -)         9   than 9)
```

More than one sort key can be used to arrange the data. A census file illustrates this. Each record for a household might contain a city, state, and a family name. The census file might be sequenced on the state, city, and name, making these three items the sort keys. When there are multiple sort keys, you must decide which key to sort on first, which second, and so on.

The sort key that is sorted first is termed the *major sort key*. The sort key that is last is termed the *minor sort key*. Consequently, when there are several sort keys, the hierarchy of the keys is specified in major to minor sequence. Changing the hierarchy of the sort keys would completely rearrange the census file.

A lower-level hierarchy (minor sort key) cannot change the sequence of a higher-level hierarchy (major sort key). That is, if the sort hierarchy is:

```
state first
city second
name third
```

All records for a particular state will sort together. Whether we sort on city second and name third, or name second and city third, or city second alone, all records for a state will still sort together.

II. SORT PROGRAM

IBM provides several versions of the sort program. In addition, two popular sort products, SyncSort (a product of SyncSort, Incorporated, Englewood Cliffs, NJ) and CA-SORT (a product of Computer Associates Intl. Inc., Garden City, NY) are found at many installations. All the sort packages have essentially the same features. They differ mainly in their efficiency.

The sort programs can be invoked by the SORT statement in COBOL and subroutine calls in PL/I and assembler language. More often they are invoked as a separate job step through a cataloged procedure as follows:

```
//SORT1 EXEC SORTD
//SORTIN   DD DSN=sort-input-file,DISP=OLD,...
    [ SORTIN specifies the input data set to sort.  It must be a
    sequential or VSAM data set. ]
//SORTOUT DD DSN=sort-output-file,DISP=(NEW,...
    [ SORTOUT specifies the output data set to contain the sorted
    records.  It must be a sequential or VSAM data set. ]
//SYSIN    DD *
  SORT FIELDS=(1,4,CH,A,20,10,CH,D),FILSZ=E1000
/*
```

The SORT statement specifies the sort order. The FILSZ = E1000 is an estimate of the number of records in the data set, 1,000 in this example, and the order is as follows:

```
1,4,CH,A
    [ Starting in character position 1, sort 4 CHaracters in
    Ascending sequence. ]
```

```
20,10,CH,D
    [ Starting in character position 20, sort 10 CHaracters in
    Descending sequence. ]
```

The general form of the SORT statement is:

```
SORT FIELDS=(sort-key,sort-key,...sort-key),FILSZ=En
```

- The SORT statement must begin in column 2 or beyond.
- FILSZ = En estimates the number of records to sort. This estimate enables the sort to be more efficient. The FILSZ option may be omitted, and the sort will proceed with a slight performance degradation.
- *sort-key* specifies the fields within the record to sort, their data types, and whether they are to be sorted in ascending or descending sequence. The keys are listed from left to right in the major to minor order in which they are applied in the sort. Each sort-key has four parts: start, length, format, order.
- *start* specifies the starting byte position in the record. The first byte is number 1. For binary fields, specify *start* in the form *byte.bit*, where *byte* is the byte number and *bit* is the bit number within the byte. (The first bit is number 1.) Hence 3.2 indicates that the key begins in the second bit of the third byte.
- *length* specifies the length of the field in bytes. For binary fields, specify the *length* in the form *bytes.bits*, where *bytes* is the number of bytes and *bits* is the number of bits. Hence 0.3 indicates that the key is 3 bits long.
- *format* specifies the format of the sort field. It must be one of the following:

Format	Description	Signed	Length in bytes
CH	EBCDIC character		1–4092.
ZD	Zoned decimal	yes	1–32
PD	Packed decimal	yes	1–32
FI	Fixed point	yes	1–256
BI	Binary		1 bit to 4092 bytes
FL	Floating point	yes	1–256
CSL	Numeric character, leading separate sign	yes	2–256
CST	Numeric character, trailing separate sign	yes	2–256
CLO	Numeric character, leading overpunch sign	yes	1–256
CTO	Numeric character, trailing overpunch sign	yes	1–256
AC	ASCII character		14–256
ASL	ASCII numeric character, leading separate sign	yes	2–256
AST	ASCII numeric character, trailing separate sign	yes	2–256
AQ	EBCDIC character, alternative collating sequence set by installation		1–256

- *order* specifies the sequence:

```
A       Ascending
B       Descending
```

The following example sorts records into ascending sequence with two sort keys.

```
SORT FIELDS=(4,6,ZD,A,12,3,PD,D),FILSZ=E2000
```

The sort order is:

- 4,6,ZD,A Bytes 4 to 9 as zoned decimal in ascending sequence.
- 12,3,PD,D Bytes 12 to 14 as packed decimal in descending sequence.

To continue the SORT statement, break it after a comma and continue it in columns 2 to 16 of the following line.

```
SORT FIELDS=(4,6,CH,A,
      12,3,CH,D),FILSZ=E2000
```

The following options may also be coded on the SORT statement:

- FORMAT=*format* may be coded if all the data fields have the same format, and the *format* may be omitted in the FIELDS parameter.

```
SORT FORMAT=CH,FIELDS=(4,6,A,12,3,D),FILSZ=E2000
    Same as:
SORT FIELDS=(4,6,CH,A,12,3,CH,D),FILSZ=E2000
```

- SKIPREC=*n* skips *n* records before sorting.

```
SORT FIELDS=(4,6,CH,A),FILSZ=E2000,SKIPREC=1000
```

- CKPT requests that checkpoints be taken at the start of the first sort phase, at the start of each intermediate merge phase pass, and at the start of the final merge phase.
- EQUALS specifies that records having identical keys are to sort in the order they appear in the input data set. EQUALS is ignored for a MERGE.
- NOEQUALS specifies that the sequence of records having identical keys need not be preserved.

III. MERGE STATEMENT

MERGE merges several input data sets having identical record formats into a single output data set in the same sequence. Merging yields the same results as if the several data sets were concatenated as input to a sort, but merging is more efficient because the input data sets are already in the proper sequence.

The JCL for a merge is identical to that for a sort, except that instead of one SORTIN DD statement describing the input, there are up to 16 SORTINnn DD statements describing the data sets to merge. A merge is written as:

```
//  EXEC SORTD
//SORTIN01 DD ...
//SORTIN02 DD ...
        .
        .
        .
//SORTOUT  DD ...
        [ The output is written on this data set. ]
//SYSIN    DD *
  MERGE FIELDS=(sort-key,sort-key,...sort-key)
/*
```

The SORTINnn DD statements name the input data sets to merge and tell how many data sets are to be merged. A maximum of 16 data sets can be merged. The *nn* in the SORTINnn DD statements must begin with 01 and continue in increasing, consecutive order: (01, 02, 03, but not 01, 03, 04).

The MERGE statement is identical to the SORT statement except:

- You write MERGE instead of SORT.
- FILSZ is not needed to estimate the total number of input records. There is only one way to merge, regardless of the number of records involved.
- SKIPREC and EQUALS are ignored if written.

The special rules are:

- The RECFM for all the SORTIN*nn* must be the same.
- The LRECL for fixed-length records must be the same.
- The BLKSIZE need not be the same, but the data set with the largest BLKSIZE must be SORTIN01.

IV. OTHER SORT STATEMENTS

The SORT statement is necessary for every sort, but there are several other statements provided for specialized use.

A. The RECORD Statement

The RECORD statement specifies the output record length and is used under the following conditions:

- For sorting VSAM data sets, the RECORD statement is required to specify the record length.

- For variable-length records, the RECORD statement is optional to estimate the record lengths to make the sort go faster.
- For changing the record length in a sort exit, for a sort called by PL/I or assembler language, or if you have no SORTIN DD statement, the RECORD statement is required to specify the record length.

You write the RECORD statement as:

```
RECORD LENGTH=(n1,n2,n3,n4,n5),TYPE=type
```

- *n1,n2,n3,n4,n5* are length parameters explained below.
- *type* is the record type, F for fixed-length, V for EBCDIC variable-length, and D for ASCII variable-length.

For VSAM data sets and situations where there is no SORTIN DD statement, RECORD is written as:

```
RECORD LENGTH=(length),TYPE=type
```

- *length* is the LRECL for the record length. Add four bytes for VSAM variable-length records.
- *type* is F for fixed, V for EBCDIC variable-length, and D for ASCII variable-length.

If the record length is changed in a sort exit, write the following:

```
RECORD LENGTH=(input-length,output-length),TYPE=type
        [ Add 4 bytes to the length for VSAM variable-length records. ]
```

To increase the sort efficiency of data sets containing variable-length records, write:

```
RECORD LENGTH=(,,,min-length,modal-length),TYPE=type
        [ The min-length is the length of the shortest record.   The
        modal-length is an estimate of the most frequent record
        length. ]
```

B. The MODS Statement

The MODS statement names an assembler language entry point to branch to during the sort. These branches are termed sort exits. With sort exits, you can supply records to the sort rather than having the sort read SORTIN, and you can retrieve the sorted records rather than having them written in SORTOUT.

Altogether, there are 18 sort exits possible during the various sort phases. Each sort exit is numbered, with the numbers ranging from E11 to E61. You are unlikely to write a MODS statement, but it is important to understand how the sort exits work. Here is the sequence in which the two most-used sort exits occur: the E15 before-sort exit and the E35 after-sort exit.

1. The Sort/Merge utility reads an input record.
2. If you have included a MODS statement for an E15 before-sort exit, Sort/Merge calls the subroutine you name on the MODS statement. Your subroutine might then modify the records being passed to the sort.
3. Sort/Merge goes back to STEP 1 until all input records are read.
4. Sort/Merge sorts the file.
5. Sort/Merge selects the next sorted record and if you have included a MODS statement for an E35 after-sort exit, Sort/Merge calls the subroutine you name on the MODS statement. Your subroutine might then modify the sorted record.
6. Sort/Merge writes the output record and goes back to STEP 5 until all output records are written.

The general form of the MODS statement is:

```
MODS exit=(routine,bytes,ddname,routine,bytes,ddname,...)
```

- *exit* is the type of sort exit, such as E15.
- *routine* is the name of the routine to receive control.
- *bytes* is the number of bytes occupied by the routine.
- *ddname* is the ddname of the data set containing the routine.

For example:

```
MERGE E15=(PROCESS,1000,LIB)
```

You probably won't use sort exits except through the COBOL SORT verb, and for this you don't need the MODS statement.

C. The ALTSEQ Statement

The ALTSEQ statement may be coded along with SORT or MERGE statements to change the EBCDIC collating sequence. ALTSEQ is coded as:

```
ALTSEQ CODE=ffll
ALTSEQ CODE=(ffll,ffll,...,ffll)
```

- *ff* is the hexadecimal representation of the EBCDIC character to change.
- *ll* is the hexadecimal representation of an EBCDIC character that the *ff* character is to sort as.

For example, to make a lower-case a (X′61′) sort as an upper-case A (X′41′), code:

```
SORT FIELDS=...
ALTSEQ CODE=6141
```

D. INCLUDE/OMIT Statements

The INCLUDE and OMIT statements, used in a sort but not a merge, test specified fields to select or exclude records from the SORTIN data set. They are placed along with the other control statements: SORT, MERGE, RECORDS, or ALTSEQ.

```
SORT FIELDS=(...
INCLUDE ...
```

You write INCLUDE and OMIT as:

```
INCLUDE COND=(logical-expression)
OMIT COND=(logical-expression)
```

The logical-expression is written as:

```
COND=(field,comparison,field or constant)

field:      Specifies a field in the record in a similar format
            to the SORT and MERGE statements:
            byte,length,format

comparison: The comparison operation:
                  EQ    EQual
                  NE    Not Equal
                  GT    Greater Than
                  GE    Greater than or Equal
                  LT    Less Than
                  LE    Less than or Equal

constant:   A decimal constant:      12 -16 222.46
            A hexadecimal constant:  x'nnnn...nn'
            A character constant:     C'character-literals'
               (write a quote as two quotes:  C'ISN''T')

INCLUDE COND=(field,comparison,field or constant)
OMIT    COND=(field,comparison,field or constant)
```

For INCLUDE, a record is accepted only if the logical expression is true. A false logical-expression results in the record being rejected. For OMIT, a record is rejected if the logical-expression is true. A false logical-expression results in the record being selected. You can write either a single INCLUDE statement or a single OMIT statement. They cannot be written together.

As an example suppose you have records such as:

```
70014AL.....
70049AL.....
80016CA.....
80049OH.....
```

To include only records having "AL" in columns 6 and 7, you write:

```
INCLUDE COND=(6,2,CH, EQ, C'AL')
```

To omit zip 70049 in columns 1 to 5 and include all others, you write:

```
OMIT COND=(1,5,ZD, EQ, 70049)
```

The following rules apply:

- Any number of AND/ORs are permitted.
- One additional set of left and right parentheses is permitted: COND = (...(...)) but not COND = ((...)...(...)) or COND = (((...))).
- Where parentheses don't specify the evaluation order, the AND conditions are evaluated before the OR.
- Only format codes BI, CH, PD, ZD, or FI are permitted.
- Any fields being compared must be in the first 4,092 bytes of a record.
- Binary fields can be compared, but must begin and end on byte boundaries.
- The maximum field length for comparison is 256 bytes.
- Character fields are padded on the right with blanks to make a shorter field equal a longer field for comparison.
- Numeric data is padded on the left with zeroes to compare a shorter field with a longer field.

E. *The INREC and OUTREC Statements*

The INREC statement reformats a record before it is sorted so that only the fields you need get passed to the sort. This may let you shorten the record length to speed up the sort. OUTREC reformats the record after it is sorted, perhaps to lengthen the record. INREC reformats after any E15 before-sort exit and after records have been selected by INCLUDE or OMIT. The SORT, MERGE, OUTREC, or SUM statements refer to the sort keys after they have been reformatted. Be sure to account for this if you change the position of fields. OUTREC reformats after any E35 after-sort exit. INREC and OUTREC are written as:

```
INREC FIELDS=(nX,byte,length,align,...)
OUTREC FIELDS=(nX,byte,length,align,...)
```

- *n*X is optional. It specifies the number of spaces to insert in the output record before moving in the field from the input record. If *n*X is omitted, no space is inserted. The *n* can range in value from 1 to 256. To allow more spaces, you can write several *n*X values: 256X,256X,10X.
- *byte* is the starting byte position of the field in the input record. (Must be 1–4,096.) Add 4 for variable-length records.
- *length* is the length in bytes of the field in the input record to move to the output record.
- *align* is optional. Specifies the alignment. H = half-word, F = full-word, D = double-word. Omit this parameter if you wish no alignment.

These four parameters together specify an input field to copy. Suppose you have the following record:

`12TEST324633ROAD25`

If you write INREC FIELDS = (3,4), the sort Record would be ″TEST″. If you write OUTREC FIELDS = (3X,7,3,13,4,2X,1,2), the output record would be ″bbb324ROADbb12″.

The rules to cover special situations are:

- The LRECL of the SORTOUT DD statement must specify the new record length if it is changed.
- For a merge or copy, you must include the RECORD statement.
- For variable-length records, you must copy to the output record the record descriptor word and the first four bytes of the input record. The proper output record length will be stored there.
- You can copy from any byte position in a variable-length input record to the end of the record by coding the byte position last, without specifying the length.

F.   The SUM Statement

The SUM statement summarizes records by letting you specify numeric fields in the input record to sum. Records having the same sort keys are summed, and a single output record is written with the summed fields. Any other fields in the record are obtained from the last record summed.

The records are summarized after sorting. You do not sort the summarized records. Instead, the input records are sorted, then summarized, and then written to the SORTOUT. You write the SUM statement as:

`SUM FIELDS=(byte,length,format,...)`

- *byte* is the starting byte position of the field in the input record to run. (Add 4 for variable-length records.)
- *length* is the length of the field to sum.
- *format* is the format of the field to sum: BI, FI, PD, ZD, or FL.

Records are summarized based upon the sort keys specified in the SORT or MERGE statement. If three sort keys are specified in a SORT statement, records are summarized only when the three sort keys are equal. You can also write the SUM statement as:

```
SUM FIELDS=NONE
```

This causes the records to be summarized without adding any fields. SUM takes only the last record of a group whose keys match, dropping any records having duplicate keys. This might be used to eliminate records with duplicate keys. The rules for SUM are:

- You can't sum sort keys.
- Sum fields cannot overlap.
- If overflow occurs, records up to the overflow are summed and a record produced. Then the summation begins over.
- For a merge, you must include the RECORD statement.
- A summed field must be in the first 4,096 bytes of the record.

V. SORTD CATALOGED PROCEDURE

Each installation will tailor the SORTD cataloged procedure to suit its own needs. Check your installation's cataloged procedure for the specific statements. The following statements will generally be included in the procedure.

```
//SORTD PROC
//SORT EXEC PGM=ICEMAN
//STEPLIB   DD DSN=SYS1.LINKLIB,DISP=SHR
      [ The installation may place the sort program in some other
      library. ]
//SYSOUT    DD SYSOUT=A
//SORTLIB   DD DSN=SYS1.SORTLIB,DISP=SHR
//SORTWKnn DD ...
      [ Three to six work data sets must be included for the sort
      work area.  The sort writes intermediate output on these data
      sets.  SORTWK DD statements are not required for a merge. ]
```

A default storage size is established by the installation for the sort program. To change this size, code the SIZE parameter in the PARM field.

```
// EXEC SORTD,PARM='SIZE=bytes'
   [ SIZE specifies the number of bytes to give to the sort. ]
// EXEC SORTD,PARM='SIZE=MAX'
   [ SIZE=MAX allocates all the available space in the region or
   partition to sort.  This is usually the installation
   default. ]
```

The sort efficiency depends on the amount of real storage allocated to the sort. Generally, the more storage allocated, the more efficient the sort.

The SORTWK DD statements must be allocated space if they are on direct-access volumes. The default set by the installation's cataloged procedure is usually adequate, but for larger sorts, you must calculate the number of tracks to allocate. The sort is more efficient if the tracks are allocated in cylinders. To calculate the total number of tracks for all the SORTWK data sets, use the following formula:

$$\text{Total tracks} = \frac{\text{\# records(\# SORTWKs)}}{K(\text{\# SORTWKs} - 1)} + 2(\text{\# SORTWKs})$$

- $K = T/LRECL$, truncated to integer. Use 1 if the value is zero. T is the usable track size:

```
12,000 for a 3330 disk
8000 for a 3340 or 3344 disk
18,000 for a 3350 disk
34,000 for a 3375 disk
45,000 for a 3380 disk
```

- LRECL is the logical record length. Use the maximum record length for variable-length records. Tracks per SORTWK = total tracks/ # SORTWKS.

As an example, suppose 100,000 500-byte records are to be sorted with three SORTWK DD statements using 3380 disk storage. The number of tracks to allocate to all the SORTWK data sets is:

```
K = 45,000/500 = 90
```

$$\text{Total tracks} = \frac{100,000(3)}{90(3 - 2)} + 2(3) = 3340 \text{ tracks}$$

The 3340 total tracks when allocated in cylinders will require 223 cylinders; there are 15 tracks per cylinder on a 3380. We should allocate 75 cylinders to each of the three SORTWK DD statements.

The sort work areas may be dynamically allocated, which allows the SORTWK DD statements to be omitted. The work area to allocate is calculated from the FILSZ value. Dynamic sort work area location is requested as follows:

```
// EXEC SORTD,PARM='DYNALLOC=(device,n)'
   [ device specifies the device type or group name.
   n is the number of sort work files to allocate. ]
// EXEC SORTD,PARM='DYNALLOC=(3380,6)'
   [ Six sort work files are allocated on a 3380 disk. ]
```

VI. SORT EFFICIENCY

You may be able to reduce the cost of sorting dramatically by using the following suggestions.

- Number of records: Sort cost varies exponentially with the number of records sorted. That is, it costs more than twice as much to sort 1,000 records as 500 records. You can reduce the number of records by selecting records before you sort. For example, if you were working with census data and wanted to list only the names of people who live in Wyoming, you could first select the records for Wyoming and then sort. That way, you would sort only about 350,000 records rather than 200 million records.
- Record length: The cost of a sort is proportional to the record length. When you select records, you can drop all the fields that you don't need to shorten the record length.
- Tag Sort: Another variation to shorten the record length is used for random-access files having record keys. You create a small record containing only the random-access key needed to retrieve the record, and the other fields of the record to be used as sort keys. Then you sort these short records on the sort keys, and later use the random-access key to retrieve the full records in the sequence wanted.
- Sort Keys: The cost of a sort is proportional to the number of sort keys. (While it isn't easy to control the sort keys, sometimes you can have an effect on them in the way you design the record.) Suppose you are sorting a data set on date. Often the date is stored as:

```
m m d d y y y y
```

This necessitates three sort keys to sort on the date: yyyy, mm, and dd. But if you store the date in the record as:

```
y y y y m m d d
```

the entire date can be treated as a single sort key to sort on date. By placing sort keys together in major to minor order and having them be the same format, you can treat several alphanumeric sort keys in a sort as if they were a single sort key.
- Block size: Large blocks reduce the amount of I/O; they reduce the CPU time required to transmit the blocks, and, properly chosen, they conserve storage space on tape or disk.

EXERCISES

Create a data set containing the following lines and place them in the sequence shown:

```
991
992
999
981
982
989
891
899
881
882
```

Sort the lines into ascending sequence, placing them in a permanent data set on disk. Then sort the disk data set back into the original sequence, printing the sort output. (Make the SORTOUT DD statement contain SYSOUT = A.)

Chapter 17

MISCELLANEOUS JCL FEATURES

This chapter wraps up some of the loose ends remaining: the command and null statements, generation data groups, checkpoint/restart, data set protection, VIO data sets, dynamically allocated data sets, subsystem data sets, and a few miscellaneous DD parameters.

I.   COMMAND STATEMENT

Operator commands are normally entered from the console, but frequently used commands can be coded on command statements to be read in through the input stream. Command statements should be limited to operator use because they affect machine operation. Command statements are ignored in JES3.

The commands must be synchronized with the execution of jobs because the commands are executed as they are read. The command statement is placed before a JOB, EXEC, null, or another command statement. They cannot be continued onto another line. Command statements are coded as:

```
// command operands
```

The *command* is the operator command, and the *operands* depend on the type of command. The following commands can be entered on command statements in the various systems.

VS1:

BRDCST	LOGOFF	RESET		
CANCEL	MODIFY	ROUTE	STOPMN	
CENOUT	MONITOR	SEND	UNLOAD	
DISPLAY	MOUNT	SET	USERID	
HOLD	MSG	SHOW	VARY	
LISTBC	RELEASE	START	WRITELOG	
LOG	REPLY	STARTF	STOP	WRITER

MVS:

CANCEL	MONITOR	SEND	UNLOAD
CHNGDUMP	MOUNT	SET	VARY
DISPLAY	PAGEADD	SETDMN	WRITELOG
HOLD	RELEASE	SLIP	START
LOG	REPLY	STOP	
MODIFY	RESET	STOPMN	

Examples:

```
// VARY 293,OFFLINE
// DISPLAY Q
```

II. NULL STATEMENT

The null statement contains // in columns 1 and 2 with the remaining columns blank and causes the system to look for the next JOB statement; any intervening statements are ignored. Back in the days of when punched cards were used, nulls were often coded on distinctive colored cards to help operators separate card decks.

III. GENERATION DATA GROUPS

A generation data group (GDG) is a group of chronologically or functionally related data sets. They are processed periodically, often by adding a new generation, retaining previous generations, and sometimes the oldest generation is discarded. For example, an income tax report is a generation data group with a new generation added each year, chronologically and functionally related to previous years. When a new generation is added, the four previous reports must be retained for legal purposes, but the fifth may be discarded.

Cataloged generation data groups are referred to by a name and a relative generation number. For example, DSN = TAX.STATE(0) would refer to the current tax report, and DSN = TAX.STATE(-1) to last year's tax report. A new generation is added by calling it DSN = TAX.STATE($+1$). A generation data group is limited to 255 entries.

The advantage of generation data groups is that all data sets have the same name, and the system keeps track of adding and deleting successive generations. Generation data groups can have sequential, direct, or partitioned organization and can reside on tape or direct-access volumes. Generation data groups must always be cataloged. Generation data groups are used like any other data set except for the relative generation number in the DSN parameter.

Two steps are required to create a generation data group: a generation data group index must be created in the system catalog, and a prototype data set must be created on the volume containing the system catalog to supply a data set label containing DCB subparameters for the generation data group. In VS1, the index is created by the

IEHPROGM utility program described in Chapter 15. In MVS the index is created by the AMP DEFINE command described in Chapter 18.

As an example, a generation data group named TAX.STATE is created. The following two steps build the generation data group index and create a dummy data set.

```
//STEP1 EXEC PGM=IEHPROGM
     [ The IBM utility IEHPROGM is used in VS1. ]
//SYSPRINT DD SYSOUT=A
//DDA      DD VOL=REF=SYS1.SVCLIB,DISP=OLD
//DDB      DD UNIT=SYSDA,VOL=SER=PACK12,DISP=OLD
//SYSIN    DD *
  BLDG INDEX=TAX.STATE,ENTRIES=5,DELETE
     [ INDEX names the generation data group, ENTRIES specifies the
     number of generations to retain, and DELETE scratches old
     generations as they are removed from the index. ]
/*
//STEP2 EXEC PGM=IEFBR14
//BUILDIT  DD DSN=TAX.STATE,DISP=(NEW,KEEP),
//            VOL=REF=*.STEP1.DDA,SPACE=(TRK,0),
//            DCB=(RECFM=FB,LRECL=80,BLKSIZE=12960)
     [ BUILDIT creates a data set with appropriate DCB
     subparameters for the generation data group.  The prototype
     data set must be on the volume containing the generation data
     group index, but cannot be cataloged if it has the same name
     as the generation data group.  DSORG, OPTCD, KEYLEN, and RKP
     could also have been coded as DCB subparameters. ]
```

A generation data group can now be created.

```
//STEP1 EXEC PGM=CREATE
     [ Assume CREATE is a program which creates a data set. ]
//GEN DD DSN=TAX.STATE(+1),DISP=(NEW,CATLG),
//       UNIT=SYSDA,VOL=SER=PACK12,SPACE=(80,200)
     [ The system searches for a data set named TAX.STATE which
     contains the required DCB subparameters. It then creates a
     generation data set and catalogs it. DSN and UNIT must be
     coded for each new generation data set. A disposition of
     CATLG must be used for all new generation data sets. DCB
     subparameters can be coded on the DD statement to override or
     add parameters from the prototype data set. ]
```

Generation (0) is always the current generation, (−1) is the preceding generation, (−2) the second generation, etc. Generation (+1) indicates a new generation and causes all generations to be pushed down one level at the end of the job. Generations are referred to by the same number throughout an entire job, and the generation numbers are not updated until the job terminates.

```
//STEP1 EXEC PGM=ONE
//INPUT  DD DSN=TAX.STATE(0),DISP=OLD
     [ This is the current generation. ]
//OUTPUT DD DSN=TAX.STATE(+1),DISP=(NEW,CATLG),
//          SPACE=(80,200),UNIT=SYSDA,VOL=SER=PACK12
     [ This creates a new generation. ]
```

```
//STEP2 EXEC PGM=TWO
//NEXT    DD DSN=TAX.STATE(+2),DISP=(NEW,CATLG),
//            UNIT=SYSDA,SPACE=(80,200)
   [ This creates another new generation.  It cannot be referred
   to as (+1) because the indexes are not updated until the end
   of the job.  At that time (+2) becomes (0), (+1) becomes (-
   1), and (0) becomes (-2). ]
```

The prototype data set can be cataloged by giving it a different name, but it must still be placed on the volume containing the system catalog.

```
//STEP2 EXEC PGM=IEFBR14
//BUILDIT DD DSN=DUMMYDS,DISP=(NEW,CATLG),
//            UNIT=SYSDA,VOL=SER=PACK14,SPACE=(TRK,0),
//            DCB=(RECFM=FB,LRECL=80,BLKSIZE=12960)
```

Any generation data group can use the DUMMYDS data set to supply DCB subparameters.

```
//STEP1 EXEC PGM=CREATE
//GEN DD DSN=TAX.STATE(+1),DISP=(NEW,CATLG),
//         UNIT=SYSDA,SPACE=(80,200),UNIT=SYSDA,
//         DCB=(DUMMYDS,BLKSIZE=400),VOL=SER=PACK12
   [ The DCB parameter points to the data set containing the DCB
   subparameters.  Subparameters can also be added or
   overridden--the BLKSIZE is set to 400 here. ]
```

The entries within a generation data group need not all have the same DCB subparameters.

Within a generation data group, the entries are individual data sets. An individual entry is referred to by DSN = *dsname*(*index-number*). The system actually saves the entry as DSN = *dsname*.G* gggg*V*nn*. The *gggg* is the absolute generation number, 0000 to 9999, and the *nn* is the version number, 00 to 99. The *nn* cannot be set through the JCL and defaults to 00. For example, TAX.STATE(0) refers to the current generation, but if it was the tenth entry added to the generation data group, its actual data set name would be TAX.STATE.G0010V00. You can refer to an entry by its relative generation number or by its actual data set name.

By omitting the generation number, the DD statement refers to all generations. The result is the same as if all the individual data sets were concatenated.

```
//NEXT DD DSN=TAX.STATE,DISP=OLD
```

IV. CHECKPOINT/RESTART

System/370 allows programs that abnormally terminate, or even those that run to completion, to be restarted so that the entire job need not be rerun in the event of an error. There are two methods of restarting a job: restarting from a step (*step restart*) and restarting from a checkpoint (*checkpoint restart*). Step restart is simpler and does not require a checkpoint to be taken. You simply code a RESTART parameter on the JOB statement to name the step from which to restart and resubmit the job.

A restart can be *automatic* (the system restarts the job immediately), or *deferred* (permitting you to examine your output and make the appropriate changes before resubmitting the job). The restart, whether automatic or deferred, is specified by the RD parameter on the EXEC statement. Automatic restart can occur only if the completion code accompanying the step agrees with a set of eligible completion codes specified by the installation when the system was generated, and if the operator consents.

Checkpoints consist of a snapshot of a program's status at selected points during execution so that if the program terminates for some reason, the run can be restarted from the last checkpoint rather than from the beginning of the run. Checkpointing is done only because of the potential cost or time limitations of restarting a large job. The checkpoints themselves are expensive, complex, and require careful planning. You may not always be able to successfully restart the run—the problem may be caused by a program error that occurred prior to the checkpoint. Checkpoints are used more as a protection against hardware, operating system, and operator errors than as protection against application program errors.

When a checkpoint is taken, the system notes the position of each data set that is open, but does not copy it. This can make restarting from a checkpoint difficult. If a data set is updated in place after the checkpoint is taken, it will not be returned to its original status for the restart. If a temporary data set is subsequently deleted, it will not be present for the restart. Data sets read directly from unit record devices rather than spooled data sets also prevent the job from being restarted.

Several checkpoints can be taken during the execution of the job step. A DD statement is included in the step to specify the data set to contain the checkpoints. For sequential data sets, DISP=OLD writes each new checkpoint over the previous one. This is dangerous because if the job terminates while a checkpoint is being taken, there is no usable checkpoint. Coding DISP=MOD writes each new checkpoint beyond the end of the previous, and is safer. Alternatively, the DD statement can point to a partitioned data set on a direct-access volume, and each checkpoint is added as a member.

Checkpointing is supported in various languages as follows:

- FORTRAN has no provision for checkpointing.
- Assembler language takes checkpoints by executing the CHKPT macro instruction. The DCB macro gives the ddname of the checkpoint data set.
- COBOL checkpoints are taken by the RERUN clause. The RERUN clause gives the ddname of the checkpoint data set.
- PL/I checkpoints are taken by CALL PLICKPT. The ddname of the checkpoint data set is SYSCHK.
- Sort/Merge checkpoints are taken by the CKPT parameter on the SORT/MERGE statement. The ddname of the checkpoint data set is SORTCKPT.
- JCL checkpoints are taken by coding the CHKPT parameter on a DD statement. The ddname of the checkpoint data set is SYSCKEOV.

A unique name called the *checkid*, assigned by you or the system, is printed on the operator's console to identify each checkpoint as it occurs. The system assigns checkids in the form C*nnnnnnn*. The *nnnnnnn* is a seven-digit number, starting with 0000001, identifying the successive checkpoints within the step. To restart from a checkpoint, you must obtain the latest checkid from the operator or your output listing.

A. CHKPT: Checkpoint of End-of-Volume

Coding CHKPT = EOV on a DD statement requests that a checkpoint be taken when the end-of-volume is reached. The DD statement must describe a multivolume sequential data set, either input or output. You must also include a SYSCKEOV DD statement in the job step to contain the checkpoint. SYSCKEOV is coded as a normal DD statement with DSN, DISP, UNIT, and VOL parameters. Do not code DCB parameters on SYSCKEOV because they are built into the program. A SYSCKEOV DD statement or any DD statement that is to contain a checkpoint must describe a sequential or partitioned data set. The record format must be undefined (RECFM = U).

```
//STEP1 EXEC PGM=WRITEALL
//OUTPUT    DD DSN=AFILE,DISP=(NEW,KEEP),
//             UNIT=TAPE,VOL=SER=(004001,004002),CHKPT=EOV
   [ A checkpoint will be taken when tape 004001 is completely
   written. ]
//SYSCKEOV DD DSN=SAVEIT,DISP=(MOD,KEEP),
//             UNIT=TAPE,VOL=SER=002000
   [ DISP=MOD should be coded so that each new checkpoint is
   written beyond the previous checkpoint. ]
```

B. RD: Restart Definition

The RD parameter on the JOB or EXEC statement controls automatic restart and may also suppress the CHKPT macro so checkpoints are not taken. The parameter is coded as RD = *restart-conditions*. The following table describes the restart conditions.

Restart-Conditions	Automatic Restart?	Suppress CHKPT?
R—Restart	Yes	No
NC—No Checkpoint	No	Yes
NR—No Automatic Restart	No	No
RNC—Restart and No		
Checkpoint	Yes	Yes

For example, RD = RNC permits automatic restart and suppresses the CHKPT macro. If automatic restart is requested, the restart is made from the last checkpoint in the step (*checkpoint restart*). If no checkpoint occurred because the CHKPT macro was suppressed or omitted, or the step terminated before the macro was executed, restart is made at the start of the step (*step restart*). If the RD parameter is omitted, automatic restart occurs only if a CHKPT macro was executed.

Automatic restart requires that the system make special disposition of data sets. When a step is automatically restarted, any data sets created in the step are deleted, and data sets existing when the step was first initiated are kept. If restart is made from a checkpoint, all data sets currently used by the job are kept. Any CPU time limit for a step is reset to its original value when restart occurs.

1.   RD on EXEC statements

```
//STEP1 EXEC PGM=CSMP,RD=R
   [ STEP1 may be automatically restarted. ]
// EXEC FORTGCLG,RD.LKED=NR,RD.GO=NC
   [ The LKED step of the FORTGCLG procedure is not automatically
   restarted.   The GO step is not automatically restarted, and
   any CHKPT macros are suppressed.   Each step in the FORTGCLG
   procedure must have a stepname, and the stepname must be
   unique for the job. ]
// EXEC FORTGCLG,RD=RNC
   [ Automatic restart is permitted, and the CHKPT macro is
   suppressed in each step of the FORTGCLG procedure. ]
```

2.   RD on JOB statements

RD coded on the JOB statement applies to each step within the job, and any RD parameters on EXEC statements within the job are ignored.

```
//FAST JOB 4562,SMAUG,CLASS=A,RD=R
        [ All steps within the job may be automatically restarted. ]
```

C. RESTART: Resubmit a Job for Restart

After examining the output from your job, you may elect to restart it later from a checkpoint or the start of a job step. A deferred restart can be used regardless of the way the job terminates—abnormally or normally—and irrespective of whether automatic restart occurred. With deferred restart you can correct or change data and fix program errors before resubmitting the job. The RESTART parameter coded on the JOB statement requests deferred restart.

1.   Step restart

A deferred restart from a job step begins execution at a specific step within the job, bypassing all preceding steps. Data sets are not passed from previous steps because the previous steps are not executed. Referbacks cannot be used except in the DCB, DSN, and VOL parameters. The VOL must refer back to a DD statement giving the volume serial number. Remember that new data sets created in the previous run may still be in existence— attempts to recreate them may cause the job to fail because of duplicate data sets on the same volume. The JCL may have to be modified to circumvent these restrictions.

Always examine the output from the previous run to reconstruct conditions so that the step may be restarted. Perhaps the step cannot be restarted. If a temporary data set passed from a previous step is deleted, restart from the step that created the data set. If a passed data set was kept, identify the data set with name, unit, volume, and label information. Only the name and volume are needed if the data set was cataloged. For data 1.11x8sets residing on direct-access volumes that are created and kept previously within the step, either change the disposition on the DD statement from NEW to OLD or MOD, or delete the data set before resubmitting the job, or define a new data set.

Restart can be simplified by cataloging data sets when they are created so they can be referred to by name without having to specify the unit and volume. Use conditional data set dispositions (the third parameter of DISP) to delete new data sets or catalog passed data sets. You can make any necessary changes to the JCL, such as requesting different devices or volumes, using different data sets, or modifying data.

Step restart is requested by coding RESTART = *stepname* on the JOB statement, where the stepname gives the name of the step from which to restart.

```
//TEST JOB 2256,ROI,CLASS=A,RESTART=STEP6
       .        .        .
//STEP6 EXEC ...
        [ Execution resumes at STEP6. ]
```

Restart may also be made from a step within a cataloged procedure by coding RESTART = *stepname.procstep*.

```
//TEST JOB 2249,DAUPHIN,CLASS=A,RESTART=RUN.LKED
//STEP1 EXEC ...
//RUN   EXEC PLIXCLG
        [ Execution resumes at the LKED step in the PLIXCLG cataloged
        procedure. ]
```

If RESTART = * is coded on the JOB statement, execution begins at the first step. (The same happens of course if the RESTART parameter is omitted.)

2. Restart from a checkpoint

The RESTART parameter on the JOB statement, in addition to specifying the step at which to restart, can also name the checkpoint to be used for the restart. All the data sets required by the original job step must be present for the restart because the checkpoint does not save them; it only notes the position in each data set when the checkpoint is taken. The restart step must not refer to data sets that are deleted after the checkpoint is taken. If data sets are passed to the restart step, modify the JCL to include the UNIT and VOL of the data sets. Use the conditional disposition to catalog passed data sets if the step abnormally terminates to eliminate having to add the UNIT and VOL.

The DD statements in the restart step must point to the same data sets on the same units and volumes as when the checkpoint was taken, but other parameters can be changed. You can add another volume for a multivolume output data set, add new DD statements, alter data, and dummy out unneeded DD statements. Referbacks cannot be used except in the DCB, DSN, and VOL parameters. The VOL must referback to a DD statement giving the volume serial number.

To restart a job from a checkpoint, code the following on the JOB statement:

```
RESTART=(stepname,checkid)
     [ Restart from a job step. ]
RESTART=(stepname.procstep,checkid)
     [ Restart from a step within a cataloged procedure. ]
RESTART=(*,checkid)
     [ Restart from the first step within the job. ]
```

The *checkid* must be enclosed in apostrophes if it contains special characters [blank , . / ') (* & + − =]; code a legitimate apostrophe as two consecutive apostrophes.

You must include a SYSCHK DD statement to describe the checkpoint data set. Place the SYSCHK DD statement after the JOB statement and any JOBLIB statement, but before the first EXEC statement.

```
//TEST JOB 2566,JONES,CLASS=A,RESTART=(STEP1.GO,CK10)
     [ Restart is made from the GO step of the PLIXCLG cataloged
     procedure invoked by STEP1.  The restart is made from the
     CK10 checkpoint. ]
//JOBLIB DD DSN=PROGLIB,DISP=SHR
//SYSCHK DD DSN=CHKPTLIB,DISP=OLD
     [ The SYSCHK DD statement follows the JOB and any JOBLIB
     statement. ]
//STEP1 EXEC PLIXCLG
```

The SYSCHK DD statement may include other DD parameters as needed. If the checkpoint data set is not cataloged, unit and volume information must be included. Do not include a member name if the checkpoint data set is partitioned. SYSCHK must imply or specify a disposition of OLD and KEEP.

Generation data groups require that the generation in the JCL be changed for deferred step restart if the data set was cataloged in a preceding step. The JCL must point to the new generation number rather than the original generation number if the generation data set was created and cataloged in steps preceding the restart step. For example, if $(+2)$ is created in STEP 1, refer to it as (0) to restart in STEP 2. Generation data groups do not have this problem if they are kept rather than cataloged. The problem also disappears with automatic restart and with deferred restart from a checkpoint.

V.   DATA SET PROTECTION

A.   RETPD, EXPDT: Retention Checks

The LABEL parameter coded on the DD statement can assign a retention period to data sets on tape or direct-access volumes. A data set with an unexpired retention date cannot be modified or deleted. When the retention period expires, the data set becomes like any other data set without a retention check—it can be modified or deleted.

To request a retention period, code LABEL = RETPD = *days*, specifying the number of days (0 to 9,999) in the retention period. Alternatively, code LABEL = EXPDT = *yyddd* to request an expiration date. The *yy* is the two-digit year, and *ddd* is the three-digit day number (001 to 366). A retention period of zero days is assumed if retention is not specified.

Retention periods are usually assigned when the data set is created, but they can be changed or removed later in any job step that opens the data set, by coding the LABEL parameter.

B.   PASSWORD, NOPWREAD: Password Protection

A measure of security can be given to data sets with IBM or ANS labels by protecting them with a password. The PASSWORD subparameter, coded when the data set is created, indicates that a password is needed to open or delete the data set. If instead you specify NOPWREAD (no password read), the data set can be read, but the password must be supplied to write or delete the data set.

The system assigns an eight-digit password when the data set is created. The operator, or in TSO the time-sharing user, must supply the password whenever the data set is used. (It need not be supplied to read a NOPWREAD data set.) If the correct password is not given in two tries, the job is canceled.

Password protection does not yield a high measure of security. A clever programmer can circumvent the protection, and a second party—the operator—must know the password. Password protection is adequate for non-critical data sets but may not be appropriate for highly sensitive data sets such as payroll. It is inadequate for national security classified information. To request that a data set be protected by a password, code LABEL = (,,PASSWORD) or LABEL = (,,NOPWREAD).

PASSWORD and NOPWREAD are positional subparameters and RETPD and EXPDT are keyword subparameters. They may all be coded in any combination with other LABEL subparameters.

```
//A DD LABEL=(2,SL,PASSWORD,IN,RETPD=30),...
//B DD LABEL=(,,NOPWREAD,EXPDT=99360),...
```

C.   RACF Protection (MVS Only)

The Resource Access Control Facility (RACF, pronounced rack-f) is an IBM program product that limits access to data sets residing on direct-access volumes.

RACF contains a list of users that may have access to a data set, along with the type of access that they may have. A data set may be given RACF protection either automatically when it is created (if the user has the automatic data set protection attribute), or through the RACF command language. If a data set is both password-protected and RACF-protected, the password protection is ignored.

1. GROUP, PASSWORD, and USER parameters

The GROUP, PASSWORD, and USER parameters are coded on the JOB statement to give access to a RACF-protected data set. The parameters are coded as follows:

- GROUP = *group-name* associates the user with a RACF group. The *group-name* is one to eight alphanumeric (A to Z, 0 to 9) or national (@ # $) characters; the first character alphabetic or national. GROUP is optional; if omitted, the default group for the user is used.
- PASSWORD = *password* identifies the current RACF password. The password is one to eight alphanumeric characters. PASSWORD = (*old-password*, *new-password*) may also be coded to change the password of RACF-protected data sets.
- USER = *userid* identifies the user by supplying the userid. The *userid* is one to seven alphanumeric or national characters; the first character is alphabetic or national. USER must be coded to access RACF-protected data sets.

```
//TEST#1  JOB 2864,'TEST',CLASS=A,GROUP=OURS,
//              PASSWORD=L22434L3,USER=METOO
```

2. The PROTECT parameter

To request RACF protection for data sets on disk or tape, add the PROTECT = YES parameter:

```
//OUTPUT DD DSN=Y2254.TEST.DATA,DISP=(NEW,CATLG),
//            UNIT=SYSDA,PROTECT=YES,
//            SPACE=(TRK,(100,10))
```

PROTECT can be used only for nontemporary data sets and then only when they are created. For disk data sets, the data set name cannot be temporary and the normal and abnormal disposition cannot be DELETE. Tape labels must be SL, SUL, AL, or AUL. Except for SUL, the data set must be stored in the first file on the tape.

D. Summary

VSAM data sets described in the next chapter may also have password protection, although it is implemented differently.

Data security is not an easy problem. Don't be lulled into complacency by the features provided by the operating system. For example, when a password-protected data set is deleted, pointers are changed in the VTOC, but the data on the volume is not erased. Someone else could be allocated the same space, making it possible to read the "deleted" data set. Temporary data sets, such as sort work files, cannot be password protected, and they too present a security problem. Likewise, real storage is not zeroed out when another program is loaded, and any data left in storage potentially can be accessed when another program is allocated the region or partition.

VI. VIRTUAL I/O TEMPORARY DATA SETS (MVS ONLY)

Virtual storage in MVS allows a large amount of data to be retained in paging storage and paged into real storage as needed. Virtual Input/Output (VIO) data sets use this same paging facility of the operating system for data sets. The advantage of VIO is that it is more efficient than normal data sets. It is simpler to code because there is a default SPACE allocated. VIO can only be used for temporary data sets. VIO cannot be used for VSAM or ISAM data sets.

The installation must generate the system with unit names for VIO data sets. You then specify one of these unit names with a UNIT parameter. In specifying VIO data sets, the following DD parameters and defaults apply.

- DSN is optional, as it is for any temporary data set. If coded, DSN = &&*dsname* is required.
- DISP: CATLG, UNCATLG, and KEEP cannot be coded.
- UNIT must specify a VIO unit name. The unit count is ignored if it is coded.
- VOL = SER cannot be coded. The unit name selects a group of eligible volumes.
- SPACE is optional. If omitted, SPACE = (1000,(10,50)) is assumed.

The following example illustrates a VIO data set.

```
//STEP1 EXEC PGM=ONE
//DD1 DD DISP=(NEW,PASS),UNIT=VIOA
     [ SPACE=(1000,(10,50)) is assumed. ]
//STEP2 EXEC PGM=TWO
//DD2 DD DSN=*.STEP1.DISP=(OLD,DELETE)
```

If a DD statement describes a temporary data set and VOL = REF is coded to refer back to a VIO data set, the DD statement making the referback also becomes a VIO data set.

VII. DYNAMICALLY ALLOCATED DATA SETS (MVS ONLY)

Data sets can be dynamically allocated and deallocated during execution. This might be done if the needs of the job are unknown before it is run or to release resources for more efficient use.

To dynamically allocate data sets, the system needs to know beforehand the number to be allocated. You can provide this number either with the DYNAMNBR = *number* parameter on the EXEC statement or by including DD statements with the DYNAM parameter. The total number of dynamically allocated data sets is the total of the DYNAMNBR value plus the number of DYNAM DD statements.

A. DYNAMNBR: Dynamically Allocated Data Sets

DYNAMNBR = *number* coded on the EXEC statement specifies the number (0 to 1,635) of dynamically allocated data sets.

```
//STEP1 EXEC PGM=ONE,DYNAMNBR=6
    [ Six data sets may be dynamically allocated. ]
// EXEC COBUCLG,DYNAMNBR.GO=3
    [ The GO step of the COBUCLG cataloged procedure may
    dynamically allocate three data sets. ]
// EXEC COBUCLG,DYNAMNBR=2
    [ Each step in the COBUCLG cataloged procedure may dynamically
    allocate two data sets. ]
```

B. DYNAM: Dynamically Allocated Data Sets

DYNAM on a DD statement is coded with no other parameters.

```
//ddname DD DYNAM
```

A DDNAME or a referback statement cannot refer to a DYNAM DD statement. A DYNAM DD statement cannot be the first in a group of concatenated data sets. To nullify DYNAM in a cataloged procedure, code SYSOUT or DSN on the overriding statement.

C. FREE: Dynamically Deallocate Data Sets

To dynamically deallocate a data set when it is closed, code the FREE = CLOSE parameter on the DD statement. For example, coding FREE = CLOSE on a SYSOUT DD statement would release the data set to be printed when the data set is closed rather than when the step terminates as is normally done.

```
//SYSPRINT DD SYSOUT=A,FREE=CLOSE
```

A data set cannot be reopened if FREE = CLOSE is coded. FREE = CLOSE cannot be coded with the DDNAME, DYNAM, DATA, or * parameters. FREE = END may also be coded to deallocate the data set at the end of the step rather than when it is closed.

VIII. SUBSYSTEM DATA SETS

A. The SUBSYS DD Parameter

The SUBSYS parameter written on the DD statement provides a means of defining data sets for subsystems and for passing subsystem-dependent data to a subsystem. (This can only be done if Subsystem Support, SU29, is installed.) The main subsystem for which this feature is used is the IBM 3800 printer. The SUBSYS parameter is written as:

```
//ddname DD SUBSYS=(name,parm,parm,...,parm)
```

- *name* is the one- to four-character name of the subsystem. The first character must be alphabetic or national. The remaining characters can be alphanumeric or national.
- *parm* can be from 1 to 253 or 254 character strings whose meaning is defined by the subsystem. Each parameter can be from 1 to 67 characters. If a string contains special characters, enclose the string in apostrophes. Code a legitimate apostrophe as two apostrophes.

```
//TEST DD SUBSYS=(SPL,A,'IT''IS',B,'IT=6')
```

No checkpoint/restart is allowed for jobs with the SUBSYS parameter. The only other parameter that can be coded with SUBSYS is the DCB. In MVS, the COPIES, DEST, DISP, FCB, OUTLIM, SPACE, and UNIT parameters can be written, but they are checked only for syntax and then ignored.

B. The CNTL and ENDCNTL JCL Statements and the CNTL DD Parameter

The CNTL JCL statement allows you to enter subsystem control statements in the job stream rather than placing them in a library. You place the CNTL and ENDCNTL JCL statements in the job stream before the DD statement that refers to it. The DD parameter refers to the CNTL statement with a CNTL DD parameter. The DD statement referring to the CNTL statement cannot be in a cataloged procedure.

```
//TEST1 CNTL *
subsystem control statements
// ENDCNTL
//INPUT DD CNTL=*.TEST1,...
```

You write the CNTL and ENDCNTL JCL statements as:

```
//name CNTL *
subsystem control statements
// ENDCNTL
```

Each *name* must be unique within the job. The *name* can be from one to eight alphanumeric or national characters and the first character must be alphabetic or national. Then on a following DD statement, you write a CNTL parameter to refer to a CNTL statement:

```
//ddname DD CNTL=*.name, ...
```

You can also include a stepname to refer to a CNTL DD parameter in a prior step.

```
CNTL=*.stepname.name
```

The CNTL JCL statement can be placed in a cataloged procedure and then referred to by a DD statement in the job stream. To write a CNTL DD parameter in the job stream to refer to the CNTL JCL statements in a cataloged procedure, you write the CNTL DD parameter as:

```
CNTL=*.stepname.procstepname.name
```

Although both the CNTL JCL statement and the DD statement containing the CNTL parameter can be placed in a cataloged procedure, you can't refer to a CNTL JCL statement in the input stream within a cataloged procedure.

IX. MISCELLANEOUS JCL PARAMETERS

A. DSID: Diskette Data Set ID

The DSID parameter coded on a DD statement specifies a data set identifier for the 3540 Diskette Reader or Writer utility. DSID is coded as DSID = (*id*,V)

- *id* is from one to eight alphanumeric, national, minus, or left bracket characters that identify the data set on the diskette. The first character must be alphabetic or national.
- V is an optional parameter for SYSIN data sets to specify that the data set label must have been previously verified on a 3741 data entry terminal.

You can also write VOL = SER on the DD statement to specify a volume serial number. And you can write DCB = LRECL to specify a logical record length.

B. QNAME: Access TCAM Messages

The QNAME = *process-name* parameter on a DD statement gives an application program access to messages received through TCAM (Terminal Communications Access Method). The *process-name* is the eight alphanumeric or national character name of a TPROCESS macro instruction that defines a destination queue for messages that are to be processed by an application program. The first character must be alphabetic or national. Only the DCB parameter may be coded on the DD statement with QNAME, and then only the BLKSIZE, BUFL, LRECL, OPTCD, and RECFM subparameters.

```
//ADD DD QNAME=STUFFROM
```

C.   TERM: Notify System of Terminal Data Set

The TERM = TS (TERM = RT in VS1) parameter on the DD statement indicates that a data set is coming or going to a time-sharing terminal. The SYSOUT and DCB parameter may be coded with TERM; any other parameters are ignored. Coding TERM on a SYSOUT DD statement sends the output data set back to the terminal if it was submitted from a terminal.

```
//SYSPRINT DD SYSOUT=A,TERM=TS
```

D.   NOTIFY: Notification when Job Completes (MVS Only)

NOTIFY = *userid* on the JOB statement requests the system to send a message to your time-sharing terminal when the batch job completes. The *userid* is from one to seven alphanumeric characters that identify you. You must LOGON with this same userid to receive the message. If you are not logged on when the job completes, the message will be saved and displayed when you next log on.

```
//XR15 JOB (2001,10),'A JOB',NOTIFY=GDB10,CLASS=A
     [ When the job completes, a message will be sent to the user
     identified by GDB10. ]
```

E.   COMPACT: Identify Compaction Table (VS1 Only)

Coding COMPACT = *table-id* on a SYSOUT DD statement identifies the compaction table for a 3790 remote work station. The table-id is from one to four alphanumeric or national characters, the first character alphabetic or national.

```
//SENDIT DD SYSOUT=A,COMPACT=PNT
     [ The data, when sent to a remote work station, is compacted
     using the PNT compaction table. ]
```

If COMPACT is omitted or if COMPACT = NO is coded, the data is not compacted.

F.   SEP, AFF: Channel Separation (VS1 Only)

The SEP and AFF parameters coded on a DD statement can direct data sets onto different channels, which may in turn make the processing more efficient. (A channel is the part of the computer that transmits data between real storage and an I/O device.) To separate a data set from a channel used by other data sets in the same step, code SEP = (*ddname,ddname,...,ddname*). The *ddname* is the name of from one to eight previous DD statements in the same step.

```
//STEP1 EXEC PGM=ALPHA
//A DD UNIT=3380,...
//B DD UNIT=3380,SEP=A,...
    [ The data set described by the B DD statement is separated
    from the channel used by the A DD statement. ]
//C DD UNIT=3380,SEP=(A,B),...
    [ C is separated from the channels used by A and B. ]
//D DD UNIT=3380,SEP=(A,B),....
    [ D has the same channel separation as C. ]
```

The AFF = *ddname* parameter copies a SEP parameter from a previous DD statement. The previous DD statement could have been coded as:

```
//D DD UNIT=3380,AFF=C,...
```

Channel separation requests are ignored if a unit is requested by hardware address, if an old data set resides on a permanently mounted volume, or if there are not enough channels for separation. Use channel separation with discretion. In a multiprogramming environment where many jobs are running concurrently, the impact of a single job on channel usage may not be significant. Channel separation restricts unit assignment and may result in unnecessary dismounting of volumes. Use channel separation only for new data sets, or old data sets on mountable volumes, where a significant savings is expected.

G. PERFORM: Performance Group Assignment (MVS Only)

The PERFORM = *n* parameter assigns a job or step to an installation-defined performance group, where *n* can range from 1 to 999. Performance groups are defined by the installation to optimize the system's performance and to give appropriate response to groups of jobs. If PERFORM is omitted, an installation-defined default is assumed—usually 1 for non-TSO jobs and 2 for TSO jobs.

1. PERFORM on EXEC statements

PERFORM coded on an EXEC statement applies to specific steps.

```
//STEP1 EXEC PGM=ONE,PERFORM=6
    [ STEP1 is assigned to performance group 6. ]
//STEP2 EXEC COBUCLG,PERFORM.COB=8
    [ The COB step of the COBUCLG procedure is assigned to
    performance group 8. ]
//STEP3 EXEC COBUCLG,PERFORM=3
    [ All steps within the procedure are assigned to performance
    group 3. ]
```

2.   PERFORM on JOB statements

PERFORM coded on the JOB statement applies to all steps within the job, overriding any PERFORM parameters coded on EXEC statements.

```
//TEST#6 JOB (3826,20),'TEST IT',PERFORM=12,CLASS=A
   [ All steps within the job are assigned to performance group
   12. ]
```

H.   MPROFILE, PROFILE: Assign Output Class (VS1 Only)

The Installation Specified Selection Parameters (ISSP) are a table of attributes assigned by an installation to assign system messages or data sets to an output class. The assignment consists of a character string that enables the installation to define meaningful names for output classes.

On the JOB statement MPROFILE = *'message-profile-string'* performs the same function as the MSGCLASS parameter (and overrides it) to assign system messages to an output class. The message-profile-string cannot exceed 120 characters.

```
//TEST JOB (1325,6),'A JOB',CLASS=A,
//          MPROFILE='FORMS=BOND,LINES=50'
   [ FORMS=BOND and LINES=50 would be installation-defined
   parameters that together define an output class. ]
```

Also on the JOB statement, PROFILE = *'sysout-profile-string'*) performs the same function as the CLASS and PRTY parameters and overrides them. The *sysout-profile-string* cannot exceed 120 characters.

```
//TEST JOB (1325,6),'A JOB',PROFILE='A'
```

Chapter 18

DIRECT AND VSAM DATA SETS

In the time-honored tradition of saving the hardest for last, this chapter describes direct, VSAM, and ISAM data sets.

I. DIRECT DATA SETS

Direct data organization permits each record to be accessed randomly, without regard to its position relative to other records. Direct data sets must reside on direct-access volumes. There are two types of direct data sets, relative and keyed.

Relative data sets contain unblocked, fixed-length records. The records are stored consecutively on the tracks of a direct-access volume. To read or write a record, the program must supply the record's relative position in the data set. COBOL RELATIVE, FORTRAN direct, and PL/I REGIONAL(1) data sets are of this nature.

Relative data sets are used like arrays or tables. Their advantage over tables is that their size is limited by the amount of storage on a direct-access volume rather than the more limited real storage. However, it is much slower to retrieve an element from a relative data set than it is from a table. Relative data sets are best for records that are easily associated with ascending, consecutive numbers, such as years (the years 1960 to 1990 could be stored with keys 0 to 30), months (keys 0 to 11), or the 50 states (keys 0 to 49). A *key* is a field within a record that identifies the record.

Keyed direct data sets are also unblocked, but may contain fixed-length, variable-length, or undefined-length records. Several records are stored on a track, and each record is stored with a key. COBOL RANDOM and PL/I REGIONAL(2) and REGIONAL(3) data sets are of this nature.

The key is not contained within the record. The system writes the key in front of each record. To read or write a record, you must supply the relative track number (*track key*) and the record key. The *record key* or just *key* is some field or fields that identify a record.

The difficult part of keyed direct data sets involves deriving the track key. The record key often comes from the record itself—for example in a personnel file it might be a social security number. There are two usual ways of deriving the track key. First, you can let the system supply the track key as the records are written, and then save this track key, along with the record key, in a separate table or data set. Then to retrieve a record, you can use the record key to search the table or data set to obtain the track key. This is both complicated and inefficient. A better way is to compute the track key from the record key and supply it to the system when the record is written.

The efficiency of the direct access for direct data sets depends primarily on the hashing method used to translate the record key into a track key. There are many techniques, and for some applications it may pay to study them to determine which might be the most efficient. In most instances, the remaindering method works well and is simple. Divide the record key by the largest prime number less than the number of track allocated, and use the remainder for the relative track number.

Consider a personnel file containing 8,000 employees in which 10 records will fit on a single track. Such a data set would require 800 tracks, but we might want to allocate 1,000 tracks to allow for growth. Also the efficiency begins to drop off when the data becomes more than about 70 percent full. To compute the relative track number, divide the social security number by 997, the largest prime number that is less than 1,000. A social security number of 520-44-1461 divided by 997 yields a remainder of 482, which becomes the relative track number.

Direct data set DD statements differ from sequential data sets only in the DCB subparameters that are needed. DSORG = DA or DAU (direct-access unmovable) must be coded to tell the system the data organization. For keyed direct data sets, KEYLEN = *length* must be coded to specify the key length in bytes. Keys must be of a fixed length and be in every record.

In reading or writing direct data sets with keys, the DCB = (OPTCD = E,LIMCT = *tracks*) parameter may be coded on the DD statement to extend the search some number of tracks. Thus if LIMCT = 10 is coded and a track is full, the system will look at as many as nine following tracks to find available space or search for a record. If LIMCT is coded to write a data set, the same value should be coded to read the data set.

Direct data sets may be processed sequentially or randomly. In sequential processing, the records are read or written in the order in which they physically occur. In random processing, the record is read or written in an order based on a record key. The term *random* does not mean that any record is selected at random, but that the next record can be accessed irrespective of the previous record accessed. Note that if the records are stored randomly based on some hashing technique, the sequential order is essentially random—random in the sense that there is no meaningful order.

Individual records in direct data sets can be processed faster randomly than with VSAM because no index search is required. However, direct organization is slower for processing sequential than is sequential or VSAM organization because direct data sets cannot be blocked.

II.   VSAM DATA SETS

Virtual Storage Access Method (VSAM) data sets are supported in assembler language, COBOL, and PL/I, but not FORTRAN. The term *virtual* in VSAM is perhaps misleading. It means that the access method has been implemented in IBM's virtual operating systems, VS1 and MVS. There is nothing inherently virtual in VSAM.

VSAM allows data sets to be processed both sequentially and randomly. The JCL requirements are very simple. However, this has a good news/bad news aspect. The good news in VSAM is that there is little JCL. The bad news is that a set of Access Method Services (AMS) commands must be used. What follows is only an introduction to VSAM.

VSAM data sets may be organized in three ways. *Key-sequenced* data sets store records in sequential order based on the record keys. A data set can be processed sequentially, in the order of the record keys, or randomly, by presenting the key of the record to access. *Entry-sequenced* data sets store records in the order they are entered. The records are usually processed sequentially in this order, but they can be retrieved or updated randomly. However, you must externally keep track of where each record is stored to access records randomly. *Relative record* data sets are the equivalent of direct data sets, and are supported only in assembler language. The remainder of this discussion is about key-sequenced data sets, and the term VSAM is used to mean VSAM key-sequenced data sets.

To understand VSAM key-sequenced data sets, suppose a public library maintains a data set containing a record for each book and there are 150,000 books. Each record might contain the title, author, publisher, and other information about the book. The Dewey Decimal Number can be used as the key to arrange the books in the stacks.

Sequential processing works well when all the records must be processed, as they would for an inventory, but suppose the record of a book titled "Zelda's Zilch" requires a change. When a single record must be changed, random accessing is much faster. Likewise, books are added and deleted from the data set directly without having to process the entire data set.

The analogy with a library is a good one to pursue because the VSAM keyed-sequenced organization is similar to the way in which a public library is organized. The basic unit of storage in a library is a shelf (*control interval* in VSAM). Books (*records*) are arranged on the shelves in the stacks ordered by their library number (*record key*). A separate index to the books is contained in the card index (*index area*). The card index does not point directly to a book, but only to the location of the shelf. Once you find the shelf, you must search it for the book with the matching library number.

When a book is added, the card index is updated, and the book is inserted on the shelf. Note that the card index has two levels: an index in the form of card trays and the index to the books within the trays. VSAM provides as many levels of index as are needed.

Let us follow this analogy a little further to illustrate how VSAM data sets are updated. When a book is added, it is inserted where it belongs on the shelf, and the remainder of the books are moved over. If there is no room on the control interval (shelf), VSAM would insert the record where it belongs, create a new control interval, and move any records forced off the end of the old control interval to the new control interval.

The index of an VSAM data set is a little different from that of a library. The library has an index card for every book. In VSAM, there is an index entry only for the last record on each control interval. Thus the index tells where the record should be on the control interval. The control interval must be searched to see if the record actually exists.

VSAM data sets may also have alternative indexes. This allows VSAM data sets to be inverted on some key. If the term *inverted* is unfamiliar, the concept is not. Libraries invert their files and provide alternative indexes. One card catalog lists the books with the titles as keys, and then this file is inverted on the author to create a catalog listing the authors as keys. This allows you to retrieve a book given either its author or title.

VSAM data sets may have password protection. This password protection is not the same as the JCL password protection coded in the LABEL parameter. VSAM password protection affords some control over data set access, and the password is supplied by the application program rather than by the operator.

VSAM data sets must reside on direct-access volume. They may contain fixed- or variable-length records. VSAM data sets must be cataloged. Before a VSAM data set can be created, a *master catalog* must be established to be used by all VSAM data sets. Separate *user catalogs* may also be created. A large amount of space termed the *VSAM data space*, often an entire volume, is then allocated to VSAM. This space is then subdivided into *clusters* and allocated to individual data sets. The VSAM data space may have up to 15 secondary allocations, and the clusters may each obtain up to 123 secondary allocations out of the VSAM data space. The system selects an optimum block size for VSAM data sets, and you cannot specify the blocking. Figure 59 illustrates the VSAM catalogs and data space.

VSAM data sets must be created sequentially. When the data set is created, you write the records ordered on their keys, and the system blocks the records and creates a separate index containing the key of the last record written in each block. Records are retrieved randomly by searching the index to find the block containing the record, and then by searching the block for a record with a matching key. VSAM data sets can also be updated by replacing, adding, or deleting records. Records are replaced by overwriting the old record.

The records in a VSAM data set are stored in control intervals. A *control interval* is similar to a block in that it contains several records, but it also contains free space as shown in Figure 60. The system selects an efficient control interval size based on the track size of the direct-access volume and the data set's record length. When the data set is created, free space can be specified in two ways: a percentage of each control interval can be left free, and a percentage of the total control intervals can be left free.

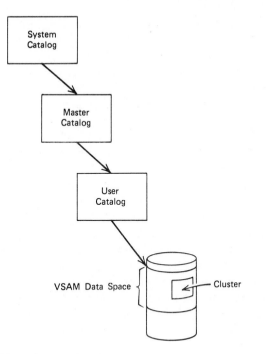

Figure 59. VSAM catalogs and data space

Record A	Record D	Record F	Free space

Figure 60. VSAM control interval

The index area also consists of these same control intervals. As the data set is created, the key of the last record stored in each control interval, along with a pointer to the control interval containing the record, is stored in the index control interval. The pointer consists of the relative byte address (RBA) of the record's location in the data set. Figure 61 illustrates VSAM indexes.

The system creates as many levels of index control intervals as needed. When an index control interval is filled, another control area is allocated, and a higher-level index control interval is created to point to the two lower-level control intervals. When this higher-level control interval is filled with pointers, another higher-level control interval is created. This continues for as many levels as needed. The lowest-level group of control intervals is termed the *sequence set*, and it points to all the control intervals containing data records. The entire data set, including the indexes and the sequence set, is termed a *cluster*.

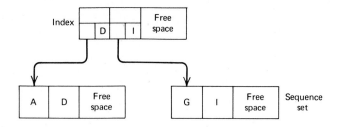

Figure 61. VSAM pointer structure

VSAM data sets are reorganized as they are updated. When a record is deleted, all the records following it are moved down in the control interval, increasing the free space. When a record is added, it is inserted where it belongs in the control interval, and the records following it are moved down, collapsing the free space at the end of the control interval. If there is not enough free space to contain the new record, a *control interval split* occurs. A new control interval is allocated, and records are moved off the original control interval so that both the old and new control interval now contain free space. The indexes are then updated. The overflow records are thus stored in the same blocked format as the original records. The result is that VSAM data sets seldom require a separate reorganization. Figure 62 illustrates a control interval split.

When VSAM data sets are updated, the records are written into the data set and the pointers are updated. If the program abnormally terminates when the data set is opened for output or update, the data set may become unusable because the pointers may not get updated. This is a serious problem if you do not have a backup. This generally requires that you back up the data set at some point and save the transactions entered until a new backup is made.

A. Accessing VSAM Data Sets

Once the data set has been created, the following DD statement suffices to access the data set.

```
//ddname DD DSN=file-name,DISP=SHR
```

OLD may be coded in place of SHR, and an existing VSAM data set can be rewritten. VSAM data sets cannot be passed.

B. AMP Parameter on the DD Statement

The DCB parameter cannot be coded for VSAM data sets. Instead, an AMP parameter serves the same purpose in specifying the items about the data set left unspecified when it was created. AMP is coded as:

```
AMP=('option','option',...'option')
```

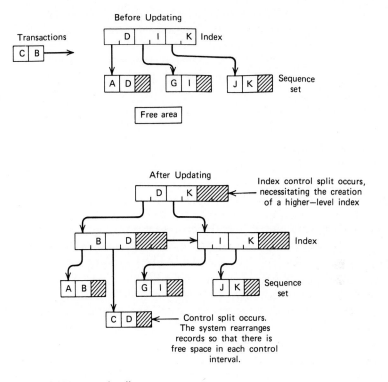

Figure 62. VSAM control split

The following options are provided:

- 'AMORG' indicates that the DD statement describes a VSAM data set and is needed if the DD statement is made DUMMY. (VSAM data sets may be made DUMMY.) AMORG is also needed if the UNIT and VOL parameters are coded on the DD statement.
- 'BUFND=n' specifies the number of buffers for the control data area data. At least two buffers must be provided. If omitted, BUFND defaults to an installation-defined value.
- 'BUFNI=n' specifies the number of buffers for the index data. At least one buffer must be provided. If BUFNI is omitted, an installation default is assumed.
- 'BUFSP=n' specifies the same number for BUFND and BUFNI and overrides both. At least two buffers must be specified. If omitted, BUFND or BUFNI or an installation default is assumed.
- 'CROPS=RCK,NCK,NRE, or NRC' (only one can be coded) specifies the checkpoint/restart option. RCK defaults. It specifies that an erase-test and data

set post-checkpoint modification test are performed. NCK specifies that data set post-checkpoint modification tests are not performed. NRE specifies that a data-erase test is not performed. NRC specifies that neither a data-erase test nor data set post-checkpoint modification tests are performed.

- 'SYNAD = *modulename*' specifies a module name to be used by the EXLIST macro instruction.
- 'TRACE' specifies that the generalized trace facility is to be used to gather statistics.
- 'STRNO = *n*' specifies the number of VSAM requests that require concurrent data set positioning.

The following options are coded for the ISAM interface:

- 'OPTCD = I, L, or IL' (only one can be coded) specifies how the ISAM records flagged as deleted are to be processed by the program. I causes records flagged as deleted not to be written if DCB = OPTCD = L was coded when the data set was created. L causes records flagged as deleted to be written. IL causes records flagged as deleted not to be written.
- 'RECFM = F, FB, V, or VB' (only one can be coded) specifies the record format of the original ISAM data set.

C. AMS Commands

The AMS commands described here have been condensed to the essential. Many nonessential commands and options are omitted. The AMS commands are invoked in a job step as follows:

```
//stepname EXEC PGM=IDCAMS
    [ The AMP program is named IDCAMS. ]
//JOBCAT DD DSN=dsname,DISP=SHR
    [ The JOBCAT or STEPCAT DD statements are required if private
    catalogs are used. ]
//SYSPRINT DD SYSOUT=A
    [ Prints the AMP messages. ]
//ddname DD DSN=...
    [ Some commands require one or two DD statements to describe
    input or output data sets. ]
//SYSIN DD *
    [ command statements ]
/*
```

The command statements are coded in columns 2 to 72. Continue a command statement by coding a hyphen after a complete subparameter, leaving at least one blank between the subparameter and the hyphen.

```
RPRO -
  INFILE(INDD)
```

1.   Creating catalogs

VSAM data sets cannot be created through JCL. The VSAM catalog and space allocation must be done with AMS commands. The data set is then loaded by writing the data set sequentially, presenting the records in ascending order on the record keys.

The first step in creating a VSAM data set is to define the VSAM catalog. This is usually done by the installation.

```
//STEP1 EXEC PGM=IDCAMS
//SYSPRINT DD SYSOUT=A
//ddname    DD UNIT=device,VOL=SER=volume,DISP=OLD
    [ This statement points to the volume that is to contain the
    catalog.  Any ddname may be used. ]
//SYSIN DD *
  DEFINE MASTERCATALOG( -
  NAME(catalog-name) FILE(ddname) VOLUME(volume) -
    [ Name the catalog and the volume that is to contain the
    catalog. ]
RECORDS(primary secondary) -
    [ Give the number of records which the primary and secondary
    areas are to contain.  Code CYLINDERS or TRACKS in place of
    RECORDS to allocate space in these units.  Up to 15 secondary
    allocations will be made if necessary. ]
MASTERPW(password) UPDATEPW(password) READPW(password))
    [ The passwords are all optional, and are 1 to 8 characters.
    MASTERPW is the master level password, UPDATEPW the password
    for reading and writing, and READPW the password for reading
    only. ]
/*
```

After the master catalog is created, user catalogs may be created. Although not required, they can speed up access by limiting the number of catalog entries. They also make the data sets more exportable because the user catalog can be copied along with the data set. User catalogs are created similar to the master catalog, except that the DEFINE statement is coded as:

```
DEFINE USERCATALOG( -
  NAME(catalog-name) FILE(ddname) VOLUME(volume) -
  RECORDS(primary secondary) -
  MASTERPW(password) UPDATEPW(password) -
  READPW(password) -
  CATALOG(master-catalog-name/password)
    [ The password is optional, and is coded only if
    MASTERPW was coded for the master catalog. ]
```

If a user catalog was specified, a JOBCAT or STEPCAT DD statement must be coded for each job or step that uses the catalog. JOBCAT applies to an entire job and STEPCAT to a single job step, similar to the JOBLIB and STEPLIB DD statements. JOBCAT is placed after the JOB statement and any JOBLIB statement, but before the first EXEC statement. STEPCAT is placed after the EXEC statement.

```
//TEST#9 JOB (5542,30),'A JOB',CLASS=A
//JOBLIB  DD DSN=PROGLIB,DISP=SHR
//JOBCAT  DD DSN=catalog-name,DISP=SHR
         [ Only DSN and DISP=SHR should be coded. ]
//STEP1 EXEC PGM=...
//STEPCAT DD DSN=catalog-name,DISP=SHR
         [ Only DSN and DISP=SHR should be coded. ]
```

After the catalogs have been created, a large amount of space is allocated to be used by several VSAM data sets. This is done with the following job step.

```
//STEP1 EXEC PGM=IDCAMS
//SYSPRINT DD SYSOUT=A
//ddname    DD UNIT=device,VOL=SER=volume,DISP=OLD
         [ This DD statement points to the volume upon which the space
         is to be allocated. ]
//SYSIN    DD *
  DEFINE SPACE( -
  VOLUME(volume) FILE(ddname) -
         [ VOLUME specifies the volume upon which the space is to be
         allocated.  FILE names the DD statement pointing to the
         volume. ]
RECORDS(primary secondary) -
         [ TRACKS or CYLINDERS can be coded in place of RECORDS to
         allocate space in these units.  Up to 15 secondary
         allocations are made as needed. ]
RECORDSIZE(average maximum) -
         [ Specifies the average and maximum record size in bytes. ]
CATALOG(catalog-name/password)
         [ CATALOG specifies the catalog to contain the entry.  The
         /password is optional and is coded only if MASTERPW was
         coded for the catalog. ]
  /*
```

The final step is to suballocate a portion of the space to an individual data set.

```
//STEP1 EXEC PGM=IDCAMS
//SYSPRINT DD SYSOUT=A
//SYSIN    DD *
  DEFINE CLUSTER( -
  NAME(file-name) VOLUME(volume) INDEXED -
  RECORDS(primary secondary) -
         [ Specify the number of records the primary and secondary
         areas are to contain.  Code CYLINDERS or TRACKS in place of
         RECORDS to request space in these units.  Up to 123 secondary
         allocations are made as needed. ]
  RECORDSIZE(average maximum) -
         [ Specify the average and maximum record sizes; they will be
         the same for fixed-length records. ]
  FREESPACE(internal-pct total-pct) -
         [ Specify the percentage of free space within each control
         interval (internal-pct), and the percentage of total
         control interval to be reserved for free space (total-pct). ]
  KEYS(lenqth position) -
         [ Specify the length of the record key and its relative byte
         position (0 to n) in the record. ]
  UPDATEPW(password) READPW(password) ATTEMPTS(0)) -
         [ The update and real passwords are optional and specify the
         passwords for updating and reading.  ATTEMPTS(0) should be
         coded if either UPDATEPW or READPW is coded. ]
  CATALOG(catalog-name/password)
         [ The /password is optional and is required only if
         MASTERPW was coded for the catalog. ]
  /*
```

2.   Defining a generation data group

The DEFINE command defines a generation data group for MVS data sets and for all VSAM data sets.

```
DEFINE GDG( -
  NAME(file-name) -
    [ Names the generation data group. ]
  LIMIT(number) -
    [ Maximum number of generations to keep (1 to 255). ]
  EMPTY -
    [ Optional.  Uncatalogs all the generation data sets when the
    limit is reached.  Omit EMPTY or code NOEMPTY to uncatalog
    only the oldest data set. ]
  SCRATCH) -
    [ Optional.  Scratch a data set when it is uncataloged.  Omit
    SCRATCH or code NOSCRATCH to keep the data set when it is
    uncataloged. ]
  CATALOG(catalog-name/password)
    [ The /password is optional.  (It is optional in the
    sense that it is not needed if password protection is not
    used.  If the data sets are protected by a password, it is
    required.) ]
```

3.   Listing catalog entries

The LISTCAT command lists catalog entries. It is coded as follows:

```
LISTCAT CATALOG(catalog-name/password)
    [ The /password is optional. ]
```

4.   Copy a data set

The REPRO command copies data sets as follows:

- Copies non-VSAM sequential data sets to VSAM.
- Copies VSAM data sets to VSAM data sets.
- Copies VSAM data sets to non-VSAM sequential data sets.
- Copies ISAM or non-VSAM sequential data sets to VSAM data sets.

Data sets are copied as follows:

```
//STEP1 EXEC PGM=IDCAMS
//SYSPRINT DD SYSOUT=A
//inddname DD DSN=...
    [ Describes the input data set. ]
//outddname DD DSN=...
    [ Describes the output data set. ]
//SYSIN DD *
  REPRO -
  INFILE(inddname/password) -
    [ Specifies the DD statement that describes the data set to
    copy.  The /password is optional. ]
  OUTFILE(outddname/password)
    [ Specifies the DD statement that identifies the output data
    set.  The /password is optional. ]
/*
```

The *inddname* and *outddname* DD statement parameters must be coded as necessary for the input and output data sets.

5. Printing data sets

The PRINT command can print non-VSAM sequential data sets, ISAM data sets, and VSAM data sets.

```
//STEP1 EXEC PGM=IDCAMS
//SYSPRINT DD SYSOUT=A
//ddname   DD DSN=...
     [ Specifies the data set to print. ]
//SYSIN DD *
  INFILE(ddname/password) format
     [ The /password is optional.  The format must be
     one of the following:

CHAR prints each record in character form.
HEX prints each record in hexadecimal.
DUMP prints each record in both character and hexadecimal. ]

  /*
```

6. Deleting data sets

The DELETE command deletes both VSAM and non-VSAM data sets. It is coded as:

```
DELETE (dsname/password) -
     [ The /password is optional. ]
FILE(ddname) -
     [ Names the DD statement that identifies the data set.
     Optional in MVS. ]
PURGE -
     [ Optional.  Deletes the entry regardless of the retention
     date. ]
ERASE -
     [ Optional.  Overwrites the deleted item with binary zeros and
     should be used for all sensitive data. ]
SCRATCH -
     [ Required to scratch non-VSAM data sets.  Omit for VSAM data
     sets. ]
CATALOG(catalog-name/password)
     [ Optional.  Names the VSAM catalog of the item to be
     deleted. ]
```

III. ISAM DATA SETS

The Indexed Sequential Access Method (ISAM) is supported in assembler language, COBOL, PL/I, but not in FORTRAN. An ISAM data set can be accessed sequentially or randomly. Each record must contain an identifying key, and the records are arranged in collating sequence on the keys. ISAM is an older access method that has largely been replaced by VSAM.

Functionally, ISAM is similar to VSAM. To the COBOL or PLI program, ISAM will look much like VSAM. The major difference between ISAM and VSAM data sets is that ISAM data sets are not reorganized as they are updated. Consequently, ISAM data sets need to be reorganized periodically. Also, you access ISAM through a rather complicated set of JCL statements.

A. Records

ISAM data sets can be created only on direct-access volumes. They are composed of records, blocks, tracks, and cylinders. Records may be fixed or variable length, but not undefined length. A record has the format shown in Figure 63.

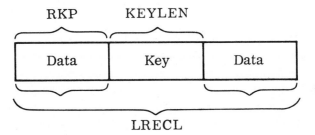

Figure 63. ISAM record

RKP (the relative location of the key within the record), KEYLEN (the key length, 0 to 255), and LRECL (the record length) are all DCB subparameters whose values are given in bytes. The RKP value for the first byte of a fixed-length record is 0; for a variable-length record the value is 4. If RKP is omitted, it defaults to 0.

The first byte of each record may be reserved for a delete byte—a byte used by the system to flag a record as deleted. Code DCB = OPTCD = L to reserve the first byte for the delete byte. A hexadecimal value of 'FF' marks a record as deleted. When a delete byte is used, the RKP DCB parameter (Relative Key Position) should have a value of 1 (or 5 for variable-length record) or larger. Records may be written with the delete byte set to 'FF' to reserve space within a track for adding records.

In our library example, a record might consist of the delete byte, 10 characters for the library number, 30 characters for the title, 20 characters for the author, 20 more characters for the publisher, and finally 19 characters for other information. The DCB subparameters would be DCB = (RKP = 1,KEYLEN = 10,LRECL = 100,OPTCD = L). (The LRECL is 10 + 30 + 20 + 20 + 19 + 1—the 1 is for the delete byte.) The records are placed on the tracks in the order of the key—the library number.

B. Blocks

Several records can be placed in a block to conserve storage space on the direct access volume and to increase the sequential processing speed. The key of the last record in the block is appended to the front of the block to aid in locating a particular key. A block has the format shown in Figure 64.

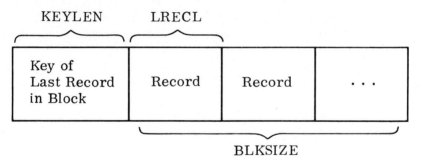

Figure 64. ISAM block

Unlike sequential data sets, blocking for ISAM does not necessarily increase the I/O efficiency. It does when the data set is processed sequentially, but not when it is processed randomly. For random access, it is less efficient to bring in an entire block of records rather than just one unblocked record. Because the access is random, it is unlikely that the next record to be accessed would be in the same block as that of the last record accessed.

C. Tracks

As many complete blocks are placed on a track as space permits. The total number of tracks containing records is called the *prime area*. The tracks must be arranged on cylinders, but the cylinders need not be contiguous.

A track index is automatically created for each cylinder on the first track of the cylinder. Two entries are required for each track: a normal entry pointing to the track, and an overflow entry pointing to an overflow area in case the records overflow the track.

As records are added to a data set, all the records following it on the track are moved down to make room. Any records forced off the track are placed in an overflow area, and an appropriate entry is made in the track index. Several records forced off a track are linked together. Records in overflow areas are unblocked and require an extra 10 bytes for the link field. A deleted record is simply flagged as deleted to save a time-consuming move-up operation, but it is discarded if forced off a track. Tracks can also be flagged as inactive in the track index to reserve space. The track index entry has the format of Figure 65.

D. Overflow Areas

Two overflow areas, a cylinder overflow area and an independent overflow area, can be reserved either singly or in combination. A *cylinder overflow area* is reserved by allocating a specified number of tracks on each cylinder for overflow. Any records overflowing tracks on that cylinder are placed in this area. This has the advantage of

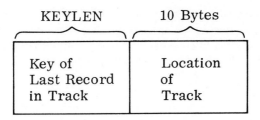

Figure 65. ISAM track index entry

minimizing access time by ensuring that overflow records are placed on the same cylinder. However, cylinder overflow areas are not shared so that if an area for one cylinder becomes full, unused space on other cylinders cannot be used. Code DCB = (CYLOFL = *tracks*,OPTCD = Y) to request cylinder overflow and indicate the number of tracks on each cylinder to reserve for the cylinder overflow area.

An *independent overflow area* can be shared by all cylinders, conserving storage space. The independent overflow area is given a separate space allocation called the *overflow area*. The price is increased access time because an independent overflow area must be placed on a different cylinder from the original data.

The best method of reserving space for overflow records is to set the cylinder overflow area at a reasonable value and to provide an independent overflow area to contain records when cylinder overflow areas become full. (The cylinder overflow area is filled first.)

E. Index Areas

The cylinder index and the master index constitute the index areas.

1. Cylinder index

A *cylinder index* is created by the system if the data set resides on more than a single cylinder. An entry is added for each cylinder and has the same format as the track index entries.

2. Master index

You can request that an entry be created in a *master index* for each specified number of tracks of cylinder index. A master index obviates having to search the entire cylinder index to locate a record, allowing the system to focus quickly on the relevant cylinder indexes, and is particularly useful for large data sets. A second- and third-level master index are also created for every specified number of tracks of lower-level index. Programs can request that the master index be held in real storage to decrease the search time. The area for the master index and cylinder index is called the *index area*. The format of each master index entry is the same as for track index entries.

A master index is created by coding $DCB = (OPTCD = M, NTM = tracks)$. NTM specifies a number of tracks, and an entry is made in the master index when this number of tracks has been filled in the index area. A second- and third-level index will be created when the lower-level index fills the number of tracks specified by NTM.

F. Locating Records

The following steps show how the system locates a record "directly" with a key.

1. If a master index does not exist, the search begins at step 2. Otherwise the master index is searched for the first entry containing a key greater than the key desired. If the master index points to a lower index, it is searched in a similar manner. Eventually a master index entry is found that points to a cylinder index known to contain the desired key.
2. If there is no cylinder index, the data set must be contained on a single cylinder and the search continues at step 3. Otherwise the cylinder index is searched for the first entry with a key greater than the key desired. When found, that entry will point to a cylinder containing a record with the desired key.
3. The track index occupying the first tracks of the cylinder is searched for the first entry with a key greater than the key wanted. The track index points to a track containing the record.
4. The track is then searched for the record with the desired key.

To speed up the search, the master and cylinder indexes should both be placed on the same cylinder. Search time is also decreased by locating the cylinders containing the master and cylinder indexes on a separate volume from the prime area. (Place it on the fastest device.) If it must be on the same volume, place it on a cylinder contiguous to the prime area.

An ISAM data set is processed sequentially by locating each cylinder in the cylinder index and processing all the tracks sequentially. Overflow tracks greatly increase sequential processing times, particularly if they are on independent overflow areas.

G. Creating ISAM Data Sets

ISAM data sets must be created sequentially by writing the records in order of their keys. The IEBISAM utility program creates an ISAM data set, or a program can be written to write the ISAM data set sequentially.

An ISAM data set may require space allocation for three separate areas: the prime area, the index area, and the independent overflow area. A prime area must always be provided, but the index and independent overflow areas are optional. The DD statements for an ISAM data set must be coded in the following order:

```
//ddname DD DSN=dsname(INDEX),...
//       DD DSN=dsname(PRIME),...
//       DD DSN=dsname(OVFLOW),...
```

The only DD parameters that can be coded are DSN, DISP, UNIT, VOL, DCB, and LABEL with EXPDT/RETPD and PASSWORD/NOPWREAD subparameters. The DCB subparameter DSORG = IS or ISU (indexed sequential unmovable) must be coded on each DD statement. Any other DCB parameters coded on one statement must be consistent with DCB subparameters coded on the other statements. Volume mounting cannot be deferred so UNIT = (,,DEFER) is not permitted.

The ddname is coded on the first DD statement only. INDEX, PRIME, and OVFLOW must always be coded in that order, maintaining the order if INDEX or OVFLOW is omitted. A temporary data set is indicated by coding DSN = &&*dsname*(..) on each DD statement. If the data set consists of only a prime area, PRIME need not be coded; that is, DSN = *dsname* and DSN = *dsname*(PRIME) are identical if the data set is created by one DD statement.

1. DCB subparameters

The following DCB subparameters may be coded for ISAM data sets.

- RKP = n gives the relative byte position of the key within the record, 0 to 255.
- OPTCD = L reserves the first byte of the record for the delete byte.
- NTM = n specifies the number of tracks to fill before creating a master index entry. You must also code OPTCD = M.
- OPTCD = R requests reorganization statistics to be kept. These can be accessed through COBOL.
- OPTCD = I requests that overflow records be placed only in the independent overflow area, even if there is room in the cylinder overflow area.
- CYLOFL = n specifies the number of tracks on each cylinder to reserve for the cylinder overflow area. You must also code OPTCD = Y.
- OPTCD = U can only be coded for fixed-length records. It requests the index area to be blocked to a full track. This is more efficient when the ISAM data set is loaded (written the first time.)

2. The SPACE parameter

The SPACE parameter must be coded in one of two ways for ISAM data sets, but the same method must be used on all DD statements describing the data set. To request an amount of space, code:

```
SPACE=(CYL,(quantity,,index),,CONTIG)
```

Space is allocated on cylinders. The *index* is optional and specifies the number of cylinders to reserve for the index area if it is to be imbedded in the prime area. CONTIG is also optional and allocates contiguous cylinders. It must be coded on all DD statements if it is coded on one. If more than one volume is requested, the specified space is allocated on each volume. The secondary amount, RLSE, MXIG, ALX, and ROUND cannot be coded.

Specific tracks can be requested by coding:

```
SPACE=(ABSTR,(quantity,address,index))
```

Space is allocated on the absolute tracks requested. The quantity must be equivalent to an integral number of cylinders, and the address must be the first track on a cylinder other than the first cylinder of the volume. If more than one volume is requested, space is allocated beginning at the address specified and continuing through the volume onto the next volume until the request has been satisfied. The VTOC on the second and succeeding volumes must be contained on the first tracks of each volume. The index is optional and specifies the number of tracks to reserve for the index area. The index must be an integral number of cylinders. The specific track method of requesting space is often used for ISAM data sets because the relative placement of the prime, index, and overflow areas affects access time.

ISAM data sets can be cataloged with DISP = (NEW,CATLG) only if the data set is created with a single DD statement. The IEHPROGM utility described in Chapter 15 can catalog ISAM data sets defined by more than one DD statement, provided that all the DD statements request the same type of unit.

3. *Example of space allocation*

Since space allocation for ISAM data sets is complicated, the library example suggested earlier is used to show each step involved. Table 3 in Chapter 11 provides the formulas for space allocation.

$$\text{Blocks/track} = 1 + \frac{\text{track capacity} - B_n}{B_i}$$

where B_i is any block but the last and B_n is the last block on the track. Track capacity, B_i, and B_n depend upon the type of device. This example will use a 3330 disk, so the equation is:

$$\text{Blocks/track} = 1 + \frac{13,165 - (191 + \text{KEYLEN} + \text{BLKSIZE})}{(191 + \text{KEYLEN} + \text{BLKSIZE})}$$

The library data set contains 150,000 records, each 100 bytes long. The library number is used as the key and contains 10 bytes. Assume there are 11 records per block, so the data set has DCB subparameters of KEYLEN = 10, LRECL = 100, BLKSIZE = 1,100, DSORG = IS, and RECFM = FB.

4. Prime area

The prime area may reside on more than one volume of the same device type. Any unused space in the last cylinder of the prime area is used as an independent overflow area. The prime area is allocated in cylinders, and the first tracks in each cylinder are used for track indexes.

1. Compute the number of records per track in the prime area.

```
                       13,165 - (191 + 10 + 1100)
Blocks/track = 1 +  ---------------------------  = 10.12
                          (191 + 10 + 1100)
```

which truncates to 10 blocks per track.

```
Records/track=Blocks/track(records/block) = 10(11) =
                                         110 records/track
```

2. Compute the number of tracks required to store the records. The system reserves the last track on each cylinder for the file mark.

```
                           number of records      150,000
Prime tracks required = ------------------ + 1 = ------- + 1 =
                           records/tracks           110
```

$$1364.64$$

which is rounded up to 1,365 tracks.

3. Compute the tracks per cylinder needed to contain the track indexes. Records are unblocked and consist of a key plus 10 bytes of data.

```
                                    13,165 - (191 + 10 + 10)
Tracks index entries/track = 1 +  ------------------------ =
                                        191 + 10 + 10

          62 index entries/track

                                     2(tracks/cylinder) + 1
Tracks/cylinder for track index =  ----------------------
                                     index entries/track + 2
```

Table 2 in Chapter 11 tells us that a 3330 disk has 19 tracks per cylinder.

```
                         2(19) + 1
Index tracks/cylinder = --------- = 0.6, less than 1 track
                          62 + 2
```

The first 0.6 tracks of each cylinder are used for track indexes. If the unused space (0.4) track on the track can contain blocks of data, it must be considered in determining the number of data records per cylinder.

```
Blocks/partial track = 0.4(10) = 4 blocks
```

The first track of each cylinder will contain 4(11) or 44 records in addition to the track index.

4. Compute the space (if any) to allocate for a cylinder overflow area. Overflow records are unblocked and require an extra 10- byte link field.

```
Overflow records/track =

        13,165 - (191 + KEYLEN + LRECL + 10)
    1 + ------------------------------------ =
            191 + KEYLEN + LRECL + 10

        13,165 - (191 + 10 + 100 + 10)
    1 + ------------------------------ = 42.33
            191 + 10 + 100 + 10
```

which truncates to 42 overflow records per track.

But for how many overflow records per cylinder should you reserve space? The size depends on how often you add records and how critical storage space and accessing times are. Faster access times are achieved at a cost in storage space for a larger cylinder overflow area. Suppose you expect to change five percent of the records, and you wish most of these changes to go in the cylinder overflow area to minimize access time. By roughly approximating the number of records per cylinder and taking five percent of this number, you can estimate the number of cylinder overflow records and tracks per cylinder needed.

```
Overflow records/cylinder =
            (data tracks/cylinder)(data records/track)(percent)
```

But you cannot compute the number of data records per cylinder until you know the number of overflow records, and the number of overflow records depends on the number of data records. However, you can approximate the number of data records fairly accurately. A 3330 cylinder contains 19 tracks, but one track is used for track indexes, and at least one track will be used for the cylinder overflow area (you can recalculate if this estimate is too far off), leaving about 17 tracks for data.

```
Overflow records/cylinder = 17(110)0.05 = 93 records/cylinder

                           overflow records/cylinder   93
Overflow tracks/cylinder = -------------------------- = -- = 2.21
                            overflow records/track      42
```

which you can round to two tracks per cylinder (you need not be exact).

5. Compute the total number of cylinders needed for the prime area.

```
Prime data tracks/cyl =
        device tracks/cyl - index tracks/cyl - overflow tracks/cyl =
        19 - 0.6 - 2 = 16.4

                            prime tracks req'd     1364
Number of cyl req'd = ---------------------- = ---- = 83.17
                            prime data tracks/cyl  16.4
```

which rounds up to 84 cylinders.

5. Index area

A cylinder index area is required if the prime area occupies more than one cylinder. A master index area can also be requested to decrease search time. The index area, comprising the cylinder and master indexes, can be imbedded in the prime area, placed in any unused space at the end of the prime area, or allocated space with a separate DD statement. If space is allocated separately, the index area need not be on the same device type as the prime area, but it must be contained on a single volume. Any unused space left in the last cylinders of the index area is used for an independent overflow area, provided that it is the same device type as the prime area.

1. Compute the space required for the cylinder index (if the prime area occupies more than one cylinder). The same formula used to compute track entries is used for cylinder entries, and since you are using the same type of device, there are 62 cylinder index entries per track.

```
Tracks for cylinder index =

        number of cylinders + 1     84 + 1
        ----------------------- = ------ = 1.37 tracks
           index entries/track        62
```

2. Compute the space required for the master index if a master index is wanted. You must decide how many tracks of cylinder index per master index entry are needed. This involves a trade between storage space and access time. Small NTM values decrease access time and increase storage requirements. Perhaps two tracks of cylinder index per master index entry is a good compromise. The master index entries are the same size as cylinder index entries so that 62 entries will fit on a track.

```
Tracks for first-level master index =
                (cylinder index tracks/NTM) + 1
                -------------------------------
                      index entries/track
```

If the cylinder index tracks are greater than NTM:

```
Tracks for second-level master index =
                (tracks for first level/NTM) + 1
                ---------------------------------
                      index entries/track
```

If tracks for first level is greater than NTM:

```
Tracks for third-level master index =

                (tracks for second level/NTM) + 1
                ---------------------------------
                      index entries/track
```

If tracks for second level is greater than NTM:

```
Tracks for first-level master index =

                ((1.37/2) + 1)
                -------------- = 0.03 tracks
                      62
```

Second- and third-level master indexes are not required, so the total index space is the tracks for the cylinder index plus the master index area: $1.37 + 0.03 = 1.40$ tracks, rounded up to two tracks. If a separate index area is allocated, it must be allocated in full cylinders, so one cylinder would be required.

6. Independent overflow area

The independent overflow area contains records overflowing from the cylinder overflow area. The independent overflow area can be allocated with a separate DD statement, but must be the same device type as the prime area and must be contained on a single volume.

Compute the size of the independent overflow area (if desired). The size of the independent overflow area depends on how often records are added or changed and how much space was reserved for the cylinder overflow area. Allow five percent for cylinder overflow; perhaps five percent is appropriate for the independent overflow area also.

```
Independent overflow area cylinders =
      prime area cylinders(percent) = 84(0.05) = 4.2
      which rounds to 4 cylinders (again we need not be exact.)
```

To summarize the space requirements, 84 cylinders are needed for the cylinder overflow area, two tracks for the index area, and four cylinders for the independent overflow area. Since a 3330 Model 1 volume has 404 cylinders, the prime area could be allocated on one volume.

H. Using ISAM Data Sets

To retrieve an ISAM data set, code DSN, DISP, UNIT, and VOL. DCB = DSORG = IS or ISU must be coded unless the data set was passed. UNIT and VOL can be omitted if the data set is contained on a single volume and was passed or cataloged. The DSN parameter is coded without the terms INDEX, PRIME, or OVFLOW.

If the prime, index, and overflow areas all reside on the same type of device, the ISAM data set can be retrieved with a single DD statement. If the index or overflow resides on a different device type, you need two DD statements. If the prime, index, and overflow all reside on different device types, code three DD statements to retrieve the data set.

The following examples show various ways space can be allocated for the library data set and the means of coding DD statements to retrieve the data set.

- Separate areas for index, prime, and independent overflow.

```
//STEP1 EXEC PGM=CREATE
//A  DD DSN=LIB(INDEX),DISP=(NEW,KEEP),
//      UNIT=3330,VOL=SER=PACK12,SPACE=(CYL,1,,CONTIG),
//      DCB=(DSORG=IS,OPTCD=YM,CYLOFL=2,NTM=2,
//      RECFM=FB,LRECL=100,BLKSIZE=1100,RKP=1,KEYLEN=10)
      [ The data set is named LIB.  Only two tracks are needed for
      the index area, but all space must be allocated in integral
      cylinders.  CONTIG must be coded on all DD statements if it
      is coded on any one. ]
//   DD DSN=LIB(PRIME),DISP=(NEW,KEEP),UNIT=3330,VOL=SER=PACK13,
//      SPACE=(CYL,84,,CONTIG),DCB=*.A
      [ Eighty-four cylinders are allocated for the prime area.  The
      prime area is allocated on a separate volume, although it
      need not have been. ]
//   DD DSN=LIB(OVFLOW),DISP=(NEW,KEEP),UNIT=3330,VOL=SER=PACK14,
//      SPACE=(CYL,4,,CONTIG),DCB=*.A
      [ The DCB subparameters must be consistent on all the DD
      statements.  The referback ensures this.  The independent
      overflow area is also allocated on a separate volume,
      although it need not have been. ]
//STEP2 EXEC PGM=READ
//B  DD DSN=LIB,DISP=OLD,DCB=DSORG=IS,
//      UNIT=(3330,3),VOL=SER=(PACK12,PACK13,PACK14)
      [ The volume serial numbers must be listed in the same order
      when the data set is retrieved as they were when the data set
      was created. ]
```

- Separate index area, independent overflow area at end of the prime area.

```
//STEP1 EXEC PGM=CREATE
//A  DD DSN=LIB(INDEX),...
//   DD DSN=LIB(PRIME),DISP=(NEW,KEEP),
//      UNIT=3330,VOL=SER=PACK12,
//      SPACE=(CYL,88,,CONTIG),DCB=*.A
      [ The prime area space is increased to provide room for the
      independent overflow area. ]
//STEP2 EXEC PGM=READ
//B  DD DSN=LIB,DISP=OLD,DCB=DSORG=IS,
//      UNIT=3330,VOL=SER=PACK12
```

- Index area placed at the end of the prime area, separate independent overflow area.

```
//STEP1 EXEC PGM=CREATE
//A DD DSN=LIB(PRIME),DISP=(NEW,KEEP),UNIT=3330,
//      VOL=SER=PACK12,SPACE=(CYL,84,,CONTIG),
//      DCB=(DSORG=IS,OPTCD=YM,CYLOFL=2,NTM=2,RECFM=FB,
//      LRECL=100,BLKSIZE=1100,RKP=1,KEYLEN=10)
//   DD DSN=LIB(OVFLOW),...
//STEP2 EXEC PGM=READ
//B DD DSN=LIB,DISP=OLD,DCB=DSORG=IS,
//      UNIT=(3330,2),VOL=SER=(PACK12,PACK14)
```

- Imbedded index area, separate independent overflow area.

```
//STEP1 EXEC PGM=CREATE
//A DD DSN=LIB(PRIME),DISP=(NEW,KEEP),UNIT=3330,
//      VOL=SER=PACK12,SPACE=(CYL,(85,,1),,CONTIG),
//      DCB=(DSORG=IS,OPTCD=YM,CYLOFL=2,NTM=2,RECFM=FB,
//      LRECL=100,BLKSIZE=1100,RKP=1,KEYLEN=10)
      [ A 1-cylinder index area is imbedded in the prime area.
      Since the index area must be contained on a single volume,
      the prime area must be allocated on one volume. ]
//   DD DSN=LIB(OVFLOW),...
//STEP2 EXEC PGM=READ
//B DD DSN=LIB,DISP=OLD,DCB=DSORG=IS,
//      UNIT=(3330,2),VOL=SER=(PACK10,PACK12)
```

- Index area placed at end of the prime area, independent overflow area placed at the end of the index area.

```
//STEP1 EXEC PGM=CREATE
//A DD DSN=LIB,DISP=(NEW,CATLG),UNIT=3330,VOL=SER=PACK12,
//      SPACE=(CYL,88,,CONTIG),
//      DCB=(DSORG=IS,OPTCD=YM,CYLOFL=2,NTM=2,RECFM=FB,
//      LRECL=100,BLKSIZE=1100,RKP=1,KEYLEN=10)
      [ The prime area is increased to reserve room for the index
      and independent overflow areas.  Since the data set is
      created with a single DD statement, it can be cataloged. ]
//STEP2 EXEC PGM=READ
//B DD DSN=LIB,DISP=OLD,DCB=DSORG=IS
```

- Imbedded index area, independent overflow area at the end of the prime area.

```
//STEP1 EXEC PGM=CREATE
//A DD DSN=&&LIB,DISP=(NEW,PASS),UNIT=3330,VOL=SER=PACK12,
//      SPACE=(CYL,(89,,1),,CONTIG),
//      DCB=(DSORG=IS,OPTCD=YM,CYLOFL=2,NTM=2,RECFM=FB,
//      LRECL=100,BLKSIZE=1100,RKP=1,KEYLEN=10)
      [ The prime area is increased to reserve room for the imbedded
      index area and the independent overflow area at the end.  The
      data set must be contained on a single volume.  ISAM data
      sets can be temporary, and they can be passed if they are
      created with a single DD statement. ]
//STEP2 EXEC PGM=READ
//B DD DSN=*.STEP1.A,DISP=(OLD,DELETE)
      [ The DSORG=IS subparameter is not needed if the ISAM data set
      is passed. ]
```

Any one of the preceding six methods may be used to create an ISAM data set. The particular method depends on the relative sizes of the prime, index, and independent overflow areas, and where these areas are placed. An ISAM data set can be extended with a DISP = MOD. ISAM data sets cannot be made DUMMY.

When an ISAM data set is updated, records may be forced onto the overflow areas, making the data set less efficient; it should be reorganized periodically. An ISAM data set is reorganized by copying it sequentially and then reloading it from the sequential copy. The IEBISAM utility program reorganizes ISAM data sets.

You should give careful consideration to backing up ISAM data sets. Since an ISAM data set is updated in place, there is no old master copy to use to restore the data set. ISAM data sets also present a danger if the hardware or system fails during updating. Both the index and the records in the prime area must be updated, and a hardware or system failure may result in only one being completed. This can make the ISAM data set unusable.

EXERCISES

Using the lines of data from the exercise in Chapter 16, sort them into ascending order and save them on disk as a permanent data set. Then use the IEBISAM utility program to create an ISAM data set. Print the ISAM data set with IEBISAM. Then create a VSAM data set, print it, and delete the data set.

Chapter 19

JES2 AND JES3

JCL statements describe your job to the system and tell what resources the job needs. As if the JCL statements weren't difficult enough, you may need to learn one of two other languages to write statements that tell a network of several computers where you want your job run and where you want the output routed. Nothing comes easy on the MVS system.

JES2 and JES3 are job entry systems used to accept jobs and run them on one of several computers connected together in a network. Usually you will use either JES2 or JES3, but both are occasionally connected on the same network. JES2 and JES3 consist of statements that you usually place after your JOB statement to direct the job to a computer in a network. JES2 and JES3 can also specify where to route the output. And you can specify some of the same parameters with JES2 or JES3 that you specify through your JCL. (The JES2 or JES3 statements override what you request on your JCL.) And finally, there is an OUTPUT JCL statement and OUTPUT DD statement parameter that can specify many of the same parameters for JES2 and JES3.

It is a problem to decide where to write the various parameters. For example, the forms overlay for a 3800 Model 3 printer can be specified on a SYSOUT DD statement, on an OUTPUT JCL statement, or on a JES2 or JES3 statement. Generally, if a parameter is an inherent part of a job step, you should write it on the DD statement. This way, if you copy the JCL into another job, you copy the parameters along with it. If you change parameters often, it is generally better to supply them in JES2 and JES3 statements. This way, you can make one change in a single JES2 or JES3 statement rather than making changes on several DD statements. The OUTPUT JCL statement and OUTPUT DD parameter have a more specialized use. They let you route the output to more than one destination with different options for each destination.

I. JES2

In JES2, the computers are connected in a network, and each computer is termed a *node*. JES2 jobs are placed in a single job queue, and each computer in the network can select jobs from its queue. JES2 is a decentralized system in which each computer

274

runs independently, selecting jobs from its queue as it sees fit. Usually each computer has its own set of computer operators.

JES2 consists of a set of statements that specify information on how to run the job. JES2 statements look like JCL statements and have the same rules for coding. JES2 statements begin with /*. Two of the statements, the Command and PRIORITY, are placed in front of the JOB statement. The remaining statements are placed following the JOB statement. You cannot place JES2 statements in a cataloged procedure.

JES2 statements cannot be continued. Instead, you can write multiple statements:

```
/*OUTPUT TEST BURST=Y,COPIES=3
/*OUTPUT TEST DEST=LOCAL,FCB=TT4
```

Many of the parameters specified on the JES2 statements are the same as those written on JCL statements. You have the option of specifying the same information on either the JCL statements or on JES2 statements. Parameters specified on JES2 statements take precedence over the same parameters on the JCL statements.

A. The ROUTE Statement

The ROUTE statement specifies the destination of a job for execution or the output for printing if you want the destination to be a specific node.

```
          XEQ
          PRINT
/*ROUTE _____ node

      XEQ routes the job for execution.
      PRINT routes the output for printing.

//RUN12 JOB (334458),'TAPE JOB',CLASS=A
/*ROUTE XEQ HOUSTON
/*ROUTE PRINT LA
```

B. The XEQ Statement

The XEQ statement routes the job to a node for execution. It does the same as the /*ROUTE XEQ statement.

```
/*XEQ node

//RUN12 JOB (334458),'TAPE JOB',CLASS=A
/*XEQ HOUSTON
```

C. The XMIT Statement

The XMIT statement sends a job or data stream to another JES2 or non-JES2 node. The job is not scheduled for execution; it is only transmitted. It is similar to the /*ROUTE statement, except the job is only transmitted—not executed. You generally use this to send data to another node.

```
/*XMIT node

/*XMIT node DLM=xx
     [ DLM=xx changes the delimiter characters from /* to the
     two characters you specify.  This is the same as the DLM
     parameter on the DD statement. ]
```

D. The NETACCT Statement

The NETACCT statement specifies an account number for the job. The account number must be the same for all the nodes (computers) on the network. This statement may or may not be required.

```
/*NETACCT account-number

//RUN12 JOB (334458),'TAPE JOB',CLASS=A
/*NETACCT 22385
```

E. The JOBPARM Statement

The JOBPARM statement specifies processing and output parameters for an entire job. (The JES2 OUTPUT statement specifies many of the same parameters, but for specific SYSOUT statements rather than for the entire job.) If the same parameters are written on the /*JOBPARM statement and on the JCL, the parameters on JOBPARM override the parameters on the JCL statements. JOBPARM is written as:

```
/*JOBPARM option,option,...,option
```

The options are:

- BURST = Y or N   Sets the default burst mode for SYSOUT data sets for the IBM 3800 printer. This is the same as the BURST parameter on the DD statement.
- BYTES = *bytes*   Estimates the maximum output in thousands of bytes. The operator is sent a message and has the option of canceling the job when this estimate is exceeded.
- COPIES = *copies*   The number of copies of output to make of the job. This is multiplied by the COPIES parameter on the DD statement. That is, if a COPIES parameter on a DD statement requests two copies and a COPIES parameter on a JOBPARM statement also requests two copies, you will get four copies.
- FORMS = *forms*   Specifies the print form to use for the job. This is the same as the third subparameter on the SYSOUT parameter: SYSOUT = (*class,program,form*).
- LINECT = *lines*   Specifies the number of lines to print on each page.

- LINES = *lines*   Gives a cutoff for the lines of output produced by the job.
- NOLOG   Specifies that you do not want the JES2 job log as output.
- PAGES = *pages*   Specifies a limit from 1 to 99,999 on the number of pages of output produced by the job.
- PROCLIB = *ddname*   Specifies the ddname of the cataloged procedure library to use for this job.
- RESTART = Y or N   RESTART = Y specifies that if the job must be restarted, it must be restarted from the start of the job. RESTART = N means that it is restarted from where it left off.
- ROOM = *room*   Specifies from one to four characters to identify the room or location where the job output is to be sent.
- SYSAFF = (*cccc,cccc,...,cccc*)   Specifies from one to seven systems that can process the job and depends on the installation.
- TIME = *minutes*   Estimates the job execution minutes (0 to 279,620). The estimate is clock time, not CPU time.

```
//RUN12 JOB (334458),'TAPE JOB',CLASS=A
/*JOBPARM LINECT=60,ROOM=322,TIME=40
```

F. The OUTPUT Statement

The OUTPUT statement specifies parameters for one or more of the job's SYSOUT data sets. If the same parameter is written on this statement and on the JCL, the parameter on this statement overrides that on the JCL statement.

```
/*OUTPUT code option,option, ...,option
```

- *code*   Specifies the SYSOUT statements to which this OUTPUT statement is to apply. The OUTPUT statement will be used for all SYSOUT statements in which the *code* matches the third subparameter of the SYSOUT statement:

```
SYSOUT=(class,program,code) .
```

- BURST = Y or N   Sets the default burst mode for SYSOUT data sets for the IBM 3800 printer. This is the same as the BURST parameter on the DD statement.
- CHARS = (*table-name,table-name,...,table-name*)   The name of a character arrangement table for a 3800 printer. This is the same as the CHARS parameter on the DD statement.
- CKPTLNS = *lines*   The maximum number (0–32,767) of lines contained in a logical page.

- **CKPTPGS**=*pages*   The number (0–32,767) of logical pages to be printed before the next checkpoint is taken.
- **COMPACT**=*nn*   Specifies a value (0–99) for the compaction table for use when sending SYSOUT output to a SNA remote terminal.
- **COPIES**=(*copies*,(*group,group*,...,*group*))   The number of copies of output to make for the job. This is the same as the COPIES parameter on the DD statement.
- **COPYG**=(*group,group*,...,*group*)   The number of copies of each page to be grouped together. This is the same as the *group* subparameters on the COPIES parameter on the DD statement.
- **DEST**=*destination*   The destination for the output data sets. This is the same as the DEST parameter on the DD statement.
- **FCB**=*image-id*   The data set forms control to use. This is the same as the FCB parameter on the DD statement.
- **FLASH**=(*overlay-name,count*)   Specifies the forms overlay to use on a 3800 printer. This is the same as the FLASH parameter on the DD statement.
- **FLASHC**=*count*   The number (0–255) of copies to be flashed with the overlay for a 3800 printer. This is the same as the second subparameter of the FLASH=(*overlay-name,count*) parameter on the DD statement.
- **FORMS**=*form*   Specifies the print form to use for the job. This is the same as the third subparameter on the SYSOUT=(*class,program,form*) parameter on the DD statement.
- **INDEX**=*nn*   Specifies the data set indexing print position offset (1 to 31 to the right) for the 3211 printer.
- **LINDEX**=*nn*   Specifies the data set indexing print position offset (1 to 31 to the left) for the 3211 printer.
- **LINECT**=*lines*   Specifies the number of lines (0–255) to print on each page.
- **MODIFY**=(*module-name,trc*)   Specifies the name of a copy modification module for the 3800 printer. This is the same as the MODIFY parameter on the DD statement.
- **MODTRC**=*trc*   Specifies the character reference table for the CHARS parameter. This is the same as the second subparameter of the MODIFY=(*module-name,trc*) parameter on the DD statement.
- **UCS**=*character-set*   Specifies the Universal Character Set. This is the same as the UCS parameter on the DD statement.

```
//RUN12 JOB (334458),'TAPE JOB',CLASS=A
/*OUTPUT LTR DEST=HOUSTON,LINECT=55
```

G. The SETUP Statement

The SETUP statement specifies tape volumes that must be mounted for a job. SETUP displays an operator message and places the job in hold until the operator mounts the tapes and releases the job. The volume must begin in column 11 or beyond.

```
/*SETUP   volume,volume,...,volume

/*SETUP   002215,003716
```

H. The NOTIFY Statement

The NOTIFY statement specifies the userid that is to receive notification of the job's completion. This is the same as the NOTIFY parameter on the JOB statement.

```
/*NOTIFY userid
     [ The userid at the job's origin is notified. ]
/*NOTIFY node.userid
     [ The userid at the node specified will be notified.  Use this
     form if someone not at the job's origin is to be notified. ]
```

I. The SIGNOFF Statement

The SIGNOFF statement terminates a remote job and disconnects the station.

```
/*SIGNOFF
```

J. The SIGNON Statement

The SIGNON statement begins a remote job session. That is, it connects the job to a work station. The remote must begin in column 16, the first password in column 25, and any second password in column 73.

```
/*SIGNON        REMOTEnnn
/*SIGNON        REMOTEnnn password
/*SIGNON        REMOTEnnn password1                        password2
```

K. The PRIORITY Statement

The PRIORITY statement specifies the priority (0 to 15) for selecting the job from the input queue for execution. This is the same as the PRTY parameter on the JOB statement. The PRIORITY statement must be placed in front of the JOB statement.

```
/*PRIORITY priority

/*PRIORITY 6
//RUN12 JOB (334458),'TAPE JOB',CLASS=A
```

L.   The MESSAGE Statement

The MESSAGE statement lets you send a message to the computer operator.

```
/*MESSAGE message

//RUN12 JOB (334458),'TAPE JOB',CLASS=A
/*MESSAGE  I AM ENCLOSING A TAPE REEL WITH THE JOB.
```

M.   The Command Statement

The command statement is used to enter JES2 operator commands in the input stream. The general form is:

```
/*$command operands
```

The command statement must be placed in front of the JOB statement. There are many operator commands but they are not described in this book.

II.   JES3

In JES3, several computers are closely connected together, and all the scheduling is done by a single computer, which is termed the *global processor*. All the jobs are placed in a single job queue. The global processor then schedules the jobs to itself or the other computers connected to it. Up to seven other computers, termed *local processors*, can be connected to the global processor. The computers on which a job may run are termed the *main processors*. JES3 is a highly centralized network. One computer and one group of operators control all the other computers.

The main processors, the computers connected closely together, are not really a network. They are more like a single computer that has multiple CPUs. JES3 can also operate in a network. A network consists of separate computers operating relatively independently that are connected by some form of communications. A node in a JES3 network consists of the main processors—the global processor and its local processors. The network can contain other JES3 nodes and JES2 nodes as well.

JES3 also lets you submit several jobs in a group and make the execution of jobs contingent on the successful or unsuccessful execution of other jobs, thereby giving you some of the flexibility for jobs that the COND parameter gives to job steps.

JES3 consists of a set of statements that specify information on how to run the job. JES3 statements look like JCL statements and have the same rules for coding. JES3 statements begin with //*. All JES3 statements except the command statement are placed following the JOB statement. You cannot place JES3 statements in a cataloged procedure.

To continue a JES3 statement, end the statement after a comma, code a //* on the next line, and continue in column 4.

```
//*MAIN SYSTEM=(CPU1,CPU4),EXPDTCHK=YES,
//*HOLD=YES
```

Many of the parameters specified on the JES3 statements are the same as those written on JCL statements. You have the option of specifying the same information on either the JCL statements or on JES3 statements. Parameters specified on JES3 statements take precedence over the same parameters on the JCL statements.

A. The NETACCT Statement

The NETACCT statement specifies an account number for the job at a node in the network. It may also supply information to identify you and your location. Each installation will specify what is required for this parameter. The NETACCT statement must immediately follow the first JOB statement and precede any //*ROUTE statement.

```
//*NETACCT option,option,...,option
```

The options are:

- PNAME=*name*   1 to 20 characters for the programmer's name.
- ACCT=*account*   1 to 8 characters for the account number.
- USERID=*userid*   1 to 8 character for your userid.
- DEPT=*department*   1 to 8 characters for your department.
- BLDG=*building*   1 to 8 characters for your building number.
- ROOM=*room*   1 to 8 characters for your room number.

```
//RUN12 JOB (334458),'TAPE JOB',CLASS=A
//*NETACCT PNAME=SMITH,ACCT=22385
```

B. The ROUTE XEQ Statement

The ROUTE XEQ statement specifies the destination of the job for execution if you do not want JES3 to decide where to run the job.

```
//*ROUTE XEQ node,vmuserid
       [ The vmuserid is needed only if the job is sent to a VM/370
       node. ]
```

The //*ROUTE statement must be placed after any JOB statement for the submitting location but after any //*NETACCT statement. Any JOB statement for the destination location must follow the //*ROUTE statement.

```
//jobname JOB ...                    <== For submitting location.
//*NETACCT PNAME=SMITH,ACCT=22385
//*ROUTE XEQ DALLAS
//jobname JOB ...                    <== For destination location.
```

C. The MAIN Statement

The MAIN statement specifies the processor (computer) requirements for the job.

```
//*MAIN option,option,...,option
```

The following options specify the processor on which the job is to be run and where the output is to be sent.

- SYSTEM = *main-name*   Specifies the processor (computer) on which to run this job. Special names are ANY for any system, JGLOBAL for running on the global processor only, and JLOCAL for a local processor only. The default is ANY. To specify several main processors on which the job can run, enclose a list of names in parentheses. If you instead want to list the processors on which the job is not to run, place a slash (/) in front of the names.

```
//*MAIN SYSTEM=(CPU1,CPU4)       (Job could run on CPU1 or CPU4.)
//*MAIN SYSTEM=/(CPU1,CPU4)      (Job could run on any processor
                                 except CPU1 or CPU4.)
```

- ACMAIN = *main-name*   Identifies the job with a specific processor (computer) even through the job was not submitted from or processed by that computer. This allows the SYSOUT data sets to be sent to some computer in the network other than the one the job was submitted from or processed on.
- ORG = *name*   Tells JES3 to treat the job as if it were submitted from this group or node name, even though it was submitted from somewhere else. The result is that the output is directed back to this device rather than the device from which the job was actually submitted.
- SPART = *partition-name*   Specifies the name of a JES3 spool partition that is to allocate spool space for the job.
- USER = *userid*   Identifies the job with a TSO user even though that user did not submit the job. This lets the TSO user enquire about the job's status, cancel the job, or retrieve the output.

The next set of options tells how the job is to be run.

- CLASS = *class*   Specifies the job class. Overrides the CLASS parameter on the JOB statement.
- DEADLINE = (*time,type*)   Specifies when the job is to be scheduled. The *time* can be *minutes*M or *hours*H to indicate how soon to start the job. Or you can write a time of day as four digits based on a 24-hour clock. DEADLINE = (1300,A) requests the job to be started by 1:00 P.M. The *type* is a single character defined by the installation to allow the job to run. You can also add a date: DEADLINE = (*time,type,mmddyy*), where *mm* is the month (01–12), *dd* is the day (01–31), and *yy* is the year. And finally, you can specify

the cycle on which to run the job as: DEADLINE = (*time,type,when,cycle*). The *cycle* can be WEEKLY, MONTHLY, or YEARLY. The *when* specifies when in the cycle to run the job. For WEEKLY, *when* is 1–7 to indicate the day of the week—1 is Sunday. For MONTHLY, *when* is the day of the month with 29, 30, and 31 treated as the last day of the month. For YEARLY, *when* is the three-digit Julian date—the day of the year.

- EXPDTCHK = YES or NO   Specifies whether the expiration date is to be checked for scratch SL output tapes. EXPDTCHK = YES is the default to check for expiration dates.

- FAILURE = RESTART or CANCEL or HOLD or PRINT   Specifies the recovery in case the job fails. RESTART restarts the job, CANCEL cancels it, HOLD holds the job for operator intervention, and PRINT prints the job and holds it for restart.

- FETCH = ALL or NONE or SETUP or *ddname* or /*ddname*   Overrides the installation-defined FETCH parameter and determines which fetch messages are issued to the operator for disk and tape mounts. ALL means all mountable volumes requested in the JCL should be fetched. NONE means no fetch messages. SETUP means that only volumes in DD statements specified in the SETUP parameter on this MAIN statement should be fetched. You can also code one or more ddnames of volumes requested in the DD statements to fetch. Enclose the ddnames in parentheses and separate them with commas. To specify instead the ddnames of the data sets not to fetch, precede the ddnames with a slash (/). You can't continue the FETCH parameter if you need to list more ddnames than will fit on one line—just write another MAIN statement.

- HOLD = NO or YES   Tells whether to hold the job until the operator releases it. HOLD = NO is the default. HOLD = YES is the same as the TYPRUN = HOLD parameter on the JOB statement and overrides it.

- JOURNAL = YES or NO   Indicates whether a job journal is to be kept for the job. The default is NO.

- MSS = JOB or HWS   MSS = JOB causes each 3330V MSS unit requested by the job to be assigned to a separate unit. MSS = HWS causes 3330V units to be reused in following job steps to minimize 3330V unit usage.

- RINGCHK = YES or NO   Specifies whether a check should be made for the write-enable ring for tape mounts. The default is RINGCHK = YES.

- SETUP = *setup*   Specifies the availability of I/O devices before the job is released for execution. The options are:

```
JOB:      All devices for the entire job must be available.
HWS:      The minimum devices required to run the job are
          sufficient.
THWS:     The minimum disk and tape devices must be available.
ddname:   The fully-qualified ddname of a DD statement whose
          device must be available.  You can name several ddnames
          by enclosing them in parentheses and separating them with
          commas.
```

```
Example:

/ddname:    All ddnames except that listed must be available for
            the job to be initiated.  You can name several ddnames
            by enclosing them in parentheses and separating them
            with commas.

//RUN12 JOB (334458),'TAPE JOB',CLASS=A
//*MAIN SYSTEM=ZIP,SETUP=(DDA,DDB)
```

The next set of options gives various estimates of the size of the job.

- BYTES = (*bytes,option*)   Estimates the maximum output in thousands of
  bytes. The *options* are W to issue a warning message to the operator and
  continue, C to cancel the job, and D to cancel the job with a storage dump.
- IORATE = MED or HIGH or LOW   Specifies the I/O to CPU ratio for the
  job to assist in job scheduling.
- LINES = (*lines*)   Estimates the lines printed by the job. You can also specify
  LINES = (*lines,option*) and give one of three options if the job exceeds the
  estimated lines. W gives an operator a warning message and continues printing, C cancels the job, and D cancels the job with an ABEND dump.
- PAGES = (*pages,option*)   Estimates the maximum number of output pages
  for the job and what to do when this maximum is exceeded. The *options* are W
  to issue a warning message to the operator and then continue, C to cancel the
  job, and D to cancel the job with a storage dump.
- TRKGRPS = (*primary,secondary*)   For spooling, specifies the number of
  primary and secondary track groups to assign to the job. A track group
  represents a number of spool space units.
- TYPE = ANY or VS2   ANY means that any JES3 system can initiate the job.
  (At this time, MVS is the only system so ANY is the same as VS2 and is the
  default if you omit the TYPE parameter.) VS2 requests the job run on MVS.
- LREGION = nK   Estimates the largest size of the region needed by the job
  and is used to improve scheduling.

```
Example:

//*MAIN SYSTEM=ZIP,LINES=(8000,W)
```

The last set of options gives information about the cataloged procedure libraries.

- PROC = *xx*   Specifies any private library to search for the cataloged procedures. The *xx* are the last two characters of the ddname of any procedure
  library to search in place of the standard procedure libraries. You can also
  write ST or omit the PROC parameter to search only the standard procedure
  libraries.
- UPDATE = *xx*   Specifies the last two characters of the ddname of any procedure library updated by this run. You can also write ST to update the
  standard procedure library. In MVS/XA, you instead write the data set name.

D. The FORMAT Statement

The FORMAT statement is used to request any special forms for print or punch data sets. You write:

```
//*FORMAT PR option,option,...,option
```

The options are:

- DDNAME = *ddname*   Specifies the ddname of the data set that this statement is from. Write stepname.procedure-stepname.ddname if necessary to qualify the reference. You can also write the ddname as SYSMSG to specify system messages, as JESJCL to specify the JCL messages, or as JESMSG to specify the JES3 and operator messages.
- DEST = *destination*   The destination for the output data sets. This is the same as the DEST parameter on the DD statement.
- EXTWTR = *name*   The name of an external writer routine at the destination node that is to print the SYSOUT data set.
- PRTY = *priority*   Specifies the priority of the printing in the output queue.

```
//RUN12 JOB (334458),'TAPE JOB',CLASS=A
//*FORMAT DDNAME=OUT,DEST=W10
```

The following options are for the printer.

- CARRIAGE = *carriage-tape-name*   Specifies the carriage control tape for a 3211, 3203-5, or 1403 printer. A "6" requests the installation's standard carriage control tape.
- CONTROL = PROGRAM or SINGLE or DOUBLE or TRIPLE   Specifies the line spacing for the printer.

```
PROGRAM:   First character of a record is control character.
SINGLE:    Forces single spacing.
DOUBLE:    Forces double spacing.
TRIPLE:    Forces triple spacing.
```

- COPIES = (*copies*,(*group*,*group*,...,*group*))   The number of copies of output to make for the job. This is the same as the COPIES parameter on the DD statement.
- FCB = *image-id*   The data set forms control to use. This is the same as the FCB parameter on the DD statement. Writing a 6 as the *image-id* requests the installation's standard forms control buffer.
- FORMS = *forms*   Specifies the print form to use for the job. This is the same as the third subparameter on the SYSOUT statement: SYSOUT =

(*class,program,form*). (STANDARD requests the installation's standard form be used.)

- OVFL = ON or OFF   Tells whether the printer program should test for forms overflow.
- TRAIN = *train-name*   Specifies the print train to use with a printer that has a print train. STANDARD requests the installation's standard print train.
- THRESHLD = *limit*   Specifies the number of data sets that are to be grouped together for printing.

The following options are for the 3800 printer only.

- CHARS = (*table-name,table-name,...,table-name*)   The name of a character arrangement table for a 3800 printer. This is the same as the CHARS parameter on the DD statement. Use STANDARD for the installation's standard character table.
- FLASH = (*overlay-name,count*)   Specifies the forms overlay to use on a 3800 printer. This is the same as the FLASH parameter on the DD statement. Use STANDARD for the installation's standard forms overlay.
- MODIFY = (*module-name,trc*)   Specifies the name of a copy modification module for the 3800 printer. This is the same as the MODIFY parameter on the DD statement.
- STACKER = S, C, or STANDARD   Specifies the stacker of the 3800 printer to use. S is the Burster-Trimmer-stacker and results in the output being burst into separate sheets (the same as BURST = Y on the DD statement), C is the continuous forms stacker, and STANDARD is the installation's standard stacker.

The following options are used for work stations.

- CHNSIZE = *number*   For transmitting from a SNA work station, specifies the number of records that are to be sent. You can write CHNSIZE = DS if the data is sent as a single SNA chain.
- COMPACT = *compaction-table-name*   When transmitting from a work station, specifies the name of a compaction table to be used.

E.   The NET Statement

The NET statement specifies dependencies between jobs. The general form is:

```
//*NET ID=net-id,option,option,...,option
```

- ID = *net-id*   The one-to-eight-character name identifying a given job with a collection of dependent jobs. All the jobs with the same *net-id* are a part of the collection. Such a collection is called a *job net*.

The options are:

- NHOLD = n Gives the number (0 to 32,767) of previous jobs that must complete before this job is to be released. A value of 0 means the job can be scheduled immediately.

- RL = (*jobname,jobname,...,jobname*)   Gives the names (1 to 50) of jobs in the job net that are to follow this job.

- NC = D or F or R   Specifies the action to take for this job when a previous job terminates normally. D means to decrement the NHOLD count by 1. The job is scheduled to be run only if the count goes to zero. F means to flush the job and any jobs following it from the system. Any output generated by previous jobs is printed. R means to retain the job and not decrement the NHOLD count. The job and any following jobs are suspended until the preceding job is resubmitted or the operator decreases the NHOLD count. The default is NC = D.

- AB = D or F or R   Same as NC, except it specifies the action when a previous job abnormally terminates. The default is AB = D.

- OH = YES or NO   OH = YES holds the job until the operator releases it. The default is OH = NO.

- RS = n Specifies when to begin the setup for the job, that is, when to begin allocating devices. The n can range from 1 to 32,767, and setup begins when the NHOLD count becomes less than or equal to this number. If RS is omitted or RS = 0 is written, there is no early setup of dependent jobs.

- NR = (*net-id,jobname*)   Specifies that this job is a predecessor to a job in another job net. The *jobname* names the following job in the other net.

- DEVPOOL = (ANY or NET)   Specifies the devices to be dedicated to this dependent job net. It should be written on the first job of the job net—it is ignored if it is not on the first job. ANY means that jobs in the net can use any device. NET means that jobs can use only devices dedicated to the net. The default is DEVPOOL = (ANY). You can follow ANY or NET with a list of *device-names* and *numbers*. The *device-name* can be the UNIT names of a DD statement or an installation-defined name.

```
//RUN12 JOB (334458),'TAPE JOB',CLASS=A
//*NET ID=TEST,NHOLD=3,DEVPOOL=(ANY,3380,2)
```

Finally, you can specify the MSS staging drive groups to be pooled for the job net. Write DEVPOOL = (NET,SDG*xx*,...) where SDG*xx* is a staging drive group.

- DEVRELSE = YES or NO   DEVRELSE = YES causes all devices dedicated to the dependent job control net to be released at the end of this job. DEVRELSE can be written on more than one job in the net and the devices are released by the first completing job with DEVRELSE = YES. The default is DEVRELSE = NO and causes the devices to be released when the last job in the net terminates.

- PC = HOLD or NOHO or FLSH   Indicates that this job has completed normally and is being resubmitted. It is not to enter the job net and all references to the job net are to be erased. HOLD means to hold the job to be released by the operator. NOHO means the job can be scheduled as system resources become available. FLSH means that the job is to be flushed (purged from the system) without being executed. The default is PC = HOLD.
- AC = KEEP or NOKP   Specifies the action to take if the job abnormally terminates. KEEP means to keep the job net in the system until either the job is resubmitted and completes normally or the operator forces the net from the system. NOKP means to purge the job net if the job that abnormally terminated has not been resubmitted by the time the other jobs in the job net have completed and there are no missing following jobs or subnets. The default is AC = NOKP.

F.   The DATASET Statement

The DATASET statement specifies the beginning of an additional input stream data set that can contain JCL or data. It is written as:

```
//*DATASET DDNAME=ddname,option,option, ...,option
```

- DDNAME = *ddname*   Assigns a ddname to the spooled data set entered in the input stream following this statement. This should match the ddname of a DD statement in the job that is to read the data set. If necessary, the ddname should be qualified by the stepname and cataloged procedure name.

The options are:

- CLASS = NO, MSGCLASS, or *class*   Specifies the class to be used for JES3 job processing. NO means that the system is to assign a default class. MSGCLASS means that the data set is to have the same class as the MSGCLASS of the job. The *class* specifies a particular class.
- MODE = E or C   Specifies the reading mode: E causes the lines to be read as EBCDIC with validity checking; C specifies the lines to be read as column binary.
- J = NO or YES   Specifies how the data set is terminated. No means that a JOB statement terminates the data set; YES means that an ENDDATASET statement terminates the data set. YES is used if the data set contains a JOB statement.

```
//RUN12 JOB (334458),'TAPE JOB',CLASS=A
//STEP1 EXEC PLIXCLG
//READIT DD ...
//*DATASET DDNAME=STEP1.PLIXCLG.READIT,J=YES
       [ lines of data ]
//*ENDDATASET
```

G. The ENDDATASET Statement

The ENDDATASET statement is used to mark the end of a JES3 input stream.

```
//*ENDDATASET
```

H. The PROCESS Statement

The PROCESS statement lets you bypass the standard JES3 job flow. You might want to do this to only check for JCL errors or bypass output processing so that the operator can check whether the job reaches completion. You write a single process-ing option on a PROCESS statement, and you can request several processing options by writing several PROCESS statements. Then you mark the end with an ENDPROCESS statement.

```
//*PROCESS process
//*PROCESS process
//*ENDPROCESS
```

There are many *processes* and many of the processes have optional parameters, but since PROCESS is seldom used, they won't be listed here.

I. The ENDPROCESS Statement

The ENDPROCESS statement marks the end of a series of PROCESS statements.

```
//*ENDPROCESS
```

J. The OPERATOR Statement

The OPERATOR statement lets you send a message to the computer operator.

```
//*OPERATOR message

//RUN12 JOB (334458),'TAPE JOB',CLASS=A
//*OPERATOR   I AM ENCLOSING A TAPE REEL WITH THE JOB.
```

K. The Command Statement

The command statement is used to enter operator commands in the input stream. The command statement must be placed in front of JOB statements in the input stream. The general form is:

```
//**command operands
```

For example

```
//**VARY,290,OFFLINE
```

There are many operator commands but since they are mainly used by the computer operators, they won't be described in this book.

L. The SIGNON Statement

The SIGNON statement begins a remote job session. That is, it connects the job to a work station.

```
/*SIGNON work    AR password1 password2

work The name of the remote work station.
               A Indicates an automatic reader.
                R Indicates that the print can be suspended if the
                  printer is not ready.
          password1 The password for the remote job processing line.
          password2 The password for the remote job work station.
```

M. The SIGNOFF Statement

The SIGNOFF statement ends a remote job stream processing session.

```
/*SIGNOFF
```

III. THE OUTPUT JCL STATEMENT AND DD PARAMETER (MVS/XA ONLY)

The OUTPUT JCL statement, along with the OUTPUT parameter on the DD statement, lets you specify special processing for SYSOUT data sets. For example, you could use an OUTPUT JCL statement to route a SYSOUT data set to a remote printer and also print it on a local printer. You place the OUTPUT JCL statement in the input stream before the OUTPUT DD parameter that refers to it. The OUTPUT JCL statement specifies the special processing. For example:

```
//STEP1 EXEC PGM=PROG1
//TEST1 OUTPUT DEST=PARIS
//TEST2 OUTPUT DEST=HOME
//SYSOUT DD SYSOUT=A,OUTPUT=(*.TEST1,*.TEST2)
```

You write the OUTPUT JCL statement as:

```
//name OUTPUT option,option,...,option
```

Each *name* must be unique within the job. The *name* can be from one to eight alphanumeric or national characters and the first character must be alphabetic or national. Then on a following DD statement, you write an OUTPUT parameter to refer to one or more OUTPUT statements:

```
//ddname DD SYSOUT=class,OUTPUT=(*.name,*.name,...,*.name)
```

You can also include a stepname to refer to an OUTPUT DD parameter in a prior step. The stepname isn't required since the OUTPUT JCL statement names must be unique. Note that you can omit the outer parentheses if you refer to only one OUTPUT JCL statement.

```
OUTPUT=(*.stepname.name)
```

Each OUTPUT DD parameter can refer to as many as 128 OUTPUT JCL statements. The OUTPUT JCL statements can also be placed in a cataloged procedure. To write an OUTPUT DD parameter in the job stream to refer to the OUTPUT JCL statements in a cataloged procedure, you write the OUTPUT DD parameter as:

```
OUTPUT= *.stepname.procstepname.name
```

You can also write an OUTPUT parameter on a DD statement to refer to an OUTPUT JCL statement in the cataloged procedure. But you can't refer to an OUTPUT JCL statement in the input stream within a cataloged procedure.

Parameters may be written on both the OUTPUT JCL statement and the OUTPUT DD parameter. If the same parameter is written on both, the OUTPUT DD parameter is used.

The JES2 /*OUTPUT statement is ignored when OUTPUT JCL statements are used. The JES3 //*FORMAT statement is in addition to OUTPUT JCL statements.

The following options can be written on the OUTPUT JCL statement:

- BURST = Y or N   Sets the default burst mode for SYSOUT data sets for the IBM 3800 printer. This is the same as the BURST parameter on the DD statement.

- CHARS = (*table-name,table-name,...,table-name*)   The name of a character arrangement table for a 3800 printer. This is the same as the CHARS parameter on the DD statement. Use STD for the installation's standard character table in JES3 and DUMP for a 204-character line SYSABEND dump.

- CKPTLNS = *lines*   The maximum number (0–32,767) of lines contained in a logical page.

- CKPTPAGE = *pages*   The number (0–32,767) of logical pages to be printed before the next checkpoint is taken.

- CKPTSEC = *seconds*   The number of seconds of CPU time to elapse between checkpoints of the SYSOUT data set being printed. The *seconds* can range from 1 to 32,767.

- CLASS = class   Specifies the SYSOUT class. You can also write CLASS = * to use the MSGCLASS parameter on the JOB statement. To use the CLASS option, you must write a null SYSOUT class on the DD statement: //OUT DD SYSOUT = (,),OUTPUT = *.TEST1.

- COMPACT = *compaction-table-name*   When transmitting from a work station, specifies the name of a compaction table to be used.
- CONTROL = PROGRAM or SINGLE or DOUBLE or TRIPLE   Specifies the line spacing for the printer.

```
PROGRAM:  First character of a record is control character.
SINGLE:   Forces single spacing.
DOUBLE:   Forces double spacing.
TRIPLE:   Forces triple spacing.
```

- COPIES = (*copies*,(*group*,*group*,...,*group*))   The number of copies of output to make for the job. This is the same as the COPIES parameter on the DD statement.
- DEFAULT = Y or N   Specifies whether the OUTPUT JCL statement can be implicitly referenced by a SYSOUT DD statement. The default is DEFAULT = N. DEFAULT = Y prevents the OUTPUT JCL statement from being named in an OUTPUT DD parameter. But SYSOUT DD statements within a step that don't have an OUTPUT DD parameter implicitly refer to these OUTPUT JCL statements.
- DEST = *destination*   The destination for the output data sets. This is the same as the DEST parameter on the DD statement.
- FCB = *image-id*   The data set forms control to use. This is the same as the FCB parameter on the DD statement. Writing STD as the *image-id* requests the installation's standard forms control buffer.
- FLASH = (*overlay-name*,*count*)   Specifies the forms overlay to use on a 3800 printer. This is the same as the FLASH parameter on the DD statement. Use NONE for no forms overlay. In JES3, use STD for the installation's standard forms overlay.
- FORMDEF = *membername*   Names a library member that contains statements to control the Print Services Facility for printing data sets on a 3800 printer. The statements in the member specify the overlay forms to use.
- FORMS = *form*   Specifies the print form to use for the job. This is the same as the third subparameter on the SYSOUT = (*class*,*program*,*form*) parameter on the DD statement. In JES3, you can specify STD for the installation's standard form.
- GROUPID = *group* (JES2 only.)   Specifies that the SYSOUT data set belongs to an output group.
- INDEX = *nn* (JES2 only.)   Specifies the data set indexing print position offset (1 to 31 to the right) for the 3211 printer.
- JESDS = ALL or JCL or LOG or MSG.   Specifies whether the JCL listing and job log are to apply to this OUTPUT JCL statement. ALL means all of the following, JCL means just the JCL listing, LOG means just the jobs hard-copy log, and MSG means just the system messages for the job.

- LINDEX = *nn* (JES2 only.)   Specifies the data set indexing print position offset (1 to 31 to the left) for the 3211 printer.
- LINECT = *lines* (JES2 only.)   Specifies the number of lines to print on each page.
- MODIFY = (*module-name,trc*)   Specifies the name of a copy modification module for the 3800 printer. This is the same as the MODIFY parameter on the DD statement.
- PAGEDEF = *member*   Identical to the FORMDEF parameter except PAGEDEF member statements specify page format: size, fonts, etc.
- PIMSG = Y or N   Y is the default and specifies that the messages accumulated by Print Services Facility should be printed with the output listing following the SYSOUT data set. N suppresses the messages.
- PRMODE = LINE or PAGE or *mode*   Specifies the process mode for the SYSOUT data set. LINE schedules the data set on a line-mode printer. PAGE schedules the data set on a page-mode printer. JES3 can be only LINE or PAGE. In JES2, the *mode* can in addition be a one- to eight-alphanumeric character name for a mode initialized in JES2.
- PRTY = *priority*   Specifies the priority of the printing in the output queue.
- THRESHLD = *limit*   Specifies the number of data sets that are to be grouped together for printing.
- TRC = Y or N (JES3 only.)   N is the default and indicates that the data set does not contains TRC codes. Y indicates that it contains TRC codes. TRC stands for Table Reference Code and is a code at the start of a line that refers to a table specified by the CHARS parameter to use to map the characters to some other character set.
- UCS = *character-set*   Specifies the Universal Character Set. This is the same as the UCS parameter on the DD statement.
- WRITER = *name*   Names an external writer to process the SYSOUT data set.

Chapter 20

TSO

TSO, which stands for Time-Sharing Option, is a system that runs under MVS and acts as a host to other on-line applications. TSO has a command language that enables you to do many of the things that you can do with JCL and the utilities, such as create, delete, and copy files. You can also store JCL in a data set and submit the data set as a batch job through TSO and retrieve the output from your terminal.

This chapter gives a brief description of the features of TSO that you are likely to use on a regular basis. TSO has many commands not covered here, but you will seldom need to use them. The intent is to give you an overview rather than an exhaustive description.

Most people use TSO to run on-line applications, and they generally are not aware that they are using TSO. For example, ISPF/PDF is usually run under TSO. You first log into TSO and then invoke ISPF/PDF, but you aren't really aware that you are using TSO because you pass right through it on your way to ISPF/PDF.

TSO is not an easy language to use. When it is expecting a response from you and you give the wrong response, it gives you the cryptic message: REENTER. If you don't know what it wants you to enter, you can sit at the terminal forever trying different responses. It makes no suggestions and gives no hints. For example, you might enter something incorrect and get the following response:

```
IKJ56712I INVALID KEYWORD, ##@%
IKJ56703A REENTER -
quit
IKJ56712I INVALID KEYWORD, QUIT
IKJ56703A REENTER -
stop
IKJ56712I INVALID KEYWORD, STOP
IKJ56703A REENTER -
help
IKJ56712I INVALID KEYWORD, HELP
IKJ56703A REENTER -
terminate
IKJ56712I INVALID KEYWORD, TERMINATE
IKJ56703A REENTER -
give me a break
IKJ56712I INVALID KEYWORD, GIVE
IKJ56703A REENTER -
```

You can usually press PA1 to force an interrupt. Sometimes your only recourse is to contact the computer operators and have them log you off of TSO. Getting into loops such as this in TSO is rather common.

I.   THE TSO LANGUAGE

You enter TSO commands from a terminal. The general form of a TSO command is:

```
command parameter ... parameter
```

The TSO command language is actually quite simple, but it appears complex because the commands have many synonyms and abbreviations. For example, the following two TSO commands are identical:

```
ALLOCATE DATASET(TEST.DATA) FILE(INPUT) OLD

ALLOC DD(INPUT) DSN(TEST.DATA)
```

You write the command first (ALLOC is an abbreviation for ALLOCATE), and then the parameters in any order for this command. (DA is an abbreviation for DATASET, which is a synonym for DSNAME, which in turn can be abbreviated as DSN. DD is an abbreviation for DDNAME, which is a synonym for FILE.) To simplify TSO for this book, only one form will be used for each command, often an abbreviation, to save typing and reduce the chance for typing errors.

The parameters must be separated by one or more blanks. You can write the command in either upper- or lower-case characters. Lower case is better because you don't have to hold down the shift key when you type.

To continue a command, you break the command at a parameter, leave a blank, type a plus sign (+), and continue the command on the next line:

```
ALLOC DD(INPUT) +
DSN(TEXT.DATA)
```

Wherever you might want to name several data sets, you can enclose the names in parentheses, separating them with a blank. For example, you can write:

```
LISTD TEST.DATA
      [ To list information about one data set. ]
LISTD (TEST.DATA RUN.DATA SAVE.DATA)
      [ To list information about several data sets. ]
```

When you name a data set, TSO automatically appends your logon userid to the front of the data set to qualify it. If you wrote:

```
LISTD TEST.DATA
```

and your userid were A1000, TSO would list the data set whose fully qualified name was A1000.TEST.DATA. If you want to supply the fully qualified data set name yourself and not have TSO append your userid to it, enclose the data set name in apostrophes:

```
LISTD 'B2020.TEST.DATA'
```

This lets you name a data set belonging to some other userid.

II. ENTERING AND LEAVING TSO

You log onto TSO with the LOGON command:

```
LOGON userid
```

The *userid* is assigned to you by your installation. The installation must establish your userid in TSO before you can log on. After you log on, you will be prompted for your password, which must also be assigned by your installation when they assign you your userid. To save time, you can specify the userid and password together when you logon:

```
LOGON userid/password
```

However, you should note that your password will display on the terminal when you type it in this way, and someone walking by can see it.

You can also request an amount of virtual memory when you log on, similar to the way you request virtual memory with the JCL REGION parameter. You add the SIZE parameter to the LOGON.

```
LOGON userid SIZE(n)     or LOGON userid/password SIZE(n)
```

where *n* is the number of 1024-byte amounts. For example,

```
LOGON A1000/SHAZAM SIZE(2000)
```

logs on user A1000 whose password is SHAZAM onto TSO and assigns a 2000K byte region.

If the connection is broken with TSO while you are logged, you can specify the REC (RECONNECT) option when you log back on. (If you don't specify REC, TSO won't let you log back on because it thinks you are already logged on.)

```
LOGON A1000/SHAZAM REC
```

After you enter the LOGON command, you may have some system messages displayed on your terminal, and then you will receive the TSO prompt:

```
READY
```

You may then enter any TSO command. To log off from TSO, you enter:

```
LOGOFF
```

III. DISPLAYING INFORMATION ABOUT DATA SETS

A. Listing the Names of Data Sets: The LISTCAT Command

The LISTC command (for LIST Catalog) lists on your terminal the names of all the data sets on disk cataloged under your ID. You enter:

```
LISTC
```

B. Listing Information About Data Sets: The LISTD Command

The LISTD (for LIST Data Set) command displays information about data sets on your terminal. The LISTD causes the RECFM, LRECL, BLKSIZE, and DSORG information to be listed. It is written as:

```
LISTD data-set-name
      [ To list a single data set. ]

LISTD data-set-name M
      [ To also list all the member names of the partitioned data
      set. ]
```

C. Listing the Contents of Data Sets: The LIST Command

The L (for List) command lists the contents of a data set on your terminal. You enter:

```
L data-set-name
      [ This lists the entire sequential data set. ]

L data-set-name(member)
      [ This lists the member of a partitioned data set. ]

L data-set-name NONUM    or    L data-set-name(member) NONUM
      [ NONUM is an option to not list line numbers when printing
      the data set. ]

 L data-set-name first-line last-line
      [ This lists only the range of lines you specify. ]
```

D. Printing Data Sets: The DSPRINT Command

The DSPRINT command prints a data set on a printer. You enter:

```
DSPRINT data-set-name printer
      [ The printer is the identification established at your
      installation for the printer on which to print the data set.]
```

To stop the listing, press PA1. PA1 acts as the interrupt key in TSO.

IV.   ALLOCATING DATA SETS

A.   The ALLOCATE Command to Associate Data Sets

When you run an on-line program, there needs to be a way of associating the ddname in the program with a data set name. The DD statement does this in JCL, but if the on-line application isn't executed with JCL, you must use the TSO ALLOC command to do this. You write:

```
                                        MOD
                                        SHR
                                        OLD
        ALLOC DD(ddname) DSN(data-set-name)  ___
```

This associates an application program with an existing data set through the ddname. If you omit the disposition, it is assumed to be OLD. The following two statements do the same thing:

```
        ALLOC DD(TEST) DSN(RUN.DATA) OLD
        ALLOC DD(TEST) DSN(RUN.DATA)
```

This is only one way of writing the ALLOC command. It most closely conforms to the names on JCL statements. The ALLOC command is also written fairly often with FI (for FILE) used in place of DD and DA (for DATASET) used in place of DSN:

```
        ALLOC FI(TEST) DA(RUN.DATA)   or   ALLOC DD(TEXT) DSN(RUN.DATA)
```

It is strictly a matter of personal preference.

B.   The FREE Command

All data sets will be deallocated when you log off. To deallocate or free data sets while you are still logged on, you enter:

```
        FREE DSN(data-set-name)     or     FREE DD(ddname)
```

To free all data sets, you can enter:

```
        FREE ALL
```

C.   Listing Allocated Data Sets: The LISTALC Command

To list all the data sets allocated to you, you can enter the LISTA command (for LIST Allocations):

```
        LISTA
```

D. The ALLOCATE Command to Create Data Sets

You've just seen how you can associate an existing data set with an application program by writing an ALLOC statement. You can also create data sets from TSO, although it is much easier to do this from ISPF/PDF or even from JCL. To allocate a data set in TSO, you write the ALLOC command as:

```
                                     KEEP
                                     DELETE
                                     CATALOG

ALLOC DD(ddname)  DSN(data-set-name)  NEW _____  +

                                     AVGBLOCK(blocksize)
                                     TRACKS
                                     CYLINDERS
          SPACE(primary,secondary)  _____  +

          DIR(directory-blocks)  UNIT(unit)  VOL(volume)  +

          RECFM(format)  LRECL(length)  BLOCK(blocksize)
```

This form of the ALLOC command gives the same information you would supply on a DD statement to create the data set. The UNIT and VOL are optional. If you omit them, a default established at your installation will be used. You write the DIR(directory-blocks) only for a partitioned data set.

Some systems do not allow the LRECL and RECFM parameters to be written on the ALLOC, and you must use the ATTRIB statement described next. And there are even more parameters that can be specified.

Here is an ALLOC command to create a data set shown with a JCL DD statement that would do the same thing, assuming your userid were A1000:

```
ALLOC DD(OUTPUT)  DSN(TEST.DATA)  NEW CATALOG +
      SPACE(100,20)  TRACKS DIR(10)  UNIT(SYSDA)  VOL(PACK12)  +
      RECFM(FB)  LRECL(80)  BLKSIZE(6320)

//OUTPUT DD DSN=A1000.TEST.DATA,DISP=(NEW,CATLG),
//           SPACE=(100,20,10),UNIT=SYSDA,VOL=SER=PACK12,
//           DCB=(RECFM=FB,LRECL=80,BLKSIZE=6320)
```

E. The ATTRIB Command

Because the ALLOC command is so complex, it is usually used in conjunction with an ATTRIB command when allocating data sets. You write the ATTRIB command as:

```
ATTRIB name attributes
```

Then you enter the ALLOC command and name the ATTRIB command to use:

```
ALLOC DD(ddname)  DSN(data-set-name)  USING(name)
```

The ATTRIB statement stays in effect until you log off. One ATTRIB command can be used by several ALLOC commands. You can name many attributes on the ATTRIB command, but the most common ones are:

```
RECFM(type)
LRECL(length)
BLKSIZE(length)
DSORG(type)
```

Here is an example of an ATTRIB command used with two ALLOC commands:

```
ATTRIB JUNK RECFM(FB) LRECL(80) BLKSIZE(6320)
ALLOC DD(OUTPUT) DSN(TEST.DATA) NEW CATALOG +
      SPACE(100,20) USING(JUNK)
ALLOC DD(SAVEIT) DSN(OUT.DATA) NEW CATALOG +
      SPACE(50,10) USING(JUNK)
```

V. SUBMITTING JOBS

A. The SUBMIT Command

You submit a data set in the batch mode as a job by entering:

```
SUB data-set-name
```

When you submit batch jobs, you may wish to modify your JOB statement to supply the NOTIFY parameter so that you are notified when your job completes. You may also want to add the HOLD = YES parameter on the SYSOUT DD statement to hold your output on disk rather than printing it. Some installations set up a special output class for holding your output. Either way, you can examine your output from your terminal rather than waiting for it to be printed.

```
//RUN#12 JOB (228766,223),'TEST RUN',CLASS=A,NOTIFY=A1000
// EXEC PGM=TEST
//OUTPUT DD SYSOUT=A,HOLD=YES
```

B. Checking the Status of Jobs: The STATUS Command

To enquire about the status of your job after you submit it, you can enter:

```
ST
```

C. Canceling Jobs: The CANCEL Command

To cancel a background (or batch) job, you enter:

```
CANCEL jobname     or     CANCEL jobname PUR
```

The *jobname* is from the JOB statement: //*jobname* JOB .... The PUR causes your output to be purged. Otherwise, it will print. If you have more than one job with the same jobname, you must follow the *jobname* with the job number enclosed in parentheses. The system gives you the job number when you submit the job:

```
CANCEL jobname(JOBnnnn)
```

D.   Retrieving Output: The OUTPUT Command

To display or print the output produced by a batch job if it is held rather than printed, you can enter:

```
OUTPUT jobname(JOBnnnn) DEST(station-id)
     ι The station is defined by your installation and is
     usually a local printer.  Your output is then removed from
     disk. ]

OUTPUT jobname(JOBnnnn)
     [ This prints your output on the system printer and removed it
     from disk. ]

OUTPUT jobname(JOBnnnn) DEST(station-id) HOLD
     [ If you add the HOLD parameter, your output is not removed
     from disk after it is displayed.  This enables you to view it
     again or print it. ]
```

VI.   USE OF TSO FOR UTILITY FUNCTIONS

A.   Deleting Data Sets: The DELETE Command

To delete a data set, you enter:

```
DEL data-set-name
```

To delete a member of a partitioned data set, you enter:

```
DEL data-set-name(member)
```

B.   Copying Data Sets: The COPY Command

To copy a data set, you enter:

```
COPY from-data-set-name to-data-set-name NONUM
```

The NONUM option tells TSO to not number your data in the rightmost eight columns. COPY allocates the data set it copies to. You can copy to or from the following types of data sets:

```
TO                                 FROM
sequential data set                sequential data set
partitioned data set               partitioned data set
sequential data set                member of a partitioned data set.
member of a partitioned data set   sequential data set
member of a partitioned data set   member of a partitioned data set
```

To copy to or from a member of a partitioned data set, enclose the member name in parentheses. This statement copies a sequential data set as a member of a partitioned data set:

```
COPY TEST.DATA LIB.DATA(SUB2)
```

C. Renaming Data Sets: The RENAME Command

To rename a data set, you enter:

```
REN old-data-set new-data-set
```

```
REN TEST.DATA PROD.DATA
```

You can also rename a member of a partitioned data set. Notice that you don't need to mention the data set name a second time, only the new member name.

```
REN LIB.DATA(SUB2) (SOMETHING)
```

Chapter 21

ISPF/PDF

ISPF/PDF is a text editor that provides many utility functions. Much of your computer usage will likely be through ISPF/PDF. This chapter gives an overview of the main functions you will need to use ISPF/PDF effectively.

The initials, ISPF/PDF, stand for Interactive System Productivity Facility/ Program Development Facility. The ISPF part consists of a dialog manager that enables you to build screens to be filled in as part of an application. The PDF part consists of a text editor and utilities and is the subject of this chapter. Unlike the other products described in this book, such as JCL, TSO, and the utilities, ISPF/PDF is easy to use and well human-engineered. ISPF/PDF is menu-driven, which means you don't have to memorize many commands.

I.   USING PDF

You invoke PDF by logging into TSO and entering ISPF or whatever else your installation has provided to invoke it. You then get the first panel that appears below. You type the number of the option you want following the OPTION $= = = >$.

```
------------------------- ISPF/PDF PRIMARY OPTION MENU -----------
OPTION ===>  _
                                              USERID   -  xxxxx
    0   ISPF PARMS  - Specify terminal and user  TIME     -  hh:mm
                      parameters                 TERMINAL -  3278
    1   BROWSE      - Display source data or     PF KEYS  -  24
                      output listings
    2   EDIT        - Create or change source data
    3   UTILITIES   - Perform utility functions
    4   FOREGROUND  - Invoke language processors in foreground
    5   BATCH       - Submit job for language processing
    6   COMMAND     - Enter TSO command or CLIST
    7   DIALOG TEST - Perform dialog testing
    8   LM UTILITIES- Perform library management utility functions
    C   CHANGES     - Display summary of changes for this release
    T   TUTORIAL    - Display information about ISPF/PDF
    X   EXIT        - Terminate ISPF using list/log defaults

Enter END command to terminate ISPF.
```

You direct PDF by one of three ways: by entering information on a menu, by pressing PF keys, and by entering commands. The standard PF key assignments are the following, but you can change them if you wish.

```
NAME      PF KEYS         FUNCTION
----      -------         --------
HELP      PF1 or PF13     Requests help--a tutorial.
SPLIT     PF2 or PF14     Splits screen.
END       PF3 or PF15     Terminates current operation and
                          goes back to previous panel.
RETURN    PF4 or PF16     Terminates current operation and
                          returns directly to PRIMARY OPTION
                          MENU.
RFIND     PF5 or PF17     Repeats the last Find command.
RCHANGE   PF6 or PF18     Repeats the last Change command.
UP        PF7 or PF19     Scrolls up.
DOWN      PF8 or PF20     Scrolls down.
SWAP      PF9 or PF21     Swaps the cursor between top and
                          bottom of split screen.
LEFT      PF10 or PF22    Scrolls left.
RIGHT     PF11 or PF23    Scrolls right.
CURSOR    PF12 or PF24    Moves cursor to COMMAND/SCROLL area.
```

A. Shortcuts with Menus

If you remember the number of the panel you want, you can go directly to it when you invoke PDF by entering:

```
ISPF n          or          ISPF n.n
```

You can enter several options at a time to go directly to the panel, assuming you remember the option numbers and their order:

```
OPTION ===> 3.2
```

If you go down several levels in menus, you don't have to press the END PF key several times to get back to the PRIMARY OPTION MENU. As a shortcut, you can just press PF4.

On any panel where "= = = >" appears, you can enter an equal sign (=) followed by the options you want. The equal sign tells PDF to return to the PRIMARY OPTION MENU and then to select the options you specify. The following takes you directly to the MOVE/COPY utility panel, regardless of what panel you enter it on:

```
COMMAND ===> =3.3
```

To enter a command and not have it erased so that you can edit the command and execute it again, precede it with an ampersand:

```
COMMAND ===> &C This That ALL
```

To stack commands in order to enter several on a line, separate the commands with semicolons:

```
COMMAND ===> CAPS OFF;C This That ALL
```

B. Split Screen

Split screen lets you place a "bookmark" on the screen you're working on, jump to the PRIMARY OPTION MENU, select something else, and work on it at the bottom of your screen. You request a split screen by moving your cursor to the point where you want to split and pressing the SPLIT key (PF2 or PF14).

To terminate split screen, just enter =X. Or you can press the RETURN key (PF4 or PF16) or END key (PF3 or PF15) to get back to the PRIMARY OPTION MENU. Then, press the END key again to get back to where you were.

C. Printing a Data Set

If your terminal is connected to a local printer, you can press the PRINT key in the lower left-hand corner of your keyboard to print a "snapshot" of the current display on your terminal screen. To produce a "snapshot" of the current display on your terminal panel to be printed on a high-speed printer when you exit PDF, enter either of these commands:

```
COMMAND ===> PRINT          (Normal print.)

COMMAND ===> PRINT-HI       (Double-strike to show
                             highlighted characters.)
```

The PRINT and PRINT-HI commands print the physical screen. That is, they print exactly what appears on the screen. You can also print the logical screen. The logical screen consists of the data on the screen, without any of the PDF menu. You print the logical screen by entering:

```
COMMAND ===> PRINTL     Print the logical screen.

COMMAND ===> PRINTLHI   Print the logical screen with highlighting.
```

II. USING PDF FOR PROGRAMMING

A. Submitting Jobs

To submit a data set you are editing as a job, enter:

```
COMMAND ===> SUB
```

Use the OUTLIST (option 8) from the UTILITIES menu (enter 3.8 on the PRIMARY OPTION MENU) to examine the output.

B. The FOREGROUND Option

Selecting the FOREGROUND option on the PRIMARY OPTION PANEL gives you
a menu of various language processing programs that you can execute interactively.
In addition, you can also use the Document Composition Facility (SCRIPT/VS). The
items available will depend on your installation.

```
------------------------- FOREGROUND SELECTION MENU  -------------------·
OPTION ===> _

    1  - System assembler          7  - Linkage editor
    2  - OS/VS COBOL compiler       9  - SCRIPT/VS
    3  - VS FORTRAN compiler       10  - COBOL interactive debug
    4  - PL/I checkout compiler    11  - FORTRAN interactive debug
    5  - PL/I optimizing compiler  12  - Member parts list
    6  - PASCAL/VS compiler
```

C. The BATCH Option

BATCH lets you select a language processor. It then generates the JCL you need and
lets you submit batch jobs. The language processors available will depend on your
installation.

```
------------------------- BATCH SELECTION MENU  ---------------------·
OPTION ===> _

      1 - System assembler         5 - PL/I optimizing compiler
      2 - OS/VS COBOL compiler      6 - PASCAL/VS compiler
      3 - VS/FORTRAN compiler       7 - Linkage editor
      4 - PL/I checkout compiler   12 - Member parts list

SOURCE DATA ONLINE ===> YES (YES or NO)
SOURCE DATA PACKED ===> YES (YES or NO)

JOB STATEMENT INFORMATION:
   ===> //jobname JOB (accounting)
```

D. Customizing PDF Features

The PDF PARMS option on the PRIMARY OPTION MENU lets you customize
various PDF features as shown on this panel:

```
------------------------- ISPF PARAMETER OPTIONS  ------------------
OPTION ===> _

      1  TERMINAL  - Specify terminal characteristics
      2  LOG/LIST  - Specify ISPF log and list defaults
      3  PF KEYS   - Specify PF keys for 327x terminal with 24 PF keys
      4  DISPLAY   - Specify screen display characteristics
      5  LIST      - Specify list data set characteristics
```

PDF maintains two data sets to record information collected during your terminal session.

- LOG—Record of significant events, such as creation, change, or deletion of data sets.
- LIST—The "snapshot" output produced by PRINT or PRINT-HI commands and other output commands.
- You can change the default LOG/LIST options by requesting the LOG/LIST option on the PDF PARMS panel.

You can change the default exit options when you exit PDF by pressing the END key (PF3 or PF15) on the PRIMARY OPTION MENU, rather than entering an X.

III. EDITING DATA SETS

To edit a data set, you select option 2 on the PRIMARY OPTION MENU. Then you name the data set to edit on the EDIT ENTRY PANEL.

```
--------------------------- EDIT - ENTRY PANEL -----------------------
COMMAND ===> _

ISPF LIBRARY:
    PROJECT ===>
    GROUP   ===>          ===>          ===>          ===>
    TYPE    ===>
    MEMBER  ===>                   (Blank for member selection list)
```

To edit a partitioned data set, you enter the member name on the line provided. If you aren't sure what member you want or can't remember its name, you can leave the MEMBER blank and press ENTER. You get a member list such as this:

```
EDIT --- data-set-name ------------------------------------------------
COMMAND ===>                                          SCROLL ===> PAGE
NAME      LIB   VV.MM   CREATED    LAST MODIFIED SIZE INIT  MOD      ID
member    1     vv.mm   yy/mm/dd   yy/mm/dd hh:mm  nn   nn    0  userid
**END**
```

The columns give the following information:

```
NAME          -  The member names.
LIB           -  The library the members come from.  You can
                 name from 1 to 4 libraries.
VV.MM         -  The version (VV) is usually 1. The modification (MM)
                 is incremented each time you save the member.
CREATED       -  Date created.
LAST MODIFIED-  Date and time last modified.
SIZE          -  Current size in lines or records.
INIT          -  Initial size of member in lines or records.
MOD           -  Number of lines added or changed since
                 version was created.
ID            -  Userid of person who created or updated this version.
```

If there are too many member names to fit on the screen, you scroll up and down to view the remainder. To edit a particular member, you move your cursor to the left of the name and type an "S". When you select a data set or member to edit, you get this panel. The top two lines tell you the data set you are working on, the columns being displayed, and the scrolling in effect.

```
EDIT --- data-set-name ---------------------------- COLUMNS 001 072
COMMAND ===>                                          SCROLL ===> HALF
****** ******************************** TOP OF DATA ********************
''''''
''''''
''''''                         This is where you
''''''                         enter your data.
''''''
''''''
****** *************************** BOTTOM OF DATA ********************
```

When you enter text and press ENTER, unused lines are removed and each line is given a line number. A line on the EDIT panel has this form:

```
nnnnnn columns 1 to 72 of text -----------------------------------------
  /|\    (You can press PF10 and PF11 to scroll beyond column 72.)
   |
   +-----(PDF numbers your lines here.  The numbers are for reference
          only.  They aren't stored as part of the data unless you
          request it with an option.)
```

To jump out and edit another data set or member of a partitioned data set while you are editing, you enter:

```
COMMAND ===> EDIT            (To get a menu allowing you to
                             enter the name of a new data set.)

COMMAND ===> EDIT member     (To name another member of this
                             partitioned data set to edit.)
```

When you press the END key, you return to the original data set you were editing.

A. Entering Text

You type your data on the lines made available for you on the edit panel. Pressing ENTER removes all the empty lines. You can use the CURSOR key (PF12 or PF24) to quickly move the cursor to the different areas of the panel. Pressing PF12 while the cursor is in the text area moves it to the COMMAND area. Pressing PF12 thereafter moves the cursor back and forth between COMMAND and SCROLL.

To enter the text free-form without having to do carriage returns (called "power typing"), type TE over the line number and press ENTER. Lines are opened up for you to type on and PDF automatically performs a carrier return when you reach the end of a line. You can't use tabs when you use TE.

To reflow the words in a paragraph, type TF over the line number of the first line of a paragraph. PDF reflows all of the text within the bounds to the end of the paragraph. A blank line or indent marks the end of a paragraph.

To split a line, type TS over the line number, move the cursor under where you want to split, and press ENTER. The split part of the line is inserted on the next line and starts in the left margin or left bounds.

To automatically place fixed data into each new line, you can use the MASK feature. Do the following:

1. Type MASK over a line number and press ENTER. Any current MASK is displayed.
2. Overtype the MASK line with whatever mask you want and press ENTER. Whatever you type as the mask will appear on each new line as you insert it.
3. Then type an I, TF, or TS command over a line number to insert new lines.

B. NULLS

The NULLS command specifies whether to place null characters or blanks at the end of a line. NULLS are an inherent weakness of the 3270-type terminal. When nulls are on, nulls are placed at the end of a line rather than blanks. This allows you to insert text within a line. The problem is that if you move the cursor with the cursor control keys in a line that contains nulls, the text will end up shifted left where the nulls begin when you press ENTER. To turn null on, enter:

```
NULLS ON    or just    NULLS
```

When nulls are off, blanks are inserted at the end of each line. The advantage of this is that you don't have to worry where nulls are on the screen when you move the cursor with the cursor control keys. The problem is that PDF won't let you move a character, including a blank, off the right of the screen. Since the line is padded on the right with blanks, you can't insert text on a line unless you first move to the end of the line and press the DELETE EOF key. To turn nulls off, enter:

```
NULLS OFF
```

Since you can't see either a null or a blank on the screen, nulls on and off is a constant problem. If you try to insert text on a line and your keyboard locks and you appear to have space to the right of the line, nulls must be off. If you space over to type with the cursor control keys and type some text, and the text shifts left when you press ENTER, nulls must be on. This feature will be very foreign to someone used to a PC.

C. Exiting the Editor

You exit from the EDIT panel by:

- Pressing the END key (PF3 or PF15). This saves the data set and returns to the previous EDIT–ENTRY PANEL.
- Pressing the RETURN key (PF4 or PF16). This saves the data set and returns to the PRIMARY OPTION MENU.
- Entering the CANCEL command. This returns to the previous EDIT— ENTRY PANEL without saving the data set.

D. Saving Data Sets

1. The SAVE command

To save a data set without leaving the edit screen, you enter the SAVE command on the COMMAND line:

```
COMMAND ===> SAVE
```

2. Packing text to save space

Text can be compressed to eliminate blanks and repeated characters with the PACK command. This saves disk space, but you can't operate on the text until you unpack it. PDF automatically unpacks packed text when you edit it. To turn packing on (to save disk space) or off, enter:

```
COMMAND ===> PACK ON   or just   PACK
COMMAND ===> PACK OFF
```

E. Displaying Text

1. Scrolling

The PF keys for scrolling are:

- PF7   or PF19—Scroll up.
- PF8   or PF20—Scroll down.
- PF10 or PF22—Scroll left.
- PF11 or PF23—Scroll down.

You set the scroll amount by entering the scroll amount in the SCROLL area at the top of the EDIT panel.

```
EDIT --- data-set-name ----------------------------- COLUMNS 001 072
COMMAND ===>                                         SCROLL ===> HALF
```

The scroll amounts can be:

- HALF or H—Scroll half a page up or down, left or right.
- PAGE or P—Scroll a full page.
- DATA or D—Scroll a full page, overlapping one line or column.
- nn—Scroll nn lines up or down, or nn characters left or right.
- CSR or C—Scroll according to where the cursor is placed on the panel.
- MAX or M—Scroll the maximum amount one time.

2. Listing specific lines

You can also list text by entering the L (for LOCATE) command on the COMMAND line:

```
COMMAND ===> L 1        Lists starting at the first line.

COMMAND ===> L 99999   Lists line 99999 of the data set.
```

Rather than listing by line number, you can plant labels in the data set and name them in a L command. The labels are typed over a line number. The label must begin with a period and be from one to five alphabetic characters (.label). The first character cannot be a Z. PDF provides three built-in labels that begin with a Z:

- .ZF   (The first line of your data set.)
- .ZL   (The last line of your data set.)
- .ZCSR   (The line your cursor is on—or the first line on the screen if your cursor is not in the data area.)

You can then use the LOCATE command to list lines by the label, just as you list them by line number: L .label. To list the first line (top) of the data set, you enter:

```
COMMAND ===> L .ZF    or    COMMAND ===> L 1
```

To list the last line (bottom) of the data set, enter:

```
COMMAND ===> L .ZL
```

3. Displaying text in hexadecimal

To turn the hexadecimal display on or off, enter:

```
COMMAND ===> HEX ON  or just  HEX
COMMAND ===> HEX OFF
```

With HEX ON, a line is displayed in text with two lines below it to display the hexadecimal code.

F.   Editing Commands

1.   Inserting lines

To insert lines following some line in the text, you type the I command over the line number:

```
I     -    inserts a line
In    -    inserts "n" lines, where "n" is a number
```

2.   Deleting lines

To delete lines, type the following over the line numbers to delete:

```
D     -    deletes a line
Dn    -    deletes "n" lines, where "n" is a number
```

To delete a range of lines, type a DD over the first and last line number of the range:

```
DD       Defines a range of lines to delete.
```

3.   Copying and moving lines

Copying or moving lines is a two step process. First you type a C or M over the line number or the lines to copy. This tells PDF which lines to move or copy. Then you must tell PDF where to move or copy the lines to. You do this by moving the cursor to the line number where you want the lines copied or moved and type an A on the line (to copy or move after), or a B (to copy or move after this line).

```
C     -    copies a line
Cn    -    copies "n" lines, where "n" is a number

M     -    moves a line
Mn    -    moves "n" lines, where "n" is a number

A     -    after this line
B     -    before this line
```

To copy or move a range of lines, termed a "block," you type a MM or CC over the first and last line number of the range.

```
MM       Defines a range of lines to move.
CC       Defines a range of lines to copy.
```

4.   Moving or copying lines from another data set

To move or copy a member or a data set into the data you are currently editing, mark where you want the data copied with a B (before this line) or A (after this line). Then enter one of the following commands to name the data set or member to copy in.

```
COMMAND ===> COPY member        To copy or move a member from the
COMMAND ===> MOVE member        partitioned data set you are
                                currently editing.

COMMAND ===> COPY               To get a panel to name a sequential
COMMAND ===> MOVE               data set or member of some other
                                partitioned data set.
```

To save lines in the data set you are working on into another data set, you first mark the lines you want to save by typing the following over the line numbers.

```
To copy:   C              To move:   M
           Cn                        Mn
           CC/CC                     MM/MM
```

Then enter one of the following commands:

```
COMMAND ===> CREATE member      For partitioned data sets only.
                                Used to store the text as a new member.
COMMAND ===> CREATE             To store in another partitioned
                                data set.

COMMAND ===> REPLACE member     To replace a partitioned data set
                                member.
COMMAND ===> REPLACE            To replace a sequential data set
                                or a member of a partitioned data
                                set other than the one you are
                                currently working on.
```

5.   Canceling move, copy, and delete

To remove any pending Move, Copy, or Delete or any PDF line message, enter:

```
COMMAND ===> RESET
```

6.   Repeating lines

To repeat lines, you type the following over the line number:

```
R      -   repeats a line
Rn     -   repeats line "n" times, where "n" is a number
RR         Defines a range of lines to repeat.
RRn        (Repeats the lines "n" times.)
```

7.   Displaying a rule

To display a rule below a line showing column positions, type COL over the line number.

8.   Shifting columns

You do column shifting left or right n spaces by typing parentheses over the line numbers. The default is 2 if you omit the n.

```
Left:   (n                        Right:   )n

        ((                                 ))
        ((n                                ))n
```

Data is lost if it is shifted beyond the left or right margin. Alternatively, you can also do what PDF terms data shifting. With data shifting, the lines are shifted, but they are never moved closer than one space of the left or right margin. You enter:

```
Left:   <n                        Right:   >n

        <<                                 >>
        <<n                                >>n
```

9.   Overlaying text

You overlay text from one set of lines onto another as follows:

1. Specify the line or lines to overlay (O), by typing the following over the line number:

```
O          One line.

OO         A block of
OO         lines.
```

2. Mark the lines containing the data to move or copy by typing the following over the line number:

```
C   or   CC/CC   or   M   or   MM/MM
```

3. Then press ENTER. Only blank character positions are overlaid.

10. Finding and changing data

a. Finding Text—The FIND Command

The FIND command is written as:

```
COMMAND ===> F word      or      F 'characters'
```

The single quotes are needed if there is an embedded blank or comma. PDF begins its search at your current cursor position (or with the first character on the screen if your cursor is in the COMMAND area) and continues forward. You can find the next instance by pressing the RFIND key (PF5 or PF17). You can tell PDF where to start the search and how to search for the characters by entering the F command as:

```
COMMAND ===> F options 'characters'    or    F 'characters' options
```

The first set of options tell where to start the search and the direction to search:

- ALL—Start with the first character, count the number of times found, and position to the first instance.
- FIRST—Start with the first character in the member or data set and search forward for the next occurrence.
- LAST—Opposite of FIRST. Start at bottom of data and search backward to find the last occurrence.
- NEXT—The default if you omit them all. Start from the cursor position and search forward for the next occurrence.
- PREV—Opposite of NEXT. Start where your cursor is (or with the last character on the screen if your cursor is not in the text area) and search backward.

The second set of options specify how to search for characters:

```
CHAR - The default.  Just find the characters.
SUF  - Find the characters as a suffix--at the end of a word.
PRE  - Find the characters as a prefix--at the beginning of a
       word.
WORD - Find the characters as a complete word.
```

PDF normally ignores upper and lower case in the search. To search for characters matching upper or lower case exactly, place a C in front of the string enclosed in single quotes:

```
COMMAND ===> F C'the'
```

b. Changing Text—The CHANGE Command

You can find characters and then change them by writing:

```
COMMAND ===> C old-word new-word or C 'old characters' 'new characters'
```

The single quotes are needed if the characters contain blanks or commas or are a PDF special word, such as ALL. You can make several changes throughout the text by:

1. Pressing the RFIND key (PF5 or PF17) to find the next instance of the old characters.

2. Pressing the RCHANGE key (PF6 or PF18) if you want to change the characters.

The search begins where your cursor is positioned (unless it is not in the data area; then it begins with the first character on the screen). You can write the same positioning options for Change and Find:

```
COMMAND ===> C options 'old characters' 'new characters'
```

c. Limiting the Search or Change

The EXCLUDE command, abbreviated X, can be used to exclude lines from a Find or Change. It is written almost identically to the FIND:

```
COMMAND ===> X options 'characters'
```

You can mark lines in the text to be excluded from the FIND or CHANGE by writing an X or XX over line numbers:

```
X       Exclude one line
XX      Exclude a block of lines.
```

The FIND and CHANGE commands operate on all lines, both included and excluded, unless you specify otherwise in the command. You do this by adding X or NX to the command:

```
            X       Scan or delete only the excluded lines.
            NX      Scan or delete only the lines not excluded.
F options __
C options __
```

The FIND, CHANGE, and EXCLUDE commands only look at data within any bounds you set; thus you can limit the search to specific columns by setting bounds. Alternatively, you can specify a starting and ending column in the command itself:

```
COMMAND ===> F ALL 20 30 'THE END'
```

The complete FIND, CHANGE, and EXCLUDE commands are:

```
                NEXT
                ALL    CHAR
                FIRST  SUF
                LAST   PRE  X
                PREV   WORD NX
F .label .label ____ ____ __ first-col last-col 'characters'
C .label .label ____ ____ __ first-col last-col 'old' 'new'
X .label .label ____ ____ __ first-col last-col 'characters'
```

You can write the characters on a FIND, CHANGE, or EXCLUDE command as:

```
'characters'
"characters"          Double quotes required if characters
                      begin or end with single quotes.
C'characters'         Searches for exact match of upper or
                      lower case characters.
```

The new characters in a CHANGE command can be:

```
word                  No blanks, commas, and can't be a special PDF word
                      such as ALL.
'characters'          Required if characters begin or end with a single
                      quote or contain embedded commas, blanks, or a
```

The search string can also be:

```
String      Searches for:
------      -------------
P'='        Any character.  (The "don't care" character.)
P'¬'        Any non-blank character.
P'.'        Any nondisplayable character--usually an
            invalid character.
P'#'        Any numeric (0-9) character.
P'-'        Any non-numeric character.
P'@'        Any alphabetic character (A-Z, a-z).  Upper or
            lower case.
P'<'        Any lower case alphabetic character (a-z).
P'>'        Any upper case alphabetic character (A-Z).
P'$'        Any special character.  (Not A-Z, a-z, or 0-9.)
```

d. Line Numbering

PDF automatically numbers your text and displays the line numbers in the first six columns of the display. However, the line numbers are not made a part of your data when you save the data set unless you request PDF to save them for you. You do this by entering the NUM ON command.

```
COMMAND ===> NUM ON  or just NUM
    (Numbers are stored in columns 1-6, 1-8 or 73-80, depending
    on the data type.)
COMMAND ===> NUM ON COBOL
    (Numbers are stored in columns 1-6 regardless of the data
    type.)
COMMAND ===> NUM OFF
```

During an edit session, you can renumber lines by entering:

```
COMMAND ===> REN
```

To remove the line numbers from the display so that your lines begin in the left column, you enter the UNN command. UNN also sets NUM OFF.

```
COMMAND ===> UNN
```

When you save a data set with NUM ON, PDF automatically renumbers the lines, beginning with 100 and incrementing by 100. To save the data set without renumbering, you enter:

```
COMMAND ===> AUTONUM ON   or just   AUTONUM
COMMAND ===> AUTONUM OFF
```

G. Setting the Editing Environment

1. Bounds and margins

You set up bounds or margins as follows:

1. Type BNDS over the line number of a line and press ENTER. Any current bounds are displayed.

2. Type a "<" and a ">" on the BNDS line where you want the left and right boundary and press ENTER.

You can also enter the BNDS command to do the same thing:

```
COMMAND ===> BNDS column column
```

2. Setting tabs

Because of limitations on the 3270-type terminal, three types of tabs are provided: software, hardware, and logical. All three have their problems. Software tabs let you tab by pressing the ENTER key. The problem with this is that the computer must be interrupted to perform a tab, and the response can be slow during busy times of the day. Hardware tabs let you tab by pressing the TAB key. Their problem is that a control character must be placed on the screen which prevents you from displaying a character in that position.

Logical tabs let you tab by typing any character that you specify as the tab by entering:

```
COMMAND ===> TABS ON character
```

For both logical and hardware tabs, you must first enable the tabs by entering:

```
COMMAND ===> TABS ON   or just   TABS
```

You set tabs by typing TABS over a line number. Then you specify the tab positions:

- Software tabs: Type dash (—) or underline (_) where you want a tab set.
- Hardware or logical tabs: Type an * in the column preceding where you want the cursor to stop.

3. Upper or lower case

CAPS OFF lets you enter text in upper and lower case. CAPS ON converts all your
text to upper case as you enter it.

```
COMMAND ===> CAPS ON     or     CAPS OFF
```

To convert lines to upper or lower case after you type them in, two sets of
commands are provided. You type the command over the line numbers.

```
UC   Convert a single line to upper case.
UCn  Convert n lines to upper case.
UCC  Convert a block of lines to upper case.

LC   Convert a single line to lower case.
LCn  Convert n lines to lower case.
LCC  Convert a block of lines to lower case.
```

4. Saving the editing environment

All the tabs, margins, and other information you set for an editing session constitute
your editing profile. PDF saves the profile when you save a data set. The profile is
reinstated when you edit the data set again.

The data type in the data set name should match the language name (COBOL,
PL/I, etc.) because PDF keeps a separate profile for you of each data type.

You can name and enter several different profiles. You name the profile on the
PROFILE NAME line of the EDIT — ENTRY PANEL. To display the profile
currently in effect, enter:

```
COMMAND ===> PRO
```

To save a profile or request a new one during an edit session, you enter:

```
COMMAND ===> PRO name
```

The *name* is a one- to eight-character name. If a profile exists with the name in the
PRO command, PDF uses it. Otherwise PDF saves the current profile under this
name.

You can make changes to your edit profile during an edit session and not save
them when you exit the editor by entering:

```
COMMAND ===> PRO LOCK
```

H. Sorting Data

The most general form of the SORT command is:

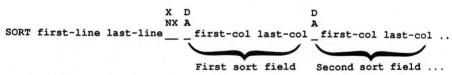

The A or D for a sort field means ascending or descending order. If you don't name the columns, PDF sorts all the columns within any bounds set. Data outside the bounds or margins is not reordered.

```
COMMAND ===> SORT D
```

If you name only one column, PDF sorts from that column to the end of the line (or the right bounds column):

```
COMMAND ===> SORT D 10
```

Ascending sort order is assumed if you don't write an A or D.

```
COMMAND ===> SORT 16 20    (sorts on columns 16-20 in ascending order)
```

You can write several sort fields. If you write an A or D for one field, you must write them for all fields:

```
COMMAND ===> SORT A 1 10 D 15 20
```

You can sort only excluded lines or lines not excluded:

```
COMMAND ===> SORT X ...      (sorts only excluded lines)

COMMAND ===> SORT NX ...     (sorts only lines not excluded)
```

You can sort from a starting label to an ending label:

```
COMMAND ===> SORT .FROM .TO D 17 20
```

IV. BROWSING TEXT

To browse a data set, select the BROWSE option on the PRIMARY OPTION MENU. The browse option differs from the edit in that browse is "look but don't touch." The reason for using a browse is that several people can browse the same data set at the same time whereas only one person can edit a data set at a time.

You can enter the following primary commands when you browse a data set:

```
DISPLAY      FIND    RESET    BROWSE
HEX ON/OFF   LOCATE  COLS
```

To jump out and browse another data set or member of a partitioned data set while you are browsing, you enter:

```
COMMAND ===> BROWSE            (To get a menu allowing you to
                               enter the name of a new data set.)

COMMAND ===> BROWSE member     (To name another member of this
                               partitioned data set to edit.)
```

When you press the END key, you return to the original data set you were browsing.

V.   THE PDF UTILITIES

Selecting the UTILITIES option on the PRIMARY OPTION MENU gives you this panel:

```
------------------------ UTILITY SELECTION MENU  --------------------------
OPTION  ===> _

    1  LIBRARY      - Library utility:
                         Print index listing or entire data set
                         Print, rename, delete, or browse members
                         Compress data set
    2  DATA SET     - Data set utility:
                         Display data set information
                         Allocate, rename, or delete entire data set
                         Catalog or uncatalog data set
    3  MOVE/COPY    - Move or copy members or data sets
    4  DLIST        - Data set list:
                         Print or display (to process) list of data set names
                         Print or display VTOC information
    5  RESET        - Reset statistics for members of ISPF library
    6  HARDCOPY     - Initiate hardcopy output
    7  VTOC         - Display or print VTOC entries for a DASD volume
    8  OUTLIST      - Display, delete, or print held job output
    9  COMMANDS     - Create/change an application command table
   10  CONVERT      - Convert old format messages/menus to new format
   11  FORMAT       - Format definition for formatted data edit/browse
```

A.   Operations on Partitioned Data Sets

Selecting the LIBRARY option from the UTILITIES SELECTION MENU lets you perform operations on partitioned data sets. You get this panel:

```
--------------------------- LIBRARY UTILITY  ---------------------------
OPTION ===> _

    blank - Display member list     B - Browse member
    C - Compress data set           P - Print member
    X - Print index listing         R - Rename member
    L - Print entire data set       D - Delete member
    I - Data set information         S - Data set information (short)

ISPF LIBRARY:
    PROJECT ===>
    GROUP   ===>
    TYPE    ===>
    MEMBER  ===>                     (If option "P", "R", "D", or "B" selected)
    NEWNAME ===>                     (If option "R" selected)

OTHER PARTITIONED OR SEQUENTIAL DATA SET:
    DATA SET NAME  ===>
    VOLUME SERIAL  ===>             (If not cataloged)

DATA SET PASSWORD ===>              (If password protected)
```

The options are:

- C—Compress the data set.
- X—Prints general information about the data set (size, record length, blocking, etc.) and prints a list of the member names. You fill in the data set name but not the member name for this. (This option can be used for sequential data sets also.)
- L—Print entire data set. Don't fill in member name. (This option can be used for sequential data sets also.)
- B—Browse through a member. (There is also a Browse option on the PRIMARY OPTION MENU that does the same thing.)
- P—Print member. Fill in member name.
- R—Rename a member.
- D—Delete a member.
- S—Displays the primary and secondary space allocated to the data set, the record format, record length, and block size.
- I—Same as S, except for a partitioned data set, displays directory size and number of members.

To print, delete, rename several members at once, you can fill in the partitioned data set name, leave the option blank, and press ENTER. You'll get a list of member names. Enter a P to print, a D to delete, or R to rename the members you want. You can also enter an R to rename and a B to browse a member. You can enter the P, R, D, or B option to the left of the names to perform the operations on them.

- P—Print the member.
- R—Rename the member. Fill in the new name in the RENAME column.
- D—Delete the member.
- B—Browse the member.

```
LIBRARY --- data-set-name -----------------------------------------
COMMAND ===>                                        SCROLL ===> PAGE
NAME    RENAME  VV.MM   CREATED    LAST MODIFIED SIZE INIT MOD    ID
member          vv.mm  yy/mm/dd  yy/mm/dd hh:mm    nn   nn   0  nnnnn
**END**
```

You fill in all the operations you want and press ENTER.

B. *Creating, Deleting, and Renaming a Data Set*

To operate on data sets as a whole, you select the DATA SET OPTION. You get this panel:

```
-------------------------- DATA SET UTILITY -----------------------
OPTION ===> _

   A - Allocate new data set             Catalog data set
   R - Rename entire data set            Uncatalog data set
   D - Delete entire data set            Data set information (short)
   blank - Display data set information

ISPF LIBRARY:
   PROJECT ===>
   GROUP   ===>
   TYPE    ===>

OTHER PARTITIONED OR SEQUENTIAL DATA SET:
   DATA SET NAME ===>
   VOLUME SERIAL ===>          (If not cataloged, require for option "C")

DATA SET PASSWORD ===>         (If password protected)
```

You enter each level of the data set name in one of two places. Normally, you write the name in the top menu:

```
ISPF LIBRARY:
   PROJECT ===>      (Enter your userid.)
   GROUP   ===>      (Enter your chosen data set group name.)
   TYPE    ===>      (Tell PDF the type of data set you are creating.
                      Words like DATA and TEXT are often used as the
                      type.)
```

But you must write the name in the bottom place if the name doesn't have three levels:

```
OTHER PARTITIONED OR SEQUENTIAL DATA SET:
   DATA SET NAME  ===> STUFF
          or
   DATA SET NAME  ===> THING.RENTAL.COST.DATA
```

To create a data set, you enter an A (for Allocate) as the option. When you press ENTER, you get this panel. You fill it in and press ENTER to allocate the data set. You specify the same data you specify on the JCL DD statement. The one main exception is that there in no equivalent of the RLSE parameter.

```
------------------------- ALLOCATE NEW DATA SET -------------------------
COMMAND ===>

DATA SET NAME: date-set-name

    VOLUME SERIAL      ===>  _        (Blank for authorized default volume)
    GENERIC UNIT       ===>           (Generic group name or unit address)
    SPACE UNITS        ===>           (BLKS, TRKS or CYLS)
    PRIMARY QUAN       ===>           (in above units)
    SECONDARY QUAN     ===>           (in above units)
    DIRECTORY BLOCKS   ===>           (Zero for sequential data set)
    RECORD FORMAT      ===>
    RECORD LENGTH      ===>
    BLOCK SIZE         ===>
    EXPIRATION DATE    ===>           (national format or blank)
```

To delete a data set, name the data set and select option D (Delete). To rename a data set, you enter the data set name and select option R. You'll get another panel on which you enter the new name. If you leave the option blank, you'll get a panel displaying the date the data set was created and the amount of space allocated to it.

C. Copying and Moving Data Sets

To copy or move a data set, you select the MOVE/COPY option from the UTILITY SELECTION MENU. You get this panel:

```
------------------------- MOVE/COPY UTILITY -------------------------
OPTION ===>  _

    C - Copy data set or member(s)        CP - Copy and print
    M - Move data set or member(s)        MP - Move and print
    P - Promote data set or member(s)     PP - Promote and print

SPECIFY "FROM" DATA SET BELOW, THEN PRESS ENTER KEY

FROM ISPF LIBRARY:
    PROJECT ===>
    GROUP   ===>
    TYPE    ===>
    MEMBER  ===>            (Blank for member list, * for all members)

FROM OTHER PARTITIONED OR SEQUENTIAL DATA SET:
    DATA SET NAME   ===>
    VOLUME SERIAL   ===>    (If not cataloged)

DATA SET PASSWORD ===>      (If password protected)
```

A move deletes the "FROM" data set. Promote is used for libraries whose access is controlled. To copy "FROM" a sequential data set, you enter the data set name. For a partitioned data set, you add one of the following on the MEMBER line:

- A member name to copy a single member.
- An asterisk (*) to copy all members.
- Blank to get a list of member names. Then you type an "S" to the left of each name you want to copy.

When you select the copy option and press ENTER, you get another panel on which to enter the name of the data set to copy to. You can copy from sequential or partitioned data sets to sequential or partitioned data sets. You can change the record format, record length, and block size when you copy. Records are truncated or padded on the right with blanks as necessary when the record length is changed.

D. Operations on Groups of Data Sets

Selecting the DSLIST option (Data Set List) on the UTILITY SELECTION MENU lets you Browse, Edit, Delete, Rename, Print, and Compress data sets, among other things. It does many of the things we have already described for the other utilities. The big advantage of the DSLIST utility is that you can list your data sets and specify several operations on them at the same time. It lets you do operations on data sets similar to the way the LIBRARY UTILITY lets you perform operations on several members of a partitioned data set. When you select the DSLIST utility, you get the following panel:

```
-------------------------- DATA SET LIST UTILITY ------------------
OPTION ===>
 Blank - Display data set list *        P  - Print data set list
 V     - Display VTOC information only  PV - Print VTOC infomation only

Enter one or both of the parameters below:
 DSNAME LEVEL  ===>
 VOLUME        ===>

SPECIFY THE FOLLOWING, IF DISPLAYING A LIST OF DATA SETS:
      DISPLAY FORMAT OPTION   ===> QUICK    (QUICK, SHORT or LONG)
      CONFIRM DELETE REQUEST ===> YES      (YES or NO)

* The following options will be available when the list is displayed

 B - Browse data set                  C - Catalog data set
 E - Edit data set                    U - Uncatalog data set
 D - Delete entire data set           P - Print entire data set
 R - Rename entire data set           X - Print index listing
 I - Data set information             M - Display member list
 S - Data set information (short)     Z - Compress data set
```

To select data sets, you can specify a DSNAME LEVEL or a VOLUME. You can use an * as a wild card character to represent any characters in the DSNAME LEVEL. Don't enclose the data set name in quotes. Specify the level 1 qualifier. Don't use an * in the level 1 qualifier. The * can only appear first and/or last in a level name.

E. Other Utilities

The remaining utilities are used less often. They are:

- RESET—Resets the version and level numbers of a library or partitioned data set.
- HARDCOPY—Prints "clean" copies of a sequential data set or single member of a partitioned data set.

- VTOC—Lists all the data sets stored within a particular volume (disk pack).
- OUTLIST—Used to examine output generated by a batch job.
- COMMAND—Used to build command tables for application programs.
- CONVERT—Used to change format messages and menus in the old version of PDF (it was called SPF then) to the new format.
- FORMAT—Used to format data using the Double-Byte Character Set.

Appendix A

Common System Completion Codes

The following codes are the most common form of ABENDs.

Code	Description
0C1	Invalid instruction. Usually caused either by wild branch into a data area of your program or data clobbering the instruction area of the program.
0C5	Invalid address. Usually caused by a wild branch or a wild index used with an array.
0C7	Invalid data. Usually caused by invalid alignment of data or packed decimal data being clobbered.
222	Computer operator canceled the job. Most often this is because the job requested a resource that isn't available. The typical example is a request for a tape volume that can't be found.
322	Exceeded the CPU time limit. Make sure that the job isn't in an endless loop and then increase the TIME parameter on the JOB or EXEC statement.
806	Couldn't find the program to execute. Make sure that you used the proper JOBLIB or STEPLIB statement and that the PGM keywork on the EXEC statement names the program you want.
80A	Exceeded the region size. Increase the REGION parameter for the step that ABENDed.
B37	No more space on the disk pack. Request a different volume or request several volumes.
E37	Exceeded the direct-access storage space. Increase the amount of space in the SPACE parameter.

INDEX